SHAILER
MATHEWS'S
LIVES OF JESUS

Shailer Mathews

SHAILER
MATHEWS'S
LIVES OF JESUS

*The Search for a Theological Foundation
for the Social Gospel*

WILLIAM D. LINDSEY

STATE UNIVERSITY OF NEW YORK PRESS

Acknowledgment is gratefully given to the following for permission to use copyrighted materials: to Mr. Craig Mathews, representing the estate of Shailer Mathews, for permission to reproduce the photograph of Shailer Mathews, and for permission to cite material from *Jesus on Social Institutions* (New York: Macmillan, 1928), and *New Faith for Old* (New York: Macmillan, 1936); to the University of Chicago Press for permission to cite material from Mathews' "The Development of Social Christianity in America During the Past Twenty-Five Years," in Gerald Birney Smith, ed., *Religious Thought in the Last Quarter-Century* (Chicago: University of Chicago Press, 1927); and to Scholars Press for permission to cite material from Diane Yeager, "Introduction," and Susan Lindley, "'Neglected Voices' and *Praxis* in the Social Gospel," *Journal of Religious Ethics* 18 (1990).

Published by
State University of New York Press, Albany

Printed in the United States of America

For information, address the State University of New York Press, State University Plaza, Albany, NY 12246

Production design by David Ford
Marketing by Patrick Durocher

Library of Congress Cataloging-in-Publication Data
Lindsey, William D., 1950–
    Shailer Mathews's lives of Jesus : the search for a theological foundation for the social gospel / William D. Lindsey.
        p. cm.
    Originally published: New York : P. Lang, 1996.
    Includes bibliographical references and index.
    ISBN 0-7914-3507-5 (hardcover : alk. paper). — ISBN 0-7914-3508-3 (pbk. : alk. paper)
    1. Jesus Christ—Biography—History and criticism.   2. Social gospel. 3. Mathews, Shailer, 1863–1941. I. Title.
[BT301.9.L56 1997
261.8 — dc21   96-52290
                                                                    CIP

To two Hatties:

both Southern women, without whose courage, compassion,

and conviction I would not be who I am:

my mother, Hattie Clotine Simpson Lindsey,

and my late grandmother, Hattie Batchelor Simpson.

To place Jesus in the world is to emphasize the freedom of his spirit. Paradoxical as it sounds, he who would be most like Jesus will be most unlike him.

– Shailer Mathews,
"The Imitation of Jesus"

The free spirit is he whose impulses are controlled and directed by an ideal that is the very anticipation in history of humanity's goal. And that is the very paraphrase of Christian faith. For that ideal is Christ.

– Shailer Mathews,
The Gospel and the Modern Man

CONTENTS

ACKNOWLEDGMENTS

As with any book, those who deserve credit for abetting me are legion. In particular, I want to thank Roger Haight, SJ, for his unfailing patience and unerring critical insight as he guided me through the writing of this book in its initial dissertation stage.

Thanks, too, to those who granted me personal interviews to talk about Mathews and his work: to the late Harvey Arnold, who graciously shared with me his guide to the Divinity School papers; to Francis Schüssler-Fiorenza; to Kenneth L. Smith; to Larry Greenfield; and to the late Stephen Wurster, who gave me a copy of his 1972 dissertation, as well as taped interviews with Bernard Meland.

I should thank as well those who through correspondence provided me with many helpful suggestions and various important materials. These include the late Larry Axel (who kindly published my Mathews bibliography in the *American Journal of Theology and Philosophy*), Robert W. Funk (who provided me with tapes of the 1969 Vanderbilt Consultation on the Chicago School), Roy A. Harrisville (who sent me a copy of his study of Frank C. Porter), and William J. Hynes.

I owe a special debt of gratitude to two colleagues who believed in the book when my faith in it flagged, and who kindly offered help as I sought a publisher: Creighton Peden of the Highlands Institute for

American Religious Thought; and Jerome A. Stone of William Rainey Harper College.

Librarians rarely receive thanks adequate to the invaluable help they offer researchers. This book could not have been written without the assistance of Linda Hayes of Emmanuel College library, Toronto, Margaret McGrath of St. Michael's College library, Toronto, Daniel Meyer, the University of Chicago archivist, and the staff of the American Baptist Archives in Rochester, New York.

I must also recognize the United Negro College Fund, which provided me with a Charles Dana Grant that enabled me to write as I taught in the theology department of Xavier University of New Orleans.

INTRODUCTION

Taking a New Look at the Social Gospel

Though critics of the North American social gospel movement[1] considered themselves to have spoken the last, dismissive word about it some decades ago, the movement has proven to be more resilient than its detractors thought it would be. Far from remaining decently buried, in recent years social gospel theology has received sufficient attention to enable theologians to begin asking whether rumors of its demise had been greatly exaggerated. Following Ronald C. White and C. Howard Hopkins's important 1976 anthology of social gospel writings, *The Social Gospel: Religion and Reform in a Changing America*, which urged scholars to "restate and re-vision" this significant chapter of North American religious history, so many fresh examinations of neglected aspects of the movement's history and reappraisals of its theology have begun to appear that one may speak of a modest contemporary renaissance of social gospel studies.[2]

This renaissance is perhaps most evident in the increasing number of works that investigate the life and thought of the social gospel's most celebrated theologian, Walter Rauschenbusch.[3] Since Rauschenbusch is widely regarded as *the* social gospel theologian, it is not surprising that reexaminations of the movement tend to focus on his contribution to it. But any discussion of the state of social gospel studies today that limits its scope exclusively or even primarily to

I

Rauschenbusch would fail to appreciate the *fundamental* significance of what is occurring in these studies. In the past two decades
works have begun to appear which suggest that our understanding of
the movement as a whole needs fundamentally to be reframed. These
works suggest that the received tradition that has long guided assessments of social gospel history and theology is so polemically
distorted that key features of this history and theology have been
neglected or misunderstood.

In the view of an increasing number of scholars engaging in
new research on the movement, our knowledge of the social gospel
is still in its infancy. What we have taken for granted may not have
been the case at all. What "everyone of course knows" about the social gospel may not be so transparent as we have thought. Recent
scholarly work has begun so significantly to revise our understanding of the social gospel that it is becoming more and more apparent
that we need a new comprehensive history of the movement.

This drive to assemble a revisionary portrait of the social gospel
movement proceeds from two primary stimuli. The first of these is
the emergence of political and liberation theologies during the 1960s
and 1970s. As a number of scholars have noted, although political and
liberation theologies sometimes deny any connection to social gospel
theology, the three theological movements have enough family re-
semblance to elicit interesting questions about possible kinship ties.

In North America, questions about such connections began to
emerge soon after Gustavo Gutiérrez's pioneering statement of liberation theology, *A Theology of Liberation*, appeared in English translation in 1973. In his 1975 volume *The Radical Imperative*, and in his
essay "The Social Gospel Today," which concludes the 1976 White
and Hopkins anthology, John Bennett observes that political, liberation, and social gospel theology have many points in common; for
example, all three find their thematic focus in the biblical symbol of
the kingdom of God.[4] In a 1980 essay, Howland Sanks reaches a similar conclusion: social gospel and liberation theology have such affin-
ity for one another, he thinks, that the two are, in important respects, variations on a single theme.[5] Roger Haight and John Langan
corroborate this thesis in a 1990 article on recent Catholic social
teaching in light of the social gospel, which discovers strong analogies between theologies of liberation, social gospel theology, and the
theology of the U.S. Catholic bishops in their 1986 pastoral letter
Economic Justice for All.[6]

In the same year, the case for a fresh scrutiny of social gospel
theology in light of the concern of many theologians today to accentuate the political and liberationist implications of the Christ-

ian gospel was stated even more forcefully by Gary J. Dorrien and
Diane Yeager. Dorrien's book *Reconstructing the Common Good* re-
assesses the Rauschenbusch heritage from the standpoint of liberation theology. It concludes that "in the life and work of . . . Walter Rauschenbusch, we confront the most instructive precedent for
the modern liberationist project."[7] Dorrien's revisionary re-read-
ing of Rauschenbusch's theology of the kingdoms of God and evil
sees him as prefiguring liberationism and as offering "a more re-
generative theological vision than the alternatives produced by his
numerous critics."[8]

Yeager's examination of the social gospel occurs in an essay in-
troducing the *Journal of Religious Ethics* (hereafter, *JRE*) theme issue
on the ethics of the social gospel in which the Haight and Langan article appears. Observing that the year 1990 marked the fiftieth an-
niversary of Charles Howard Hopkins's comprehensive critical assessment of social gospel history, *The Rise of the Social Gospel in
American Protestantism, 1865–1915*, she notes that Hopkins consistently referred to the social gospel in the past tense. In Yeager's
view, Hopkins's historiography was dominated by a negative theological assumption—namely, that the social gospel was best understood "not as a theologically original endeavor but as a kind of ger-
rymandering of theological boundaries under the pressure of various
external cultural changes."[9] In this reading of its significance, the
social gospel movement was fated to die, when the cultural situation
to which it had adapted itself ceased to exist. Hopkins therefore intended his study to be a *definitive* summary of social gospel history,
one that would "close the book on a movement that drove to the
extreme the tendencies of Protestant liberalism and made incontrovertibly plain its weaknesses."[10] For Yeager, Hopkins's closing the
book on social gospel history, and the theological judgments this
closing enfolds, continue to represent "the reigning consensus" of
scholars regarding the movement, despite Hopkins's own 1976 in-
vitation to scholars to reappraise the movement.[11]

Yeager is not content to give Hopkins the last word about social
gospel theology. As she argues, the development of political theologies in the period after Hopkins wrote has opened new vistas of interpretation on the movement. In Yeager's judgment, the time is
ripe for a critical history of the social gospel that employs a hermeneutic more sensitive to the primary concerns of the movement and less
polemically distorted than that of neo-orthodox critics:

> What was so clear to so many in 1940 is less clear in
> 1990. Political theologies flourish; efforts to define

a faithful Christian social philosophy abound. It seems likely that a full-scale critical history of the social gospel constructed today might offer an analysis rather different from that of Hopkins, setting these preachers, teachers, and activists in the context of the several waves of kingdom theology which have characterized theology in this century. From this perspective, a movement which had seemed to be the last muscular twitching of an already moribund theological liberalism might be rehabilitated.[12]

Yeager's *JRE* theme issue on social gospel ethics aptly sketches the contours of such a rehabilitated historiography of the social gospel: with articles on Rauschenbusch, Francis Greenwood Peabody, the "neglected voices" of the social gospel movement, and the analogies between recent Catholic social teaching and social gospel theology, this issue demonstrates how much that is genuinely new and interesting may still be said about the social gospel, in the wake of political and liberation theology.[13]

Political and liberation theologies have not been the sole stimulus to scholarly reexamination of social gospel theology. An equally powerful impulse for such reexamination has been the recent development by historians of new historiographical approaches "from below" that accentuate the contributions of hitherto overlooked marginal persons and groups to the so-called mainstream of history.

Conventionally, critics have accused social gospel theologians of having largely ignored African Americans's and women's aspirations to justice in the late nineteenth and early twentieth century. In the received tradition that governs scholarly appraisals of the movement, this charge has been repeated so often and for so many years now that it has become a byword, something that everyone of course knows about the social gospel, something that does not have to be demonstrated in order to be believed.

Underlying this charge is a theological judgment: that is, that social gospel theologians were culture Protestants who so adapted religion to culture that they lost any critical vantage point from which to call culture to conversion.[14] For such classic analysts of the movement's social ethic as James Dombrowski (*The Early Days of Christian Socialism*, 1936), social gospel theologians were bourgeois reformers whose vision of the shortcomings of North American society was superficial, and whose prescriptions for social reform were moralizing rather than structural, revisionary rather than radical.[15] This critique, and the accusation that social gospel theologians were tone-deaf to appeals for racial and gender justice, continue to appear in assessments of the movement up to the present, including Bennett's *Radical Imperative* and "The Social Gospel Today," Christopher Lasch's *Haven in a Heartless World* (1977), Janet Forsythe Fishburn's *The Fatherhood of God and the Victorian Family* (1981), Martin Marty's *Modern American Religion* (1986), and Dorrien's *Reconstructing the Common Good* (1990).[16]

As anyone who reads more than cursorily in the massive body of literature produced by the movement's spokespersons will soon discover, this charge is not without some foundation. In the work of leading social gospel theologians such as Washington Gladden, Josiah Strong, Rauschenbusch, or Shailer Mathews, one *can* sometimes find insensitivity to racism and the oppression of women. The movement *was* dominated by white Protestant men of middle-class backgrounds and professional standing. Social gospel theologians often unthinkingly reflected the interests and prejudices of their cultural background.

Yet recent investigations are beginning to indicate that this is not the whole truth.[17] In a theological movement that foregrounded the prophetic heritage of Judaism and Christianity, one might also expect to find glimmers of a consciousness that sometimes transcends the limitations of the class, gender, and cultural interests of its writers. Here again, White and Hopkins's 1976 anthology has been seminal. The anthology contains texts that have escaped the notice of critics of social gospel racism or antifeminism, including a 1903 sermon by Gladden against racism, an excerpt from Willis D. Weatherford's *Negro Life in the South*, a portion of Frances E. Willard's *Glimpses of Fifty Years* commenting on her involvement in the social gospel movement, and an excerpt from Mary Earhart's biography of Willard.[18] These texts demonstrate that the charge that social gospel theologians were racist or antifeminist is too monolithic, too easy. The picture was more complicated, and deserves to be examined more carefully. By including these texts, the White and Hopkins anthology addresses the lacunae of previous studies and pioneers a new historiography of the social gospel.

Following the lead of White and Hopkins, important first steps are now being made both to retrieve the "neglected voices" of the social gospel,[19] and to reconsider the evidence regarding the purported racism and sexism of "mainstream" social gospel theologians. Though so much new evidence needs to be sifted and old data reconsidered that a decisive statement about these matters cannot yet be formulated, research done in the last decade supports the conclusion that these theologians were not uniformly insensitive to racism and sexism, and were, indeed, in some cases vocal proponents of black and women's liberation.

A provocative example of such revisionary historiography is Fishburn's 1984 article "The Methodist Social Gospel and Woman Suffrage." The article is an interesting counterpoint to her 1981 volume on the fatherhood of God and the Victorian family, which had argued that social gospel theologians uncritically accepted late-Victorian notions regarding the role of women, including beliefs that the middle-class family is the building-block of society, that the family is brought into crisis by urbanization and industrialization, that men and women have complementary natures and tasks, and that such complementarity requires women to remain at home and "feminize" society by exercising their "feminine" virtues in the family circle. In Fishburn's view, Rauschenbusch assumed such ideas, and thus abhorred feminism and rejected woman suffrage.[20]

What is noteworthy about Fishburn's 1984 article is how it implicitly corrects her previous relentlessly negative assessment of the social gospel's relation to the women's movement. In the article, Fishburn maintains that while social gospel men did indeed resist woman suffrage until this was a *fait accompli*, the Methodist social gospel movement included women such as Willard who were simultaneously suffragists and social gospellers.[21] In retrieving the voices of Willard and other Methodist social gospel–cum–suffragist women, the 1984 article challenges the judgment that the social gospel movement was unabashedly opposed to the aspirations of women, and paves the way for other such projects of retrieval.

I attempted to engage in such retrieval in a 1992 article, "The Social Gospel and Feminism," which shows that Rauschenbusch's fellow Baptist social gospeller Shailer Mathews explicitly championed the women's movement throughout his long career. Mathews considered the feminist movement to be "epoch-making," and argued that "no social revolution in progress is so critical in its influences as this movement toward the emancipation of women."[22]

While it is certainly true to say that, despite their avowed sympathy for the women's movement (a sympathy that may have been more thoroughgoing in the case of Mathews), both Mathews and Rauschenbusch sometimes unreflectively accepted the patriarchal assumptions that deeply imbued the culture of late Victorian America, to say that either thinker was entirely insensitive to women's aspirations to justice would be altogether too simple.[23] In Mathews's case, a great deal of textual evidence points in quite the opposite direction. My essay notes that, because Mathews is relatively unknown today and his voluminous body of writings has not always been read carefully even by those commenting on his theology, scholars who return to the sources may find in Mathews—and, by implication, other major social gospel figures—new evidence that corrects some sweeping judgments about social gospel theology.

This call for a reconsideration of the evidence occurs as well in Jean Miller Schmidt's 1991 volume *Souls or the Social Order*, which reprints her 1969 dissertation on the social gospel movement. In a valuable introductory essay entitled "A Twenty Years' Retrospective," Schmidt notes that, had she written her survey of the movement today, some twenty years after it was originally composed, she would have done things very differently. In particular, she would have sought to incorporate the perspectives and stories of women and racial minorities. In Schmidt's view, the primary task of social gospel historiography at present is to correct the exclusive focus of previous histories of the movement on its white male proponents.[24]

The year 1991 also saw the publication of a study that provides important correctives to the view that social gospel theologians were blind to racial injustice. This study, Ralph Luker's *The Social Gospel in Black and White*, challenges the influential thesis of Arthur Schlesinger's classic 1932 essay "A Critical Period in American Religion, 1875–1900" that the social gospel movement was a cultural response to nineteenth-century industrialization, and not a movement of profound theological reflection.[25] Luker thinks that this view overlooks the theological basis of the movement: to see the social gospel as *primarily* a movement of cultural response is to neglect ample proof that the social gospel was equally a theologically creative movement. It is to overlook the culturally transformative, and not merely culturally adaptive, nature of the movement. As may be evident, Luker's critique of Schlesinger is also implicitly a critique of Hopkins's 1940 history of the social gospel movement; Schlesinger's thesis hovers within Hopkins's final-word judgment about the movement.

The response of social gospellers to movements for racial reform in the latter part of the nineteenth century and the early decades of the twentieth century illustrates the difficulty of making uniform judgments about *the* social gospel attitude to race. As Luker demonstrates, the movement incorporated a greater variety of perspectives on this (and other questions) than has hitherto been recognized.[26] It included African American figures whose contributions historians have neglected. And, Luker argues, the response of the leading white male theologians of the social gospel to race was considerably more nuanced and complex than has often been thought.

Mathews exemplifies the interpretive problem. His analysis of racism sometimes displays that shallowness critics have discerned in much social gospel thought about this phenomenon. In 1911, he was, for example, one of many social gospellers who endorsed the Supreme Court's decision to disfranchise black voters. Yet the testimony of one of Mathews's African American students, R. R. Wright, himself a neglected social gospel voice, suggests that Mathews was revered by black acquaintances with whom he had close friendships, who regarded him as a champion of the rights of African Americans. Wright credits Mathews with having "wrought a revolution" in his thinking.[27] Through Mathews and other social gospel professors, the movement's theology has had important influence on reform-minded African American preachers throughout the twentieth century.[28]

One of the most interesting recent attempts to come to terms with the complexity of social gospel attitudes regarding race and feminism is another article from the *JRE* issue on social gospel ethics, Susan Lindley's "'Neglected Voices' and *Praxis* in the Social Gospel." As do Fishburn and Luker, Lindley seeks to qualify previous critiques of social gospel imperviousness to the just demands of African Americans and women by retrieving three neglected voices—those of Vida Scudder, Reverdy Ransom, and Nannie Helen Burroughs. But she also pushes the historiographical argument considerably further than previous "from below" studies had done. Lindley argues that the attempt of historians to hear suppressed voices represents something more than the desire merely to embellish previous histories of the social gospel movement. In her view, the historiography from below deconstructs the view dominant in studies of the movement up to the present, and raises acute questions regarding all that we have taken for granted about the social gospel.

For Lindley, these are questions that drive to the very heart of interpretive traditions about the social gospel, and demonstrate how little we actually know about this movement and how fundamentally wrong some deeply entrenched judgments about the movement may be:

> But was the social gospel primarily or exclusively tied to particular responses to certain historical conditions, i.e., urban labor in the late nineteenth and early twentieth centuries? Was a particular theology, classic liberalism, definitive? What, in short, "counts" as part of the movement?
>
> The questions are made more acute by recent concern of scholars in all fields to listen for the voices of

those who were not educated white males. . . . Serious listening to the neglected voices means more than adding their sound around the edges of a finished composition; rather, the whole question of the meaning and impact of the social gospel must be re-opened and re-evaluated.[29]

In Lindley's formulation, the project of retrieving neglected social gospel voices moves to a conclusion similar to that reached by those who wish to re-examine the social gospel in light of contemporary political and liberationist theology: the movement is ripe for historical reassessment.

THE RECEIVED TRADITION
ABOUT THE SOCIAL GOSPEL

For anyone wishing to reassess the social gospel movement and its contribution to North American religion, the received tradition that continues to govern theological and historical appraisals of the movement is a formidable obstacle. The controlling view of the social gospel was established by Reinhold and H. Richard Niebuhr. In such influential studies as *Moral Man and Immoral Society* (1932) and *An Interpretation of Christian Ethics* (1935), Reinhold Niebuhr zeroed in critically on the social gospel's love ethic. Charging social gospel theologians with having uncritically accepted assumptions about the inevitability of progress that prevailed in late nineteenth-century European and American philosophies of history, Niebuhr maintained that their naive belief in progress led social gospellers to assume that intractable social problems would easily yield to sentimental preaching about love. In Niebuhr's view, the social gospel theology of sin is not radical enough—indeed, in one of those apotheg-matic pronouncements with which his theology abounds, he goes so far as to proclaim flatly that "proponents of the Social Gospel . . . did not believe in sin."[30] As a consequence, social gospel theology's analysis of how moral change occurs in social structures is crucially weak: love is emphasized to the exclusion of justice; and the social gospel cannot deal adequately with the fact that, in human collectives flawed by sin, conflict will be an inevitable concomitant of every attempt to effect reform.[31]

H. Richard Niebuhr's 1936 essay "The Attack upon the Social Gospel" and 1937 volume *The Kingdom of God in America* echo this critique, but with a slightly different focus. For H. Richard Niebuhr, the social gospel's fatal penchant for evolutionary philosophies of history is most evident in social gospel use of the biblical symbol of the kingdom of God. Niebuhr charges social gospel theologians with having held an "institutionalized view" of the kingdom of God: that is, social gospel theology expected Christian reformers to establish the kingdom of God gradually in this world; as sinful social structures gave way to love-based reform efforts, the kingdom would be built bit by bit, until the whole world had been transformed into God's reign.[32] As in his brother's critique of the social gospel's love ethic, underlying H. Richard Niebhur's negative evaluation of social gospel kingdom theology is a presumption that the social gospel lacked a strong doctrine of sin. Because this doctrine was weak in social gospel theology, Niebhur argues, the kingdom theology of the social gospel ultimately represents a "strategy of self-salvation."[33] Ignoring the radically pernicious effects of original sin on human nature, social gospellers assumed that moralizing appeals to the "higher nature" of human beings could easily overcome selfishness and bring in the kingdom.[34]

Their neo-orthodox critique proved so persuasive that, even in the lifetime of the brothers Niebuhr, it quickly became the hegemonic understanding of social gospel theology, an understanding that (in the phrase of White and Hopkins) has been "set in granite" since the 1930s.[35] And, as Lasch and Dorrien have recently observed, various attempts of scholars since White and Hopkins's anthology to reappraise the movement have done little to efface this granite critique. Lasch notes that the negative judgment the Niebuhrs passed on social gospel theology "remains the standard line on the social gospel and the progressive movement in general."[36] In Dorrien's view, the Niebuhrian assessment of the social gospel is now so entrenched that many theology students approach the social gospel *only* via the Niebuhrs's critique of it:

> By then [i.e., 1936] it had become commonplace to assume, as W. A. Visser't Hooft argued in *The Background of the Social Gospel in America*, that the Social Gospel theologians were pantheistic utopians who had failed to take seriously enough the transcendence of God and the pervasive reality of evil. This assessment (sometimes without the pantheism) was advanced over and over again by the Niebuhr brothers and others throughout the 1930s and afterward, providing the point of departure for a new the-

> ological consensus. . . . This argument has been so
> influential over the past sixty years that in many
> seminaries the Social Gospel tradition has often been
> taken up only in light of the Niebuhrian criticisms
> upon it.[37]

The Niebuhrian theological appraisal now so completely permeates most historical and theological presentations of the social gospel movement that it appears to be well-nigh incontrovertible. It has been so long repeated—as what everyone of course knows about the social gospel—that it is has become a received tradition about the movement, one that can now claim validity without demonstrating its correctness via close textual study of social gospel works, or careful argumentation.

Harry Antonides' 1985 *Stones for Bread: The Social Gospel and Its Contemporary Legacy* illustrates how scholars have come to rely on second-hand appraisals of social gospel theology. Antonides attacks political and liberation theology by tracing their genealogy to the social gospel, which descends, he maintains, from the discredited liberal theology of nineteenth-century German Protestantism:

> A direct line can be traced from the social gospel
> movement which flourished just after the turn of the
> century to the social and political activism in Protes-
> tant and Roman Catholic churches today. Both move-
> ments derive their main inspiration from liberal the-
> ology, that is, the adaptation of Christianity to the
> spirit of modernity.[38]

What is noteworthy about Antonides's treatment of social gospel theology is that it elides argument based on appeals to particular texts. Antonides' critique of social gospel theology is anecdotal, rather than well-grounded in textual appeal; it prescinds from historical proof, in the apparent expectation that readers will concur in his negative judgments because of what we all already know about the social gospel. Though even in the period in which Antonides painted the preceding picture, scholars were turning up impressive counterevidence to indicate that an accurate picture of the social gospel may be vastly more complicated than his description would have us believe, Antonides speaks as if there is no need to engage this counterevidence. In the face of the questions new evidence raises, Antonides' untroubled confidence that we all really know what social gospel theology was about is astonishing. In the final analysis, this confidence appears to rely more on received tradition than painstaking scholarship and cogent argumentation.[39]

Both the dominance of the received tradition and its tendency to degenerate into anecdote, as it is repeated over and over again without scholarly substantiation, are crucially apparent in what continues to be handed down about the social gospel's theology of the kingdom of God, a doctrine which, in Visser't Hooft's view in his classic study of the background of the social gospel, is "the heart of the social gospel."[40] Visser't Hooft argues that, particularly among European theologians, the kingdom theology of the social gospel is the ultimate criterion by which the movement is to be judged theologically valid or invalid. An important implication of this argument is that kingdom theology is an *articulum stantis et cadentis* not merely for social gospel theology, but also for the received critique of it: to the extent that social gospel use of the kingdom symbol is theologically invalid, to that extent will social gospel theology in general be invalid; but to the extent that the received tradition's critique of the kingdom theology of the social gospel can be shown to be incorrect, to that extent can the entire received tradition itself also be called into question.

As we have seen, according to the view that predominates in critical traditions, the social gospel's understanding of the kingdom of God harks back to liberal Protestant theology and suffers from the defects of its parent theological tradition. As does liberal theology, it "relieves the actual tension between the existing social reality and the absolute Christian ideal."[41] When this tension is collapsed, God's immanence in history is stressed to the exclusion of God's transcendence of history. As in the theology of Albrecht Ritschl, for which the kingdom of God was also an organizing principle, the kingdom is understood by social gospellers in this-worldly terms, and is to be achieved through human effort. Because liberal and social gospel theologians uncritically adopt the myth of progress, they expect God's kingdom to come as the capstone to developments that are occurring progressively and irresistibly in Western civilization. Like liberal Protestants, social gospellers are *culture* Protestants, believers who have so uncritically endorsed the myth of progress and evacuated divine transcendence of meaning that they have no sound theological basis for speaking a divinely other Word to culture. Their kingdom of God is identified with cultural developments.

Visser't Hooft's sketch of the kingdom theology of the social gospel sums up this critical argument in classic fashion:

> It [i.e., the Kingdom] is the ideal set before humanity
> by Jesus. It is essentially a new social order in which
> His principles will become supreme and which will
> be established on this earth through the gradual
> Christianization of all human relationships. Both the
> apocalyptic conception according to which the King-
> dom does not belong to this dispensation at all but
> will come as a catastrophic act of God Himself and
> the individualistic conception of a purely inward
> Kingdom are, from this point of view, distortions of
> Jesus' real teaching. The Kingdom is not interpreted
> from its background in the Old Testament prophets
> or from its relationship with the Jewish eschatolog-
> ical hope in the days of Jesus.[42]

For historians and theologians who adhere to this dominant critique of social gospel theology, World War I was the *kairos* moment for social gospel theology, the moment in which the fatuity of its belief in progress was definitively exposed, and its uncritical acceptance of cultural standards revealed for what it really is—not prophecy, but the blind blessing of Western culture, even as that culture walked into the nightmare of the twentieth century through the door of a world war.

The extent to which the received tradition's critique of the kingdom theology of the social gospellers still powerfully determines appraisals of social gospel theology, even as this tradition is being called into question, is evident in two recent theological commentaries on the theme. Arguing that the most serious objections to social gospel theology have to do with its use of the kingdom symbol, in his 1976 essay on social gospel theology today John Bennett contrasts the social gospel's theology of the kingdom with that of Gutiérrez, which sees the kingdom as a gift of God not to be identified with any this-worldly cultural achievement. Bennett believes that "the full weight of New Testament scholarship" is against the social gospel's understanding of the kingdom as "the fulfillment of human ideals" and its failure to recognize that the kingdom transcends history and judges all human achievements.[43]

In similar fashion, P. Travis Kroeker's 1991 article on the social gospel quest for a public morality critiques the social gospel's liberal Protestant historicization of the kingdom of God, argues that the social gospel identified God's will with historical progress, and maintains that the kingdom theology of the social gospel depended on an ideal of "anthropocentric immanence." For Kroeker, in its kingdom theology "the social gospel clearly stands in the liberal Protestant tradition of Schleiermacher, Ritschl, and Troeltsch."[44]

CRITICAL QUESTIONS ABOUT

THE RECEIVED TRADITION:

The Case of Shailer Mathews

Is the received tradition's critique of social gospel theology judicious? Is it substantially correct? Should historiographical approaches to the movement continue to take this tradition as their hermeneutical starting point? Or, if mounting evidence indicates that the picture of the social gospel painted by historians under the influence of this tradition is a partial and inaccurate one, should the received tradition itself be engaged critically, with a hermeneutic of suspicion, by those who seek to understand the movement's history?

In the following study of Shailer Mathews's lives of Jesus, I raise such critical questions regarding the neo-orthodox critique of social gospel theology by focusing on the kingdom theology (and the philosophy of history it incorporates) of a leading social gospel theologian, Shailer Mathews. The study confronts the historiography of the social gospel movement that depends uncritically on the received tradition's negative assessment of social gospel theology with a critical question: Have sweeping polemical generalizations about social gospel theology for far too long passed for informed scholarly assessment of the movement and its main players? As our preceding analysis of this tradition suggests, after the ascendancy of neo-orthodox theology and the consequent demise of the social gospel, scholars of North American religious history employing a neo-orthodox theological optic have sometimes passed wholesale judgment on social gospel theologians without even reading their texts closely and grappling with their thought in its historical context.[45]

Though recent decades have witnessed a revival in Rauschenbusch studies, other seminal social gospel thinkers remain virtually unknown today, even to trained theologians. Among the neglected parents of the social gospel, perhaps none deserves new, post-neo-orthodox scrutiny more than does the Chicago theologian Shailer Mathews (1863–1941). Mathews's claim to rescue from historical obscurity rests both on his historical importance to the movement and the continuing viability of aspects of his theology. As Sidney Ahlstrom's magisterial religious history of the American people notes, though Rauschenbusch eclipses Mathews today, in their lifetime the latter exerted more influence on the course of the social gospel movement than did the former.[46] Mathews was an eminent social gospel foundational figure; as the second dean of the Chicago Divinity school, as author of some thirty books and hundreds of articles, as editor of influential journals such as the *Biblical World*, and as a veritable "peripatetic loquacity"[47] on the Chautauqua lecture circuit and at universities throughout the United States, Mathews spread the social gospel with evangelical fervor. His impact was so widespread and so formative for the movement that, as Leander Keck's foreword to the 1970 reprint of Mathews's *Jesus on Social Institutions* observes, "There can be no substantive dialogue with our own theological tradition which ignores these influential figures, [Mathews and his Chicago colleague, Shirley Jackson Case] though today they are scarcely read at all."[48]

As the following study will demonstrate, a close contextual reading of Mathew's extensive body of theological writings reveals that the story the received tradition tells about social gospel theology is far from the whole story. In particular, as the study tracks Mathews's attempt to provide a solid foundation for the social gospel in response to the challenge posed to social gospel kingdom theology by Johannes Weiss's 1892 work *Die Predigt Jesu vom Reiche Gottes*, which "discovered" that Jesus had not proclaimed a this-worldly, but an eschatological, kingdom, it turns up abundant evidence that Mathews's social gospel theology (and, by implication, social gospel theology in general) represents something more than a liberal Protestant collapse of religion to culture.

The charge that Mathews was a culture Protestant has run rather consistently through studies of his theology and of social gospel theology in general. Beginning with Henry J. Cadbury, who accused him of transforming the gospel of Matthew into the gospel of Mathews, and who attacked his "social interpretation" of the gospel (even while admitting that Mathews eventually recanted the social interpretation of the kingdom set forth in his 1897 study *The Social Teaching of Jesus*),[49] North American theologians critical of the social gospel have unambiguously categorized Mathews as a prototypical liberal Protestant who never recognized that the eschatological turn German theology took with J. Weiss and Albert Schweitzer undermined the social interpretation of the kingdom, and thus the social gospel itself. In his *Christ and Culture*, H. Richard Niebuhr lists Mathews as a culture Protestant—though Niebuhr's misspelling of

Mathews's name as Matthews causes one to wonder a bit about how familiar he actually was with Mathews's work.[50]

Accusations that the social gospel never perceived the import of eschatology for its social interpretation of the kingdom, and continued to build its theology on an evolutionary, this-worldly idea of the kingdom right up to the moment of its demise, have long been part and parcel of the received tradition's critique of social gospel kingdom theology. These accusations appear in such classic works as Visser't Hooft's study of the background of the social gospel, and in Waldo Beach and H. Richard Niebuhr's *Christian Ethics*.[51]

Norman Perrin elaborates on these charges in his volume *The Kingdom of God in the Teaching of Jesus* (1963), which supposes that social gospellers came into contact with consistent eschatology only in the decade 1920–30, and that when they did so, they denied the apocalyptic framework of Jesus' kingdom proclamation. Perrin maintains that the first English-speaking theologian to deal with the topic of consistent eschatology was William Sanday, in his 1907 *The Life of Jesus in Recent Research*. Perrin sees B. S. Easton (*Christ in the Gospels*, 1930) as "probably unique" among North American scholars of his period in admitting the apocalyptic backdrop of Jesus' kingdom teaching. Furthermore, Perrin flatly dismisses Mathews's reading of the kingdom in the 1921 *Dictionary of Religion and Ethics* as a progressivist, anti-apocalyptic, liberal one.[52] Writing two years later, Amos Wilder echoes Perrin by noting that it is "well known" that the social gospel built its social ethic around a this-worldly interpretation of the kingdom of God.[53]

Two studies of Mathews's kingdom theology that appear in 1963 and 1981 volumes are particularly revealing; they demonstrate the extent to which we are often dealing with received opinion in what has been passed down in the chain of transmission originating with neo-orthodox critiques of social gospel kingdom theology. In the case of the two studies in question, one can see how this chain of received opinion is formed, as one scholar's interpretation of the movement links to another's. The 1963 work is John Macquarrie's *Twentieth-Century Religious Thought*. Arguing that his kingdom theology replaces "the prophetic evangelical faith" with "a sophisticated evangelical theology," Macquarrie distinguishes Mathews from social gospellers such as Rauschenbusch and Gladden, whom he takes to be bona fide evangelicals.[54] R. K. O. White's 1981 *Christian Ethics* repeats the statement, adding that Mathews "obscured the Christian message," and citing Macquarrie as his source for this claim. Having said this, White proceeds to examine Mathews's *Social Teaching of Jesus* (hereafter, *STJ*) and *Growth of the Idea of God*

(1931), paraphrasing Macquarrie's analysis of these works with uncanny literalism. White replicates an entire paragraph of Macquarrie's study, phrase by phrase, with only a few minor syntactical changes and without quotation marks; only in a footnote at the end of the paragraph does he informs his readers that he is not actually appealing to Mathews's works, but to Macquarrie.

A comparison of Macquarrie and White on Mathews is revelatory because it indicates that the received tradition about social gospel theology is so taken for granted and thought to be so impervious to challenge, that theologians can critique social gospel theology merely by appealing to previous critiques, without advertising the fact that they are repeating these critiques, and apparently without engaging in careful study of the texts on which they appear to be commenting. I make this point not merely for pedantic reasons, but because recognition of what is going on in White's questioning of the evangelical foundations of Mathews's "sophisticated evolutionary theology" raises critical counterquestions about the validity of his conclusions regarding Mathews's kingdom theology.

White concludes that at some unspecified late date, Mathews became aware of criticisms of his evolutionary theology and began to ground the social gospel in the teachings of Jesus.[55] The date to which he refers is rather ambiguous: though he states that it was "later" than some previous date at which Mathews still held an evolutionary position, he does not specify either the former or the latter date. His footnote here cites the *Dictionary of Religion and Ethics* that Mathews co-edited with G. B. Smith in 1921. Since he had previously cited *STJ* and *Growth of the Idea of God*, and since the latter work was published a decade after the 1921 volume, one can only conclude that White is claiming that Mathews abandoned his evolutionary theology for an evangelical one in the period 1897–1921. As our close reading of Mathews's work in this period will demonstrate, this claim is simply incorrect. The 1897 work was itself an attempt to ground social gospel theology in the teaching of Jesus—in an *evangelical* reading of Jesus' teaching—and Mathews had already become aware of the work of J. Weiss and its implications for social gospel kingdom theology as he wrote the 1895–96 articles that comprise the 1897 book.

Indeed, patent proof exists that, far from ignoring consistent eschatology, Mathews was in the *forefront* of North American theological response to J. Weiss. *STJ*'s recognition of the significance of J. Weiss's work is remarkable for being one of the *first* such references in a North American theological work, one that follows hard on the heels of Weiss's 1892 study of Jesus' teaching regarding the kingdom of God. And Mathews does not merely refer to J. Weiss in the 1897 book. There, and for almost a decade thereafter, he grapples with J. Weiss's challenge, and begins the process of rethinking the foundation of his social gospel theology in response to that challenge. Far from having ignored the problems the eschatological reading of the New Testament posed for the social gospel, Mathews stands out as a pioneer among North American theologians who saw the importance of eschatology for twentieth-century theology, and who sought to integrate the turn to eschatology in their theology.

When one examines Mathews's attempt to develop a foundational theology for the social gospel carefully, and notes how central his concern to respond to the eschatological thesis of J. Weiss is to that attempt, one is puzzled that scholars commenting on the social gospel in general and Mathews in particular can continue to speak so airily about social gospel theologians' ignorance of the eschatological turn that occurred in German theology with Weiss and Albert Schweitzer, whose 1906 *Vom Reimarus zu Wrede* decisively exposed the fatuity of the liberal quest for the historical Jesus.[56] As recently as 1971, in their introduction to Weiss's *Jesus' Proclamation of the Kingdom of God* in the Fortress Press "Lives of Jesus" series, Richard H. Hiers and David Larrimore Holland maintain that *"Predigt Jesu vom Reiche Gottes* . . . strangely has been neglected by British and American New Testament critics and theologians."[57] Hiers and Holland note that there is virtually no mention of Weiss's *Predigt Jesu* or eschatology in the *Journal of Biblical Literature* and the *American Journal of Theology* in the decade after 1892.[58]

Observing that "for such American writers as Shailer Mathews and Benjamin W. Bacon, the leading authorities remained [i.e, in the decade 1892–1902] B. Weiss, H. H. Wendt, and W. Beyschlag," Hiers and Holland state that only in 1903 did Bacon begin to grapple with J. Weiss's work, and then without naming J. Weiss.[59] Hiers and Holland arrive at the following conclusion regarding the influence of J. Weiss on North American and British theology: "From the lack of attention it has been given, one receives the impression that the *Predigt* has been generally unknown in Britain and America, in part because copies of it have been unavailable."[60]

As our examination of *STJ* and Mathews's subsequent work will demonstrate, to say that the prototypically liberal Protestant theologians named above were Mathews's exegetical authorities in the period from 1892 to 1902 is true only in a qualified sense. In the years 1895–97, Mathews was already beginning to question some fundamental assumptions of liberal Protestant exegesis and to acknowledge the persuasiveness of J. Weiss's work. In the period 1902–5, his exegesis veers even more sharply away from liberal Protestant mentors. By 1905, in his work *The Messianic Hope in the New Testament* (hereafter, *MHNT*), Mathews explicitly repudiates the social interpretation of the kingdom of God, and grants that J. Weiss's eschatological reading of the biblical symbol is substantially accurate.

RETRIEVING THE HISTORY

OF THE SOCIAL GOSPEL

What is one to make of the puzzle of the received tradition's claims about Mathews's kingdom theology? As our study of Mathews's attempt to discover a theological foundation for social gospel theology will show, there is clear (and abundant) evidence in texts from every period of his long career that Mathews not only grappled seriously with J. Weiss's work, but that, having accepted the eschatological interpretation of the kingdom of God, he built his social gospel theology around this interpretation. At the very least, scholars' continuing insistence that social gospel theologians ignored the eschatological turn of German theology in the face of such abundant textual evidence to the contrary in Mathews's work demonstrates that we need careful (and carefully controlled) reinvestigations of the theology of the social gospel, and in particular of its exegesis, since (as Robert Funk argued in 1976) the waters of North American biblical scholarship in the period from 1892 to 1920 are "still uncharted."[61]

Though the received tradition's critique of social gospel theology was undoubtedly warranted in some respects, it was also tendentious and partial. John Bennett views the tendency of neo-orthodox critics to exaggerate the shortcomings of the social gospel in psychological terms: theologians such as the Niebuhrs were children of the social gospel, and often acknowledged their indebtedness to their social gospel forebears.[62] As frequently happens when children seek to confirm their own identity by rebelling against their parents, neo-orthodoxy exaggerated—even caricatured—key features of the thought of its theological mentors in order to establish itself. The case of Mathews and the kingdom of God points to the need for a new historiographical retrieval of the social gospel movement, in which scholars employ hermeneutics of suspicion to cut away the thicket of neo-orthodox overgrowth that has hidden many of the movement's features from view. Once that thicket has been removed, hermeneutics of retrieval need to be applied, as scholars ask, in this age of renewed interest in the political and liberationist implications of the gospel and in the neglected voices of history, What *was* this enigmatic movement that has exerted such influence on North American Christianity? [63]

Ultimately, the rationale for such a project of historiographical retrieval rests on the premise that we still know far less about that movement than we have presumed to know. If a student of the social gospel of no less stature than H. Richard Niebuhr could conclude that it was a "multifarious thing" defying easy analysis, as he did in *Kingdom of God in America,* then one wonders how theologians and historians have found it possible to remain so long content that the primary features of the movement's history have already been satisfactorily delineated. [64] An address entitled "The Social Gospel and the Mind of Jesus," which Niebuhr presented to the American Theological Society several years before the book's publication, explicates the statement. Until Diane Yeager edited the essay in 1988, it had not been in print. In it, Niebuhr insists,

> The phrase "mind of Jesus in the social gospel" seems to make the assumption that the social gospel is a simple thing. As a matter of fact it is extremely varied. There is a vast difference between the social gospels, let us say, of Rauschenbusch and Peabody, an even greater difference between Shailer Mathews and Harry Ward. [65]

If Niebuhr is correct, then the movement's history deserves to be approached from hermeneutical standpoints that permit scholars to see its intricacies better than polemical hermenuetics have done, as they have sought to tar all social gospel theologians with one brush. As Yeager argues, "In the midst of vigorously renewed efforts to define the social and political task—or even mission—of Christians and their churches, the theology of Christian social activism which constitutes the legacy of the social gospel continues to deserve balanced and discriminating review." [66]

To say this is also to say that our approach to something so complex as social gospel history ought to be considerably more tenuous than it has been in the past. If we know less rather than more, far-reaching generalizations about some composite phenomenon called *"the* social gospel" need to await the results of new examinations of discrete portions of social gospel history and thought. Efforts to put the whole puzzle together—that is, to make new critical judgments about social gospel theology in its entirety—need to be preceded by painstaking historical investigation in which individual thinkers and their texts receive focused scrutiny, and the historical context of these thinkers and texts is satisfactorily sketched.

In his 1949 dissertation on George D. Herron, and in a prescient article published the subsequent year, Robert Handy points the way toward just such a revisionary project in social gospel history. Noting that studies of social gospel theology have far too commonly relied on vague generalizations rather than informed historical observation, he argues that what is required are "more intensive studies of certain periods and aspects of the larger movement." [67] Handy's groundbreaking study of Herron illustrates what is to be gained by such a close reading of an aspect of the social gospel: maintaining that much work remains to be done on the social gospel by historians, and that this work should begin with "intensive concern with some of its leaders," he constructs the first extended account to that date (and still one of the best) of the significant role played by the enigmatic Herron in the foundational period of the movement.[68] Unless one appreciates Herron's contributions to the social gospel movement (and one cannot do so without placing his thought in the context of his biography),[69] one cannot understand Shailer Mathews's reflections about the foundations of social gospel theology, particularly in the crucial years of his career in which he dealt with Herron's ideas while composing his first life of Jesus. Putting the Mathews piece in its place in the larger puzzle requires finding and placing the Herron piece as well.

Handy wrote a decade after the publication of Hopkins's magisterial history of the social gospel movement. If that history still remains the standard overview of the movement (as Yeager insists is the case), then Handy's description of the trajectory to be followed by revisionary historians of the social gospel remains as pertinent today as it was when he formulated it. If anything, the demand for a new comprehensive history of the movement is even more pressing now than when Handy wrote, since, while no new history has appeared, another significant historian of North American religion has seconded Handy's call for new historical analysis of the social gospel. The scholar is William Hutchison, who, in a 1975 article on the social gospel, appeals for "sharply focused" and "fairly minute" studies of discrete aspects of the movement.[70] In Hutchison's view "students of the social movement [in American Christianity] simply have before them a task of historical and historiographical 'unpacking'." [71]

Just as rewriting the history of the social gospel movement will require scholars to take a second look at the received theological critique of the social gospel, it will also entail asking some critical questions about the central thesis of the hegemonic historiographical tradition. As we have seen, Hopkins's history of the movement employs an interpretive framework borrowed from Schlesinger, which sees the social gospel in the first instance as a cultural movement, and only secondarily as a theological one.

This thesis has been challenged very directly recently by Donald K. Gorrell, whose study of the movement from 1910 to 1920 maintains that, though the social gospel was in some respects a response to cultural factors such as industrialization, it was also a theologically innovative movement. In Gorrell's view, "the message of the social gospel was both initiative and response." [72] Gorrell argues that historians who view the movement as adaptationist fail to recognize its important theological roots. He argues that the development of social gospel theology in the period from roughly 1910 to 1920 has been insufficiently appreciated by historians, who have focused either on the formative period of the social gospel, or its response to critics after World War I. [73]

SHAILER MATHEWS'S

LIVES OF JESUS:

An Outline of the Argument

The following study of Shailer Mathews's lives of Jesus situates itself within the new quest for social gospel history sketched above. It does so in the first place by heeding Handy and Hutchison's call for intensive, sharply focused, fairly minute studies of periods and aspects of the movement, particularly its leaders. Its close reading of a discrete portion of one major social gospeller's work seeks to be such a carefully delimited study. With Handy and Hutchison, I am interested in discovering whether a fine-toothed analysis of several representative social gospel foundational works—an analysis sensitive to their historical context and their place within a large corpus of other works by the same author—turns up new information about the theology of one social gospel leader, information that may also suggest that "the" social gospel was considerably more polychromatic than its critics have taken it to be. My investigation of Mathews's lives of Jesus aspires to a deliberate inconclusiveness: rather than seeking to comment on social gospel theology as a whole, or even on "the" kingdom theology of the social gospel, it attempts to recover one small piece of a much larger puzzle, one that can be assembled satisfactorily only when other historical projects of this nature have been undertaken.

I will argue that Mathews's 1897 life of Jesus, *STJ*, was a *foundational* social gospel work. Mathews wrote the book out of keen concern to find a compelling exegetical and sociological basis for social gospel theology. In both his work preceding *STJ* and that of his former teacher and mentor, Albion Small, a founding figure of American sociology, there is strong evidence of such concern. This concern forms the background to *STJ*; unless one appreciates how much Mathews's intent to develop a solid foundation for social gospel theology is primary in the 1897 work, one cannot fully understand the significance of the volume, or adequately interpret it.

Soon after Mathews wrote the 1897 social gospel foundational work, he became discontented with its treatment of the kingdom of God. *STJ* had constructed its social gospel foundational theology around a this-worldly understanding of the kingdom. Though Mathews took the work of J. Weiss into account in the book, he rejected Weiss's reading of the kingdom symbol because he considered it a threat to social gospel ethics. In his view, if one accepted that Jesus proclaimed an apocalyptic kingdom to come either in his lifetime or at some unspecified point thereafter, one removed Jesus' redemptive import from this world and robbed the church of any strong basis on which to build its social ethic.

At the same time, *STJ*'s concern to ground social gospel theology in scientific exegesis compelled Mathews to take J. Weiss's eschatology seriously. His work in the years following *STJ* shows that, for a number of years after he published his first life of Jesus, he struggled forthrightly with Weiss's thesis about the eschatological framework of Jesus' kingdom proclamation. In various essays and book reviews in the period from 1897 to 1905, he attempts to deal with the apparent quandary Weiss had created for social gospel theology. In these articles, Mathews gradually but inexorably yielded ground to Weiss, until, in 1905, with his definitive statement of social gospel exegesis, *MHNT*, he explicitly repudiated the social interpretation of the kingdom *STJ* had defended, and substantially accepted J. Weiss's reading of the kingdom symbol. The stance Mathews adopted here is one that I call eschatological realism: by 1905, he recognized that Jesus' proclamation of the kingdom of God was eschatological and not this-worldly; but he did not at this point or at any later point in his career endorse the interim ethic of consistent eschatology. In his view, if one believed that the ethical teaching of Jesus was given *ad interim*, to disciples awaiting the imminent coming of the eschatological kingdom, one made that ethical teaching ineffectual for all history between Jesus and the kingdom's final coming.[74]

Once Mathews had moved to a position of eschatological realism, he began the process of reconstructing his social gospel foundation. He did so by shifting the focus of social gospel foundational theology away from the kingdom symbol itself and toward what he called social process. The theology of social process envisages social evolution in idealistic terms. It draws from insights of such influential thinkers of the period as Small, Richard Ely, and Lester Ward, who saw social structures unfolding in response to ideals that reformers brought to bear on these structures. In the view of Mathews's sociological mentors, social ideals point to the goal of history and spur social evolution by drawing social structures toward this goal. Effective reform is that which inspires historical development toward a goal in keeping with the inherent tendencies of social structures.

In Mathews's view, a foundational social gospel theology could advantageously conjoin such sociological theory and the eschatological reading of the kingdom symbol. If the kingdom is the goal of history, a goal never perfectly realized in any cultural development within history, but one proleptically present in social structures, then it is also an ideal toward which the evolution of both church and society can justifiably be directed. A social process foundation for social gospel theology thus allows one both to affirm the eschatological nature of the kingdom of God, and to speak of the eschatological kingdom as drawing history, or social evolution, toward itself. Mathews begins the development of such a foundational theology for the social gospel in *MHNT* itself, as he endorses the eschatological interpretation of the kingdom. In the years after 1905, he paves the way for his revised foundational statement of social gospel theology, the 1928 *Jesus on Social Institutions* (hereafter, *JSI*), by continuing to elaborate a process theology and to reflect on the centrality of eschatology to Christian faith.

JSI is a revision of *STJ*. Mathews's autobiography *New Faith for Old* specifies that he revised the first social gospel foundation because he had repudiated its interpretation of the kingdom of God. Since the first life of Jesus *was* clearly a theological foundation for the social gospel, and since Mathews revised this work to take the eschatological turn of German theology into account in his social gospel foundation, the second life of Jesus provides an interesting test case of the social gospel's response to the eschatological school. To examine the two texts side by side is to see what one major social gospel thinker did with the challenges this school presented to social gospel theology. It is to see, in other words, how, at a *foundational* level, the social gospel dealt with the question of eschatology.

The study concludes that Mathews's attempt to discover a foundation for social gospel theology needs to be reappreciated by theologians and historians of the social gospel. In some respects, the neo-orthodox critique of social gospel theology certainly continues to obtain in Mathews's case. Even after he had made the eschatological turn with German theology after J. Weiss, he continued to speak of love to the exclusion of justice. His theology of sin is perhaps not so weak as critics have imagined was the case with social gospel theology. But it *is* rhetorically impoverished. Mathews speaks of sin too often as the "backwards drag" of evolving human nature; he speaks too little of the radical tendency to evil within "evolved" human nature and "evolved" social structures.

But in one central respect, the neo-orthodox critique of Mathews's theology is simply to a great extent beside the point. Far from having ignored the question of eschatology, Mathews dealt with that question straightforwardly, and with considerable acumen. In fact, he built his mature theology around an exegesis of eschatological realism. If Visser't Hooft is correct in maintaining that kingdom theology is the heart of the social gospel, then a reading of Mathews's foundational theology suggests that social gospel theology may have continuing viability, even after it has been subjected to valid critique by neo-orthodoxy.

In key respects, Mathews's social gospel theology anticipates important insights of political and liberation theologians today. His careful attempt to find a viable social ethic in light of the discovery that Jesus' kingdom proclamation was eschatological—his attempt *both* to foreground the eschatological kingdom *and* to emphasize the proleptic effect of that kingdom on history—deserves consideration today, because of the ways in which it prefigures the thought of theologians such as Johannes Baptist Metz, Jürgen Moltmann, and Gustavo Gutiérrez. And his awareness that the kingdom of God is not to be identified with, but stands in judgment on, any historical attempt to realize it also makes his foundational social gospel theology worthy of reconsideration today.

In these and other respects, Mathews's social gospel theology breaks decisively with liberal Protestantism. In fact, Mathews's treatment of eschatology in the period after *STJ* rather interestingly echoes the theology of such critics of liberal Protestantism as the French Roman Catholic modernist theologian Alfred Loisy. If contemporary theologians want to find parallels between social gospel theology and political or liberation theologies, then perhaps they need to look more closely at the ways in which the social gospel represented a new moment in twentieth-century theology, and not a faint echo of the discredited liberalism of the nineteenth century. To the extent to which social gospel theology critiqued liberal Protestant theology and its tendency to adapt faith to culture, to that extent it represents a prophetic forebear of political and liberation theology today. For North American theologians and North American Christian social activists, aspects of the social gospel may be continuingly viable. This indigenous movement remains worthy of theological and historical attention.

While some aspects of social gospel theology are clearly dated and ought to fall into abeyance—in particular, those marred by the naiveté of late-nineteenth progressivist optimism—in other respects the movement may have been far more theologically astute than its critics have given it credit for having been. In the final analysis, Keck appears to be right: North American theologians cannot engage in substantive dialogue with their theological traditions while ignoring such influential figures as Mathews. If we reopen that dialogue as the twentieth century nears its close, we may find that Mathews and other social gospellers are far more interesting and instructive dialogue partners than we have imagined them to be.

An Outline of the Book

The following investigation of Mathews's foundation for social gospel theology is divided into four parts. Chapter 1 presents a brief account of Mathews's life, intellectual development, and significance. Since he is a figure who has fallen into relative historical obscurity, the object of this short history is to "place" Mathews for the reader. In addition, the opening chapter seeks to provide a basis for the subsequent study of Mathews's lives of Jesus by delineating the progression of his theological thought, by situating that thought within the historical context both of Mathews's life and of broader historical currents, and by noting the most important works in an extensive bibliography that may not be immediately familiar to many readers.

Chapter 2 concentrates on Mathews's first social gospel life of Jesus, *STJ*. A primary objective of this section of the book is to demonstrate that Mathews wrote the life to provide a foundation for social gospel theology. To show this, the chapter tracks very closely Mathews's statements of concern regarding the question of discovering such a foundation in the period immediately prior to the composition of the 1897 volume.

After the chapter examines the background of concern from which *STJ* emerged, it moves to a close reading of the text of *STJ*. One of my overriding intents here is to locate Mathews's lives of Jesus within an intellectual and historical context. Broadly speaking, this context is, of course, his desire to provide a solid foundation for social gospel theology. But in a more immediate sense, Mathews wrote *STJ* to respond to a variety of theological thinkers of his period who had undertaken similar projects to base the social or political reform programs of the period on the social teachings of Jesus.

Mathews responded to these exegetes, sociologists, and social reformers both negatively and positively in the text of *STJ*. On the one hand, as both *STJ* and his articles and reviews in the years prior to the publication of *STJ* reveal, Mathews composed his foundational study as a critique of reform proposals he considered to be invalid, either because they were sociologically ill-informed or because their exegesis was not scientific. On the other hand, he also clearly drew on the work of contemporary sociologists and theologians whose research he regarded as well-founded. Both sets of thinkers, those Mathews wished to combat and those on whom he depended, create the intellectual context within which Mathews composed *STJ*. In my view, studies of the work need to reconstruct that context, if the full significance of his social gospel life of Jesus is to be apparent. In addition, since *STJ* is a pioneering social gospel foundational statement, to uncover the background of Mathews's thought in *STJ* is by inference to provide significant information about the intellectual context within which North American social gospel thought emerged. For this reason, the chapter devotes considerable attention to the question of whom Mathews was reading as he wrote the 1897 life of Jesus.

Finally, as the second chapter combs the text of *STJ* carefully, it asks precisely how this text provides a foundation for social gospel theology. Since Mathews's writings before *STJ* suggest that among his chief considerations was the desire to find an exegetically appropriate basis for Christian involvement in social reform movements, and to show that this basis intersected with what sociologists were saying about effective social change, the social gospel foundation that *STJ* elaborates was double-layered. Chapter 2 studies both the exegetical and the sociological foundation in detail, with particular attention to how Mathews handled the kingdom of God symbol.

The third chapter moves to an examination of Mathews's reflections about a social gospel foundation in the period spanning the two lives of Jesus. Above all, this section of the study wishes to track how the inner logic of Mathews's understanding of social gospel foundational problems unfolds as he deals with the challenge of eschatology. Since the 1905 *MHNT* represents a watershed for Mathews's understanding of eschatology, and since this is his culminating social gospel exegetical statement, this work receives primary consideration in chapter 3. Finally, as in the previous chapter, this section of the book continues to reconstruct the intellectual context within which Mathews's thought unfolded.

To a great extent, the years to 1905 were the seminal period for Mathews's social gospel thought, and indeed for his entire theological system. This is evident *inter alia* in the following: by 1905 he had already arrived at the eschatological formulation that his 1928 revision of the 1897 study of Jesus' social teaching would presuppose; and, in his later work, Mathews never significantly alters the exegetical basis he had developed for social gospel theology in *MHNT*. After 1905, he puts this question to rest, and in all his subsequent theology consistently employs the understanding of eschatology at which *MHNT* had arrived.

Since this is the case, study of Mathews's thought about the foundations of social gospel theology over the period 1897–1928 must give proportionately greater attention to the 1897–1905 period than to that after 1905. Indeed, a strong case can be made on behalf of more intensive study of *all* aspects of Mathews's early theology. Most studies of Mathews to date focus on the *later* Mathews, and, in particular, on such key works as *The Atonement and the Social Process* (1930) or *The Growth of the Idea of God* (1931). Such important early works as *MHNT*, *The Church and the Changing Order* (1907), or, for that matter, *STJ*, receive considerably less attention in studies of his theology.

Yet one can justifiably argue that Mathews's work after 1905 was somewhat less creative or pioneering than it had been in the earlier period. As he became increasingly involved in administrative, editorial, and other responsibilities such as lecture tours and political committee work, Mathews tended to do less groundbreaking theological thinking than he had done in his early career. In significant respects, the post-1905 theology simply develops insights that he had already attained in the first years of his theological work.

One can sometimes track the dependence of Mathews's later work on his earlier in a quasi-empirical way by comparing the texts of Mathews's postwar works with those published prior to the war: again and again, whole sections of previously published material crop up later with only slight emendations. Indeed, in some cases Mathews seems to have been in such haste to compile his later volumes that he even reproduces mistakes from previous works. Intellectual biographers would not do Mathews an injustice, then, if they focused on the first period of his career and life. Such a disproportion of emphasis is entirely to be expected in the case of a thinker who draws heavily on his early writings in his later ones. And it is perhaps a welcome corrective to the emphasis already placed on his later works by many scholars—an emphasis that too often presumes that one can understand these works without examining the historical context within which they arose.

The fourth chapter focuses on *JSI*. The controlling question of this portion of the study will be to ask how the second foundational statement of social gospel theology revises or advances on its predecessor. Here, the issue of eschatology is obviously crucial, so the chapter will seek in particular to identify how *JSI* incorporates Mathews's 1905 exegesis of eschatological realism and his interesting application of that exegesis in various works from 1905 to 1928. Since the fourth chapter examines both how *JSI* revises *STJ* and how the latter work advances on the former's formulation of kingdom theology, a preliminary focus of this chapter will be a close textual comparison of the two lives of Jesus.

What is true of Mathews's writings in general—that his later texts replicate portions of previously written texts, to such an extent that a rather lengthy volume might be written about the redactional history of his works—is true *pari passu* of the relationship between *STJ* and *JSI*. The 1928 work reproduces entire sections of the 1897 work, changing some of them superficially, others substantially. Though Kenneth Cauthen's valuable introduction to the recent Fortress Press reprint of *JSI* tracks some of these textual changes, it misses some revealing revisions, and assumes that some portions of the text that had appeared in the 1897 volume are new to the 1928 one. One of my leading objectives in chapter 4 is to compare the two texts and show how the revisions incorporated by the second life of Jesus reflect Mathews's intent to provide a new, eschatologically realistic foundation for social gospel theology.

The final goal of the fourth chapter is to assess Mathews's mature foundation for social gospel theology. Since an underlying intent of our examination of Mathews's lives of Jesus is to ask whether the social gospel produced a theology that dealt effectively with the threat consistent eschatology appears to pose to theologies that premise arguments for believers' political engagement on the this-worldly significance of Jesus' kingdom proclamation, this chapter asks whether Mathews dealt successfully with the challenge of consistent eschatology. The chapter also asks whether the neo-orthodox critiques of Mathews's theology are, in the final analysis, justifiable. If not, do any aspects of his theology remain useful; and in particular, does the foundation he laid for social gospel theology after his eschatological turn compel any assent?

Our assessment of Mathews's second life of Jesus forms a bridge to the book's afterword, which develops the argument that Mathews's kingdom theology represents a point of intersection between his social gospel theology and political or liberation theology today. Mathews's case may demonstrate that the social gospel's kingdom theology is both its potentially most valuable contribution to later theologies, and its least understood contribution. If one reads Mathews's attempt to find a foundation for social gospel theology carefully, one discovers that he coped, and coped rather well, with the challenge of the eschatological school. Having read J. Weiss at an early date, and having analyzed social gospel theology from the standpoint of Weiss's analysis of eschatology, Mathews made the eschatological interpretation of the New Testament central to his social gospel theology.

Mathews not only dealt with the apparently mortal threat of eschatology successfully. In the face of this apparent threat, he also retrieved a strong social ethic for Christian theology. And he did so without diminishing the critical force of Christian theology vis-à-vis culture. In these respects, Mathews's theology anticipates the theology of Metz, Moltmann, and Gutiérrez, and thus deserves to be critically retrieved. The afterword will develop this argument at length.

Some Concluding Methodological Considerations

In delineating the two poles of Mathews's thought regarding the foundations of social gospel theology and reconstructing the process of thought that moves between the first and the second, I am engaging in a project of retrieval that employs tools of intellectual biography. In my view, retrieval of the thought of a historical figure about a given subject, or intellectual biography, is primarily a reconstructive enterprise. In the first place, intellectual biography needs to reconstruct the context of the thought of the person it studies. If it focuses on particular texts, as the present study does, it must ask questions such as the following: to whom is the thinker responding in this passage; on whom is she relying; whose works does he cite, or whose books does she review? If one is writing intellectual biography of a theologian, one must ask such questions with a concern to discover what contemporary theological debates are reflected in the texts one is studying.

As the preceding discussion has suggested, such questions are particularly pertinent when one studies a social gospel theologian. As we become aware that what has passed for informed historiography of the movement's origins may sometimes be at best tenuous, and at worst tendentious, historiography, it becomes increasingly apparent that we know comparatively little, in hard empirical terms, about the genesis of the social gospel. Was the movement spearheaded by North American epigones of German liberal Protestant theologians, of Ritschl in particular, as has often been maintained? Or was it primarily a North American phenomenon, a Christian theological adaptation of themes running through North American thought of the nineteenth century? Even to ask these questions (as recent theological and sociological research is doing) is to suggest how much clarity we lack about the beginnings of the movement. If we are to know more, we have to fine-tune our study of the movement by examining the historical context presupposed by its key texts, and the influences at work in these texts.

The task of the intellectual biographer is reconstructive in another sense. Texts not only situate themselves vis-à-vis texts of other writers, but also in the context of their author's entire body of work. In Mathews's case, it is crucially important that particular texts be interpreted in the context of the whole. It is so in the first place because previous studies have too often isolated themes in Mathews's theology, and sought to analyze his thought about these chosen themes, without paying sufficient attention to the historical development of his thought in a dauntingly large corpus.[75] The partiality of some assessments of Mathews's theology can be traced to this tendency to ignore the multifaceted, sometimes bewilderingly vagarious, nature of his theological development, as it is reflected in that large body of writings.

Though accurate perception of either facets of Mathews's theology, or of his entire theological corpus, demands wide-ranging examination of his works—and this is particularly true in the case of a theologian who has fallen into such obscurity—no previous study of Mathews's theology appears to have attempted to base itself on a reading of his whole body of writings.

The following survey of Mathews's reflection about the foundations of the social gospel depends on a reading of every book, article, and editorial by Mathews I have been able to discover, and on a wide sampling of his book reviews. The comprehensive listing of Mathews's works appended to this study is the first attempt that has been made to arrive at a complete bibliography.[76] Once again: an overriding concern of my examination of Mathews's lives of Jesus is to discover what Mathews actually said; until we can be relatively assured that we know what social gospel theologians said, we cannot begin to speak with confidence about what "the" social gospel itself said.

When Mathews's social gospel works (which represent a limited portion of his entire corpus both chronologically and numerically) are read in the context of the whole, two recognitions leap out. The first is that his social gospel theology presupposes concepts that reappear in virtually all his theological works, and not merely in the social gospel ones. A primary example is the notion of social process. Even though Mathews did not develop a full-blown definition of the term until after he composed his seminal social gospel works, a social process perspective both informs STJ and runs through everything he ever wrote. One cannot fully understand STJ without reading later studies (e.g., *The Atonement and the Social Process, The Growth of the Idea of God*) in which he defines and applies the notion.

(In passing, I might note that one reason some studies of Mathews's theology tend to view aspects of his thought in isolation from other aspects is that they have assumed that one *may* productively study a theologian's understanding of a topic in systematic theology without paying attention to the nexus of concerns and interests out of which that understanding arises. An advantage of attempting to set analysis of an aspect of the theologian's thought in the context of the theologian's overall body of work is that one avoids such systematic reductionism. As Stephen Wurster's valuable 1972 historical study of Mathew's modernism argues, accurate assessment of Mathews's theological system sorely needs as its foundation preliminary historical work on his life and thought.[77] It is only when we have done a thoroughgoing reconstruction of the historical context in which a theologian's thought is set that we can confidently begin to delve into the intricacies of that thought—particularly when that theologian has become all but unknown to contemporary readers.)

A second recognition that flows from a comprehensive reading of Mathews's works is that he was a theologian with disparate theological interests. Mathews was certainly a social gospel theologian. Throughout his long theological career, even in the years when the social gospel was under fiercest attack, he remained a loyal advocate of the movement. But he also claimed labels other than that of social gospeller. He was as well a North American modernist and a member of the Chicago school of theology—indeed, a founding figure of both theological movements. Even a cursory perusal of his extensive bibliography reveals the breadth of his theological interests, a not surprising breadth, when one considers that his training and academic appointments spanned areas as diverse as history, historical theology, exegesis, social ethics, religious education, and systematics.

In conclusion, the study that follows is a retrieval of Mathew's thought regarding the foundations of the social gospel in the 1897 and 1928 lives of Jesus, and in selected texts between these two works. The word "retrieval" can be misleading. It might be taken to imply that the past is simply *there*, like an artifact, to be picked up, dusted off, and displayed on a museum shelf. In my view, such an understanding of the historian's task is seriously flawed. It rather naively assumes that historians can step outside their worldviews, with the manifold commitments and interests these worldviews enfold—*ideological* commitments and interests—and approach the past as an archaeologist approaches a field-site.

Every project of historiographical retrieval presupposes ideology. For those who seek to understand classic texts in their historical contexts (as I am doing in this study of Mathews's lives of Jesus), it is ideology that orients one to these texts, that allows one to ask interesting (and interested) new questions about it, that provides one with a perspective which enables one to see in the text what no has seen there before, or at least not in quite this way. Our ideological commitments and interests are what attract us to classic texts and allow us to submit ourselves to these texts even when they seem alien to us, when our worldview is far from that of the text. Ideologies of attraction bring us into dialogue with classic texts, and keep us in that dialogue even when we find our presuppositions about the text shattered, our worldviews challenged or expanded.

My quarrel with the received tradition's reading of social gospel texts is not that this reading has been ideological, then, but that its polemical intent has too frequently caused it to function as an ideology of occlusion, rather than attraction. Ideologies of occlusion insist on finding in texts what readers have already decided to discover in them. Occlusive readings of texts do not respect texts or enter into dialogue with them; instead, they distort texts, and wrest them to readings that conform to preconceived ideas.

The following study of Mathews's lives of Jesus approaches several classic social gospel texts in light of the emergence of political and liberation theologies, and of new historiographies "from below." Both developments have opened new space around social gospel texts. Both enable interpreters to read these texts anew, asking questions that arise out of a new set of interests and commitments. This book represents what I have found when I have done so.

CHAPTER ONE

SHAILER MATHEWS

Life and Significance

U nderlying every theological work Shailer Mathews published over the course of his long and productive career is the question of how the Christian church is to deal with the phenomenon of social change. Mathews was concerned with this issue both at the practical level of church involvement in social reform, and at the academic level of theological reflection on the implications of such change for Christian doctrine. Indeed, the two concerns so intertwine in his thought that one has great difficulty distinguishing them from each other: since his understanding of the role of the church was strongly tinged with missionary assumptions, Mathews found it impossible to conceive of academic theological reflection as something that ought to occur in isolation from the church's involvement in social reform. And as a scholar, Mathews was also keenly aware of the need for theologians involved in the social gospel movement to correct the anti-intellectual and merely activist stance taken by some Christian social reformers. In his view, the history of Christian thought is full of instructive examples of how social change and Christian belief interact to the mutual benefit of one another, to produce both desirable social reform and the development of new expressions of traditional Christian doctrines.

The accent on social change in Mathews's thought and in that of other social gospellers who began their careers at the end of the nineteenth century reflects their own historical experience, which was one of coming to maturity in a period of explosive social and technological change in the Western world. When Mathews was born on 26 May 1863, most North Americans lighted their dwellings with tallow candles or kerosene lamps and used horse-drawn conveyances as their ordinary means of transport. At his death on 23 October 1941, widespread electrification, the automobile, the airplane, and the mechanization of agriculture (to isolate four among many important technological developments of the period) had so altered the life of most North Americans that the America of Mathews's youth seems more akin to that of the founding fathers and mothers than that of the mid-twentieth century.

One measure of the distance between the worlds of Mathews's birth and death is less benign than the replacement of kerosene lamps by electric lights. Mathews was born during one of the first of modern wars, a war that, despite the carnage it entailed, was fought with saber, rifle, and cannon. Had he lived less than four years longer, he would have known of the deployment of a weapon that, for all practical purposes, relegates the technology of the Civil War to the military museum and, as the Roman Catholic bishops of the United States noted a decade ago, calls for theological reflection about the morality of war that must move at a sharp disjuncture from all previous moral teaching about war and peace.[1]

From the "one-hoss shay" to the airplane, from the Winchester repeater to the atomic bomb, Mathews lived through a period of rapid technological development perhaps unprecedented in human history. Technological change inevitably implies and entails social change. During Mathews's lifetime, the fabric of North American society was subject to a series of reweavings with imports as far-reaching as those of the technological restructuring of North American life during the same period. Mathews's distinctive contribution to modern North American theology, the theology of social process, addresses the period of rapid social transition through which he lived. The notion of social process forms the framework of all Mathews's theological work: the term implies that interchange of mutual effect between church and society which is, for Mathews, the matrix within which Christian theological reflection must always take shape. The unifying theme of Mathews's theological writings is his constant desire to understand and articulate the reciprocal relationship of church and society in a period of social flux.

MATHEWS'S EARLY YEARS

The preceding interpretation of Mathews's theological significance is one he himself proposed. His 1936 autobiography, *New Faith for Old (NFO)*, is an *apologia pro vita sua* justifying Mathews's involvement in the theological controversies that troubled North American Protestantism in the post–World War I period. *NFO* presents Mathews's life as a parable of shifting Christian response to the social developments that had occurred in the late nineteenth and early twentieth centuries: the mid-Victorian evangelicalism that sufficed for his boyhood in a town in a nonindustrial area of New England could no longer meet his mature religious needs in the complex society of modern, urban, industrial America. New faith must supplant old.[2]

Mathews was born in Portland, Maine, at a time when that small city remained a solidly Yankee stronghold, a community hardly touched either by industrialization or the influx of immigrants having other than Anglo Protestant ancestry who had begun to alter the character of other New England cities such as Boston. Mathews's own lineage was in all respects Yankee; both his maternal and paternal forebears were seventeenth-century British settlers of New England.[3] Through his mother, Sophia Lucinda Shailer, he was the descendant of several generations of teachers and ministers.[4] Mathews's maternal grandfather, Dr. William H. Shailer, was a Baptist minister and man of influence in Portland.[5] In *NFO*, Mathews recalls (with a mixture of wry amusement and slight condescension characteristic of his recollections about his upbringing) the traditional New England sabbath Dr. Shailer kept:

> With him Sunday was still the Puritan Sabbath. During its hours no cooking was to be done except boiling water for his tea. The family always had cold corned beef which had been cooked on Saturday, which was uniformly treated in New England as a "baking day." How strict was his Sabbatarianism may be observed from a curious regulation of the house. The piano had a melodeon attachment which, by turning a switch, could be played with the piano keys. On Sunday only the melodeon part of the instrument could be played.[6]

As the passage suggests, in his autobiography Mathews views his formative years as typical of those who came of age in middle-class households in the mid-Victorian evangelical culture of the northeastern United States.[7] Though New England evangelicalism had strong Puritan overtones, by Mathews's youth revivalism and romanticism had effected significant changes in its character. Stressing the primacy of the affective dimension of religious experience, both allowed religious feeling a prominence that tended to mitigate the sterner implications of rigorously held Calvinist theology. To illustrate what the shift from orthodox Calvinism to Victorian evangelicalism entailed in New England families such as his, in *NFO* Mathews notes that his father endured a religious crisis regarding the punitive justice of God: as a Baptist deacon, Jonathan Mathews felt obliged to hold the orthodox position that love and justice have equal weight, as God decides the fate of sinners; but his consideration of the matter gradually led him to conclude that God's love always outweighs God's justice. When Jonathan Mathews had reached this decision, he "was rather terrified lest his conviction that God was swayed by love rather than by justice was heretical."[8]

Mathews's formative years were spent in a social milieu in which gradual change was occurring not only in small-town New England's religious beliefs, but also in its economic structures. During his adolescence, Mathews worked as a bookkeeper for his father's wholesale tea and flour business in Portland.[9] This experience introduced him to what was to be a lifelong concern of both his social gospel theology and activism, the problem of justice in the workplace. Critics of Mathews's political views have sometimes charged him with adopting an unreflective pro-capitalist stance regarding labor-capital disputes.[10] The charge has some merit: a lifelong (and a politically active) Republican, Mathews tended to view organized labor's appeal for substantive change in the economic sector as threatening to social stability. This view certainly reflects the reformist (as opposed to radical) sociological presuppositions he was to derive from his association with Albion Small. But it also stems from his upbringing. Though *NFO* depicts the commercial life of Portland during Mathews's boyhood as relatively uncomplicated in comparison with that of the twentieth century, and though it notes that the structure of New England economic life in the latter half of the nineteenth century did not differ radically from that of the early 1800s, it observes that businessmen such as Jonathan Mathews feared the increasing activity of organized labor, strikes, and riots, and resisted government "interference" in the economic sector, favoring the laissez-faire economics of John Stuart Mill.[11] Something of this social and economic conservatism was to tinge Mathews's own thought about economic issues throughout his career.

Mathews's adolescent experience of the practical problems inherent in the complex changes to which North American economic life was being subjected appears to have influenced him to such an extent that he chose as the topic of his high school graduation address in 1880 the theme "Mechanical Industry." In 1936 he recalled that the address opened with the following declamatory flourish: "In these days of strikes and riots our minds naturally turn to that branch of industry in which they occur." [12] As a social gospel theologian who would write frequently on the theme of labor-capital relationships, Mathews recognized the need to transcend his tendency to uncritical identification with the interests of management over against those of labor, and to reframe his understanding of this question. In this respect, Mathews's intellectual development closely parallels that of his mentor Small, who, despite his penchant for progressivist reformism, also expressed severe criticisms of capitalism that often echo Marx.[13] Both Mathews and Small appear to have been critically aware of how significantly their formative experiences and class background tinged their mature theology, though neither was perhaps ever entirely successful in overcoming these formative influences on his thought.

In conclusion, Shailer Mathews's coming of age took place in a rather conventionally pious middle-class New England evangelical home. Even when one allows for that golden patina that memory often casts on elderly people's recollections of their childhood, one cannot read Mathews's account of his childhood without imagining Norman Rockwell or Winslow Homer scenes of straw-hatted, freckle-faced children with dogs and fishing poles. The Chicago in which Mathews was to spend his mature years was more than geographically distant from his New England home; in the first half of the twentieth century, the burgeoning Midwestern urban center was a microcosm of the pluralistic, bustling society of an urban twentieth-century North America, an America Mathews and other social gospellers liked to call "America in the making." In appealing for Christian reformist response to this new society, Mathews sometimes exhibits a certain visceral nativism.[14] But as with his economic views in general, as a social gospeller Mathews also demonstrates a critical awareness of his tendency to see North America as the community of the New England saints writ large—as in the gently mocking observation with which he sums up his upbringing in the autobiographical essay "Theology as Group Belief": "We had no serious anxieties about the social order. Indeed I do not remember that we knew there was a social order. We knew God had been good to New England." [15]

THE EDUCATIONAL YEARS

In 1880 Mathews entered Colby College, some eighty miles from his home. Viewing his educational years with the same optic of wry amusement he had employed in remembering his boyhood, he characterizes his Colby education as one that reinforced, and did not cause him to question, the provincialism of his upbring-ing.[16] During his years at Colby, most of the college's students were drawn from the region surrounding the college, and were from back-grounds similar to that of Mathews. As was the case with most North American colleges at the time, the curriculum was calcu-lated to uphold the traditional cultural values that such students' rearing presupposed. In two respects, however, Mathews's college work evidently challenged him to begin the process of thinking critically about his cultural heritage in ways that were to deter-mine the course of his academic career. The first of these stimuli came from a charismatic professor of history and political econ-omy, Albion W. Small, who was eventually to become president of the college. Small owed his *entrée* to the profession to Mathews's grandfather, Dr. Shailer, who (despite misgivings) had recommended him for his first teaching post in Portland.[17] Mathews's recollection of Small's classes indicates that he was a dynamic teacher whose ped-agogical methods diverged from the rote memorization employed in most schools at this period.[18]

Small was a founding figure of North American sociology. In Berlin and Leipzig, he had studied under such notable social scientists as Gustav Schmoller and Adolf Wagner, members of the German historical school of economic thinking. The fundamental insight of historical economics—that economic organization is a social con-struct, rather than a function of rigid natural laws capable of scien-tific formulation and manipulation—informed Small's progressivist understanding of social change, a notion that had seminal influence on Mathews's thought.[19] From Small, Mathews derived a sociologi-cal perspective and a theoretical framework for understanding so-cial change that were to exercise a continuous architectonic influence in his theological work. Small's 1892 appointment to the chair of sociology at the new University of Chicago, from which he worked to establish this academic discipline in America, insured that his impact on Mathews was to outlast the Colby years.[20]

Another initiatory experience of Mathews's college years occurred in connection with his study of the natural sciences. In *NFO*
Mathews recalls that in a biology class at Colby, he committed Hux-
ley's *Physiology* to memory. As he undertook this mammoth task,
he asked his biology teacher, William Elder, to recommend a book
that would demonstrate the errors of the theory of evolution. In re-
counting Elder's response some fifty years later, Mathews once again
paints that portrait of callow naiveté shattered that appears again
and again in his recollections of his youth:

> "Why do you want to know it is untrue?" he asked.
> "Because," I replied, with the assurance of complete
> ignorance, "it is contrary to Christianity." "If sci-
> ence shows," said the professor, "a fact which is con-
> trary to Christianity, Christianity must be
> changed." [21]

The shock he experienced at Elder's remark provoked Mathews to
read extensively on the topic of evolution. In doing so, he seems to
have cast his intellectual net so wide that, as he dryly observes in his
autobiography, "I have the impression that I am the only living person who [has] read through Lionel Beale's *Protoplasm*." [22]

For those living in the wake of modernity, it is perhaps difficult
to appreciate what an intellectual lightning bolt Darwinism was for
Western Christian thinkers of the late Victorian period. Reminiscences such as Mathews's concerning the impact of this intellectual revolution have for us the faded charm of locks of children's
hair in old family bibles: Can people ever have thought this, have
cared so much about the discovery that the biblical account of creation is not literally true? But as crucial documents of this intellectual revolution, such as Edmund Gosse's *Father and Son* (1907), indicate, Victorian religionists were correct to see the rise of
evolutionism as the beginning of the end of their world, for the paradigm shift that this scientific development represented was one designed not merely to change significantly the way people thought, but
how they lived as well. The theory of evolution was integral to a
cultural shift out of whose far-reaching effects we still live. Mathews
does not overstate the case when he sees his struggle with the idea
of evolution as "the beginning of what independent thinking I may
have done." [23] In informing his mature work's understanding of how
social structures develop, and in providing a framework for his social
process theology, evolutionary thought had a profound impact on
Mathews and other theologians of the period. Mathews's concern

with the topic of evolution was not confined to the apologetic problem of reconciling Christianity and modern science; the evolutionary metaphor is basic to Mathews's entire theological system.

After his graduation from Colby in 1884, Mathews entered
Newton Theological Institution. Although he felt no particular calling, his family (and so he himself) took for granted that his post-
graduate study would prepare him for a career in the ministry.[24] However, the Newton years ended with Mathews's decision not to receive
ordination: NFO suggests that he arrived at this decision in part as
a result of his conviction that the pastoral fieldwork he had been required to do at the seminary had been a dismal failure.[25] Other factors may also have been at work: throughout his theological career,
Mathews's lay status was a point of touchy honor with him; his
punctilio may indicate that he considered it important for Christian churches of the day to have lay theologians willing to venture into
fields which ordained theologians might hesitate to enter.

At Newton Mathews was introduced to biblical exegesis. Having learned Hebrew and Greek, he read the Bible through in its original languages.[26] The exegetical method taught at Newton at the
time was almost exclusively philological, and higher criticism was
presented primarily by way of refutation.[27] On the whole, then, Mathews insists, the Newton education did not unsettle his mid-Victorian
evangelical presuppositions any more than had the Colby years. As
he remarks in NFO, "Evangelicalism was too thoroughly presumed
to be self-conscious or introspective."[28] In 1936, from the vantage
point of more than fifty years of involvement in the turbulent events
that shaped the course of North American Christianity in the first part
of the twentieth century, Mathews remembered his seminary days as
ones of uncritical pietism.[29]

Mathews's memoirs do, however, recount a seminary incident
akin to those at Colby that caused him to subject his settled theological presuppositions to critical scrutiny and to move towards his
mature theology. Having read Kenningale Cooke's The Fathers of
Jesus (a pioneering English language work of historical exegesis which
the Newton librarian had purchased under the misapprehension that
it was a history of the Roman Catholic Society of Jesus), Mathews
started to reflect on the historical context of the New Testament
writings.[30] His persistent questions about the rabbinic background
of Paul's theology so vexed his New Testament professor, Alva Hovey,
that Hovey set him the task of writing a paper on the topic. In this
way, Mathews says, he "came upon what was to be an enduring interest, that is to say, historical study as a means of understanding
and evaluating Christian doctrine."[31]

Having graduated from Newton in 1887, Mathews decided on a career in education. A vignette in *NFO* describes in parabolic form both that charming disingenuousness his upbringing and education had inculcated in him, and his emergence from that disingenuousness as he began his professional life. Mathews tells how his discernment that his talents lay in the field of education rather than ministry was "confirmed":

> My last year in the theological seminary was to de-
> mand decisions as to what in those days seemed to be
> providential guidance. A few months ago when I was
> in Madras I was reminded that during the last months
> of my theological course I made a solemn promise
> to myself and, as I believed, to my God that I would
> go to Madras as a missionary if a decision as to a po-
> sition at Colby was not reached within two weeks.
> Probably it was fortunate for the work in Madras that
> the decision was reached and that I became Assis-
> tant Professor of Rhetoric and Instructor of Elocu-
> tion at my *alma mater*.[32]

As parabolic *apologia*, *NFO* intends not merely to justify Mathews's own theological divergences from those historic forms in which Christian orthodoxy had found expression for several centuries. The autobiography wants as well to suggest that the course of develop-ment followed by a North American Christianity confronting cul-tural diversity, urbanization, and rapid technological change was to a certain extent inevitable; a church that wishes to remain viable in modern culture must always look back nostalgically on the snows of yesteryear.

Mathews's return to Colby brought him back into close asso-ciation with Small, whose influence continued to be decisive. When Small became president of Colby in 1888, he had Mathews trans-ferred from the department of rhetoric, in which he was a professor from 1887–89, to Small's former position in the department of his-tory and political economy. Small also encouraged Mathews to do studies in these fields in Germany, and in 1890, having married Mary Philbrick Elden (who had been an acquaintance of several years) on 16 July of that year, he entered the University of Berlin.[33]

Theologians commenting on Mathews's theology commonly stress the foundational importance of his year of study in Berlin for his mature theological outlook.[34] To some extent, Mathews him-self corroborates the judgment that his German education exercised a constant formative influence on his thought when he insists, as he does in *NFO* and other writings, that the grounding in rigorous critical historical methodology he received in Berlin from historians such as Hans Delbrück and Ignaz Jastrow laid an indispensable foundation for his social process theology.[35] Delbrück and Jastrow were close associates of the famous historian Leopold von Ranke. Through these historians, Mathews appears to have been strongly influenced by Ranke's understanding of the historian's task as recovering the past *wie es eigentlich gewesen*. Though, as historians today note, this assumption that historians can ever have access to the past as it actually was skates rather glibly over insuperable hermeneutical difficulties, Ranke's insistence on thorough and painstaking research represents an important methodological contribution to the field of historiography. In Berlin Mathews was to acquire habits of sound scholarship that were to undergird all his theological research, and to make him acutely aware of the cultural influences at work in every credal formulation at any moment in history. The sociohistorical method that Mathews and his Chicago colleague Shirley Jackson Case were later to pioneer draws on the rigorous, non-apologetic approach to history that these theologians learned in their Berlin studies.[36]

But historiographical influence is not necessarily theological influence—that is, not in the sense that Mathews's Berlin education was also instruction in German liberal theology. To the chagrin of critics who wish to see liberal theologians as Mathews's primary theological mentors, his autobiography notes that his work in Berlin was so detached from theological interests that, in the year he was there, he heard only one theological lecture, and this not a lecture by Harnack—despite the fact that Harnack's Berlin lectures of the 1890s were attracting flocks of hearers.[37] If Mathews's theology does show explicit Harnackian tendencies (and that should probably not be conceded until his works have been combed for explicit references to the German theologian), these tendencies must be attributed to a general impact of German liberal Protestantism on North American theology, rather than to any direct impact deriving from Mathews's year of study in Germany.

In addition to the effect of Ranke mediated through Delbrück and Jastrow, a more decisive influence on Mathews's thought from the Berlin year was Small's teacher Adolf Wagner, a leading proponent of historical economics. From Wagner Small derived that emphatically reformist understanding of effective social change that was to play a determinative role on Mathews's thought. From Wagner to Small to Mathews, a penchant to think in reformist ways clearly informs social gospel thought. Indeed, Wagner's seminal influence on the movement as a whole has not yet been sufficiently appreciated: in addition to Mathews and Small, such prototypical social gospellers as Ely and Rauschenbusch also expressed indebtedness to Wagner. Through him, the social-construction reading of economic institutions represented by German historical economics powerfully shapes the social and economic thought of the social gospel.[38]

THE CALL TO CHICAGO

In 1892, Albion Small was made head of the new department of sociology at the new University of Chicago. As Mathews's 1933 autobiographical essay "Theology as Group Belief" notes, when Small went to Chicago, he did so intending to bring Mathews into the department as soon as this could be arranged.[39] In accord with this intent, Mathews began an intensive study of the discipline, beginning with the works of Herbert Spencer.[40] Before Small's plan could be put into effect, however, Mathews was invited by Ernest Dewitt Burton, formerly his professor at Newton, to come to Chicago as associate professor of New Testament. Mathews hesitated to take the position: he did not see his academic work as theological; and a visit to the Columbian Exposition in 1893 had left him with an unfavorable impression of the city.[41]

Despite Mathews's misgivings, Burton prevailed, and in 1894 Mathews came to Chicago as professor of New Testament history and interpretation. As *NFO* suggests, a decisive factor in his decision to come to Chicago was the new school's missionary self-understanding.[42] The possibility of implementing this missionary spirit to effect social reform appealed to the idealistic young theologian with a head full of exciting new sociological ideas.[43] His decision to take the Chicago position resolved the tension between Mathews's missionary inclinations and his desire to be a teacher—a tension evident in the inner struggle he underwent prior to taking the Colby position in 1887.[44]

The Chicago context is indispensable for any understanding of the theological thought of Shailer Mathews. The new university saw the role of the educator as not merely imparting knowledge, but actively participating in the making of twentieth-century North American society.[45] The university was itself an experiment in which new pedagogical techniques were developed. Its emphasis on interdisciplinary work encouraged collaborative research and led to the implementation of novel educational techniques. The concern to innovate educational methods and the stress on cross-disciplinary conversation reflected the progressivist social philosophy that permeated the thought of the university's founders.

The setting for this novel educational experiment was a city in the rough: as Mathews notes, within its newly minted urban boundaries, the university "sprawled over an all but unredeemed prairie."[46] The Chicago of the early twentieth century was that of Carl Sandburg's *Chicago Poems:* raw, somewhat unstable on its new legs, but optimistic about its place in the America to be built in the new century. From a small huddle of buildings on the prairie, the city had grown rapidly in the first half of the nineteenth-century to become a large urban center of factories and slaughterhouses. It was in this very American context—with its bustling air and its ethnic and religious diversity, a context very *differently* American than that of his idyllic New England boyhood—that Mathews's career was to unfold and his theological thought take shape. It was this new urban North America that Mathews and other social gospellers intended to evangelize with a fervor akin to the zeal the Puritans brought to their task of building a city on a hill.

As might be expected, the divinity school partook of the missionary spirit of the new university established in this microcosm of America in the making. The president of the university, William Rainey Harper, who had formerly served as professor of New Testament at Morgan Park Seminary, was a dynamic educator who had spearheaded the development of modern methods of teaching Hebrew.[47] In 1881, he had begun the Institute of Hebrew, a correspondence school whose purpose was to introduce the scholarly study of the Bible to a wide popular audience. To extend the scope of what he called his "democratization of religious scholarship," Harper expanded the work of the institute by creating the American Institute of Sacred Literature (hereafter, AISL) in 1889. This institute operated in conjunction with that phenomenon of North American educational progressivism known as Chautauqua.[48] In Dorothy Ross's view, Harper was "surely the most entrepreneurial biblical scholar America ever produced."[49]

With Harper's assumption of the presidency of the University of Chicago, the AISL moved to Morgan Park, where it was closely associated with the Divinity School. In 1896, Harper formed a Council of Seventy composed of theological teachers whose expertise was to be made accessible to the community at large through the institute. Mathews was an early member of this council, and under its auspices an indefatigable lecturer on the Institute and Chautauqua circuits.

The missionary self-understanding of the Chicago Divinity School, with its intent to foster the democratization of religious scholarship through the work of the AISL and Chautauqua: these form the matrix of Mathews's theological thought, apart from which it cannot be adequately assessed. The work of the early Chicago school of theology was decidedly evangelical in outlook; its sense of urgency about contributing to the formation of the "social mind" of a rapidly changing, rapidly industrializing America, had affinities with (and saw itself as counter to) the missionary outreach of premillennialists of the period.[50] When Mathews and his protégés spoke of a culture's "social mind," they intended the term to signify a composite of the culture's preeminent traits and paradigmatic optics for interpreting the social and physical world—a concept not unlike, though far more crudely formulated than, T. S. Kuhn's "paradigm" or Stephen Toulmin's "map" of social reality.[51] Through Harper's journal, the *Biblical World* (hereafter, *BW*), the Divinity School theologians wanted to disseminate the results of current biblical scholarship among North American Christians, and thereby to contribute to shaping a progressivist, idealistic, "Christian" social mind in the nation of their day. No less than premillenialism, the social gospel modernism of the early Chicago school was a strongly evangelical strategy for Christianizing the nation.[52]

THE PREWAR PERIOD:

Mathews and the Real World

In the educational-cum-missionary ventures established by Harper to democratize religious scholarship, Mathews found his métier. A man of unflagging energy (as was Harper), optimistic and irenic by nature, and little given to torturing self-doubt, Mathews was temperamentally suited to the evangelistic work of the Divinity School. From the beginning of his tenure at the university, he involved himself with gusto in both academic activities and the broader task of shaping the social mind of the nation and its churches, to such an extent that (as we have seen) he felt himself in danger of becoming a "peripatetic loquacity" on the AISL and Chautauqua lecture circuits.[53] In 1895, for example, Mathews's schedule included a Chicago AISL course on the history of New Testament times and the life of Christ, six AISL lectures in February at Wheaton College on the times of Jesus, four lectures in March for the Christian Union at the University of Chicago on the times of Jesus, and a summer

AISL course at the University of Chicago on the social history of New Testament times.[54] These commitments were in addition to his regular classes. In 1936 Mathews estimated that his career had given him the opportunity to lecture at more than 190 colleges.[55]

Mathews's attempt to mold the social mind of the first decade of twentieth-century America was not limited to disseminating the findings of recent theological and biblical scholarship to academic and popular audiences. Since the Divinity School professors viewed themselves as academics with a cause, they sought as well to influence society through active involvement with what they liked to call the "real world," that of business and politics.[56] Through his editorship of the journal *Christendom*, a short-lived endeavor started in 1903 by a group of progressivist businessmen acting in collaboration with Harper, Mathews commented on "current events from the point of view of Christian idealism."[57] When *Christendom* failed and merged with the *World Today*, Mathews remained as editor until, in 1911, this periodical also ran into financial difficulties and was bought out by William Randolph Hearst.[58] In his *World Today* editorials about topics as diverse as Theodore Roosevelt and the reform of football in the twenties, Mathews attempted to reach the social mind of the culture by bringing idealistic considerations to bear on issues of everyday interest to his readers.[59]

In addition, in the prewar years Mathews plunged directly into both politics and progressivist reform activities. With other reform-minded Republicans in Chicago, he entered the turbulent sphere of Chicago politics by assisting in the establishment of the Voter's Clearing House, whose purpose was to screen candidates for the Chicago Republican primaries.[60] Another cause was the settlement-house movement: soon after his arrival in Chicago, he had visited the settlement sponsored by the University of Chicago, and the experience convinced him that this social reform movement ought to have his strong support. Throughout most of his academic career, Mathews served on the board of the university settlement.[61]

Mathews's conviction that "no social revolution in progress is so critical in its influences" as the "epoch-making" feminist movement led him in 1913 to assume the editorship of a series of textbooks entitled the *Woman's Citizen's Library*.[62] The instigator of the series was the former business manager of the *World Today*, who designed the series to make available to women a wide range of edifying literature that would educate them to make intelligent choices about things political at a moment in which women were being permitted to assume political responsibility in ways unprecedented in United States history. In 1936 Mathews would remark that the enfranchisement of women had been one of the most significant factors contributing to the development of reformist legislation in the United States in the first part of the century.[63]

Mathews saw his involvement with the "real world" as one in which a reciprocal effect occurred: not only did he address the economic and political community through his editorials, lectures, and political activism; but this community taught him something as well. From his attempts to instill social idealism in business leaders, with whom he had close ties because of his background, to his grappling with the nitty-gritty problems that social reformers inevitably face when they apply that idealism to the actual structures and situations of the everyday world—in all the multifaceted ways in which he participated in shaping the social mind of his day, Mathews considered himself to have learned valuable lessons about the effectiveness and limits of social reformism. Of these lessons, the one to which he most constantly recurred was that of the need for process, rather than revolution, in social change.[64] Throughout his career Mathews was to insist that his active engagement with reform in the "real world" had confirmed what he had received from Small and Wagner: that is, that revolutionary programs of social reform rarely succeed, because they too radically disrupt the social order they seek to transform, whereas sober, measured progressivism usually effects long-lasting and ameliorative changes. Clearly, in "proving" to himself the validity of process (as opposed to revolution), Mathews was reaffirming that cautious, conservative outlook with which his bourgeois evangelical upbringing had equipped him.

Mathews gave theological substance to his prewar activism by developing a program of "theological reconstruction." In the prewar years, the phrase connoted a turn beyond liberalism that was occurring in North American theology. North American theologians who promoted theological reconstruction argued that liberal theology, as represented by Harnack and Ritschl, must move in a new direction.[65] The liberalism of the latter part of the nineteenth century had had a primarily critical intent, a goal of dismantling theological systems constructed on outmoded premises regarding revelation or inspiration. In the view of North American heirs of the liberal project, the emphasis on deconstruction was one-sided: mere leveling of old systems was only half the task lying before post-Enlightenment Christian theology; what must now take place was a *constructive* move, an attempt at theological reconstruction.[66]

As a social gospel theologian, Mathews was committed to such a constructive understanding of the evangelical theological program of the first decades of the twentieth century. Indeed, the extent to which North American theologians understood the challenge facing twentieth-century theology as reconstruction rather than deconstruction is perhaps a touchstone for the extent to which the social gospel represents a departure from nineteenth-century European liberal theology. As Hutchison and Gorrell have demonstrated, the note of culture crisis in theological writings in the prewar decade was sounded particularly by theologians who identified with the social gospel movement.[67] When social gospellers spoke of culture crisis, they were speaking in theologically loaded terms; their crisis rhetoric represented a challenge to liberal theology to articulate a sound basis on which Christian churches could involve themselves in social reform. The clear implication of such rhetoric was that a *merely* liberal, merely deconstructive, theology could not meet the crucial needs of a culture in crisis. Mathews cast his lot with such critics of culture Protestantism: when he succeeded William Rainey Harper as editor of the *Biblical World* in December 1912, the editorial announcing the change of editorship noted (tellingly) that under Mathews's direction the journal intended to devote itself to theological reconstruction.[68]

Mathews's prewar reformist activism expressed itself not only in social movements; it also sought ecclesiastical expression. With Harper and the AISL, in 1903 he was instrumental in founding the Religious Education Association, an ecumenical organization that strove to implement John Dewey's pedagogical philosophy in religious education.[69] In 1907–8, Mathews helped create the Northern Baptist Convention, of which he was president in 1915 and 1916.[70] In 1912, Mathews became director of religious work for Chautauqua, a position he held until 1934. From 1912 to 1916, he was president of the Federal Council of Churches of Christ in America. Mathews was also president of the Chicago Council of City Missions (1908–15) and of the Baptist Executive Council of Chicago (1910–19).[71]

True to his nature, in the same years in which he engaged in these numerous social and church reform activities, the unflagging scholar also pursued his academic work aggressively, and began an auspicious ascent up the ladder of academic rank. In 1899, he was made junior dean of the Divinity School, and in 1908 succeeded Dean Eri Baker Hulbert to the deanship of the school, a position he held until 1933.[72] When George Burman Foster ran afoul of the university administrators by publishing *The Finality of the Christian Religion*, a probing Nietzschean reflection on Christianity's claims to absolute truth that rattled the cage of conservative Christians of the day, Harper (who had close ties to John D. Rockefeller and acted as his "surrogate" in the university to discourage radical thought) decided to provide a countervailing theological position in the systematic theology department.[73] With his irenic temperament and penchant for cautious reform, Mathews appeared to be the logical choice, and so was transferred to the department in 1906. Until 1933, his professorship in historical and comparative theology was to be his primary academic "housing" at the Divinity School.

During the prewar era, Mathews published extensively. His writings of the period include both numerous journal articles and various books and study guides. While at Colby, he had published a collection of documents for the study of the medieval church in its relation to the empire; this collection, entitled *Select Medieval Documents*, collected materials he had gathered during his year in Berlin. Reprinted as recently as 1974, the volume is still useful to historians.[74] In 1901 a second historical work, *The French Revolution*, appeared.[75] This monograph relies strongly on insights regarding social psychology that were coming into vogue as it was published. It applies what Mathews had learned in his study of sociology in the 1890s by arguing that any revolutionary movement presupposes and sets into motion a social psychology of revolution, and attempts to achieve successful revolutionary change must begin with attempts to clarify the underlying psychology of the revolutionary movement. This way of envisaging revolution was to have a strong impact on Mathews's interpretation of the messianism of the Jesus movement in works such as *STJ*, *MHNT*, and *JSI*.

Three prewar works were in the field of New Testament studies. The first of these was *STJ*, which will be examined in detail in the following chapter.[76] The second book, *A History of New Testament Times in Palestine, 175 B.C.–70 A.D.*, published in 1899 and modelled on Emil Schürer's monumental *Geschichte jüdischen Volkes im Zeitalter Jesu Christi*, provides a political, social, and religious history of New Testament Palestine.[77] In accord with the intent of the Chicago theologians to make recent New Testament scholarship accessible to a broad but serious reading public, the study is simultaneously academic and popular. The combination is not always felicitous, however; while the book manages to be readable, it is often tedious and plodding. For those who might wish to plumb the academic depths of the subject, the volume is substantially documented. This history is one in a series of such New Testament handbooks Mathews was to edit during the years 1899–1910.

Mathews's third New Testament study of this period, *The Messianic Hope in the New Testament* (1905), pioneers the application of social psychology to the New Testament period.[78] Whereas *New Testament Times in Palestine* had approached late Palestinian

Judaism primarily through the external events of political and social life, *MHNT* was "the outgrowth of a growing perception of the real meaning of the history of New Testament times as the history of ideas and social attitudes."[79] Obviously Mathews's work on the French Revolution was a significant motivating factor in his shift in interpretive focus; in *NFO*, he observes that his attempt to shape the social mind of the real world during this period also influenced his reading of messianism in the 1905 volume.[80] In addition, the treatise's concentration on the central role played by messianic expectation in the New Testament clearly reflects Mathews's attempt to come to terms with the eschatological school then coming to prominence in German biblical scholarship. Though Mathews himself recognized the dryness of the work—"If being uninteresting is a proof of scientific accomplishment I think I may be very well said to have succeeded in being scientific"[81]—the book has earned a secure place in the pantheon of North American biblical scholarship. As we have seen, *MHNT* consolidates the important eschatological turn Mathews took in the period 1897–1905, and for this reason alone deserves recognition among early North American historical critical studies of the scriptures. And that recognition is not entirely lacking: though some historians of North American exegesis have ignored or refused to credit Mathews's acceptance of the eschatological reading of the kingdom of God in the work, other scholars have accorded the book the attention it deserves as a pioneering attempt of North American exegesis to come to terms with consistent eschatology. In the words of F. C. Grant, in exploring the relation of Christianity to its Jewish cultural matrix, in setting early Christianity in its social context, and in aiming at exacting scientific exegesis, subsequent North American exegetical works have "sunk paying shafts into veins of rich ore where he [i.e., Mathews], long ago, began his digging."[82]

Three books by Mathews in the prewar years are more directly in the popular social gospel vein. In his 1907 *The Church and the Changing Order*, he sought to join sociological analysis to reconstructive theology in order to provide solid sociological and theological grounding for attempts by Christian reformers to deal with those social conditions he had discovered through his involvement with the "real world."[83] Coincidentally, the volume appeared almost simultaneously with Rauschenbusch's *Christianity and the Social Crisis*, and when read together, the books provide an instructive diptych of social gospel theology in the first decade of the twentieth century. As did Rauschenbusch's book, *Church and Changing Order* warned of an impending crisis in Western culture, and called for the application of Christian principles to avert the crisis. In later years Mathews was generously to say that Rauschenbusch's explicitly socialist analysis of the economic order had been more incisive than his own more timid critique—a contrast that will be explored in some detail in the following chapter.[84]

The Gospel and the Modern Man (*GMM*) is a collection of lectures Mathews presented at Haverford College.[85] Though also in the social gospel vein, the work is more explicitly theological than *Church and Changing Order*. Indeed, it may be seen as a type of twentieth-century *Reden über die Religion* which, as did Schleiermacher's work, reaches for a correlation between evangelical constants and shifting historical thought-patterns. Throughout, Mathews expresses his conviction that a rational apologetics is as much needed today as at any previous transitional period of Christian history. Thus, the basic motif of *GMM* is theological reconstruction— but, in keeping with its social gospel coloring, theological reconstruction with a view to social reconstruction.[86] The method the study employed was one Mathews had developed when he was transferred to the systematic theology department in 1906: (1) New Testament teaching is presented with historical accuracy; (2) this teaching is critically evaluated; (3) and it is then translated into contemporary thought patterns. In *NFO* Mathews criticizes the indirect Ritschlianism of such an understanding of the task of theology by remarking that its "total effect was a restatement of evangelicalism as if there had not been any contribution to Christianity from the days of the New Testament."[87]

Mathews's other social gospel work of this period is *The Making of To-morrow: Interpretations of the World To-day* (1913), a volume consisting for the most part of editorials reprinted from *Christendom* and the *World Today*. The work's chief interest lies in how it spells out concrete details of Mathews's reformist program of social change. Though some details of this program are now patently dated (as, for instance, when Mathews inveighs passionately against vacations and for whole-year schooling on the ground that children's hands need to be kept from that idleness so inviting to the devil), in other respects they indicate that even the cautiously reformist Mathews (and by implication the social gospel in general) envisaged social changes surpassing many of those considered unthinkably radical today, in the post-Reaganomics United States. For example, he argues that the growth of trusts and the consequent concentration of wealth in the hands of a few play into the hands of socialism. To avert revolution, Mathews calls for repeal of laws permitting formation of trusts and for a progressive inheritance tax.[88]

WORLD WAR I

With the outbreak of war in Europe in 1914, the crisis in Western civilization that social gospellers had seen developing and sought to stave off with the proposals for reform outlined in works such as *Church and Changing Order* and *Christianity and the Social Crisis* reached a climax. The failure of their attempt to stem the tide of crisis in Western culture presented social gospel thinkers with a difficult challenge: on the one hand, they had built their theologies on the premise that Christian idealism could, indeed must, "leaven" cultural development; yet on the other hand, cultural development had not taken the progressivist route expected by the social gospellers. Prewar optimism about the success of Christian attempts to assist in bending the social process toward the kingdom of God had played the social gospel false. With the war, social gospellers must ask themselves whether fatuity was *inherent* in their theology, or if it was found primarily in their overly sanguine appraisal of cultural development and of the ability of Christian reformers to move that development to idealistic ends.

At the same time, as the war forced social gospellers to engage in such radical self-criticism, another group of North American Christians began to mount an attack on social gospel theology from without. These were the premillennialists, whose belief in the irreformability of the world by human effort and in the need for some final divine intervention via apocalypse as a solution to the mess of history caused them to center on the social gospel's this-worldly reading of the kingdom of God as *the* theological problem of social gospel theology. And, it goes without saying, if the social interpretation of the kingdom was awry, then so were the reform programs of the social gospel: hovering always behind the front in premillennialist sorties against the social gospel were criticisms of social gospel reform programs that presupposed a cultural base radically different from that of the premillennialists themselves, who tended to ally themselves with groups in North American society that looked nostalgically back to the various holiness movements of the eighteenth and nineteenth centuries, with their resistance to modernity. To say that the premillennialist–social gospel conflict of the World War I period represents a culture war, a battle between conflicting evangelical visions of the future of North American culture, is not to overstate the case. If World War I was a watershed moment for Western culture in general, then, it was no less a watershed for Western Christianity and Western Christian theology. With the war, Christian organizations and theologies both in Europe and in the United States came into open competition, and this competition so polarized the churches that the results of the shift that occurred in conjunction with World War I are still with us.[89]

As with most social gospellers, Mathews initially supported United States isolationism as the war began. That this stance was not a particularly morally courageous one should perhaps be noted; an isolationist mood prevailed in the country at large for some time after the outbreak of war. Through 1916, Mathews's writings consistently endorse a pacifist position vis-à-vis this war. Though his 1909 social gospel study guide, *The Social Gospel,* had maintained that some wars of the past had been justifiable, and, indeed, that a long historical perspective demonstrates that war "has been a necessary and valuable factor in human progress," [90] the study nevertheless concludes that, in general, war is a failure to extend gospel principles to social evolution, and it perceptively analyzes what it calls the "arms race" of the day as a manifestation of European imperialism grasping to control Africa and Asia.[91] Up to the entry of the United States into the war, Mathews's writings follow this line of thought, as does the editorial policy of *BW*, which is succinctly stated in the following aphoristic observation of an unsigned 1914 editorial: "The ultimate issue is between Jesus and Nitsche [*sic*]. If we take Jesus seriously, we shall not war." [92]

With the United States's declaration of war on Germany, Mathews sharply altered his stance. *The Social Gospel*'s notion that social evolution sometimes demands war as a defense of national ideals gave him a ready justification for this particular war: that is, the war had released sanitizing forces that, properly channelled, could ultimately make the world safe for democracy—an argument he presses strongly in the 1916 *The Spiritual Interpretation of History.*[93] The 1917 article "The Spiritual Threat to Democracy" defends a similar thesis by urging that "the world-war in begetting a world-spirit has begotten a new world order"—words with a macabre resonance for Americans living in the wake of Operation Desert Storm.[94] In these rationales for World War I, social gospel faith in the ability of Christian ideals to penetrate the social process joins hands with John Dewey's pragmatic (and astonishingly chauvinistic) justification of the United States' involvement in the war as a channelling of the destructive energies of the conflict.

As Mathews himself was later to grant, this defense of American involvement in the war exhibited strong tinges of war hysteria. As did his colleague Case, he tended to see sinister German influence lurking within many movements that did not march to the martial

beat of the day; when United States socialists made an official declaration of their neutrality, Mathews and Case concluded wildly that
the group had been infiltrated by Boche sympathizers.[95] To his discredit, his distrust of things German even led Mathews to maintain
that the motives of those conscientious objectors who had German
accents were under suspicion: "The conscientious objector—provided that he does not speak with a German accent—should not be
persecuted."[96]

A so-called Christian Embassy to the churches of Japan involved
Mathews at a high official level in American activities during the
war. In 1915, after anti-Japanese legislation in states such as Cali-
fornia had created a great deal of anti-American sentiment in Japan,
Mathews went with Sidney L. Gulick (a former American missionary to Japan) as a "Christian ambassador" of goodwill to Japan. Before
departing, Mathews and Gulick had an interview with President Wilson and Secretary of State William Jennings Bryan. In Japan, their
embassy appeared to have the official endorsement of the United
States ambassador to Japan.[97]

As the preceding paragraphs suggest, Mathews has been justly
criticized for his tendency to identify Christian ideals with North
American democracy. This tendency was particularly pronounced
in his writings during the First World War. In these years, Mathews
sometimes even equates democracy (presumably, in its North American formulation) with the kingdom of God, as in the 1917 article
"Present Co-Operative Action by the Churches," in which he speaks
of the "democracy of the Kingdom of God."[98] The 1918 *Patriotism
and Religion* presses the claims of democracy even further: "Only
where the spirit of democracy is working is there creative religious
thinking."[99]

Yet any appraisal of Mathews's understanding of democracy
that stops at these critical observations would not be a balanced one.
Running through Mathews's reflections about democracy is also a
strand of thought that (again, echoing Dewey) sees democracy as an
"unobtainable abstraction," an "undefined symbol" that, because it
is unspecifiable, challenges the imagination and provokes creative response on the part of those seeking "to make the future."[100] As is
perhaps to be expected, these chastened perspectives on democracy
(and, by implication, North American culture in general) grow more
pronounced in Mathews's writings in the period after World War I.[101]
The increasing appearance of these themes in Mathews's theology
after the war certainly reflects sensitivity to critiques of his uncritical support for the war, and remorse about that support. But it also
reflects a theological development in Mathews's thought: the as-

sessment of democracy as a yet-to-be-attained ideal toward which the creative tendencies of social evolution stretch arises out of Mathews's theology of social process.

In several important articles written during the period 1910–25, Mathews lays a methodological foundation for the social process theology. These articles have great significance both for Mathews's intellectual biography and for the history of the Chicago school of theology: they were to play an important seminal role in the theology of that school.[102] In the essays Mathews hinges social process theology on what he calls the sociohistorical method, a theological method of viewing Christian doctrinal statements as both function of and creative response to the dominant "social mind" of a given culture at a given period in history. The 1915 article "Theology and the Social Mind" defines the nebulous concept as follows: a social mind is "a more or less general community of conscious states, processes, ideas, interests and ambitions which to a greater or less degree repeats itself in the experience of individuals belonging to a group characterized by this community of consciousness."[103] The term itself may have come from Lester Ward's *Dynamic Sociology*, a study that, as will be seen, had a great impact on the sociology of Small, and, through Small, on Mathews.[104]

With Small, Mathews understands society to be in a process of continuous evolution, a process in which human activity and creativity play an indispensable role. The concept of social mind presupposes this process perspective. Thus, Mathews distinguishes between "creative" and "counter" social minds: the former include yet-to-be-realized ideals around which the creative activity of a given culture coalesces; the latter represent those cultural norms that are incapable of producing creative social change, and that must therefore be resisted by those who wish to move the social process to a new stage of development. This distinction gives Mathews a framework for understanding what takes place in Christian doctrinal development: he argues that such development occurs as a process of response to the creative social minds of successive cultural periods, in which Christian thought refashions fundamental Christian beliefs in accord with the dominant metaphors of the social mind of the period.

In his articles describing the sociohistorical method, Mathews identifies six major creative social minds in the history of Western Christianity: these are Semitic monarchial, Hellenistic monarchial, imperialistic, feudal, national, and bourgeois. In Mathews's view, the bourgeois social mind is giving way in the early twentieth century to a new social mind, a scientific-democratic one. In creating such typologies, Mathews wants to point the study of Christian doctrinal development toward a historical consciousness that will make students of Christian history aware of how, as it flows down the stream of history, Christian doctrine has both carried along certain constants and has also adapted to the new channels in which that stream has flowed. As may be apparent, this developmental point of view provides a useful starting point for doing historical theology that is both acutely conscious of the contributions of previous eras (as Mathews thought the liberal Protestant theology of Harnack and Ritschl had not been), and geared to the hermeneutic needs of the present era (as he thought various forms of traditionalism were not).

In important respects, Mathews was to work out of this sociohistorical schema for the rest of his theological career.[105] Both in the 1910–25 articles and the later monographs on the doctrines of God and the atonement, Mathews sought to identify constants in the varying expressions of Christian faith found over the course of Western history, and to restate the constants from a contemporary vantage point—always, it goes without saying, a vantage point that requires attention to the *social ethical* applications of Christian doctrine. His work on the doctrine of God is an instructive case study in the implications of the sociohistorical method: in his articles and book on the subject, Mathews argues that the Jewish-Greek cultural matrix within which the church was born inevitably caused the first Christians to formulate their doctrine of God according to the analogy of the Semitic and Hellenistic monarch. With the Constantinean turn, it was to be expected that God would be seen more and more as the imperial ruler writ large. The development of feudalism enacted a new analogy, that of the feudal lord, whereas the emergence of the nation-state caused the church to speak of God in terms drawn from the monarchial structure of the nation-state. In the early modern period (the period Mathews considered to be the cultural base out of which many "orthodox" Christians in the twentieth century still operated), the appearance of bourgeois capitalism required a new formulation of basic Christian belief. In Mathews's view, this cultural framework for Christian faith is no longer applicable: Christians at the beginning of the twentieth century live on the threshold of a new cultural era with a new cultural paradigm, the scientific-democratic social mind. It is in response to this mind that Christians today need to rethink their fundamental beliefs.[106]

As this brief sketch of one concrete application of Mathews's sociohistorical method suggests, when Mathews speaks of democracy as providing the creative social mind according to which Christian doctrine must be reformulated today, he is plainly speaking of an ideal not yet realized by any concrete cultural development, a utopian symbol, as it were.[107] The 1916 study *The Spiritual Interpretation of History* spells this out very provocatively. In the book Mathews contends that the "fundamental conception" of democracy is that advantages monopolized by individuals and classes and protected as rights by social sanctions are not inviolable. As he does so, he observes, "How far we are from this condition of ideal democracy is easy to see, but the movement within history toward such an ideal is also traceable."[108] Democracy is for Mathews in the 1916 work "an ideal to which neither we nor humanity at large have yet attained."[109] Similarly, the 1918 *Patriotism and Religion* cautions: "We are apt to forget the concrete if limited character of the only democracy the modern world has yet enjoyed, and to speak as if, like the Idea of Plato, democracy somewhere existed complete and approachable."[110] And, for the 1920 article "The Deity of Christ and Social Reconstruction," democracy is the "process of democratizing privileges, rather than an ultimate static social order."[111] Even if we wish to conclude, then, as we must do, that Mathews's defense of North American democracy during World War I at times blindly conceded to Caesar what ought to belong to God, we must come to this conclusion with the counterawareness that strands in Mathews's social process theology move in the opposite direction, to the recognition that no cultural development is the kingdom of God, and that Christian faith requires us both to seek ever new expressions of our belief, and constantly to critique those cultural patterns in which we express that belief.

Before we leave the World War I period, we ought to give further attention to Mathews's two major works of the period, *The Spiritual Interpretation of History* (hereafter, *SIH*) and *Patriotism and Religion*. The first is a compilation of Mathews's William Belden Noble lectures at Harvard in 1916. In the lectures he is unquestionably developing his *Antwort* to attacks on the social gospel's idealistic interpretation of history. Written in the gathering gloom of the war, the lectures respond to philosophies of history that, in Mathews's judgment, diminish the possibility for constructive human involvement in social evolution. Among the positions he considers are the economic interpretation of history, the scientific materialism of thinkers such as the German philosopher Ernst Haeckel (whose mechanistic *The Riddle of the Universe* provided a constant focus of critical concern in Mathews's work), and the social Darwinism of Herbert Spencer. Chapter 3 will examine in more detail precisely how Mathews responds to these philosophies of history, and how he defends the idealistic position.

The second major work of the war years, *Patriotism and Religion*, also reproduces a series of lectures—in this case, Mathews's 1918 McNair Lectures at the University of North Carolina. The 1918 lectures strongly reflect Mathews's increasing conviction of the rightness of the United States's entry into the war. In them he grants that he has come to such a conviction after having defended isolationism, but argues that such active support for the war will help to make a new democratic world order that will prevent the recurrence of war. It is in this study that the strongest tinges of war hysteria in Mathews's World War I writings occur: he sees possible German influence in the ascendancy of Bolshevism in Russia, for example, and he thinks that United States socialists (who are, he surmises, largely of German extraction) disseminate "secret propaganda" favoring the German cause.[112] *NFO* admits that the 1918 study is "not untouched by war psychology": that it is, Mathews notes in an aside rarely revelatory of his feelings, may reflect the fact that he gave the lectures immediately before bidding goodbye to his son, who was being shipped to the front in France.[113]

THE POSTWAR YEARS

In some respects, the twenty-odd years of Mathews's life and career after World War I provide the most daunting obstacles for an intellectual biographer. It is not that the bare facts are inaccessible: from 1908 until his retirement in 1933, Mathews served as dean of the Divinity School; from 1933 until his death on 23 October 1941, he was professor emeritus; he lectured at Wesleyan University in 1921, at Vanderbilt in 1926, at Harvard in 1933, in India in 1933–34; he served as president of the Chicago Church Federation in 1929–32, as a member of the executive committee of Chautauqua and director of its religious work from 1912 until his retirement, on the executive committee of the World Conference on International Peace through Religion from 1928 until his death, and as head of the Kobe College Corporation from 1920. And he continued to publish extensively, some of his most important works having appeared in the period in question.[114]

The historiographical problem is not that Mathews's biographer has a dearth of material for the latter period of his life. It is more precisely a problem of finding in this material anything new to say about Mathews's thought. His brief intellectual biography "Theology as Group Belief" indicates the difficulty: in it, he talks in great detail about how the events of his life up to the war impacted his work; but when he comes to the postwar period, he shifts to a rather disembodied, sketchy examination of his later works. The focus is on his writings, and not on connections between his work and his life.

Perhaps such a shift in focus is to be expected after a person of such prodigious authorship and teaching activity has established a career. As one struggles to settle down and stake out a piece of the intellectual globe for one's own, one is far more likely to encounter interesting ideas, events, possibilities, and checks that decisively shape one's thought. But when one has secured one's place, one tends to stand there and speak out of that territory: a transfer of energy takes place akin to what developmental psychologist Erik Erikson calls *generativity*—that is, rather than taking in novel ideas, one begins to share the wisdom one has accumulated in one's struggle, to pass that wisdom on to others.[115]

Mathews's postwar theological writings look backward rather than forward for another crucial reason: they are for the most part *defensive* writings. Though Mathews and other social gospel theologians had foreseen the crisis to which the so-called Christian nations of the world were heading, and had sought to avert it, the war and the ensuing critique of the progressivist assumptions of liberal and social gospel theologies placed them on the defensive.

Mathews's sparring with critics began during the war itself, when, under his editorship, *BW* had initiated an attack upon premillennialism. In editorials such as "The By-Products of a Creative Age" and "The Social Optimism of Faith in a Divine Jesus" (1914), Mathews had inveighed against what he saw as an "extraordinary attempt to force Christianity against the current of modern culture" taking place in North American Christianity at the time.[116] That this observation is directed against premillennialism is evident from a *Constructive Quarterly* article of the previous year, "The Awakening of American Protestantism," in which Mathews laments the establishment of premillennialist Bible institutes in Chicago, New York, Minneapolis, and Los Angeles.[117] Mathews stigmatizes premillennialism as "frankly anti-modern," a charge that reverberates throughout his writings on the topic, and which he was to extend to that variety of premillennialism representing itself as a return to the fundamentals of Christian faith.[118] In Mathews's estimation, fundamentalism involves an unworkable attempt to revert to a prescientific, precritical theological stance that severs the gospel from contemporary culture. The 1923 article "Ten Years of American Protestantism" puts the point succinctly: "Fundamentalism is seventeenth-century confessionalism *redivivus*."[119]

The AISL also enlisted in *BW*'s battle to divert the theological imagination of evangelical America from premillennialism and fundamentalism. Both Mathews and Case published AISL tracts combating premillennialism; Case's 1917 tract *The Truth about the Book of Revelation*, reprinted by Mathews in *BW*, was a prelude to his 1918 book *The Millenial Hope*, which was the most substantial contribution of the Chicago theologians to the debate.[120] Mathews's 1917 AISL leaflet *Will Christ Come Again?*, which maintains that Christ will never come again in the literal sense asserted by premillennialism, provoked a violent reaction.[121] The Hyde Park office of the AISL was deluged by letters attacking the leaflet, and a number of tracts were published in response, including I. M. Haldeman's *Professor Shailer Mathews' Burlesque on the Second Coming of Our Lord* and Philip Mauro's *Dr. Shailer Mathews on Christ's Return.*[122] Nor were these attacks entirely by *fringe* members of the North American religious establishment: Haldeman was pastor of the First Baptist Church of New York City.

More substantive than the premillennialist reaction to theologians such as Mathews was that of neo-orthodox theology. As a recently discovered cache of editorial correspondence from the early years of the *Journal of Religion* (hereafter, *JR*) has revealed, Mathews and Reinhold Niebuhr were in correspondence as early as 1919.[123] Among the letters in this cache is one from Niebuhr to Mathews, in which Niebuhr expresses dissatisfaction with Mathews's request that he rewrite an article submitted to *JR*. Mathews appears to have found the article's criticism of the church too general. As Mathews's writings of the postwar period demonstrate, he was disturbed by what he took to be the pessimism of neo-orthodox theology (and its consequent opposition to social gospel reformism), as well as its penchant for socialist critiques of capitalist society. In these works, Mathews rarely cites Niebuhr or other North American neo-orthodox theologians by name, nor does he often refer directly to neo-orthodoxy itself. In a rare reference to Niebuhr's *Moral Man and Immoral Society* in the 1934 study *Christianity and Social Process*, Mathews argues against the thesis that Christian moral standards cannot be expected to apply to nations.[124] In the following year, however, in his essay "The Church and the Social Order," Mathews recommends *Moral Man and Immoral Society* in a short list of suggested readings appended to the essay.[125]

Neither does Mathews often explicitly address either Barth or the Barthian theology of the Continent. The 1927 article "The Development of Social Christianity in America during the Past Twenty-five Years" has a passing reference to the "'crisis theology' of Germany," which Mathews compares with premillennialism—though he admits that there is a large difference between the two movements in quality of thought and leadership.[126] Elsewhere in these years, Mathews characterizes crisis theology as an attempt to develop "a somewhat mystical reliance upon and conformity to the will of God as over against the Christian transformation of society and civilization."[127] Another brief indirect notice of the Barthian school occurs in *Christianity and Social Process,* in which Mathews expresses dismay about "the cult of pessimism and futility" coming out of European disillusionment with democracy, and the flirtation of this "cult" with socialism.[128]

This indirect characterization of neo-orthodox theology in both its North American and European manifestations as indicators of a cultural shift to pessimism is repeated in several of Mathews's postwar writings. The 1935 study *Creative Christianity,* for example, argues against the tendency toward pessimism in the "second generation of liberals," who find in "coerced uniformity" of thought and social structures the only solution to the problems of a troubled civilization.[129] The 1938 *The Church and the Christian* echoes the charge: in the study Mathews expresses astonishment at the "curious renascence" of the idea that the church and the world are in opposition to one another.[130] In his estimation, such a viewpoint arises from a "certain type of absolute thinking born of the collectivism of pessimistic distrust of democracy that has swept over Europe."[131]

Mathews's most pointed response to neo-orthodoxy occurs in the 1938 article "Unrepentant Liberalism." In this article, Mathews again insists that neo-orthodoxy is most precisely a second-generation liberalism, a variation on liberal theology, and not a literal reassertion of the theology of classic Protestant orthodoxy as represented by confessional statements such as the Westminster Confession.[132] The neo-orthodox are thus, Mathews argues, liberals who differ from "evangelical liberals" in one telling respect: they radically disagree with liberals of Mathews's ilk in their assessment of and strategies for Christian response to contemporary society.[133] Mathews locates the divergence between the two types of postliberal theology in their differing responses to socialism. In his view, neo-orthodoxy's sanguine appraisal of socialism yields a social mind characterized by sympathetic response to collectivism, and this response arises out of Continental despair about the effectiveness of democracy.[134] As he notes this, Mathews repeats a *bon mot* that seems to have been circulating at the time among North American theological liberals, that the watchword of neo-orthodox theology is "forward to Moscow and back to sin."[135]

If one wishes to see how Mathews works out his defensive response to critiques of liberal theology in extended fashion, one must turn to one of his best-known postwar books, the 1924 *The Faith of Modernism*. The study targets in particular J. Gresham Machen's *Christianity and Liberalism* (1923). *Faith of Modernism* continues the insistence of Mathews's previous sociohistorical theology articles that if Christianity is to have a transformative effect on modern culture, it must seek to express its fundamental beliefs in terms of the creative social mind of the day. As in the essays, in the 1924 volume Mathews argues that the creative social mind of the modern West—that social mind making the future—is characterized by two prominent characteristics: the desire to extend liberty and justice to all social relations (i.e., democracy), and the desire to extend our knowledge of physical reality (i.e., science).

If Christianity is to be a contributor to a future shaped by these creative tendencies, Mathews thinks, it must recast its ideals and values (born of what the later Mathews consistently calls "loyalty" to Jesus) in response to modern democratic and scientific thought patterns. The phrase "loyalty to Jesus," which runs like a bright thread through all Mathews's late writings, signals his growing awareness (after he developed his sociohistorical method) that Christianity is inescapably caught in a state of continuous historical process paralleling that of society itself. Thus, whereas his earlier theological works (notably *GMM*) depict the development of Christianity as a constant interaction of the eternal and unchanging gospel with a changing culture—as if, in the interactive process, Christian doctrine is always the catalyst and culture the base—the later works see that what is of perduring significance in the Christian movement is loyalty to Jesus as savior, which issues in a new ethical life in the believer and the community.[136] The values, attitudes, convictions, ideals (Mathews never formulates this essence precisely, using various terms in various contexts) arising out of believers' response to Jesus as savior: these, rather than an unchanging core of truth, are the genetic heritage transmitted by one generation of Christians to another. The twin foci of the Christian movement throughout its adaptive interactive process with culture are, then, for the later Mathews, Jesus the savior and Christian loyalty to Jesus. As *NFO* notes, in asserting the necessity of the church's adaptation to culture even as it maintains and transmits transcultural constants, *Faith of Modernism* defends a theological methodology that seeks to discover "permanent evangelical values," and to reexpress these according to the creative social mind of a culture.[137] For *Faith of Modernism*, "the true watch-word of Christianity is not truth, but faith vitalized by love."[138]

One of Mathews's preferential theological self-designations—
modernist, rather than liberal—strongly reflects this understanding
of the development of Christianity as creative interchange between
fundamental Christian convictions and culture. In Mathews's usage
both in *Faith of Modernism* and elsewhere, modernism is a *via media*
between two extremes, one attempting impossibly to repristinate
Christian faith, the other disavowing any constant factor in Christian development. Though Mathews can and does refer to his theological stance as liberal, particularly in the postwar period as liberal
theology comes under attack from various sectors, he more commonly identifies it as modernist. Throughout his theological career
he seeks to distinguish his modernist theological viewpoint from a
liberalism that on the one hand laments doctrinal development as a
departure from the primitive gospel, and a liberalism that on the
other hand tends to ignore the constants within the historical forms
of Christian faith and so concedes too much to culture in the adaptive process.[139]

If one imagines that the postwar Mathews was some Johnny-
come-late opportunist who saw the shortcomings of liberal theology only after they had been exposed by critics, one would be mistaken. Pointed critique of liberal Christianity is evident even in
Mathews's early *BW* editorials. The 1901 editorial "Certain Hopeful
Tendencies in Today's Theological Thought," for example, refers to
liberalism as reductionistic, and regards it as "apt to minimize the
darker moral facts."[140] As the editorial "Two Obligations of the
Church to a Christian Society" (also from 1901) insists, if the church
is to be effective in the modern world, it "must stand for something
other than creed-reduction; it must stand for definite convictions as
to sin and God and salvation through faith."[141] The 1907 *Church
and Changing Order* echoes this critique of liberal theology as reductionistic:

> The so-called liberal movement, while justly criti-
> cising evangelicalism in the old, crude, popular sense,
> has too often confused religion with ethical culture,
> and, with all its undeniable services as a corrective of
> a too often irrational orthodoxy, lives institutionally
> today largely by the adoption of dissatisfied products
> of evangelicalism.[142]

As is evident, these editorials reflect Mathews's strong interest in
and commitment to the enterprise of theological reconstruction—an
enterprise that, as we have seen, saw itself as a dialectic response to

the propadeutic deconstructive moment that had occurred in German liberal theology of the nineteenth century.

In a parallel move, from early in his theological career Mathews argues that classic doctrinal formulations such as those that define the significance of Jesus for the believer (as, for example, the Nicene and Chalcedonian creeds) are valid and necessary developments "implicit" in the thought of Paul and the later New Testament authors.[143] *Church and Changing Order* disagrees sharply with the notion that all theological formulations ought to be discarded in some deluded attempt to recover the "unsystematized" gospel: in Mathews's view, "the history of Christian thought cannot be wholly a history of mistakes."[144] Mathews's 1938 *apologia* for his modernistic rendition of liberalism, the article "Unrepentant Liberalism," clearly distinguishes modernism from both reductionistic liberalism and culture Protestantism. In particular, the article argues that modernists (who "wish to express the values of Christian faith and moral endeavor in terms of contemporary culture") should be distinguished from those liberals who are interested in the philosophy and history of religion, rather than with Christianity and evangelical values.[145] While both spring from the same cultural process, he surmises, the two theological viewpoints have diverged in their assessment of what is required in the Christian response to modern culture.[146]

Up to this point in our survey of Mathews's postwar theological work, we have focused on those works (such as *Faith of Modernism*) that most clearly exhibit the sharp defensive tendency in Mathews's theology during the period. While it is quite true to say that such a defensive posture characterizes Mathews's later theology, to say this without qualification would be to misrepresent the significance of some important books published after World War I in which Mathews continues his creative theological reflection of the prewar period, albeit with a combative edginess not to be found in the earliest works. Among the most important of Mathews's late studies are two that apply his sociohistorical method to specific Christian doctrines, the atonement and the doctrine of God. *The Atonement and the Social Process* (1930) and *The Growth of the Idea of God* (1931) are among the books for which Mathews is perhaps most remembered. The treatises trace the modifications of the doctrines of the atonement and of God through the successive stages of Western Christian civilization and social minds outlined above. Each study ends with a constructive theological proposal for the translation of the doctrine into terms of thought congenial to the modern believer — above all, into premises drawn from what Mathews calls the democratic-scientific social mind that he considers to be making the future.

Mathews's final theological statement, *Is God Emeritus?* (1940), furthers *Growth of the Idea of God*'s attempt to develop a conceptual theism reflecting the modern scientific and sociological understanding of cosmic and social reality as process.[147]

Another important postwar work, *Christianity and Social Process*, is less well known than the previous studies, but deserves attention. The volume consists of Mathews's 1933–34 University of Chicago–sponsored Barrows Lectures in India. The lectures are an extended reflection on religion in general and Christianity in particular as an aspect of social behavior, with particular emphasis on the relation between religion and social change. The issues on which the lectures focus still occupy the attention of Christian theologians, and, if for no other reason, the volume merits rereading as a statement of a mid-twentieth-century North American theological response to these issues, which include the relationship of Christianity to Western civilization, economics, and internationalism, and the question of the applicability of Christian moral standards to nations. In this summary statement of Mathews's theology, one can see clearly at work that chastened theological imagination he had acquired in his battle with postwar critics. One finds this new critical imagination at work in his insistence that Christian influence on the social process has occurred primarily through the impregnation or cross-fertilization (rather than deliberate direction) of the process at crisis or tension moments, as one social mind gives way to another. This insistence allows Mathews to speak of the interplay between Christianity and cultural development as reciprocal—a notion that is certainly present in everything he had written previously about this theme, but that had never been so carefully delineated. And it also allows him to grant the desirability of some cultural influences on Christianity. For example, he warns against Christian smugness about the role of the church in emancipating women: in his view, this cultural development is taking place in modern society primarily because of the activities of secular emancipatory movements, and not due to the action of the church on the social process.[148]

The 1935 study *Creative Christianity*, a compilation of Mathews's Cole Lectures of the previous year at Vanderbilt University, develops this thesis. In it Mathews argues that "strictly speaking, Christianity has been a ferment in social changes rather than an initiator of such changes."[149] This somewhat somber formulation of the place occupied by Christianity in the social process suggests that in his dialogue with neo-orthodox critics of his theology, Mathews has assimilated a neo-orthodox awareness of the need for Christian theologians to recognize the radical *devolutionary* force sin brings to the movement of the process. This recognition militates against any naive glorification of "progress," and it reminds Christian social activists that attempts to "Christianize" the process may be fraught with difficulties and ironies that mere optimism cannot surmount, and that optimism may even gloss over, and, in doing so, gloss over structural injustices that do not yield easily to reform programs based on progressivist ideologies of social change.

One may validly conclude, then, that Mathews's encounter with neo-orthodox critics was not a one-way street: in his dialogue with these theological opponents, Mathews both defended his theological presuppositions and accepted certain presuppositions of his sparring partners. As our examination of the 1928 life of Jesus *JSI* will demonstrate, Mathews's later theology exhibits a realism that may fairly be called neo-orthodox. This realism is apparent above all in Mathews's later understanding of the Christian love ethic, in his growing awareness that a love ethic does not include specific prescriptions for social reform. Or, as Mathews sometimes puts the point, Christian "attitudes" must be distinguished from the "techniques" by which such attitudes are to be implemented in concrete situations.[150] In this vein, *Creative Christianity* observes the following:

> The Christian movement preserves and expresses values that are final, but Christian men and women must implement these values in changing human relations. They must be intelligent because love itself involves the choice of a best known course of conduct.[151]

Again, the point is not that such insights are entirely new in Mathews's thought at the end of his career. As the following chapter will show, even in his earliest social gospel writings Mathews was moving against a tendency in less critically self-reflective social gospellers to assume that the Christian gospels *automatically* yield a minutely embroidered social reform program. Mathews regarded this assumption with extreme suspicion, not only because he saw the reform agenda of social gospellers such as Herron as a slipshod hobbling together of gospel verses and ill-defined idealism, but also because he suspected that the gospels never automatically yield a social ethic. Nonetheless, the encounter with neo-orthodoxy enabled him to make the point with much more acuity at the end of his career, in a way that both safeguards the love ethic and forecloses attempts to use it in an uncritical fashion.

And on such notes, the career of a complex, influential, and ill-remembered North American theologian of the first half of the twentieth century closes. As our examination of Mathews's life has sought to indicate, this career is one with both a strong main current and several unexpected twists and eddies. Running as a continuous current throughout Mathews's theological concern is the question of the social ethical applicability of Christian doctrine. Whether Mathews writes explicit social gospel works such as *STJ* or *Church and Changing Order*, or systematic theological treatises such as *Growth of the Idea of God*, he intends to foreground the problem of finding a theological basis on which to move from affirmations of Christian belief, to the social ethical implications that these affirmations enclose. Ironically, even those modernist works such as *Faith of Modernism* that critics most violently attacked as transmutations of the gospel of Matthew into the gospel of Mathews are, when read at the end of the twentieth century, rather benign attempts to "translate" the eternal gospel into thought patterns congenial to contemporary persons. And not merely benign attempts: attempts imbued as well with an evangelical warmth and zeal to Christianize society that elicit a certain embarrassment in jaded postmodernist readers of Mathews's works.

Yet it would be wrong to say that Mathews wrote about *nothing else* than the applicability of the gospel to society. As the preceding survey of his life and thought has revealed, throughout his career Mathews the academic theologian was intent to pitch his theology to notes predominating in the theology of the day. From his early attempt to deal with the eschatological school emerging strongly in German theology in the work of J. Weiss, to his concern to respond to liberal and neo-orthodox theology in the pre– and post–World War I decades, Mathews constantly reconsidered and reframed his fundamental presuppositions. In doing so, he composed an impressive body of theological literature that continues to have both theological and historical pertinence for scholars of North American religion. Its theological importance lies in what a close contextual reading of Mathews's entire corpus uncovers: that is, that this theology *is* far more contextual, more critically aware of its shortcomings, and therefore more intent to revise itself in response to critics and epiphanic moments in history, than its detractors have admitted. And its historical importance lies in this: Mathews's theology is a virtual compendium of North American theology from the last decade of the nineteenth century to the middle of the twentieth. To read it is to track the development of our theological history through an exciting and perhaps still inadequately understood moment out of whose effects and influence we live even today.

CHAPTER TWO

THE SOCIAL
TEACHING OF JESUS

A Foundation for
Social Gospel Theology

THE MILIEU OF CONCERNS

FROM WHICH *STJ* EMERGED

In the latter half of the nineteenth century, North American Christian churches found themselves challenged to make common cause with the various social reform movements of the day. Writing in the second volume of the *American Journal of Sociology* (hereafter, *AJS*)—a journal founded by Albion Small, which in its early years was to be an important forum for social gospel thought—Walter Rauschenbusch formulated this challenge succinctly: "One of the special tasks of our generation is the work of wedding Christianity and the social movement."[1] To wed Christianity to reform movements in which increasing numbers of churches were involving themselves, to find common cause between the churches and the social movement, to lay a theological foundation for Christian collaboration with secular reformers: this was the foundational task facing social gospellers as the nineteenth century neared its close.

Significantly, the same volume of *AJS* in which Rauschenbusch's article appeared also carried a series of articles by the young

Chicago theologian Shailer Mathews.[2] The series, entitled "Christian Sociology," was written at the behest of Albion Small, and in 1897 would be published as a single volume entitled *The Social Teaching of Jesus.* This study, which would go through numerous reprintings, was to have "an immense influence, especially here in America, where for a generation and longer it was one of the two or three major textbooks of the social-gospel school of New Testament interpretation."[3]

Albion Small and Christian Sociology

Since Small urged Mathews to write the *AJS* articles that constituted the social gospel work *STJ*, any attempt to interpret this volume must begin by asking about Small's concern with social gospel theology. As close investigation of his involvement in the social gospel movement in the early 1890s reveals, Small shared the preoccupation of Rauschenbusch and Mathews to find a solid foundation for social gospel theology, and that preoccupation clearly underlay his commissioning of the "Christian Sociology" articles. In particular, Small's writings of the 1890s indicate that a persistent and central focus in his thought during this period was the question of the relationship between the social gospel movement and the new academic discipline of sociology. To appreciate the point, one must give some attention to the historical context within which sociology emerged as an academic discipline in the United States.

Recent research into the North American origins of the discipline of sociology has demonstrated that to a considerable extent the rise of sociology as an academic discipline and the development of the social gospel form interrelated aspects of a single cultural phenomenon. Indeed, the connection between early sociology and the social gospel appears to have been so close that, in the judgment of sociologist J. Graham Morgan, "to a large extent sociology in America may be seen as an *outgrowth* of the social gospel."[4] Morgan has uncovered evidence that early North American sociology and the social gospel shared a single agenda: as he has discovered, almost one-third of the 298 professors teaching sociology in United States colleges at the turn of the century had received theological training; and a sizable proportion of these were, in fact, ordained ministers.[5] In Small's Chicago department, the connections between the social gospel and sociology may have been even more pronounced. As Arthur J. Vidich and Stanford M. Lyman note, a central prerequisite for joining the department was that one have a "Christian spirit of uplift."[6] Vidich and Lyman have found that "every member of Small's faculty during its first fifteen years—until Harper's death—was associated with ministerial work, settlement houses, and Social Gospel."[7]

That many theologians-cum-sociologists had pronounced social gospel sympathies is indicated, Morgan thinks, by the fact that key texts used in sociology departments in the early years of the discipline were actually social gospel works, and not sociology textbooks, per se.[8] For Cecil Greek, such data represent the tip of the iceberg: in Greek's view, "the ties between early sociology in America and the social gospel movement were much more significant than earlier commentators had either realized or been willing to admit."[9]

In the reciprocal relationship between the social gospel and North American sociology of the 1880s and 1890s, social gospel concerns not only decisively colored sociology, but social gospel thinkers also derived from sociology a sociological perspective that had a determinative influence upon their thought. In particular, sociology contributed to the social gospel a pragmatist perspective on how reform is to be effected, and an evolutionary theoretical framework in which to set its reflections about social change. In the thought of those founding figures of sociology who had most influence on the social gospel movement in the latter part of the century (including Small and Ward), sociological theory was clearly oriented to practical application.[10] Both Small and Ward stringently opposed the social Darwinism of Herbert Spencer and his American disciple William Graham Sumner. In opposition to the laissez-faire approach to social evolution Spencer and Sumner deemed desirable—an approach that extrapolated Darwin's principle of the survival of the fittest from its naturalistic context and applied it to things social—Small and Ward insisted that the evolution of society can and indeed must be directed toward goals deemed socially desirable.[11]

As with their German historical school mentors, the founders of sociology sought to understand social mechanisms in order to implement social reform. In Small's view (echoing Marx's famous observation that the point of philosophy is not to understand but change the world), "Science is sterile unless it contributes at last to knowledge of what is worth doing. . . . The ultimate value of sociology as a pure science will be its use as an index and a test and a measure of what is worth doing."[12] Again paralleling the hermeneutical insights of German historical economics, sociologists such as Small and Ward saw the pragmatist orientation of sociological theory as dovetailing with the evolutionary perspective that predominated in both natural and social sciences in this period. For both

Small and Ward, society is a continuously evolving organism whose evolution is spurred by ideals that serve as end points toward which the growth of social structures is to be directed.[13] From an evolutionary standpoint, the task of social reformers can be described in this way: they are to observe the "tendency" of social evolution in order to discover indications of the ends to which social evolution is pointing; and they are to apply to that process ideals that are intelligent in that they respect this "tendency." Constructive social change is accomplished, Small and Ward insist, only when the ideals proposed as the *telos* of a society's growth accord with the potentials of the evolving society, when they safeguard the integrity of the process in that they are within the range of the concrete capacities of a given society at a given moment.[14]

The pragmatist orientation and evolutionary schema of sociologists such as Ward and Small appealed to those reform-minded Christians of the latter part of the century who sought, with Rauschenbusch, to wed Christianity to the social movement. Above all, sociology appeared to illuminate an important point of contact between Christianity and the various reform movements of the period—the ideals towards which reform was to be directed. If constructive social change is effected when reformers impose ideals on social evolution, then one can easily demonstrate that Christianity and the social movement share common ground, if "Christian" ideals can be shown to be congruent with those of social reformers.

The sociological perspective that social gospel thought incorporated assured that the late nineteenth-century attempt to wed an already pragmatically oriented evangelicalism and the social movement would focus on the question of the "practical application" of Christianity. The Christocentrism of the social gospel was an outgrowth of North American evangelical piety of the latter part of the nineteenth century. Recognition of the North American evangelical derivation of social gospel Christocentrism is important for correct interpretation of Mathews's project in *STJ*. In North American evangelicalism of the latter half of the century, theological concern with the teaching of Jesus had come to center on the *practicability* of Jesus' teaching—specifically, its practicability for guiding the disciple of Jesus in the modern world. The pragmatic orientation of North American evangelical Christocentrism sought to ascertain how to implement the teachings of Jesus in a social order that he had not, and could not have, envisioned. This utilitarian preoccupation caused the social gospel movement to seek to couple the ideals of Jesus with the idealistic reformist impulses emerging in late nineteenth-century America.

In the final decades of the century, a number of studies appeared that explore this question in some detail. These works purported to be justifications for a new field of theological analysis, that of Christian sociology. As exemplars of such foundational reflection, the studies attempted to survey Christian beliefs and their biblical foundation from the standpoint of the new science of sociology, in order to isolate a set of Christian ideals that would intersect with those of secular reformers of the period. Among important seminal works in this vein were J. H. W. Stuckenberg's *Christian Sociology* (1880), *The Age and the Church to Come* (1893), which proposed to present the sociological teachings of the New Testament, and *The Christian Society* (1894); Washington Gladden's *Applied Christianity* (1886); and Richard T. Ely's *Social Aspects of Christianity* (1889).

This sudden exuberance of treatises styling themselves studies of Christian sociology forms the immediate backdrop to Mathews's 1895–96 "Christian Sociology" articles. As Small's writings of the period indicate, he encouraged Mathews to write the articles as a direct response to these studies, because he was alarmed at the growing diversity of works claiming to be accurate representations of Christian sociology. Though as a social gospeller Small wholeheartedly endorsed the call for the wedding of Christianity and the social movement, he had serious misgivings about the viability of some of the reforms advocated by those calling themselves Christian sociologists in the 1880s and 1890s. In particular, he appears to have been greatly alarmed by the turn of social gospeller George Herron to Christian socialism in 1893.[15]

Small had previously been in sympathy with Herron and had even praised his seminal essay on Christian sociology, "The Scientific Ground for a Christian Sociology." But in 1893, at the publication of Herron's *The New Redemption*, which advocated a Tolstoiean interpretation of the Sermon on the Mount as the "social constitution" of Jesus, Small broke with Herron. In an 1894 letter to Ely, who had been his teacher at Johns Hopkins in 1889, Small expresses his distaste for Herron's increasing radicalism, and encourages Ely to sever all ties with him.[16] In 1892, Herron had begun to offer retreats in Christian sociology at Iowa (later Grinnell) College, where a wealthy follower, Mrs. E. D. Rand, had established a chair of Applied Christianity for him in 1893. In 1893, Ely and Herron had been instrumental in founding the American Institute of Christian Sociology at Chautauqua; Ely was elected president of the new institute, Herron principal of instruction.[17] But in 1895, at the appearance of Herron's *The Christian State*, which advocated the establishment of a theocratic polity in United States government, moderate social gospellers including Ely definitively parted company with him.[18]

The publication of Christian sociological works such as Herron's 1893 and 1895 volumes provoked Small to a consideration of the fundamental meaning of the term "Christian sociology." As his writings of the 1890s indicate, in Small's view the range of concrete applications evoked by the term (from Herron's revolutionary platform to his own reformist agenda) pointed to a lack of clarity regarding the foundational aspects of what was being touted as Christian sociology. Small thought that this lack of clarity stemmed from the indeterminacy of the line separating the "Christian" aspect of Christian sociology from its sociological aspect. He wished to raise a number of critical questions about this line. Was Christian sociology sociological research pursued with Christian presuppositions? Or was it instead the sociological study of the New Testament, as most Christian sociological works of the period claimed to be? Did a sociological reading of the New Testament yield a definite agenda for the structuring of contemporary society, as Herron thought? Was there a necessary Christian program for the economic or political organization of society?[19]

In Small's judgment, because it failed to give due attention to questions about its precise meaning, much Christian sociology of the 1880s and 1890s was inadequate in two important respects: it was poor sociology; and it misrepresented the biblical foundation for Christian involvement in the social movement. Since this assessment of Christian sociology lies behind his encouragement of Mathews to write the 1895–96 "Christian Sociology" articles, Small's critique of Christian sociology deserves careful attention.

In Small's writings of the 1890s, a constant charge levied against Christian sociologists was that they lacked regard for the scientific nature of sociology. Of particular concern to Small was the cavalier indifference he believed many Christian sociologists exhibited about the need to test their sociological hypotheses (that is, their concrete proposals for social reform) against empirical data. In Small's view, not a few Christian sociologists of the day indulged in a type of Christian sociological fideism: having appealed to what they took to be the *ipsissima verba* of Jesus, they regarded themselves as dispensed from the hard work of amassing and analyzing social scientific evidence to back their claims.

The 1896 essay "The Limits of Christian Sociology" makes this critique pointedly. Here, Small inveighs against Christian sociologists who appear to think that mere quotation of scripture provides them with sufficient warrant for proposing any and every agenda for social reform that appeals to them. Against such an assumption, Small argues,

> [w]e do not object to the use of the term "Christian Sociology," but we decidedly object to ignorant and opinionated abuse of it. The fundamental principles of human relationship which Jesus expounded must be recognized and applied in any permanent successful social program. . . . However, this does not exhaust the subject matter of sociology.[20]

Small's *An Introduction to the Study of Society* (1893) had begun to move toward this critique of Christian sociology by lambasting Christian sociologists who substituted "loose criticism and silly utopianism" for social scientific research.[21] As an 1895 letter from Small to Harper proposing the institution of a journal of sociology indicates, among the concerns motivating Small to found *AJS* was his wish to offset facile appropriations of sociology by social reformers, Christian and otherwise. In the letter, Small tells Harper that,

> Every silly and mischievous doctrine which agitators advertise claims sociology as its sponsor. A scientific journal of Sociology could be of practical service in every issue, in discrediting pseudo-sociology and in forcing social doctrinaires back to accredited facts and principles.[22]

Small's inaugural essay in *AJS* leaves no doubt that Christian sociologists are included in this indictment of "pseudo-sociology":

> To many possible readers the most important question about the conduct of the Journal will be with reference to its attitude toward "Christian Sociology." The answer is, in a word, toward Christian sociology, sincerely deferential, toward alleged "Christian sociologists," severely suspicious.[23]

Small's critique of Christian sociology in the 1890s reflects his struggle to specify the terrain proper to his new academic discipline. As occupant of the first chair of sociology in the United States and as founder of *AJS*, during the 1890s Small was preoccupied with the problem of defining the research field proper to sociology, and developing methodological guidelines for it.[24] Given the haziness of the line separating early sociology from the social gospel, this preoccupation is rather easy to understand. Did the sociologist develop theory to understand and explain the operations of society, and then relinquish to the social gospeller the task of implementing this theory in social reform? Or were the two tasks, theoretical and practical, intertwined constitutive aspects of the fundamental charge of sociology itself?

In the early 1890s, Small appears to have opted for a division of labor in which sociology would provide a theoretical framework and a scientific methodology, while the social gospel would concern itself with the practical application of sociological theory.[25] From Ward's *Dynamic Sociology*, whose distinction between dynamic and static sociology exerted a seminal influence on Small's understanding of sociology, Small derived a comprehensive vision of the sociologist's task.[26] In his view, sociologists must constantly be on guard against lapsing into facile deductions on the basis of a limited range of data. Small thought that scientific investigation (e.g., statistical research) must constantly attend the elaboration of sociological theory, acting as a check against ideological distortion, and serving to keep the theoretical process open-ended, in a state of constant revision.[27] Scientific explanations of social phenomena are most adequate, Small believed, when they seek to incorporate as many viewpoints as possible. The multilayered complexity of social realities demands a superperspectival social theory.

This understanding of the theoretical basis of a scientific sociology underlies Small's critique of Christian sociologists such as Herron. In his consideration, the "sociology" of such reformers was divorced from controlled observation of social phenomena: thus their proposals for social reform were completely dominated by preconceived fixed ideas.[28] As a result, not a few of the reforms they advocated would, he believed, be liable to do damage rather than to effect constructive change. In his *Introduction to the Study of Society*, Small argues that due attention to the need to revise theory in light of ongoing research should check the reformer's "mischievous tendencies to construct mountainous social philosophies out of molehills of social knowledge."[29]

Small's concept of effective social reform derives from the organic, evolutionary model of society presupposed by his sociology. Since he understands society to be a continuously evolving organism, Small holds that "gradualism rather than catastrophism is the universal manner of social cause and effect."[30] The stress on social evolution leads both Small and Ward to insist that amelioration rather than radical revision of social institutions is the best means of achieving lasting social reform—an assumption that would have determinative influence on Mathews's social gospel theology.[31]

The political context of Small's penchant for gradualism rather than catastrophism in social reform is not without significance.[32] Though throughout his career he remained an outspoken critic of North American capitalism, Small was skeptical about the feasibility of socialism as an alternative model for North American society. This skepticism emerges early in his thought. In his 1888 report to the trustees of Colby College, for example, he argues that the French Revolution presents us with the timeliest of all historical lessons, that is, that considered reform is more effective than ill-conceived socialist experimentation.[33] Once again, this is a perspective that powerfully shapes Mathews's thought: in his study of the French Revolution, Mathews would demonstrate the extent to which his understanding of this event was indebted to Small's sociological assessment of revolution.

Implicit in Small's concern to discover a sociologically sound foundation for Christian sociology was also an interest in grounding Christian sociology in accurate exegesis. This interest obviously hovers within Small's critique of Herron's *New Redemption*. To see this, however, one must tease out of Small's remarks about the foundational aspects of Christian sociology his exegetical criticisms and recommendations, since these are never brought to the fore in his writings to the extent that his reflections on the sociological base of Christian sociology are. However, though implicit, these exegetical interests are nonetheless clearly evident.

A distinct critical perspective regarding the exegetical base of some Christian sociologists's work shows itself in writings such as "The Limits of Christian Sociology." Here, as he argues against the tendency of certain Christian sociologists to elide the scientific demands of the discipline of sociology by citing scripture, Small notes that what disturbs him above all is the tendency of some social gospellers to assume that the gospels contain *explicit* prescriptions for the structuring of contemporary social institutions.[34] Against such a notion, he contends that the "fundamental principles" of Jesus' teaching must be "applied in any permanent successful social program."[35] This observation reflects an insight voiced distinctly in various of Small's writings: that the sayings of Jesus as recorded by the gospel writers do not provide concrete directions for political, economic, or social life. Rather, underlying Jesus' words are "fundamental principles" and ideals that have to be applied variously in various historical situations. An interesting passage in an 1895 letter to Ward regarding the Reverend L. T. Chamberlain's assumption of the leadership of the American Institute of Christian Sociology expresses Small's assessment of the relationship between the Jesus of the gospels and the Christian social reformer: "My personal belief is that Christ's life was the most effective object lession [sic] in history as to the quality of rational human life, but that it showed comparatively little about the process." [36] Or, as Small's 1913 social gospel novel *Between Eras* would observe: "The importance of Jesus' message does not lie in a blueprint for structures, but of presenting us with the moral attitude a man ought to take up when creating structures or performing tasks." [37]

This understanding of the biblical foundation of Christian sociology runs counter to Herron's. In calling for the literal political and economic implementation of Jesus' "social constitution," the Sermon on the Mount, Herron presupposes that the teaching of Jesus in the gospels provides clear directives for the organization of contemporary society. Small and Herron's differing points of view regarding exegesis yield two very different political stances for the Christian social reformer: whereas Small's attempt to discover "moral attitudes" rather than explicit norms in Jesus' message is congruent with his reformist bias and undercuts a radicalism fueled by biblical literalism, Herron's radicalism is genetically related to his belief that the gospels provide us with the *ipsissima verba* of Jesus and that these words are a literal prescription for the organization of a moral society.

Small's critical solicitude about the sociological and biblical dimensions of Christian sociology forms the ground of concerns out of which Mathews's 1895–96 "Christian Sociology" articles emerged. Small's concerns were *foundational* ones: he perceived the need for a study that would provide a sociologically astute and exegetically sound foundation for Christian sociology. Such a work would constitute an adequate theological ground for the wedding of Christianity and the social movement. Drawing on the insights of the developing science of sociology, it would recognize that the attempt to discover in the "social teaching" of Jesus clear directives for the political or economic organization of contemporary society is fraught with complexities overlooked by reformers untutored in sociology.

Moreover, an adequate foundation for Christian sociology would seek in the gospels warrant for the ethical idealism presupposed by the sociology of sociologists-cum-social gospellers such as Small. If society is an organism evolving in response to idealistic impulses, then the social teaching of Jesus must be found at base to be commensurate with a set of ideals—those on which both Christian reformers and other social reformers can readily agree. By transferring the weight of Jesus' social teaching from precise prescriptions to ideals that must incarnate themselves variously in various social settings, Christian sociology would avoid collapsing the entire project of social reform into a set of gospel verses. An idealistic interpretation of Jesus' social teaching leaves room for the scientific study of society, for the revision and growth of the reformer's understanding of the requirements of a given society at a given time. An idealistic interpretation of Jesus' teaching is susceptible to a reformist application of Small's belief that "gradualism rather than catastrophism is the universal manner of social cause and effect."

Mathews and Christian Sociology

These foundational concerns are clearly apparent in Mathews's search for a theological foundation for the social gospel in the 1895–96 articles.[38] As was Small, in the early 1890s Mathews was intently preoccupied with the question of the meaning of Christian sociology, and in particular with the problem of developing a sociological and biblical foundation for this sociology. An important interest that surfaces in his writings of the 1890s is to determine precisely how Christian sociologists ought to use the scriptures to buttress their proposals for the reform of society.

Such a preoccupation is manifest in Mathews's reaction to the work of Christian sociologist Z. S. Holbrook, whom the journal *Bibliotheca Sacra* appointed in 1894 as editor of its new department of Christian sociology. In an October 1894 *BW* synopsis of Holbrook's article "Christian Sociology," Mathews complains of the vagueness of the term "Christian sociology"—a vagueness that leaves it open to a variety of interpretations and applications.[39] Underlying this observation seems to have been a quarrel between Mathews and Holbrook about the exegetical basis of Christian sociology, since, in a subsequent synopsis of an article by John Sewall on Jesus' social ethic, Mathews notes disapprovingly that Holbrook's approach to the social teaching of the gospels is systematic rather than exegetical. In opposition to such a point of departure, Mathews argues that the first question to be asked by Christian sociologists is, "What does Jesus *really mean* by the term kingdom of God, Father in heaven, brother, neighbor . . . ?"[40] The point is indicative of Mathews's underlying concern in *STJ*: in his search for an adequate theological foundation for the social gospel, he intends to lay great stress on the need for exegetical precision in any attempt to determine the social teaching of Jesus.

Mathews's interest in the exegetical foundation of Christian sociology in the early 1890s exactly parallels Small's. As does Small, he combats the tendency of some Christian sociologists to base entire programs of reform on isolated scripture texts. Moreover, as with Small, in Mathews's judgment not only do some Christian sociologists naively presume that the social teaching of Jesus is easy to ascertain and apply to contemporary social problems, but these reformers in fact often simply read their own presuppositions about the needs of contemporary society back into the gospel texts. In his synopsis of Holbrook's "Christian Sociology," Mathews contends with uncharacteristic acerbity, "We have had more than enough of undigested, hysterical studies based upon what it is supposed the New Testament teaches."[41] An 1895 editorial entitled "Sociology and New Testament Study" makes the point even more trenchantly: "Just at present it is fashionable to buttress sociological sentimentality—too often called `Christian sociology'—with an uncritical and deluding citation of Scripture."[42]

As in Small's thought as well, Mathews's wish to oppose such anachronistic misuse of the gospels appears to have had a patent political intent. This is evident in an 1891 essay for the International Sunday School lessons of the year. Mathews's lesson-outline is a commentary on 2 Kings 25:1–12. He uses the commentary to drive home a social gospel point: that is, if it wishes to avert revolution, the church must make common cause with the reform movement:

> We to-day are confronted with many of the same
> questions that confronted and conquered Judah. The
> social condition of our people will sooner or later
> bring revolution or readjustment. Our one hope lies
> in Christ's teachings. . . . The one great lesson of the
> Captivity of Judah is this: the fearless application of
> Christianity to living questions is the duty of both
> clergy and laymen, and the hope of the state.[43]

As Dennis Smith's study of the Chicago School of sociology notes, the concern of Chicago sociologists/social gospellers to avert revolution grew even stronger in 1894, as strikes—including a Pullman strike— crippled the city.[44] One cannot adequately interpret *STJ* without keeping in mind that this text was composed in the midst of such labor unrest.

Political preoccupations surface in several of Mathews's 1895 editorials on Christian sociology. In an editorial on sociology and New Testament study, for example, Mathews observes that if Christian sociology is to make a sound contribution to New Testament exegesis, it must avoid loose use of terms such as "anarchist" and "socialist."[45] The remark is evidently turned against social gospellers such as Herron who would find in Jesus a model for Christian socialism. Another editorial of the same year criticizes those who seek to make Jesus a social reformer in the modern sense of the term, or the champion of a particular class. Against what he takes to be such misappropriations of Jesus' example and teaching, Mathews maintains that "good politics and equitable distribution of wealth, it is to be hoped, will result from Christian civilization, but Jesus stands committed to no scheme or ready-made millennium."[46]

Mathews demonstrates concern with the sociological and biblical foundation of Christian sociology in the late 1880s and early 1890s not only in his published writings, but in unpublished documents. As his correspondence with E. D. Burton regarding the New Testament position that Burton offered him reveals, Mathews went to Chicago intent on combining New Testament exegesis with the new discipline of sociology. When he had begun to read extensively in this discipline in the expectation that he would be brought to Chicago as a member of Small's sociology department, among the authors he placed on his reading list (in addition to Herbert Spencer) were Ely, Gladden, and Josiah Strong. Ely seems to have exerted a particularly strong influence on Mathews at this time; Mathews adopted Ely's *Outlines of Economics* for use in his economics classes at Colby.[47] Once again, this links Mathews closely to Small, since Ely had been not merely Small's teacher at Johns Hopkins, but a director of his dissertation, and the two remained lifelong friends and associates.[48]

In addition, as he began to read widely in sociology, Mathews became actively involved in the social gospel movement. In the early 1890s, he associated himself with a group of reform-minded Baptists identified by Stephen Wurster as the Baptist Congress for the Discussion of Current Questions.[49] The group, described by C. H. Hopkins as "an unofficial denominational forum," met yearly from 1892 to 1907.[50] Among its members were several social gospellers destined to become leading figures in the movement, including Samuel Zane Batten, Charles P. Henderson, and Rauschenbusch.

When Mathews came to Chicago in 1894, therefore, he brought to his New Testament work both expertise in the new field of sociology and a background of active participation in the social gospel movement. As the correspondence with Burton shows, in negotiating the position Mathews initially asked Burton to make him professor of Christian sociology with a cross-appointment to Burton's

New Testament department and Small's sociology department.[51] Though Burton eventually prevailed on Mathews to drop from his title the sociological designation, he did so by assuring him that his New Testament work could be pursued from a sociological standpoint.[52] Mathews accepted the appointment with such a proviso, and proposed to develop a course in "The Exegetical Sociology of the New Testament."[53]

As this correspondence also demonstrates, Mathews regarded himself as singularly qualified to develop a sociological exegesis for another important reason: his Berlin historiographical training had instilled in him a regard for historical accuracy that he found lacking in the exegetical work of some other Christian sociologists.[54] The influence of Ranke's concern for exacting research, and his disdain for theoretical departure from texts and artifacts examined in their historical context, would be strongly evident in Mathews's attempt to create a theological foundation for Christian sociology in STJ.

One final point regarding how the preoccupations of Small and Mathews interplayed to yield STJ's foundation for social gospel theology: Small's desire to discover a compelling foundation for Christian sociology was not merely a function of his sociological interests. He himself was an active social gospeller. As with Mathews, he had deep Baptist familial roots: the son of a Baptist minister in Maine, Small had studied at Colby (graduating in 1876), and had then trained for the ministry at Newton, from which he took his degree in 1879. Small followed his work at Newton by studying in Berlin and Leipzig from 1879 to 1881. Like Mathews, he chose not to be ordained, but was throughout his lifetime a Baptist lay preacher.[55]

Various writings of the early 1890s exhibit Small's social gospel leanings. For instance, the volume of the International Sunday School Lessons in which Mathews's social gospel interpretation of the captivity of Judah appears also contained a lesson by Small on "Christ Comforting His Apostles" (a commentary on John 14:22).[56] As does Mathews's, Small's commentary draws a pointed social gospel moral. Social gospel inclinations are also clearly discernible in Small's reviews of Wilbur F. Crafts's *Practical Christian Sociology* and Gladden's *Ideas of the Present Age*, which appear in the first volume of *AJS*. Both reviews note that the kingdom of God is the organizing principle of the thought of Christian social reformers of the day; the tone of the texts suggests that Small was not at all opposed to such applications of the concept, and that he sees his sociology as moving on a track intersecting with that of social gospel thought.[57] Plainly, at work in the deliberation of both Small and Mathews in the early 1890s regarding the foundation for Christian sociology is an intent to bring the new discipline of sociology into a symbiotic relationship with the social gospel, in which theological analysis will animate sociological theory, and theories of social process will validate reformist interpretations of the gospels.[58] What remains to be seen is how Mathews works these insights out in his social gospel foundational study.

STJ:

Mathews's Foundation for

Christian Sociology

Mathews first develops his theological foundation for Christian sociology in the nine 1895–96 articles collectively entitled "Christian Sociology." The initial article discusses the meaning of the phrase "Christian sociology," and sets forth what Mathews considers to be a valid understanding of the phrase. Included in this article is an important discussion of the exegetical presuppositions upon which Mathews will draw in the study.

The introductory examination of the definition of Christian sociology is followed by eight articles proposing to present the social teaching of Jesus on the topics man [*sic*], society, the family, the state, wealth, social life, the forces of human progress, and the process of social regeneration. In each, Mathews applies exegetical principles established in the introductory article: having isolated texts that he takes to represent Jesus' teaching on the topic, he attempts, by means of historicocritical analysis, to get at the "actual thought" of Jesus underlying the gospel writers's editorial presentation of his teaching.

When the "Christian Sociology" articles appeared as a single volume in 1897, each article constituted one of the nine chapters of *STJ*. Though *STJ* contains a prefatory note declaring that the articles were considerably rewritten for the 1897 edition, a careful textual comparison reveals that the text of *STJ* is in substance that of the 1895–96 articles. Revisions of significance appear only in the chapter entitled "Society," which treats the important question of the kingdom of God, and that entitled "Wealth," in which socialist readings of the gospels are discussed. Even though *STJ* incorporates several major revisions of the 1895–96 articles on these topics, these are not in fact substantive, but rather seem intended to sharpen and refine Mathews's position on these topics of central importance to social gospel thought.

In the following analysis of Mathews's first social gospel foundational statement, unless otherwise noted, all references will be to the 1897 volume. Where textual comparison reveals a revision of the "Christian Sociology" articles that deserves attention, this will be indicated. Our object is to ascertain how *STJ* seeks to provide an adequate theological foundation for Christian sociology. The first section of our discussion focuses on Mathews's attempt to define Christian sociology in critical dialogue with those social gospel works he regarded as ill-founded. In the next section, *STJ*'s concern to develop an exegetical foundation for Christian sociology will be considered, with particular emphasis on the question of the meaning of the kingdom of God, since this question is of central importance to the foundation of Christian sociology. Section three examines Mathews's pursuit of a theological foundation satisfying the demands of Small's sociological critique of previous Christian sociological works.

What Is Christian Sociology?

In the presentation of the definition of Christian sociology with which *STJ* opens, Mathews's tactic is to critique those definitions of Christian sociology that fall short of the mark, and to establish a cogent working definition. Mathews's critique of insufficient notions of Christian sociology is illuminating: it demonstrates the extent to which Small's critical insights regarding the foundation of Christian sociology inform Mathews's investigation of the social teaching of Jesus. Above all, the introductory portion of *STJ* reveals that Mathews is seeking a secure theological basis for the participation of Christian reformers in the social movement. As in Small's reflections on the topic, Mathews's concern with the problem of Christian sociology centers on questions such as the following: What is an adequate biblical foundation for Christian involvement in social reform? How does the reformer properly make use of the scriptures? What is the particular contribution of Christian sociological exegesis? What is the relationship of Christian sociology to the academic discipline of sociology? How is Christian reformism to be grounded in scientific sociological theory and research? As Mathews addresses these questions, the "episcopal presence" of his mentor Small hovers powerfully over his thought.[59]

Mathews begins by noting the ambivalence of the phrase "Christian sociology." Is it sociology that employs a specifically Christian methodology? Or is it sociological investigation whose conclusions may be given a Christian application?[60] Since objective scientific methodology is by definition neither religious nor ethical, he peremptorily rules out the first understanding as nonsensical.[61] With regard to the notion of Christian sociology as "the formulation and application of results derived by Christian students," Mathews thinks that, though admissible, this definition is open to such a wide range of concrete applications as to be virtually useless.[62]

To be more precise: some applications of Christian sociology are in Mathews's view adequate neither from a Christian nor a scientific standpoint:

> The champions of some so-called Christian sociology
> are dangerously open to criticism similar to that
> which Voltaire passed upon the Holy Roman Em-
> pire—it is neither scientific nor Christian. It cer-
> tainly is desirable that an end should come to such
> pious christening of scientific progeny of at best very
> questionable parentage.[63]

This observation is telling. It reveals that Mathews's concern is specifically with the foundational aspects of Christian sociology. In particular, he is evidently troubled by the use some Christian sociologists make of the biblical warrants for social activism (i.e., the "Christian" aspect), and of the new academic discipline of sociology (that is, the "scientific" aspect). Mathews's study of Jesus' social teaching is thus a sharply focused critical response to studies that (as he judges) misrepresent the exegetical and sociological foundations of Christian sociology.

Mathews follows his consideration of inadequate appraisals of the task of Christian sociology with that definition he thinks most valid:

> Christian sociology should mean the *sociology of
> Christ;* that is, the social philosophy and teachings of
> the historical person Jesus the Christ. In this posi-
> tive sense the term is both legitimate and capable of
> an at least tentatively scientific content.[64]

This definition precisely establishes Mathews's project in *STJ*: he will seek to provide an adequate theological foundation for Christian sociology by examining the *social philosophy* of Jesus. *STJ* will thus be an exegetical exposition of the teaching of Jesus as recorded by the gospel writers. But it will be an exposition with an eye to the sociological applicability of what the exegete discovers. Clearly reflected in this formulation of Christian sociology is Mathews's own academic self-understanding: as his correspondence with Burton notes, he sees himself as a New Testament scholar who conjoins exegesis and sociology.

As Mathews recognizes, his definition of Christian sociology is open to a variety of critical objections. His response to possible counters to his definition in the subsequent sections of the introductory chapter of *STJ* is important, because it demonstrates his awareness of the noteworthy exegetical difficulties lying in the path of such a definition. The first critical challenge Mathews considers is this: May one properly speak of a sociology of Christ? Was Jesus not a teacher of religion and ethics? Given the historical context in which he lived, how could he have elaborated social teaching in the modern sense of the phrase?[65]

Mathews's response incorporates an argument that will be crucial to *STJ*'s interpretation of Jesus' social teaching: that is, granted that Jesus did not deliver a body of social teaching comparable to the prescriptions of a modern social reformer, nevertheless his religious teaching is possessed of a certain "sociological content."[66] If this is not the case, then how is one to account for the manifest social and political influence Christianity has exercised from its inception: "Is it altogether impossible that He whose followers have rebuilt empires and founded new civilizations should have been quite unsuspicious of the social and political forces that lay within his words?"[67] In asking this, in speaking of the "sociological content" of Jesus' teaching, Mathews is obviously casting about for some tool of analysis to use to uncover the social ethical significance of all Christian doctrinal statements; here one can see the germ of the later Mathews's systematic theological insistence that discussions of Christian doctrine which exclude the question of the social applicability of Christian symbols are incomplete discussions.

This important argument for the sociological content of Jesus' teaching thus makes a tactical move that will be fundamental to Mathews's social gospel theology in particular, and the social process theology in general. That is, it draws a neat cleavage between Jesus' precise words, and the "social and political forces that lay within his words." Such a move is calculated to undercut criticism of Christian sociology on the grounds that the "social teaching" of Jesus is either so sparse as to be cryptic, or is inapplicable to a historical context other than that in which he lived. This distinction between Jesus' precise teaching and the "forces" contained by his teaching frees the Christian reformer to apply Jesus' teaching in ways that a literalistic approach to the gospels would prevent. As is apparent, this formulation of Jesus' social teaching is nicely congruent with Small's thought.

To argue for the sociological content of Jesus' teaching is, however, to elicit a second critical objection: that is, if the gospels have such sociological content, how does one account for the fact that this content has been largely overlooked by previous exegetes? In Mathews's view, the answer lies in post-Reformation Christian theology's preoccupation with the salvation of the individual believer.[68] In both the theology and the popular faith of the post-Reformation church, a decisive theological tendency to "unmodified individualism" has been present, Mathews thinks, and this tendency has operated to the virtual exclusion of the question of the salvation of society. With its recognition of the "essential sociability of human nature," sociology illuminates for the exegete an aspect of the gospels missed by the rather limited scope of previous theology.[69] The wedding of sociology and exegesis promises to revolutionize biblical studies:

> Whether for weal or for woe, the underlying premises
> of the social sciences that isolation is abnormality
> and that society is itself an object of study, promise
> some day to prove as revolutionary in biblical inter-
> pretation as was the new conception of the worth of
> the individual in the sixteenth century. . . . The future
> of a man is known; the future of mankind is now to
> be discovered.[70]

The claim that the rise of the social sciences in the nineteenth century opens new room for Christian theology to discover the social significance of its soteriological affirmations is also central to such key social gospel texts as Rauschenbusch's *Theology of the Social Gospel*.[71] To a great extent, social gospel theology in the first decades of the twentieth century was an "unpacking" of this important foundational claim.

The final obstacle that Mathews finds confronting the sociological exegete is the presupposition that it is relatively easy to extract from the gospels prescriptions for social reform. In Mathews's estimation, such a presupposition fails to advert to significant exegetical considerations, including the historical context, dating, and intent of scriptural texts.[72] Because much Christian sociology fails to broach important exegetical questions, it is for Mathews simply philanthropic sentimentalism decked out with scripture verses:

> Disregarding the mischievous tendency for every
> good man to dub as "sociology" his hasty thinking

and hopes as to society; disregarding the refreshing
certainty enjoyed by many amateur though earnest reformers that in the preparation of millenniums the ac-
cumulation of figures and statistics is wholly super-
fluous; disregarding the fact that much so-called
sociological teaching is nothing more than relabeled
ethics; granting that sociologies are as easy to produce as political panaceas, the fact remains that as yet
Christian sociology has been too much at the mercy
of men who have mistaken what they think Christ
ought to have taught for what he really did teach. . . .
Too often modern prophets to a degenerate church,
in sublime indifference to the context, time of authorship, and purpose of a New Testament book, and
with an equal neglect of the personal peculiarity and
vocabulary of a New Testament writer, have set forth
as the work of Christianity views which are but bescriptured social denunciation and vision.[73]

This important critique of the work of previous Christian sociologists clarifies Mathews's fundamental intent in *STJ*. In defining Christian sociology as the social philosophy and teachings of
Jesus, he assumes that the teaching of Jesus is in some sense accessible to the sociological exegete. However, as this passage amply
demonstrates, Mathews also recognizes that the gospels are hardly
perspicuous: even if accessible, the teaching of Jesus is nonetheless
to be discovered only through painstaking exegetical work. Contrary
to the assumption of some Christian sociologists, in Mathews's estimation the employment of a sociological perspective in exegesis
will not automatically yield an exegetically precise statement of
Jesus' social teachings.

Moreover, as Mathews points out, in the practice of some Christian sociologists the "sociological perspective" is less a fresh vantage point for reading the gospels, than a determinative bias which assures that reformers will discover in the gospels what they already
believe to be Jesus' social teaching. Compounding the problem is
the sociological naiveté of so many Christian sociologists, who sub-
stitute for rigorous social scientific analysis a vague utopianism.
Here again, the influence of Small is clearly evident. The impatience
with the tendency of some Christian sociologists to eclipse the scientific dimension of sociology; the presupposition that the plotting
of effective strategies of social reform demands wide-ranging research;
the dismissal of much Christian sociology of the day as "but be-

scriptured social denunciation and vision": all these elements of Mathews's critique strongly reflect Small's critical assessment of Christian sociology. The exact congruence of Mathews's critique of some social gospel programs with that of Small allows one to make an important deduction about Mathews's agenda in *STJ:* when he insists on the necessity of basing programs of reform on accurate exegesis, he is doing so over against the work of "radical" Christian sociologists such as Herron. Despite his protests about the need for objectivity in approaching the gospels, Mathews's exegetical analysis of the social teaching of Jesus will have a patent underlying hermeneutical interest, one he shares with Small. This is to find in Jesus' teaching grounds for gradual reform of social institutions.

The Biblical Foundation: Mathews's Exegetical Presuppositions

STJ follows its preliminary examination of the definition of Christian sociology with another groundlaying discussion. Here, the focus is on exegesis, on the exegetical presuppositions and principles Mathews will bring to his study of Jesus' social teachings. Mathews begins this portion of the introductory chapter by declaring:

> There is but one way to the apprehension of the teachings of Jesus, whether religious or social, and that is the patient study of the gospels with the aid of all modern critical and exegetical methods. . . . Here, as in all scientific processes, the aim of the investigator must be the discovery of what is, not the substantiation of some notion as to what ought to be.[74]

This declaration sets forth the prevailing exegetical consideration of the study: in *STJ*, Mathews seeks to discover what the gospels actually say, rather than what an exegesis of wish-fulfillment desires to see in them; and he intends to accomplish this by the application of "all modern and critical methods." This is an important formulation of the task of sociological exegesis. With it, Mathews is deliberately linking historicocritical exegesis with the Christian sociological quest for the social teaching of Jesus. Since it is his insistence on the necessity of scientific exegesis that will lead Mathews, both in *STJ* and *MHNT,* to recognize the importance of eschatological readings of the New Testament, the move to ground social gospel theology in a scrupulously accurate interpretation of the gospels is of momentous importance both to Mathews's own theology, and that of the social gospel in general.[75] To appreciate the point, one must give attention to the development of Mathews's understanding of exegesis in other writings of the period.

The question of the legitimacy of higher criticism and of its implications for Christian faith is perhaps the single topic that occurs most frequently in Mathews's writings of the 1890s. Both the frequency with which the topic appears and the nature of his reflections suggest that Mathews was himself struggling to come to terms with the sometimes profoundly disturbing implications of higher criticism for evangelical Christians.

Since his introduction to contemporary exegesis at Newton had been primarily refutatory, when Mathews was offered the New Testament position at Chicago, among the reasons for his hesitancy to accept the offer was his recognition of the inadequacy of his training in the field.[76] Though none of his autobiographical statements specifies how he sought to overcome this inadequacy after having accepted the position, Mathews's writings of the 1890s allow one to infer that he began to read widely in New Testament scholarship during this period. Moreover, a number of sources suggest that his reading in these years focused primarily on the work of German higher critical exegetes, including Bernhard Weiss, Emil Schürer, H. H. Wendt, and Willibald Beyschlag.[77]

Mathews's *BW* editorials of the 1890s are particularly useful for exposing his specific concerns as he studied the work of these exegetes. Almost all the editorials from 1894 to 1898 deal with the theological problems posed by higher criticism.[78] Though most of these postdate the composition of the "Christian Sociology" articles, the issues they address were certainly preoccupying Mathews as he wrote the articles. Indeed, these issues would continue to concern him (as they did other North American theologians) well into the first decades of the next century.

In general, Mathews's *BW* editorials on higher criticism represent a manifest appeal for North American theologians and pastors to accept the new methodology. To this end, they employ a twofold tactic: they argue that higher criticism does not (indeed cannot) erode the foundations of Christian faith; and they attempt to disseminate the most important conclusions that higher critical exegesis of the scriptures has reached.[79] In keeping with the popularizing intent of *BW*, in his summaries of the findings of higher critics, Mathews employs a soft-sell approach that mitigates the threatening implications of higher criticism and highlights what seems of pertinence for Christians concerned with the evangelical application of exegesis—an approach in keeping with that of Harper, who found himself simultaneously intellectually drawn to higher criticism in the 1880s and emotionally repulsed by it, and whose writings on the topic employed a rhetorical conservatism designed to introduce North American readers to the subject without alienating them.[80]

In his editorials of the 1890s Mathews uses an argument typical of this period in North American theology, one that represents a strategic move designed to undercut reservations some believers might have about the destructive tendencies of higher criticism. He characterizes the theological situation of the period as transitional: arguing that in such a transitional period higher critical work will to a certain extent necessarily be destructive, he notes that not every tenet of previous theological systems will be able to withstand the assault of destructive critical findings, particularly in the areas of revelation and Christology.[81] However, Mathews assures his readers, this transitional stage of criticism is only propadeutic. Destructive critical work will be succeeded by theological reconstruction. Thus, though higher criticism appears to be shaking the foundations of Christian faith, its threat is only apparent; indeed, rather than threatening the foundation of Christian faith, critical exegesis is actually exposing its sure historical foundations. Simultaneous with the extension of critical methodology has occurred a laudable theological "return to Christ." The confluence of modern theological Christocentrism and higher critical research has assured that "the historical character of Jesus, his personality, the authenticity of his teachings, his death and subsequent manifestations . . . —all these are far more credible today than half a century since, as the result of criticism."[82]

The 1890s editorials are thus clearly optimistic about historical criticism's potential to recover the "essential Jesus" from gospel texts that are the faith-interpretation of the early church.[83] In an 1897 editorial, for example, Mathews observes that "the highest function of criticism is to bring us face to face with the original material—the words of eyewitnesses—out of which to construct our character sketch [i.e., of Jesus]."[84] Such a critical recovery of the "original material" will allow the exegete to group the gospel materials into a "working 'harmony'" so that "from them shall emerge as nearly as possible the actual Jesus."[85]

The arguments set forth in Mathews's *BW* editorials of the 1890s regarding the function and possibilities of higher criticism are reflected in the exegetical presuppositions of *STJ*. Full comprehension of what Mathews is attempting in the study demands that one recognize that, as an exercise in higher criticism, *STJ* is a pioneering example of North American historicocritical exegesis. When

Mathews declares that the "one way to the apprehension of the teaching of Jesus" is "the patient study of the gospels with the aid of all modern critical and exegetical methods," he is breaking important ground for a sociological analysis of the text that moves beyond prescientific philological analysis to an effort to come to terms with the worldview of the author of the text.

As Mathews begins to specify his exegetical principles, this intent to implement scientific exegesis in Christian sociology becomes even clearer. He declares first that, though the social teaching of Jesus is to be drawn primarily but not exclusively from the words of Jesus himself, mere quotation does not constitute exegesis. Although for many theologians an appeal to the *ipsissima verba* of Jesus ends all discussion, in Mathews's view "the thought of Jesus is sometimes so genuinely Oriental as to elude any process of interpretation that is purely verbal."[86] The exegete who seeks to go beyond mere quotation must situate a given text within its context, and must pay attention to the milieu of thought in which the text came into being.

Moreover, exegetes cannot fully appreciate the thought of Jesus until they recognize that Jesus was not a systematic teacher, but a "creator of impulses."[87] This being the case, one may isolate texts that appear to affirm a particular position, and then discover other texts that contradict the position. Mathews insists that the teaching of Jesus on a given point (as recorded in this or that text) must be understood within the context of his teaching as a whole.[88]

In arriving at this conclusion, Mathews evidently wishes to stipulate an exegetical procedure that he employs throughout the study. This is a method of collation: in Mathews's view, scrupulous exegetes must collate *all* gospel texts that treat a given topic; then they must weigh text against text, in order to arrive at a nuanced synthetic statement of Jesus' teaching on the given topic. The procedure has patent affinities with Small's sociological methodology, with its insistence that the theoretical process must be kept open-ended and must seek to incorporate the findings of ongoing research, to avoid facile applications. Mathews seems to opt for his synthetic exegetical procedure in order to offset deductions based on a too limited range of data. And again as with Small, in Mathews's application this synthetic procedure sometimes has a political intent, as in *STJ*'s chapter on wealth, where he argues that the "distorted applications" often made of Jesus' "economic" sayings are due to "an incomplete collection of the data to be found in the gospels."[89]

Having established his basic exegetical presuppositions, Mathews broaches a question of fundamental importance to any study of the social teaching of Jesus: that is, "Are the teachings of Jesus commensurate with the teachings of the entire New Testament?"[90] In response, he first allows that one may validly speak of the writings of the New Testament canon outside the gospels as informed by "the spirit and purpose of Christ."[91] Yet a rigorous historical approach demands, Mathews thinks, that the exegete distinguish between the social teaching of the gospels and the epistles: for "in the latter we have the application of the former to the needs of the growing Christian societies of the first century."[92] In the social teaching of New Testament writings other than the gospels, we can discern the passage "from constitution to statutory law, from principle to attempted realization of principle, from philosophy to conduct."[93] A foundational study of the social teaching of the New Testament must, therefore, begin with the gospels themselves.[94]

The distinction Mathews is drawing between the teaching of Jesus as spirit, philosophy, or principle, and the teaching of the epistles as statute or legislative enactment of Jesus' principles, is important. It obviously parallels his previous assertion that the sociological content of Jesus' teaching may be extrapolated from the precise formulations in which the gospels enshrine this content. Once again, the move away from grounding Christian sociology in a literalistic reading of the gospels, to grounding it in Jesus' principles or ideals, is fundamental to the social process theology that Mathews's later works will develop. Once one has separated the principles of Jesus from their situational utilization, one has at one's disposal a body of ideals that can then be enacted in the social process in various ways.

Mathews's distinction between the social teaching of Jesus in the gospels and the application of this teaching in the epistles defines the boundaries of his project in *STJ:* in this study, he will restrict himself to an exegesis of the teaching of Jesus as presented by the gospel writers. As Mathews recognizes, this definition of his project raises the crucial exegetical question of the historicity of the gospels. The next section of his consideration of the exegetical principles underlying *STJ* addresses this problem, initially by acknowledging that "it is beyond serious question that in their present form the accounts they [i.e., the gospels] contain are the work of writers who lived at least a generation after the death of Jesus."[95] But if this is the case, how may the sociological exegete determine with any precision what Jesus' teaching actually was?

Mathews's frank avowal of the gospel problem is somewhat remarkable, if one considers the infant state of critical exegetical studies in this country at the time in which he is writing. It clearly underscores his intent to inculcate in social gospel exegetes an acumen that surpasses mere collecting, classifying, and citing of texts. However, Mathews makes several qualifications that tend somewhat to soften the force of his recognition of the gospel problem. In the first place, he argues that the exegete must distinguish between the words of Jesus as reported by the gospel writers and the "editorial" material with which the writers accompany Jesus' teaching.[96] Moreover, Mathews supposes that criticism may fairly easily discern Jesus' actual teaching within its editorial elaboration.[97] Furthermore, the gospel writers have clearly employed "sources" that "can be shown to date from the contemporaries of Jesus."[98] As is evident, these exegetical provisions echo the *BW* editorials of the 1890s, with their urgent intent to disseminate the findings of higher-critical exegesis to North American Christians in such a way that their most cherished evangelical presuppositions will not be unseated.[99]

In addition, in *STJ* as in his *BW* editorials, Mathews argues that the gospels incorporate an editorial improvisation "of the utmost value" to the student of Jesus' teaching. This is the narrative of his life, which in Mathews's view is "in most cases . . . demonstrably from eyewitnesses and in its essential elements is beyond suspicion."[100] This narrative complements what an exegetical investigation of his teaching is able to turn up, and so provides another point of entry for interpreting his teaching: "Speaking generally, the doings of Jesus, when once viewed in the light of their attending circumstances, quite as much as his words, are materials from which to construct a systematized statement of his social teachings."[101]

Finally, the sociological exegete must not overlook another essential source for understanding Jesus' social teaching, Mathews insists. This is his silence.[102] With regard to such important social problems of his day as slavery, Jesus did not deliver any moral teaching at all.[103] The Christian social reformer must not attempt to read into Jesus' teaching what is not there. Jesus' silence is "significant of a distinct element in what we venture to call his social philosophy."[104] To vocalize this silence is "to make exposition presuppose, if not dangerously resemble, imposition."[105]

The Biblical Foundation:
The Kingdom of God

As Mathews applies the exegetical principles sketched in the first part of *STJ*, a matter of central importance is to determine the correct significance of Jesus' proclamation of the kingdom of God. That this topic occupies a large part of his attention in this foundational study is not surprising. With the rise of higher criticism, theologians of the latter part of the nineteenth century had become increasingly aware that the message of the coming kingdom constituted the substance of Jesus' preaching. Systematic theologians such as Ritschl had seized upon the exegetical "discovery" of the kingdom and had built their theology around this biblical symbol. In Ritschl's usage, the kingdom becomes a linchpin for a theology accentuating the ethical demands of Christian faith.

As we have seen, Christian sociologists had also appropriated the kingdom theme to a theological use. In the thought of Christian sociologists, the kingdom became the organizing principle for the theological attempt to wed Christianity and the social movement. Building upon the exegetical recognition that Jesus' fundamental proclamation was the coming of the kingdom, Christian sociologists argued that Jesus intended to proclaim a kingdom that began with his ministry, continued to grow through the activity of his followers, and will be "brought in" in its fullness when the entire world has acceded to the ideals of Jesus.

For Christian sociology constructed on such theological premises, Johannes Weiss's 1892 *Die Predigt Jesu vom Reiche Gottes* was a knell of doom. Weiss showed that the "social interpretation" of the kingdom promulgated by the Ritschlian school and Christian sociology rested on a fundamental misapprehension of Jesus' kingdom proclamation. Far from intending to establish a present kingdom, Weiss argued, Jesus had viewed the kingdom as an eschatological event to be brought in at the end of history through God's action. Furthermore, Weiss urged, Jesus had not supplied his disciples with a set of ethical precepts by which the world could be transformed into the kingdom; rather, since he had expected the imminent arrival of the eschatological kingdom, Jesus had preached an "ethics of preparation" for the coming kingdom.

Weiss's work exacerbated the difficulties of exegetical inquiry into the meaning of the kingdom of God in the gospels. Obviously, the question of the precise meaning of Jesus' kingdom proclamation was particularly urgent for Christian sociologists. The writings of both Mathews and Small in the early 1890s demonstrate their awareness of this urgency. In an 1895 synopsis of an article "Social Ethics of Jesus," Mathews notes that sociological exegesis of the teaching of Jesus must begin by asking what the phrase "kingdom of God" meant to Jesus himself.[106] As *STJ* reveals, Mathews had read Weiss's *Predigt Jesu* by 1894–95, when he composed the "Christian Sociology" articles, and he was intent to respond to Weiss in the articles. The drive to ascertain what Jesus actually intended by his proclamation of the kingdom of God is *STJ*'s central exegetical impulse.

As previously noted, *STJ*'s exegetical inquiry into the meaning of the kingdom of God occurs primarily in the chapter entitled "Society." The chapter is divided into five sections. In the first, Mathews considers three prevailing interpretations of the kingdom—political, subjective-ethical, and eschatological—each of which he thinks to be inadequate. In the next section, he follows this examination of alternative views of the kingdom with a presentation of that interpretation which he considers warranted by a comprehensive examination of Jesus' teaching: this is the social interpretation. Mathews concludes the chapter with three sections defending and explicating his social interpretation of the kingdom.

The chapter on "Society" begins with an important warning about the perils of modernizing Jesus and his teaching:

> To speak of Jesus as anticipating a regenerate society may appear to some as savoring of literalism and to others as a mere modernizing of the simple records of the gospels. Both objections would not be altogether without foundation. There is constant danger that, in the attempt to restate the teachings of Jesus in the terms of to-day's thought, exposition may wait too subserviently upon desire. The first century, albeit surprisingly like the nineteenth, was nevertheless not the nineteenth, and Jesus the Jew was not a product of Greek syllogisms and German hypotheses.[107]

This passage is significant. That Mathews chooses to preface his discussion of the kingdom with such a proviso indicates that *STJ*'s defense of the social interpretation of the kingdom is to a great extent a response to the charge that the Christian sociological use of the kingdom symbol represents a "modernizing of the simple records of the gospels." The passage itself provides no indication of those particular critics to whom Mathews is responding; but since *STJ* initiates an important ongoing dialogue with J. Weiss's *Predigt Jesu* that will culminate in the 1905 work *MHNT*, both the defensive tone of *STJ*'s discussion of the kingdom and Mathews's continuing preoccupation with Weiss's *Predigt Jesu* over the years 1895–1905 strongly suggest that *STJ*'s attempt to vindicate the social interpretation of the kingdom is already in part a critical response to Weiss's eschatological thesis.

Mathews follows his prefatory warning about the perils of modernizing Jesus with a preliminary vindication of the notion that the goal of Jesus' preaching and ministry was "the establishment of an ideal society quite as much as the production of an ideal individual."[108] Had this not been Jesus' intent, Mathews argues, how does one explain that his listeners were encouraged in their hopes that he would reestablish the Hebrew kingdom?[109] Moreover, Mathews maintains, that Jesus so uniformly referred to himself as son of man attests to his identification with the messianic expectation of his people.[110]

Above all, the term "kingdom of God" itself "suggests social relations," Mathews thinks.[111] "No other term, unless it be Son of Man, is so characteristic of Jesus; none is more certainly his."[112] Since the concept is central to Jesus' understanding of himself and his mission, contemporary theology must seek to determine precisely what Jesus intended in using the term: "If any weight is to be given to the teachings of Jesus, it is imperative that the meaning of this term as he used it should be accurately gauged."[113]

This appeal for a precise exegetical determination of what Jesus understood by the term "kingdom of God" leads into a critical assessment of the political, subjective-ethical, and eschatological interpretations of the kingdom. Mathews deals rather summarily with the political and subjective-ethical approaches. With regard to the former, he thinks that "it is easy to discover that Jesus does not mean a merely political kingdom, or theocratic state."[114] The critical edge of this observation is apparently turned against Christian sociologists such as Herron: noting that "it is as easy for political enthusiasts today as it was in his own time to mistake here," Mathews glosses (in a footnote), "as do some of the Christian Socialists."[115] Appealing to his synthetic exegetical principle, Mathews comments that while one may discover isolated statements of Jesus that bear a political interpretation, one must "canvass the entire field before recording decisions" about the meaning of Jesus' kingdom proclamation.[116]

Mathews dismisses the subjective-ethical view of the kingdom as flatly as the political. In his judgment,

> [t]here is but one saying [i.e., Lk. 17:20–21] of Jesus that in any way lends support to the view that he thought of the kingdom as a subjective state of the individual, and even that can hardly be used as a basis upon which to build an individualistic system of self-culture.[117]

As in his critique of the political idea of the kingdom, Mathews specifies the object of this critical observation, in this instance naming a particular theologian. Though Tolstoi's *The Kingdom of God Is Within You* is cited once, Mathews is chiefly concerned here with the philosophical use made of the kingdom idea by the Ritschlian theologian Julius Kaftan. Kaftan's *The Truth of the Christian Religion* is cited three times, in each instance with a rebuttal.[118]

Mathews's primary critique of Kaftan is that he has misappropriated to a philosophical service a term that, in its original context, has a very different sense than that which Kaftan prefers to see in it. Whereas Kaftan maintains that "the kingdom is the rational idea of the chief good" which must not be identified with the "universal moral society which is being developed in the world,"[119] in Mathews's view the gospel use of the term is concrete and objective.

Mathews explicates his critique of such philosophical misappropriations of the kingdom in an important passage:

> It is one thing to appreciate the exact position of Jesus, and it is quite another to translate it into the terms of one's own philosophy. The first step is one of interpretation and must always condition the second. The chief criticism of this appropriation of the kingdom as the capstone of a philosophy is the same that must be passed upon so much of the work of the theologian—it is attractive, it is doubtless in the main true, but it is not the thought of Jesus. With him the kingdom was not a subjective but a concrete, objective reality: one that could be expected and enjoyed if not here and now, at any rate in another world and age.[120]

This critique of Kaftan appears to have two underlying motivations. In the first place, Mathews's insistence on the concreteness and objectivity of the kingdom idea in Jesus' preaching safeguards the social ethical implications of the kingdom proclamation against philosophical interpretations that, by removing the kingdom to a subjective realm, threaten to reduce its social content. Later in *STJ* Mathews will make a parallel criticism of those theologians of the "newer Ritschlian school" (specifically, Hermann [*The Communion of the Christian with God*]) who remove regeneration from the realm of experience.[121] Against such a tendency, Mathews argues that Jesus' notion of divine sonship had a concrete import that Hermann's theology evacuates of significance. In saying this, Mathews is clearly insisting on the concreteness of biblical concepts as a counter to philosophical abstractions that diminish their ethical significance.

Mathews rejects Kaftan's philosophical appropriation of the kingdom for another important reason. As he maintains, appreciation of the "exact position of Jesus" (i.e. , the biblical meaning of the kingdom) must precede and condition philosophical or theological usage of the kingdom idea. This stress on the necessity for grounding systematic theology in historically realistic exegesis is characteristic of Mathews's theology. It is precisely this stress that will lead him in the period from 1895 to 1905 to an ever greater appreciation of the eschatological interpretation of the kingdom. Significantly, Mathews's first reference to Weiss's *Predigt Jesu* occurs in the context of his critique of Kaftan's use of the kingdom. Not only does Mathews cite Weiss in this discussion: he cites Weiss *against* Kaftan.[122] The point is crucially telling: given a choice between the subjective-ethical interpretation of the kingdom defended by Ritschlian theologians such as Kaftan, and Weiss's eschatological interpretation, Mathews finds himself in sympathy with the latter approach.

This judgment regarding the tendency of Mathews's thought is borne out by his consideration of the eschatological interpretation. In contrast to the summary way in which he has dealt with the political and subjective-ethical views, Mathews's investigation of the eschatological interpretation proceeds from the conviction that "there is much that is worthy of consideration" in this view.[123]

Harnack's argument that Jesus' teaching reflects an apocalyptic background carries historical weight, Mathews thinks.[124] And, from an exegetical standpoint, the thesis of theologians such as Meyer, Schmoller, and J. Weiss that Jesus saw the kingdom as the fulfillment of the prophetic idea of the messianic kingdom is also compelling.[125] Mathews thinks that these historical arguments deserve particular consideration.[126] In fact, he grants, the apocalyptic background of the New Testament literature deserves further exploration—a prescient insight, when one considers that Mathews is writing in the mid-1890s, before the full import of consistent eschatology had dawned upon North American theologians: "Probably the recognition of the importance of the apocalyptic literature in the formation of the early Christian vocabulary, if not Christology, may yet be still further emphasized."[127] Mathews's recognition of the apocalyptic context of New Testament thought leads him to make another important concession to the eschatological interpretation of the New Testament: that is, Jesus sometimes used statements that, taken in isolation from other of his sayings, "would be sufficient to justify the sweeping statement [i.e., of Harnack, *History of Dogma*] that 'the gospel entered into the world as an apocalyptic eschatological message, apocalyptical and eschatological not only in its form, but in its contents'."[128]

Though Mathews thinks the eschatological view worthy of serious consideration, he concludes that this interpretation is insufficient. In his view, those gospel sayings in which Jesus appears to speak of the kingdom in eschatological terms must be weighed against those in which he refers to the kingdom as present.[129] When one makes a comprehensive survey of the passages in which Jesus presents his understanding of the kingdom, Mathews concludes, one finds that "Jesus thought of the kingdom as a concrete reality rather than an idea, and . . . this reality was not to be left as an unattainable ideal, but was to be progressively realized, perhaps evolved."[130]

The discussion of the eschatological interpretation of the kingdom concludes the first section of the chapter on "Society." Having ruled out three prevalent interpretations of the kingdom, Mathews proceeds to present that reading he thinks warranted by a comprehensive survey of Jesus' teaching. For Mathews, "by the kingdom of God Jesus meant an *ideal* (though progressively approximated) *social order in which the relation of men to God is that of sons, and* (therefore) *to each other, that of brothers.*"[131]

Mathews follows this social definition of the kingdom with an exegetical defense. He argues first that "the point of departure for any interpretation of the term must be the historical expectation of the Jews in the days of Jesus."[132] What was this expectation? As the intertestamental literature demonstrates, it was nothing less than hope for the reestablishment of the Jewish kingdom through divine intervention.[133] It should be noted that this argument carries through on the insight (expressed in Mathews's consideration of Harnack's historical argument for the eschatological interpretation) that Jesus' notion of the kingdom reflects the messianic expectations of his hearers. As the next chapter will show, it is this line of thought that will lead Mathews by 1905 to grant that Jesus' understanding of the kingdom was eschatological.

Jesus built, then, on the concrete messianic hope of his people. Echoing Harnack, Mathews argues that Jesus "took the hope as he found it," and elevated it to an entirely new plane of expectation.[134] Rejecting the particularistic ideas of the kingdom that prevailed among his religious confreres, Jesus universalized the messianic expectation by making membership in the kingdom dependent not on birth, but on decision.[135] Since the Jewish messianic expectation on which Jesus built was a hope for a new society, the kingdom Jesus proclaimed was, Mathews maintains, itself a new social order.[136] As the gospels indicate, Jesus intended to inaugurate the kingdom through his ministry; this new social order was to stand in relation to the present order (as Mathews understands the gospel term "world") as the ideal stands in relation to the actual.[137] As an ideal order, the kingdom is to grow slowly but apace within the actual order, through the conversion of individuals to the ideals enunciated by Jesus in his preaching. When the final growth of the kingdom will have been attained, the kingdom of this world will have become the kingdom of the Christ.[138]

The concluding sections of the chapter on "Society" are devoted to an explication of two aspects of the preceding statement of Mathews's own definition of the kingdom. These are the assertion that Jesus understood life in the kingdom to be human brotherhood under divine fatherhood; and the assertion that the kingdom is an *ideal* order within history. The first question, that of the kingdom as human fraternity under divine paternity, is one that evidently preoccupied Mathews during these years. The issue appears often in his editorials and book reviews of the 1890s, and was apparently among the motivating concerns of his search for an adequate biblical foundation for Christian sociology.

To be specific: Mathews wishes to determine whether Jesus understood the terms "fatherhood of God" and "brotherhood of man" (which "for many minds" constitutes the "substance of Christianity") in a universal sense, or whether he restricted the application of the terms to members of the kingdom.[139] In Mathews's view, if these terms apply universally, then the necessity for moral transformation as a prerequisite for membership in the kingdom is undermined.[140] As in his consideration of the subjective-ethical interpretation of the kingdom, at this exegetical juncture Mathews's overriding intent is to preserve the social ethical import of biblical concepts. Thus (and on exegetical grounds), Mathews argues that Jesus clearly restricted application of the terms "fatherhood of God" and "brotherhood of man" to anyone other than those who had entered the kingdom by conversion. As an ideal social order in which the relation of men to God is that of sons and to one another that of brothers, the kingdom grows as those dominated by the antifraternal impulses of this world choose to accede to the ideals proclaimed by Jesus.

Mathews concludes his defense of the social interpretation of the kingdom with a discussion of the operative principle of his kingdom definition: this is the term "ideal."[141] Mathews is concerned to preclude any understanding of the ideal kingdom as incapable of realization within history. He asks, "Does Jesus regard this ideal [i.e., of brotherhood] as a Utopia, an idealist's heaven which is to hang forever over the world an unattainable dream? Or does he think of it as at least partly realizable in human life?"[142]

Mathews answers this question by arguing that, far from being a utopian dream, in Jesus' kingdom sayings the kingdom appears as a "social force capable of expressing itself in a universal society." [143] Jesus clearly anticipated that the kingdom and the world would one day be coextensive. [144] How would this be brought about? By the spiritual forces latent within the kingdom:

> In this spiritual character of the kingdom lie its energy and its practicability. Membership within it is possible for all since all are spiritual. It can move not merely in organized but in unorganized ways. It can remake alike the ambition of one of its members and public opinion and social conceptions. In a word it is dynamic—a power as well as a condition. [145]

This passage clarifies what Mathews means when he speaks of the kingdom as ideal. As an ideal order existing in the midst of the actual social order, the kingdom has the power to remake society by infusing the actual order with its ideals. Or, as Mathews will insist in his social process writings, the kingdom ideals "seed" the social process, or they "draw to themselves" the evolution of the process. Mathews's important 1916 work SIH will seek to provide a philosophical rationale for such an idealistic interpretation of history by maintaining that the ideal is capable of realization under historical forms, that it carries within itself the germinative principles by which it may be attained. STJ's definition of the kingdom already anticipates this understanding of the ideal by insisting that "the ideal is the evolution of the attempted," and "if it would beget duty, the ideal must be possible." [146]

Moreover, the kingdom accomplishes its transforming work precisely as an ideal or spiritual order. As ideal, the kingdom can exist universally, and can move "not merely in organized but in unorganized ways." [147] In STJ as in all his later reflections on the topic, Mathews repudiates any ecclesiology that would see the church and the kingdom as coextensive: in his view, the kingdom is "as much grander than the church as an ideal is grander than the actual . . . ; as much more catholic as Christianity is more catholic than ecclesiasticism." [148]

STJ's insistence on the possibility for the ideal kingdom to be realized in history sounds curiously defensive, and raises questions about why Mathews is so concerned to justify his construction of the term "ideal" against those who might see the ideal kingdom as a utopian dream. His later work may provide a clue to his intentions in this discussion. In it Mathews carries on a polemic against the *ad interim* thesis of the consistent eschatology school, holding that theologians such as J. Weiss and Albert Schweitzer remove the ethical significance of the gospels to a utopian realm only tangentially related to the concerns of everyday existence. For example, in his 1913 article "Awakening Protestantism," Mathews argues against Weiss and Schweitzer that Protestantism will have lost all significance for the modern world, "when Jesus Christ becomes a well-intending neurasthenic and his ethics a call to impossible ideals born of a mistaken expectation of the speedy end of the world." [149] The close parallel between this critique and *STJ*'s argument against the utopian interpretation of the kingdom suggests that Mathews's defense of the notion of the ideal as attainable is in part a critical response to Weiss's eschatological view of the kingdom.

Against an eschatological interpretation of the kingdom, *STJ*'s exegetical analysis of Jesus' kingdom proclamation concludes that "the kingdom is thought of by Jesus as present as well as future, and . . . its history is an evolution." [150] This evolution will proceed by "the gradual leavening of all social environment" with the ideals of the kingdom until—incumbent on some "catastrophic completion"— the final age of the kingdom, in which it will have attained its full growth, will be inaugurated. [151] Prior to this final moment of the kingdom's growth, the kingdom will have been realized within the social order insofar as social existence approximates life within the kingdom. [152] This, in a nutshell, is the social interpretation of the kingdom for which Mathews opts in his first foundational social gospel study, and which he was gradually to dismantle in the period leading up to 1905.

The Biblical Foundation:
An Assessment

From the vantage point of contemporary exegesis, the exegetical presuppositions and deductions of *STJ* are in important respects flawed. Mathews's assumption that the redaction of the gospels represented an "editorializing" process by the gospel writers, in which Jesus' sayings (accessible in sources dating from contemporaries of Jesus) were stitched together with clearly identifiable editorial stitches; his sanguinity regarding the possibility of separating Jesus' teachings from their editorial context; his contention that the gospels contain a narrative account of the life of Jesus "demonstrably from eyewitnesses"; his defense of the social interpretation of the kingdom: none of these notions can withstand the critical assault of postliberal exegesis of the New Testament. Insofar as these exegetical presuppositions constitute the biblical foundation of *STJ*, the work partakes of the liberal quest for the historical Jesus, and will have no more than passing historical interest for contemporary theologians.

However, any assessment of the biblical foundation of *STJ* that stops with these critical observations fails to recognize where the real contribution of the study lies. If *STJ* is viewed from within its historical context, its accomplishments are striking. The study is in the first place a pioneering work of North American historicocritical exegesis. Mathews's insistence that biblical terms must be understood in their historical setting, and that theological use of the terms must begin with accurate historical reconstruction of their original signification; his recognition that Jesus' teaching presupposes the thought world of late Palestinian Judaism; his insistence that the apocalyptic background of early Christianity had not received the attention it deserved from exegetes: these are groundbreaking exegetical insights for the North American theological community. The early work of Mathews makes an important and often overlooked contribution to American theology: in an ecclesial community (and, at times, an academic one) in which the methodology and findings of German exegesis at the end of the nineteenth century were often still thoroughly unfamiliar or anathema, the early Mathews disseminates these findings and introduces this methodology. To no small degree, *STJ* was a teaching tool designed to break down North American theological resistance to higher criticism and to demonstrate that, as it called for Christian social activism, the social gospel could indeed appeal to the latest critical scholarship.

The seminal insights that Mathews brought to this work pointed a direction for North American biblical studies that was to establish the course of subsequent American exegesis. As Robert Funk has convincingly argued, among the signal contributions of the Chicago school of theology to North American theology, perhaps none has had such formative influence on American biblical and theological studies as its insistence that historical consciousness ought always to accompany all theological inquiry.[153] As a founding figure of the school, one whose academic background convinced him of the indispensability of a strong awareness of the historical development of any theological problem one approached, of the influence of cultural considerations on it, and of the need for accurate historical research, Mathews deserves credit for having set the course of Chicago school theology—and *STJ* merits recognition as a trail-blazing example of North American historical critical theological research.

As a higher critic seeking to consolidate the biblical foundation of Christian sociology, Mathews imports into the search for a social gospel theological foundation a *historical realism* that transforms Christian sociology from "bescriptured social denunciation" into serious exegetical inquiry into the original meaning of New Testament texts. Mathews's insistence that "the aim of the investigator must be the discovery of what is, not the substantiation of some notion as to what ought to be," and his impatience with facile anachronistic appropriations of scriptural concepts that dispense with the hard work of exegesis, move the North American discussion of the "social teaching" of Jesus to an entirely new level of reflection.

An investigation of Mathews's exegetical mentors in *STJ* substantiates the preceding interpretation of the book as an attempt to disseminate the findings of German historicocritical exegesis among North American exegetes. The exegetical authority *STJ* most frequently cites is the German liberal theologian H. H. Wendt; his *Die Lehre Jesu* appears eleven times in the footnotes of *STJ*.[154] Wendt's influence is particularly evident in the article that subsequently became *STJ*'s chapter on the kingdom, where Mathews's deference is apparent in his astonishment that "even Wendt" commits Jesus to the view that the kingdom was to be "hardly more than an extended Israel."[155] Another frequently cited source is the English-language study *The Life and Times of Jesus the Messiah*, by the Anglo-Austrian exegete A. Edersheim.[156] As well, *STJ* appeals to W. Beyschlag's *Neutestamentliche Theologie*,[157] E. Issel's pioneering Leiden dissertation on the kingdom of God *Die Lehre vom Reiche Gottes im Neuen Testament* (which preceded and influenced Weiss's *Predigt Jesu*),[158] W. Lütgert's *Das Reich Gottes nach den Synoptischen Evangelien*,[159] E. Schürer's *Geschichte des jüdischen Volkes im Zeitalter Jesu Christi*,[160] and A. Harnack's *Lehrbuch der Dogmengeschichte*.[161]

Though the theological standpoint of most of these scholars may be characterized as liberal Protestant, the monochromatic designation "liberal" actually covered a wide spectrum of theological viewpoints in Germany at the turn of the century. As George Rupp's acute analysis of German culture Protestantism at the turn of the twentieth century has demonstrated, by the end of the century an important fissure had developed in the German liberal theological project.[162] On one side of the divide were theologians whose primary intent was to "translate" fundamental Christian beliefs into the thought patterns of modern Western culture; on the other were those chiefly concerned to discover the original meaning of biblical concepts, as a *sine qua non* prior to theological translation, and as a check against precisely that anachronistic maladaptation of the tradition with which liberal theologians have been charged. As we have seen, in his critique of Kaftan and Hermann's application of the kingdom symbol, Mathews notes the existence of these two emphases in liberal theology, and observes that, while they are not mutually exclusive, each theological emphasis requires a focus of attention that moves toward a conclusion at some variance from the conclusions reached by the other emphasis. The implication to be drawn from this critique is that the different allocations of emphasis in German liberal theology at the turn of the century bring the two theological projects into tension.

Rupp sees this tension as a creative one, one that indicates the extent to which the liberal theological venture had become self-critical by the end of the nineteenth century. In the drive to a historically realistic exegesis initiated by one sector of German liberal theologians was the beginning of that dialectical impulse that would dissolve the theological synthesis achieved by Ritschl, and provoke further productive examination of topics such as the exact meaning of Jesus' proclamation of the kingdom of God. In this reading of liberal Protestant theology, theologians such as J. Weiss and Schweitzer who acerbically attacked the Ritschlian-Harnackian interpretation of the gospels were liberals of a different stripe, whose emphasis on historical realism in exegesis paved the way for Barth's scathing critique of liberal theology. Barth's onslaught could produce such devastating results precisely because liberal thinkers appealing to a historical imagination had begun to question the theological presuppositions of liberals dominated by a philosophical imagination.

Viewed through the optic of Rupp's analysis, Mathews's critique of Kaftan and Hermann indicates his strong sympathy for that branch of liberal theology that thought it necessary to appreciate the historical sense of biblical concepts before correlating these concepts with contemporary thought patterns—even if historical investigation showed the concepts to be strange and unsettling to contemporary thinkers. In citing Weiss against Kaftan, Mathews allies himself with that wing of German theology in which a drive to historical realism is an indispensable preliminary to all theological analysis. By building into his search for a theological foundation for the social gospel an overriding concern to discover the original historical significance of biblical concepts, soon after the publication of *STJ* Mathews will force himself to deal with the tensions inherent in *STJ*'s solution to the eschatological problem. Mathews's historical imagination—an imagination that proceeds from liberal Protestant theology, as a dialectical moment within this theology—will require him to reconsider the meaning of Jesus' kingdom proclamation.

The Sociological Foundation

As our investigation of the matrix of concerns from which *STJ* emerged has shown, in addition to raising critical questions about the exegetical work of some Christian sociologists, both Small and Mathews expressed reservations about the shaky sociological foundation of some Christian sociological studies of the late nineteenth century. Small's critical concern had focused on these studies's purported lack of scientific basis, their disregard for empirical research, and the "silly utopianism" of their belief that one could move from text to social reform without consideration of the potential for change within a given society. He believed that the task of Christian sociologists was to discover in Jesus' teaching ideals that pointed to ends consonant with the capacities of society. And he considered that a sociologically astute reading of Jesus' social teaching must legitimate reformist, and undercut revolutionary, applications of Jesus' ideals.

As with *STJ*'s exegetical foundation, in Mathews's treatment of the sociological question there is such a close fit between his sociological assumptions and those of Small that it is tempting to view *STJ* as homework Small had assigned Mathews, in that close pedagogical relationship they still shared at the beginning of Mathews's career. Mathews focuses his foundational statement precisely on that theoretical aporia Small had isolated in Christian sociology, the gap between Christian reformism and academic sociology. His focus requires him to develop a theological rationale for the conjunction of Christianity and the social movement, premised on the assumption that the growth of the kingdom and the progressive evolution of society are linked by numerous points of contact. With this conviction that reforming society may also bring in the kingdom of God, the Christian reformer can justifiably make common cause with secular reformers.

In support of his contention that social progress connects to the this-worldly growth of the kingdom of God, Mathews argues that Jesus' social teaching is at base the enunciation of principles and ideals that are within the range of the natural possibilities of humanity. Moreover, he maintains, Jesus' kingdom proclamation may be reduced to a set of ideals, chief among which is that of brotherly love. Society evolves in response to ideals; Jesus' kingdom proclamation is the proclamation of brotherly love; the growth of the kingdom and the evolution of the social order can thus intersect; the two will eventually be synonymous: this is the underlying logic of *STJ*'s sociological foundation for social gospel theology.

A fundamental presupposition of Mathews's argument is the notion that human nature is inherently social. As we have seen, in *STJ*'s introductory comments about the individualistic preoccupation of post-Reformation theology, Mathews maintains that until recently Christian theologians have overlooked the "essential sociability of human nature." [163] In saying this, he is not simply commenting on post-Reformation theology. He is also implicitly making a claim about a primary contribution sociology makes to Christian theology: the inherent sociability of human nature was stressed by early sociologists as much as by theologians wishing to correct the excessive individualism of Christian theology in the past. As he makes this claim, Mathews draws—as in so many other respects—from Small. With Ely and the German historical school thinkers, Small regards the individualistic philosophy dominant in modern Western life and thought as one of the factors chiefly thwarting the establishment of a just and humane society in the industrial West.

In his essay on the significance of sociology for ethics, Small stresses that individuals cannot be adequately understood apart from their social contexts. Though the individual does indeed have an inherent personal worth—an affirmation both Small and Mathews consider necessary as a balance to what they see as socialist overemphasis on the essential sociability of human nature—the full potential of a person is attained only through interaction with his or her social environment. By its very constitution, human nature is unfinished; in isolation from others in society, it remains incomplete. Its essential sociability requires it to be in social relationship.[164]

Such a sociological assessment of the individual runs throughout *STJ*, but is most strongly apparent in the chapter entitled "Man." Here Mathews argues that "the ideal human life, as Jesus conceives of it, consists in transcending the limits of an egoistic individuality." [165] Jesus' teaching assumes that the "capacity for union" is a constitutive factor of human nature. Thus, the call to union with others is "deep in the ideal which he sets before mankind." [166] This sociological argument fits neatly into the theological argument of the entire study: what Jesus commands is what sociology understands as necessary for human fulfillment: the kingdom of God and social evolution present human beings and the social order with the same challenge.

Mathews's understanding of the individual as inherently social forms the framework for his presentation of Jesus' teaching about sin and righteousness. If the individual realizes her or his full potential only in union with others, then righteousness is for Jesus more than union with God, Mathews maintains. It is also living in harmony with others.[167] Conversely, unrighteous living is living without regard for the capacity for union that is constitutive of full human nature.[168] The sociological insight that human nature is essentially sociable thus provides a critical vantage point from which one may view sin as isolation that thwarts and distorts the individual. In Mathews's view, because sin exacerbates the individual's self-containment, Jesus teaches that "selfishness—that is, an over-developed individualism—must according to the laws of nature result in abnormality and consequent suffering." [169]

In addition to the notion of the inherent sociability of human nature, a second controlling perception of *STJ*'s sociological foundation is the presupposition that society is an organism constantly subject to evolutionary change, and that social evolution occurs as idealistic impulses stimulate the unfolding of seminal principles within the social organism. This sociological presupposition, clearly derived from Small and other sociologists of the period, is never developed at any single point in the study, but is rather a fundamental assumption informing the entire study. For example, in *STJ*'s chapter on "The State," in which he argues against those who read the teaching of Jesus as an anticipation of modern political philosophies such as anarchism, Mathews stresses that Jesus saw society as an organic whole and not a body politic based on the social contract:

> The union which he holds up is not that of an aggregation, but is organic. The kingdom of God is the union of brothers over whom God himself is to reign. Mankind is not composed of insulated individuals, but of social beings, who seek not a convenient association for exchange and other economic purposes, but an absorbing and organic union with one another as members of a family.[170]

Similarly, in the chapter on "Social Life" Mathews observes that, while iconoclasts may sometimes provide a useful stimulus to social reform, long-lasting and constructive social change demands reformers who respect the organic unity of society. In defense of this tenet, he notes that,

> Jesus was never so crude a thinker as to imagine that society is a mechanical mixture of elements into which it must be disintegrated as a step towards a happier recombination. With him progress was biological, an evolution rather than a revolution.[171]

As is apparent, this understanding of society borrows heavily from the Darwinian notion that the evolution of species in the natural world presupposes an integral connection between higher and lower forms of life. What social gospellers such as Mathews and Small wanted to add to this biological theory when they applied it to society was the necessity for ideals to spur the evolution of the social organism. Without such an argument, their use of the evolutionary framework might imply precisely that which they combated in social Darwinists—that is, that the social organism ought to evolve just as natural organisms do, without interference and by a process of natural selection.

If society *is* an organism that evolves in response to ideals, then the task of the Christian reformer is to discover a set of "Christian" ideals that may be used to stimulate desirable evolutionary change within the social organism. But where is the reformer to find those ideals? If they are not literally present in the gospels—a position both Small and Mathews obviously wished to discount—then some way has to be found to shift the focus of Christian sociology from citation of texts and toward the ideals or principles Jesus' teaching enshrines.

STJ makes such a shift, and in doing so, demonstrates once again how faithfully its sociological logic follows Small's. In his chapters examining Jesus' teaching on the family, the state, and wealth, Mathews argues against social gospel attempts to create a too pointed formulation of Jesus' teaching on these topics, and stresses instead that the ideals underlying Jesus' teaching form the substance of his thought on social matters. In the chapter entitled "The Family," for example, Mathews denies that Jesus delivered a body of detailed directions for the organization of family life. Rather, he presented his followers with an ideal that could be trusted to work out its particular expressions as society evolved:

> He could afford to leave his ideal society with its details not filled in, because with the ideal he gave also evolutionary forces. Once possessed by the ideal of brotherhood, and once, be it never so feebly, under the influence of these spiritual forces, each generation could be trusted to transform the world in which it lived into a greater or less approximation to the kingdom.[172]

A similar preoccupation surfaces in the chapters entitled "The State" and "Wealth." In each, Mathews addresses certain political and economic interpretations of Jesus' teaching being advanced at the time, which he regards as inappropriate. In the chapter on wealth, he considers Christian socialism. Though the topic will be considered in more detail below, it is worth noting at this point that Mathews's argument against Christian socialism leans heavily on the contention that the gospels do not contain a neatly formulated economic teaching—as he assumes many Christian socialists believe. In contrast to those who appropriate Jesus' sayings to modern political or economic uses, Mathews contends that the historical Jesus could not have presented his followers with political or economic prescriptions anticipating complex social arrangements about which he himself knew nothing, in his first-century A.D. Palestinian social context: "An itinerant preacher in Judea could hardly be expected to know of the great trade combinations of Alexandria and Rome, to say nothing of those economic changes through which the centuries were to pass."[173]

Versus those who saw Jesus' "political" or "economic" teaching as precisely articulated, Mathews maintains that Jesus enunciates principles, principles that are general and scattered.[174] Rather than seeking to discover a set of sayings that clearly delineate Jesus' teaching on these points, the exegete who aspires to scientific exactitude must survey *all* his sayings in order to find the underlying principles that give unity to his thought:

> His view of wealth is not to be found in this or that particular saying, but in the entire scope of his life and teachings. We do for Jesus simply what we do for every teacher whose method was like his, if we attempt the discovery of a principle which underlies and a philosophy that binds together all special teachings.[175]

In working out the inner logic of Small's sociological foundation for Christian sociology, Mathews must not only reduce Jesus' social teaching to ideals and principles that demand collation of texts without dogged fidelity to any single text. He must also demonstrate that the ideals underlying Jesus' teaching correspond with the inherent capabilities of individuals and of societies. He does so in *STJ*'s chapter entitled "The Forces of Human Progress," which (with its companion chapter "The Process of Social Regeneration") forms the concluding portion of the study. This chapter's argument is prefigured at several points in *STJ* as Mathews suggests that the ideals Jesus set before his followers are "not beyond human attainment, but [are] the natural possibility for man's social capacities and powers." [176] In the chapter on "Man," for instance, he observes that the ideal the exegete discerns "beneath prayer and analogy, maxim and exhortation" in Jesus' teaching is present in "the possibilities of every member of the race," as are "psychical capacities that make this ideal a possibility." [177]

"The Forces of Human Progress" explicates these suggestions about the realizability of Jesus' ideals. Here, Mathews argues that Jesus was not a utopian who imposed ideals unsuited to his followers's concrete capabilities. Rather, Jesus tailored his idealistic expectations to human nature:

> Jesus trusts the inherent powers and capacities of the race. The ideal he portrays was not intended for creatures less or more human than the men with whom he associated and out of whom he hoped to form his kingdom. Individual and social regeneration is possible because man and society are inherently salvable. [178]

Moreover, Jesus did not merely enunciate the ideal of the brotherhood of humanity under the fatherhood of God. By his life and example, he presented a "revelation of the possibility of the divine sonship of man." [179] Jesus was himself a revelation of the possibilities of human life, a revelation intended to move his followers to emulation of his ideal type of character. As Jesus has done, so his followers may do.

As may be apparent, this argument for the realizability of the ideals implicit in Jesus' social teaching closely parallels Mathews's formulation of the relationship of the kingdom to the social order as ideal:actual. If the kingdom proclamation of Jesus is at base the ideal of human brotherhood under divine fatherhood, this ideal intersects with the possibilities of the social order, so that the kingdom's growth and the progressive development of society constitute intertwined processes. Elaboration of this point forms the final step in *STJ*'s development of a sociological foundation for Christian sociology. The chapter on "The Process of Social Regeneration" is the primary locus for the discussion of the topic.

In this chapter, Mathews returns to a discussion of Jesus' understanding of the kingdom. He notes that the not uncommon view that Jesus expected the kingdom to be a new Israel established in his lifetime appears to preclude interpretations of the kingdom such as that *STJ* offers: that is, that Jesus expected the kingdom to be progressively established, and that this establishment would at some point be universal. [180] Mathews grants that there is valid exegetical uncertainty about the point, and that the reading of Jesus' kingdom proclamation as an appeal for a new Israel has historical warrant.[181] Yet, echoing his previous exegetical discussion of the kingdom of God, he maintains that Jesus' sayings in the latter part of his career strongly indicate that he had dispensed with a nationalistic understanding of the kingdom (if indeed such an understanding represents his early thought) and foresaw the progressive establishment of the kingdom throughout the societies of the world.[182]

To make this claim is implicitly to ask how Jesus expected such a universal kingdom to be established. Mathews immediately moves to this subsequent step in his argument by noting that, in his view, Jesus deliberately eschewed the delineation of a program of social reform precisely *because* he trusted the kingdom ideals to express themselves "through such institutions as the process of evolution might show necessary."[183] Thus, even though the historical Jesus could not have used the term, he foresaw an *evolutionary* growth of the kingdom as it transformed the "existing powers" of society.[184] Moreover, "this process [i.e., of the kingdom's growth] is by analogy organic."[185] That is, the kingdom will grow as it assimilates to itself the social environment in which it is present.[186] This assimilation will ultimately transform the social environment to such an extent that the world will cease to be distinct from the kingdom.[187] Jesus envisaged the eventual triumph of his ideas not as a cataclysm overtaking the social order, but as the growth of a seed into a great tree.[188]

However, Mathews insists, this is not to imply that the kingdom process will unfold ineluctably, without effort on the part of Jesus' followers. On the contrary, the assimilation of the world to the kingdom can only occur by conversion—both of individuals and of society—as cells of the kingdom are extended through the social environment.[189] Such a process of gradual conversion will involve "struggle and "anguish" over an extended period of time.[190] Eventually, when the possibilities for extending the kingdom through this "slow and painful process" will have been exhausted, the kingdom's growth will be supplanted by a cataclysm effected "through some exercise of the supreme power of the heavenly Father and King."[191]

Mathews places the finishing touch on his sociological framework with a final emphatic appeal for the followers of Jesus to seek to realize his ideals in their societies:

> For it is no dream or apocalypse that meets us in the
> words and life of Jesus, but rather a teaching the em-
> bodiment of which is well worth an effort. He who

> to-day feels humanity's need and appreciates the cri-
> sis in which the world is gripped, will not rashly
> push to one side the ideals and powers that he re-
> vealed who, by his life and words, has already
> rewrought civilizations as has no man or teaching.[192]

The concluding allusion to dream and apocalypse is suggestive: as we have noted, in his later writings Mathews will often insist that a consistently eschatological reading of Jesus' kingdom vision can remove this vision to a dream world tangential to the world of history. The fact that this observation constitutes the concluding note of the study once again compellingly indicates that *STJ*'s attempt to validate a social interpretation of the kingdom is taking place in critical response to the work of J. Weiss. Mathews is already keenly aware of the implications the discovery of eschatology has for social theologies constructed around the "kingdom ideals" of Jesus; he is searching for a sound theological defense against those who charge that the social gospel's interpretation of the kingdom is an illicit application of Jesus' kingdom teaching. As we shall discover, his preoccupation with the problem of finding such a defense, one both exegetically accurate and scientifically persuasive, will become increasingly evident in the period immediately following the publication of *STJ*.

The Sociological Foundation and Christian Socialism

In any comprehensive examination of Mathews's attempt to provide a sociological foundation for the social gospel, a topic that deserves particular attention is his response to Christian socialism. As our preliminary survey of the concerns underlying *STJ* has shown, a major motivating factor in Mathews and Small's desire to develop a foundation for Christian sociology was the turn of some Christian sociologists to "radical" interpretations of Jesus' social teaching, and specifically to Christian socialism. Since both Small and Mathews were determined to offset such radical appropriations of Jesus' teaching, a question of some importance as one scrutinizes the foundational theology of *STJ* is how Mathews deals with socialist readings of the gospels.

Before answering this question, one needs to recognize that, despite his pretensions to scientific objectivity in exegesis, Mathews reads the gospels with a clear political penchant. Indeed, his very insistence on the obligation of social gospellers to ground social, political, and economic applications of Jesus' teaching in an exeget-ically exact interpretation of the gospels is a politically oriented *parti pris.* The move to discover ideals at the base of Jesus' social teaching, and the drive to exegetical exactitude that presumably underlies it, is a political move, one that hopes to turn the social gospel from a so-cialism based in biblical literalism, to a reformism grounded in king-dom ideals that run beneath the surface of the text. Thus at various points in *STJ* when Mathews advances the argument that the at-tempt to substantiate political or economic applications of Jesus' teaching by appealing to specific texts is ultimately futile, he does so by noting that such biblical literalism often leads the reformer into visionary utopianism.

For example, when he observes that "a conviction in the ab-solute authority of each unrelated word of Scripture has of neces-sity plunged many earnest souls into profound difficulties," Mathews follows this observation by noting that one such earnest (read: "mis-guided") soul, Tolstoy, located the entire significance of Christian dis-cipleship in the Sermon on the Mount's injunction against resisting evil.[193] In Mathews's estimation, though Tolstoy's renunciation of his judgeship and military commission in response to the verse was an admirable action, such a fideistic interpretation of Jesus' sayings is theologically insupportable, because it leads to a utopian stance that divests Jesus' teaching of significance for "the world in which we live." [194] Since Herron's 1893 *New Redemption* had advocated a read-ing of the Sermon on the Mount similar to that of Tolstoy, one hardly need state that he was chief among the "misguided souls" of the day who, Mathews thought, had been led into profound difficulties by their conviction of the absolute authority of each unrelated gospel text.

When Mathews's skepticism regarding the viability of this method of using the scriptures is compared with Small's critique of Christian socialism in essays such as "The Limits of Christian So-ciology," the parallels between the two positions are striking. In his essay Small argues that the social significance of Jesus' teaching must be extracted from the gospel text: the task of the Christian re-former is not slavish fidelity to the very words of Jesus, but rather the implementation of the ideals of Jesus in existing institutions. As we have seen, Small says this not merely on exegetical grounds, but with a transparent antirevolutionary intent.

In shifting Christian sociology's focus from text to ideal or spirit, Mathews is thus following Small in seeking a formulation of Jesus' social teaching that allows Christian idealism to penetrate the existing structures of society and transform them from within by a process of measured evolutionary change. Such an intent is evident throughout *STJ*. In "The Process of Social Regeneration," for example, before maintaining that the kingdom's growth is to occur in an evolutionary process connected to the social process itself, Mathews first notes that "there is disappointment in store for the man who looks to Jesus for specific teachings as to reform."[195] The two ideas—Jesus left few prescriptions for reform; Jesus' principles are to imbue institutions with new life—are genetically linked in Mathews's foundation for social gospel theology.

This process perspective, which is present throughout *STJ* more as a seminal insight than in any single theoretical articulation, lies behind an important formula in which Mathews expresses his understanding of the relationship between Jesus' teaching and his followers's application of that teaching. The formula is the capstone to a short consideration of how the kingdom is to be established. Mathews contends that the kingdom "spirit of brotherliness" will gradually transform society, as each age and community incorporates this spirit in its own fashion, according to its needs. As a summary statement to the argument, Mathews delivers the following aphoristic observation: "Jesus gives a constitution; men can frame statutes."[196]

The insight this formula seeks to convey is pivotal to Mathews's social process thought. Unless one recognizes the reformist intent that underlies it, the full significance of the insight will not be apparent. By undercutting Christian reformers's appeal to the *ipsissima verba* of Jesus, by transferring the weight of Jesus' social teaching to the ideals that it enshrines, by arguing that succeeding generations of Christians must seek to realize these ideals in their particular historical circumstances: in each respect, Mathews wants to move Christian sociology away from revolutionary formulations and toward reformism. When he says that Jesus gives a constitution, while his followers frame the statutes of the constitution, what he means is that the social teaching of Jesus is always open-ended, and open-ended in a way that only reformist sociologists can fully appreciate, because they alone recognize that no single formulation of social ideals captures all the needs of the social process over the course of social evolution.

Mathews's option for a Christian sociological reformism is also evident in *STJ*'s contention that "not the agitator but the arbitrator has been the real conserver of . . . progress."[197] With Small, in laying the sociological foundation for *STJ*, Mathews consistently assumes that revolutionary social change is largely destructive, whereas gradual amelioration of the political or economic institutions of society is generally constructive. In the chapter "Social Life," for example, he contests the notion that Jesus desired the sudden destruction of all class distinctions. While he grants that iconoclasts sometimes stimulate reform, Mathews thinks that "social revolutions quite as likely produce political demagogues." [198] In his view, Jesus' approach to the question of social class was marked by a "constructive spirit": Jesus saw, Mathews thinks, that the attempt to effect constructive social change by dissolving society into its elements is usually unavailing. Rather, "with him progress was biological, an evolution rather than a revolution." [199]

Significantly, as he develops his reformist interpretation of Jesus' teaching, Mathews appeals to the example of the French Revolution to illustrate precisely that reformist lesson Small had seen in this historical occurrence in his 1888 report to the trustees of Colby College. In denying that Jesus attempted the dissolution of society into its elements, Mathews echoes Small as he adds that the "amateur reformer" often employs the methods of "Robespierre and other doctrinaires: that of breaking absolutely with the past and seeking to recreate society *de novo*." [200] In Mathews's judgment, such amateur reformism will accomplish nothing constructive, unless it is supplemented by Jesus' fraternal impulse: "Pleas and battles for justice have wrought revolutions and wrecked institutions; but only when they have been supplemented and corrected by this fraternal impulse have they yielded the peaceable fruits of righteousness." [201]

The French Revolution (1901) develops this claim at length, and seeks to provide historical corroboration for Small's belief that reform represents a more viable method of social change than revolution. As he was later to claim, in doing the research for this volume, he was to learn a valuable lesson about the correctness of Small's insight—but the appearance of Small's argument in *STJ* suggests that Mathews had already learned this lesson before writing *STJ*. In this respect, the early Mathews is once again irrefutably the pupil of Small the sociologist. [202]

To see Mathews's antiradical propositions as aimed primarily at Christian socialists requires little stretch of the imagination. The question of the legitimacy and viability of socialism arises often in Mathews's writings subsequent to *STJ*, with a frequency that suggests that the problem of responding to socialist influence in United States politics and on the social gospel was a predominant concern in his thought. [203]

Given the predominance of this preoccupation throughout his career, one must interpret Mathews's social gospel foundational theology as a politically engaged theology with a particular critical bent, one turned against socialism. *STJ* does in fact contain an explicit response to Christian socialism. As noted previously, this response occurs in the chapter on wealth, in which Mathews considers Jesus' "economic" teaching. Throughout the chapter, Mathews is concerned with radical appropriations of Jesus' economic teaching. It is here, for example, that he observes that the arbitrator, rather than the agitator, has been the conserver of economic progress; in this chapter he also critiques "those prophetic hearts . . . who see in his [i.e., Jesus'] words panaceas of their own unconscious devising."[204] Furthermore, it is here that Mathews insists stringently that distorted applications of Jesus' words generally derive from a lack of comprehensive consideration of his teaching, and from a lack of recognition that the substance of this teaching is a "principle which underlies it."[205]

But what principle dominates Jesus' so-called economic teaching, in Mathews's estimation? It is, he thinks, that of regarding wealth as a means by which the brotherhood ideal of the kingdom is to be realized.[206] Mathews's attempt to establish an exegetical basis for this interpretation of Jesus' economic teaching leads to his consideration of Christian socialism, since, as he grants, this notion of the role of wealth apparently "brings Jesus close to the general position of socialism."[207] And does not the New Testament itself corroborate a socialist interpretation of the life of the first Christians, he asks; did not Jesus and his followers have a common purse, and did not the Jerusalem community in Acts hold all things in common?[208]

With such apparent biblical warrant for Christian socialism, Mathews thinks "it is . . . by no means strange that there have always been those who have maintained that in some form of socialism lay the true programme of Christianity."[209] In fact, Mathews allows, the combination of Christianity and modern socialism has "great attractions"; indeed, if socialism is only what Frederick Denison Maurice considered it to be, "'the acknowledgement of brotherhood and fellowship in work'," it is, Mathews thinks, simply a phase of Christianity.[210]

Yet, in Mathews's view, ultimately "it is futile to attempt to discover modern socialism in the words of Jesus."[211] Jesus' notion of charity may not be equated with *modern* communism; nor do the common purse of Jesus and his followers and the common life of the Jerusalem community indicate communism in the modern sense.[212] In contrast to those sayings that corroborate socialism are those in which Jesus presupposes commercial competition and recognizes the employer's right to reward his or her workers according to merit: "'Unto him that hath shall be given' comes with ill grace from a socialist."[213] Moreover, "farthest possible was Jesus from the curse of most socialistic programmes—the assumption that the ideal social order is based upon an increase in creature comforts."[214]

On the whole, then, the attempt to ground modern socialism in Jesus' words is an enterprise doomed to failure, Mathews thinks. Jesus could not have anticipated economic arrangements presupposing a historical context radically different from his own. In response to Christian socialist exegesis, Mathews once again insists that, properly understood, Jesus' social teaching is at base a principle— the principle of brotherly living—which is concordant with a variety of political or economic structures. Jesus transcends the claims of a particular ideology or a particular social class:

> To be more specific, Jesus was neither a sycophant nor a demagogue. He neither forbids trusts nor advises them; he is neither a champion nor an opponent of *laissez-faire*; he neither forbids trades unions, strikes and lockouts, nor advises them; he was neither socialist nor individualist. Jesus was a friend neither of the working man nor the rich man as such.
> . . . He was the Son of Man, not the son of a class of men. But his denunciation is unsparing of those men who make wealth at the expense of souls; who find in capital no incentive to further fraternity; who endeavor so to use wealth as to make themselves independent of social obligations and to grow fat with that which should be shared with society,—for those men who are gaining the world but are letting their neighbors fall among thieves and Lazarus rot among their dogs.[215]

This passage provides an apt summary of *STJ*'s position on Christian socialism. While Mathews is suspicious of socialism, his social gospel theology also has a sharp critical edge, one turned against a capitalism that enables the owner to ignore moral obligations to use wealth for the benefit of the whole of society. Though his economic stance is capitalistic, it is capitalistic in a very particular sense: as social gospel writings such as *Making of To-Morrow* in which Mathews sets out his own reform program indicate, he wishes to limit the privileges of capital and enact laws that curb the rapacious greed of those who amass wealth without regard for the common good. Once again, Mathews's outlook in this regard is strongly reminiscent of Small's, where (as we have seen) one finds both a critique of Christian socialism, and a sympathy for aspects of socialism, with an insistence that the rights of capital are far from absolute.

The Sociological Foundation: An Assessment

As the preceding chapter's survey of Mathews's life and work indicated, the key motif of Mathews's theological thought is the idea of social process. Throughout his theological career, Mathews understands societies to be in a state of continuous evolution. Although his works can employ various terms to describe the spur of social evolution, he most often sees societies evolving in response to ideals operating as teleological ends. Because the social process requires such ideals to evolve progressively, social evolution should not be random, but guided by those who can identify ideals that most adequately point to the ideal, but real, future of a given society. As Mathews's prewar writings demonstrate, his preferential use of the term "process" (as opposed to "evolution") is a means of emphasizing that social evolution requires the constructive efforts of idealistic reformers: whereas evolution may connote development that is random, the term "process" means the opposite in Mathews's use. It means that social evolution can and must be directed.

This theoretical formulation of social process does not receive full expression in Mathews's writings until the World War I period, in the important sociohistorical theological articles of 1911–14 and in the 1916 philosophical statement of social process thought, *SIH*. Yet when one reads these works carefully, and compares their understanding of social process with the sociological foundation *STJ* establishes for the social gospel, it becomes apparent that, though the term itself occurs very infrequently in *STJ*, the seminal insights of Mathews's social process system were already present in this volume. The idea of directed social evolution, the understanding of ideals as the telesis of process, the development of the notion that, though transcendent, the ideal is attainable, the reduction of Jesus' teaching to ideals: all these insights, which are crucial to the social process theology, are already beginning to crystallize in *STJ*.

Since the concept of social process is central to Mathews's theology, and since its rudiments are already discernible in his initial foundation for social gospel theology, a question of some importance for those who wish to identify the influences in Mathews's social gospel thought—and in the social gospel in general—is where Mathews got the concept. In analyzing the exegetical foundation provided by *STJ*, we found that a close tracking of Mathews's citations yielded valuable information about his exegetical mentors. If one applies this method to *STJ*'s social foundation, however, one discovers that the study makes no reference at all to sociologists.

But the problem of determining the source of Mathews's sociological ideas is not insurmountable. As we have seen, Small's influence is everywhere in *STJ*. He urged Mathews to undertake the study, and Mathews's sociological thought parallels his at so many points that this foundational statement is as much Small's as Mathews's. The concept of social process was key to Small's thought as to Mathews's—so key that, as Dennis Smith notes, Small's definition of sociology revolves around the concept: "Small considered that sociology was the science of the social process."[216]

Yet to say that *everything* in *STJ*'s sociological foundation derives immediately from Small would perhaps be an overstatement. As Richard Hofstadter's classic work *Social Darwinism in American Thought* demonstrates, the notions that constitute the basis of Mathews's social process system were generally present in the intellectual milieu of social gospel-minded sociologists in the latter half of the nineteenth century. As we have seen, in addition to Small, Mathews had read (and been impressed by) Ely; he had certainly studied Ward as well, since this sociologist's critique of Spencerian determinism and notion of telesis are strongly apparent in *STJ*'s sociological foundation. In addition, since all these thinkers had been formed in the mold of the German historical school of economics, the direct influence of that school on Mathews and the social gospel must not be discounted.

In general, in the absence of intratextual evidence, but on the basis of abundant extratextual evidence, one may confidently conclude that *STJ*'s sociological perspective—and the notion of social process in particular—are rooted in early sociology, and above all in the sociology of Small, Ward, and Ely.[217] To come to such a conclusion is to challenge interpretations of Mathews's theology that have accented his indebtedness either to such prototypically liberal Protestant theologians as Harnack or Ritschl, or to pragmatist philosophers such as John Dewey. If our analysis of the social gospel foundation of *STJ* has been correct, the primary formative influence on Mathews's theology is early North American sociology. If this is true of Mathews, it is perhaps true *pari passu* of the social gospel in general. The genetic connections between sociology and the social gospel, and the shared agenda of the two in the early days of sociology in the United States, deserve further attention, and need to be explored in detail before we can conclude with any assurance that we understand the intellectual matrix from which social gospel thought emanates.

CHAPTER THREE

THE ESCHATOLOGICAL TURN AND THE FOUNDATION OF SOCIAL GOSPEL THEOLOGY

From STJ to JSI

REVISION OF THE BIBLICAL FOUNDATION:

The Turn to Eschatological Realism, 1897–1905

Mathews's initial foundational statement for social gospel theology was one of the most influential social gospel handbooks to have been written. Though it is ponderously footnoted, in the heyday of the social gospel this popularly accessible overview of social gospel theology circulated widely, going through reprinting upon reprinting. Indeed, one could justifiably maintain that Mathews's first life of Jesus was *the* social gospel textbook, the single volume that introduced the largest number of people to the theology of the movement and had the widest influence of any social gospel work. Rauschenbusch's *Theology for the Social Gospel* has attracted more scholarly attention, and deservedly so. But at a popular level, *STJ*'s influence was perhaps broader. Why, then, did Mathews revise the text?

In his 1936 autobiography, he answers this question by noting that he had become dissatisfied with the way in which his first life of Jesus dealt with the issue of eschatology:

> It [that is, *STJ*] represented what might be called a transitional view of the kingdom of God as a social order to be reached progressively. In later years I came to see that this term was really eschatological and I rewrote the volume, publishing it under the title *Jesus on Social Institutions.*[1]

On the face of it, this statement seems to imply that Mathews repudiated the social interpretation of the kingdom shortly before he undertook the revision of *STJ*. Lacking evidence to the contrary, one might suppose that Mathews revised the 1897 work to offset criticism from postwar opponents of the social gospel, when the social gospel was being sharply attacked by critics. *NFO*'s statement might be taken to indicate that the period of polemical exchange between social gospellers and their detractors after World War I was the context in which Mathews recognized the inadequacy of *STJ*'s treatment of the kingdom and decided to revise the work.

These deductions are erroneous. A close reading of Mathews's writings following the publication of *STJ* discloses that soon after the work appeared, he had become dissatisfied with its treatment of the kingdom and had begun to search for an alternative biblical foundation for social gospel theology. Indeed, as Mathews's books and articles demonstrate, in the period from 1897 to 1905 (when his *MHNT* definitively repudiated *STJ*'s social interpretation of the kingdom), the problem of discovering an adequate biblical foundation for the social gospel—in particular, dealing with the eschatological view of the kingdom—was perhaps his primary theological concern during these years. And, as in *STJ*, in his 1897–1905 writings Mathews continued to develop his theology of the kingdom as a deliberate response to the theology of J. Weiss.

What caused Mathews's discontent with *STJ*'s presentation of the kingdom symbol? As the writings of 1897–1905 make apparent, the factor chiefly responsible for dissolving *STJ*'s exegetical synthesis was the drive to historical realism that Mathews had built into his quest for an exegetical foundation for the social gospel. *STJ* had made the crucial admission that Jesus thought and acted as a Palestinian Jewish rabbi of the first century. To move from this admission to the recognition that Jesus' conception of his mission was strongly colored—indeed, determined—by the religious concepts of late Palestinian Judaism requires but one short step. As a trained historian, Mathews was well aware of the prevalence of apocalyptic messianic ideas in the Judaism of Jesus' time. By 1905, this historical awareness would lead him to grant that Jesus and his first followers comprehended the kingdom of God in eschatological terms.

However, in his search for a social gospel foundation that could incorporate the turn to eschatology taking place in contemporary exegesis, a constant mitigating factor was Mathews's concern that, by endorsing the eschatological idea of the kingdom, the social gospel would divest itself of any basis on which to construct a Christian social ethic. The eschatological interpretation of the New Testament appeared to present the social gospel with a quandary: in order to compel theological assent, the social gospel must ground itself in accurate exegesis; yet if it conceded that Jesus and his followers did await the imminent coming of the kingdom, on what biblical basis could they construct a social ethic? An important aspect of Mathews's work from 1894, when he accepted the New Testament appointment at Chicago, until 1905, when he published his definitive statement of social gospel exegesis, was his attempt to negotiate this quandary.

The biblical foundation Mathews was seeking in these years was one that would satisfy the demands of both historical realism and ethical idealism. Though soon after 1897 he could frankly admit that Jesus proclaimed an eschatological kingdom, throughout his theological career Mathews remained a critic of the consistent eschatology school, on the ground that this school reduced the ethical content of Jesus' kingdom proclamation to an *ad interim* ethic, and so robbed Christian faith of its social ethical import. Although Mathews would accede to the eschatological interpretation of the New Testament by 1905, he would do so in a way that safeguarded the ethical basis of the social gospel. *MHNT*'s solution to the quandary facing social gospel exegesis would be an exegesis that seeks to hold together eschatological realism and ethical idealism.

"The Social Teaching of Paul" (1902)

After *STJ*, Mathews's first serious attempt to deal with the problem of eschatology occurred in 1902, in a series of articles in *BW* entitled "The Social Teaching of Paul," which use the concept of messianism as a point of entry to the thought world of early Christianity.[2] In them Mathews argues that Jesus both endorsed and rejected aspects of the messianism of late Palestinian Judaism. Though he still wishes to uphold the social interpretation of the kingdom, in 1902 Mathews is willing to make an initial, and crucial, concession to the eschatological interpretation of the gospels by admitting that "apocalyptic in many ways gives form to his [i.e., Jesus'] thought."[3]

In order to appreciate what Mathews accomplishes in the 1902 articles, it is important to recognize that "Social Teaching of Paul" incorporates a new exegetical approach that significantly departs from his previous methodology. As we have seen, his study of the French Revolution, which culminated in his 1901 book, convinced Mathews that periods of revolutionary change are best approached by the historian through the underlying social psychology that induces revolution. "Social Teaching of Paul" seeks to apply this insight to exegesis. Whereas the 1899 work *A History of New Testament Times in Palestine* had focused on political events as a framework for understanding the Christian scriptures, "Social Teaching of Paul" sees Jesus' teaching as a reflection of and response to the social psychological phenomenon of messianism.

Mathews's social psychological exegesis in the 1902 articles provides the impetus that initially unsettles his 1897 solution to the problem of the kingdom, and urges him toward eschatological realism. As he investigates the social psychology of late Palestinian Judaism, Mathews identifies two predominant types of messianic expectation: among the masses, a hope for a deliverer who would initiate a social revolution; and among the Pharisees, a hope for a final cataclysmic intervention of God in history. This latter hope was conveyed through the medium of apocalyptic literature.[4]

Since Jesus lived within a social psychological milieu charged with such messianic fervor, his understanding of his ministry would undoubtedly have incorporated elements of popular and/or pharisaic messianism. Mathews raises the question of Jesus' own messianic self-understanding in the fourth article of his "Social Teaching of Paul" series, "The Messianism of Paul."[5] As he does so, he begins to dismantle the social gospel foundation *STJ* had set in place, and to rebuild that foundation according to a new exegetical pattern.

In "Messianism of Paul," Mathews develops the thesis that Jesus both presumed and rejected elements of popular and pharisaic messianism. He argues that Jesus' messianic ideal was distinctly at variance with those of his contemporaries; as in *STJ*, in "Messianism of Paul" he continues to find the substance of Jesus' kingdom proclamation in the ideal of the brotherhood of humanity under the fatherhood of God.[6] Jesus' apotheosis of messianism represents, in Mathews's view, a "de-Judaizing" of both the popular and the pharisaic messianic expectations. Having discarded the "archaeological elements" of both types of messianism, Jesus gave an entirely new content to his people's hope for deliverance.[7]

Yet, Mathews believes, Jesus' teaching also preserves aspects of both popular and pharisaic messianism. In his understanding of the kingdom, Jesus presupposes with the masses that, "if God is to deliver men from misery or sin, social results are inevitable. To postpone all effects of divine assistance to an indefinite future is to ostracize God and to threaten the very foundation of religion."[8] And with the Pharisees Jesus speaks of an apocalyptic kingdom to come, and of the Son of Man who would reward the righteous and punish the wicked.[9] Thus, although the 1902 articles still maintain the social interpretation of the kingdom, their discussion of the relationship of the pharisaic idea of the kingdom to that of Jesus betrays an awareness of the complexity of the issues not present in *STJ*'s treatment of the problem of eschatology.

In "Messianism of Paul," Mathews perceives an important exegetical objection to his attribution of the provenance of the idea of a present kingdom to Jesus: namely, if Jesus proclaimed the kingdom as present, why did his followers persist in believing that the kingdom was yet to come? [10] Mathews first addresses this issue in a significant footnote that will later appear in the text of *MHNT*. Naming J. Weiss, the note disputes Weiss's thesis that the notion of a present kingdom represents a reading back of the gospel writers' presuppositions into the gospels. In Mathews's view, to argue thus is "precisely to reverse the facts at our disposal": since the eschatological view predominated in apostolic Christianity, the idea of a present kingdom must have come from Jesus himself.[11]

Yet, as Mathews recognizes, such an argument fails to account for the predominance of the eschatological viewpoint in the New Testament community: "That they [i.e., the apostles] and the early church should have so utterly misunderstood his words as always to see eschatology where he intended a divinely directed social evolution is quite inconceivable." [12] As this conclusion to his consideration of Jesus' understanding of the kingdom makes evident, Mathews recognizes that the concessions he has made to the eschatological viewpoint unsettle his defense of the social interpretation of the kingdom. To admit any validity in the eschatological interpretation, as he had done tentatively in *STJ* and now more boldly in the 1902 articles, is to raise urgent questions about why exegetes ought to prefer the social to the eschatological interpretation.

Mathews leaves his 1902 treatment of the messianism of Jesus with a divided mind. The social psychological viewpoint he has adopted abets historical realism: as his understanding of the cultural milieu in which Jesus and his disciples moved is refined, his appreciation for apocalyptic deepens. As Mathews recognizes, an exegesis that incorporates social psychology leads inexorably in the direction of eschatological realism. Yet to yield to the eschatological interpretation of the kingdom is, as Mathews thinks at this point, to concede to eschatology the entire ethical basis of a social gospel. Mathews is unwilling to yield any ethical ground to the eschatological school. This determination underlies "Social Teaching of Paul"'s insistence that, if God is to deliver people from sin, social results are inevitable. To postpone all effects of divine assistance to the future is to ostracize God from history and threaten the very foundation of religion.[13] That this was Mathews's predominant concern in combating the eschatological reading of the kingdom is evident in an article in the 1902 series entitled "The Social Content of Apostolic Christianity in General," which opens with this observation:

> The kingdom of God, as portrayed by Jesus, involved inevitable social and political change. However great its apocalyptic and eschatological element, one cannot fail to discover in the teaching of Jesus a distinct recognition of the ethical significance of the family, of wealth, and even of the conventionalities of life. It is special pleading to claim that his words upon such social matters were but incidental to a persistent and predominating eschatology.[14]

The solution that the "Social Teaching of Paul" articles throws up to the quandary facing social gospel theology is thus provisional. That is, "neither conception [i.e., social or eschatological] can be used as a critical standard by which to annihilate the other."[15] Since both the social and the eschatological interpretations are in Mathews's view essential to an adequate social gospel exegetical foundation, the two must be held in balance, albeit a balance still weighted in favor of the social interpretation.

At the same time, Mathews perceives that this attempt to hold the two approaches in tension is a stop-gap solution to the eschatological problem, in just the way *STJ*'s solution had been. As he recognizes, there *is* no compelling exegetical reason for maintaining such an artificial tension between the social and eschatological interpretations of the kingdom. Mathews ends his treatment of the topic casting about for "possible" explanations of the presence of apocalyptic themes in Jesus' teaching: "possibly" apocalyptic is the husk, social regeneration the seed; or "possibly" Jesus merely presumed incidental ideas with which the intellectual atmosphere of his day was charged.[16]

Since this artificial solution to the eschatological problem depends primarily on Mathews's determination to avoid conceding ethical terrain to eschatology, rather than on a persuasive exegetical basis, it is easily upset by further probing. Such probing occurs on the heels of the 1902 articles, in a 1903 series entitled "The Gospel and the Modern Man," in which Mathews moves to a frank eschatological realism that will be worked out more carefully in his 1905 *MHNT.*

"The Gospel and the Modern Man" (1903)

"The Gospel and the Modern Man" series is an early venture by Mathews into theological reconstruction.[17] The essays employ a threefold reconstructive tactic: they first attempt to arrive at a precise statement of New Testament thought on a given topic, such as salvation or the atonement; then they seek to discern within its interpretive garb the "essence" of this idea, that which constitutes its permanent validity for the believer; and, finally, they communicate this essence in modern philosophical and scientific terms.[18]

Since the articles are primarily theological rather than exegetical, Mathews does not address the issue of eschatology directly. However, the eschatological interpretation of the New Testament is in evidence throughout. In each essay Mathews conspicuously eschews reference to the kingdom as present, and sketches the outlines of a theology that is at the same time eschatologically realistic and ethically idealistic. For example, as he strives to ascertain the essence of messianism, Mathews argues that the messianic evaluation of Jesus by his followers was compelled by the "facts" of Jesus' life, and by the cardinal fact of his resurrection in particular.[19] In those who acknowledged Jesus' messianic identity, an experience of ethical renewal occurred. This new ethical life constitutes, Mathews thinks, the essence within the culture-bound concept of messianism. Grounded in the facts of Jesus' life and resurrection, the ethical renewal that follows on faith in Jesus points toward the immortality of the believer.[20]

With this interpretation of the messianic hope, Mathews has hit on a formulation of the essence of Christianity that allows him to accept eschatological realism without abandoning ethical idealism.

He now freely admits that among the first Christians, "the precisely Messianic work of Jesus was in the future and formed the substance of the hope of the church," [21] because he does so on the basis of an exegesis that separates the substance of messianism from the cultural framework of that substance. Therefore, he can agree without reservation with those such as J. Weiss who maintain that the New Testament writers "conceived of their own times as a sort of intermediate period" in which the absent Christ had imparted his Spirit as a "first installment of the life of the coming kingdom." [22] Though "the kingdom had not come, . . . eternal life had begun." [23] The Spirit-endowed believers awaiting this coming kingdom were its "prospective citizens." [24]

In the 1903 articles, Mathews is so confident that he has removed the sting of the eschatological interpretation that he can even *appeal* to eschatology to corroborate the ethical demands of Christian discipleship. Anticipating a theme that *The Church and the Changing Order* will strongly develop, Mathews insists that the eschatological interpretation of the New Testament highlights the ethical demands of the gospel more than does the interpretation of the essence of Christianity as "progressive moral change." [25] This insistence implicitly critiques *STJ*'s interpretation of the kingdom, and demonstrates the extent to which Mathews's thought from 1897 to 1903 has eclipsed the biblical foundation of his initial social gospel foundational study.

Several noteworthy book reviews support the conclusion that 1903–4 represents the watershed moment in Mathews's understanding of eschatology. In a 1903 review of Orello Cone's *Rich and Poor in the New Testament*, Mathews declares that,

> [t]hough he [i.e., Cone] has not given due weight to the exceptions to the statement, he is undoubtedly right in seeing in the term "kingdom of God," as used generally, an eschatological, rather than a present, social content, and in assigning so prominent a place to apocalyptic elements in the New Testament. Few of us who have written on the matter would deny that he very properly insists that the thought of Jesus was religious and ethical rather than sociological. [26]

Significantly, Mathews faults Cone, however, for failing to recognize that "the eschatological sayings embody ethical teachings." [27] As he insists, "Jesus and Paul both have a distinct conception as to the present ethical significance of the age-life that awaits members of the coming kingdom."[28] In these two observations, his "solution" to the eschatological quandary is sharply delineated: a frankly eschatological reading of the kingdom of God safeguards social ethical application of this biblical symbol.

The insistence that eschatology implies ethics and does not detract from but enhances the ethical demands of the gospel appears again in a 1904 review of Paul Wernle's *The Beginnings of Christianity*. Here Mathews notes that Wernle's historical realism represents an important advance on Weiszäcker's *Apostolic Age*. He applauds Wernle for the prominence he gives to eschatology in his treatment of the thought of Jesus and his followers. He also praises Wernle for his insistence that the theologian must separate the essence of eschatology from the apocalyptic scenario in which the New Testament presents this essence. Mathews concludes his review with the following judgment, significant because it evidences the shift that has taken place in his thought about the kingdom:

> If his volume has no other effect than to impress upon biblical students the commanding position of eschatology in the gospel, it will not have been in vain. The tendency for the last generation has been steadily toward the minimizing of those elements in the New Testament which are concerned with immortality. Christianity has been made increasingly an ethical system or bald mysticism, regardless of the very central thought of all the New Testament documents.[29]

Messianic Hope in the New Testament *(1905)*

The culmination of Mathews's search for a social gospel foundation capable of holding together eschatological realism and ethical idealism occurred in the 1905 *Messianic Hope in the New Testament (MHNT)*. In this study, which is an exegetical consideration of messianism in Judaism and early Christianity, Mathews explicitly disavows *STJ*'s understanding of the kingdom and concedes that "any strict definition of the kingdom of God as used by Jesus must be eschatological."[30] Whereas in 1897 and 1902, Mathews had argued that the eschatological interpretation is to be subordinated to the social, in *MHNT* he precisely reverses this argument, and maintains that sayings of Jesus which refer to the kingdom as present must be understood in relation to the eschatological motif that predominates in his kingdom proclamation.

A revealing indicator of the important turn that Mathews's understanding of eschatology has taken between 1902 and 1905 is that, though *MHNT* incorporates virtually the entire text of "Social Teaching of Paul," it omits that portion of "Messianism of Paul" in which Mathews argues for a balance between the eschatological and the social interpretations of the kingdom. In its place, *MHNT* includes an entirely new consideration of the eschatological dimension of Jesus' teaching. This reexamination of the eschatological problem obviously provides an exegetical basis for Mathews's 1903–4 turn to eschatological realism.

As a preliminary to its careful reconsideration of the kingdom concept in its chapter "The Kingdom of God in the Teaching of Jesus," *MHNT* examines the Jewish roots of the messianic idea. The argument of this preliminary section of the book is on the whole that of "Social Teaching of Paul"; indeed, the chapters reproduce, with minor revisions, virtually the entire text of several of the 1902 articles. As do the essays, *MHNT* holds that divergent formulations of the messianic hope existed in late Palestinian Judaism—a popular revolutionary messianism drawing on prophetic literature, and an apocalyptic version that evacuated messianism of sociopolitical content.

However, the first section of *MHNT* includes something novel: a consideration of John the Baptist, which illustrates how much Mathews has advanced on his 1902 exposition of the background to Jesus' kingdom teaching. Here, Mathews argues that popular messianism often availed itself of the vocabulary of apocalyptic, and (in seeming contradiction to his thesis in those preceding chapters of *MHNT* reproducing the text of the 1902 articles) that apocalyptic expectation prevailed among both the masses and the Pharisees at the time of Jesus. John the Baptist would, then, have presupposed an apocalyptic understanding of the kingdom, and this understanding forms the immediate backdrop to Jesus' ministry.[31]

Clearly, Mathews has come to this recognition via the breakthrough insight of the 1902 articles that Jesus' kingdom teaching is properly understood in light of the social psychology of his culture. If apocalyptic messianism prevailed in late Palestinian Judaism, it prevailed in Jesus' thought, Mathews the historian concludes.[32] Once again, what is driving him into the arms of the eschatological school is his recognition that historically accurate exegesis must begin with the thought world of the text it studies, and must not torture that text into terms of thought congenial to one's culture.

Mathews's enhanced appreciation for the influence of apocalyptic ideas on Jesus is evident in *MHNT*'s key chapter on "The Kingdom of God in the Teaching of Jesus," which dialectically engages the thesis of "Social Teaching of Paul" that Jesus both accepted and rejected elements of the messianism of his day. The initial section of the chapter reproduces virtually intact the introduction to "Messianism of Paul": as previously, in *MHNT* Mathews still maintains that, "from one point of view," Jesus "seems" to repudiate both popular and pharisaic messianism.[33] Moreover, Mathews allows to stand his 1902 statement that Jesus "apparently" expected the kingdom ultimately to transform society into a great brotherhood of love and service.[34]

However, in *MHNT*, Mathews appends to this statement a crucial qualification, one that changes completely the tenor of his treatment of the kingdom. The qualification, which occurs in a footnote to the statement, constitutes Mathews's first unambiguous repudiation of *STJ*'s interpretation of the kingdom:

> This social view of the kingdom of God has played a considerable, and doubtless helpful, role in recent literature. I have myself adopted it in my *Social Teaching of Jesus*, chap. 3. Such a definition, however, is not the proper point of departure for a study of the social teachings with which the gospels abound.[35]

This note is of great import for understanding Mathews's fundamental intent in *MHNT*. With it he is cutting the moorings that tie social gospel theology to the social view of the kingdom, and he is declaring that an exegetically adequate social gospel theology must discover some other biblical anchorhold.

To put the point otherwise: Mathews's move to eschatological realism is from one standpoint a negative one. Insofar as it endorses the eschatological interpretation of the kingdom and undercuts the biblical basis of social gospel theology, it necessitates the search for a new biblical foundation. If eschatology can be shown to imply ethics, then a more exegetically astute basis, in which a transfer of focus occurs from the gradual growth of the kingdom to the gradual growth of Christian ideals within the social process, may be articulated. Though this formulation is far from antithetical to *STJ*—indeed, it is to some extent what Mathews means by his interpretation of the kingdom in 1897—it is at the same time one that decisively leaves behind social gospel theologies premised on this-worldly interpretations of the kingdom.

MHNT intends above all, then, to provide justification for a shift in Mathews's social gospel theology from kingdom-language to process-language. The chapter on the kingdom in Jesus' teaching grounds such a shift by creating a social gospel exegesis in which the eschatological interpretation of the kingdom is central. Having argued that from one point of view a social interpretation of Jesus' kingdom teaching appears warranted, Mathews goes on to argue (as in "Messianism of Paul") that apostolic teaching would be inexplicable, if this had been the *only* form taken by Jesus' kingdom teaching. Though at this point *MHNT* is still reproducing the text of "Messianism of Paul," Mathews makes several revisions to give more weight to the eschatological viewpoint. For example, he adds the statement that "Jesus' teaching must also have contained and emphasized the eschatological hope."[36] And, whereas in 1902 he had claimed that Jesus "appropriated elements of the apocalyptic messianism of the Pharisees," in *MHNT* Mathews notes more emphatically that "the extant sayings of Jesus show beyond doubt his acceptance of elements of pharisaic eschatological messianism."[37]

This declaration precedes that section of the chapter that constitutes an entirely new text not drawn from the 1902 articles.[38] The subsequent portion of the chapter is thus that in which is to be found Mathews's rationale for the shift to eschatological realism that had taken place in his thought after 1902. Though *MHNT* still wants to maintain that the gospels occasionally understand the kingdom as present, Mathews begins with a critique of the exegetical basis on which the social interpretation purportedly rests: that is, that the parable of the seed and the saying of Luke 17:20–21 presuppose a present understanding of the kingdom. In all probability, Mathews thinks, the reverse is true: both texts assume an eschatological perspective.[39] This is a noteworthy admission, since both *STJ* and the 1902 article had appealed to these texts to establish their social interpretation. In addition, Mathews notes that gospel vocabulary and concepts overlap to a striking degree with those of apocalyptic literature.[40] In support of this statement, he cites, *inter alia*, the second edition of J. Weiss's *Predigt Jesu*.[41]

These observations lead Mathews to the following deduction: of the seven elements that characterized apocalyptic messianism, six are integral to Jesus' teaching.[42] To say this is to face precisely the dilemma he had faced at the end of his 1902 articles. If Jesus speaks "far more commonly" of a future than a present kingdom, then how does the exegete decide what his kingdom proclamation meant?[43] *MHNT* approaches this question via a brief survey of how two opposing schools of criticism, the social and the consistently eschatological, deal with the topic. The discussion is illuminating, because it situates Mathews's 1905 theology vis-à-vis the exegesis of his day.[44]

Mathews states his position with regard to the first school rather peremptorily. This theological group insists with Ritschl that the apocalyptic element in the gospels derives from the interjection of the apostolic viewpoint into Jesus' teaching. In Mathews's view, this school's Ritschlian insistence that apocalyptic is an apostolic retrojection into Jesus' teaching is "under the influence of dogmatic presuppositions."[45] This is "a rough and ready treatment of a genuinely difficult problem" that "clearly begs the question."[46] Mathews is equally dubious about another tactic of the school: that is, to suppose that Jesus used eschatology strategically, to bring himself into touch with his hearers, while he himself understood the kingdom in an entirely different way. Perhaps because he had proposed precisely such an answer to his dilemma in 1902, Mathews is willing to grant this tactic plausibility, but he sees it as a far from satisfactory answer to the problem.[47] If Jesus' understanding of the kingdom did differ from the apostles', then why do the gospels never clearly display these contrasting notions of the kingdom?[48] One would expect the text to reflect such fundamental differences of view.

But Mathews is equally suspicious of consistent eschatology's denial of the authenticity of all gospel passages referring to the kingdom as present.[49] Mathews's primary argument against this school is that if one grants the validity of *any* passages referring to the kingdom as present, then one must also grant that the idea of the present kingdom *must* have come from Jesus, since we know that the prevailing conception of the kingdom in apostolic Christianity was eschatological. In developing this objection to consistent eschatology, Mathews repeats "Messianism of Paul"'s insistence that Weiss's attempt to attribute the idea of a present kingdom to the apostles reverses the facts at our disposal.[50]

This critique of both the Ritschlian and the consistently eschatological positions leaves Mathews himself between the two. To clear ground for his attempt to establish the path his own thought will follow, he rules out two final "ingenious attempts" to deal with the kingdom quandary by "exegetical *tour de force.*"[51] The first surmises that Jesus' apocalyptic sayings are genuine but figurative. Against this, Mathews points to the context of Jesus' thought.[52] Employing the rule of thumb he had used in *STJ* against those who read the kingdom idea philosophically, he asserts that to claim that Jesus used apocalyptic merely figuratively is to import extratextual philosophical generalization into the text that destroys the content of apocalyptic notions.[53]

Mathews also dismisses the proposal that "the eschatological kingdom represents a completed kingdom, the beginnings of which are to be seen in Jesus and the community of disciples about him."[54] In response to this conjecture, he argues that the gospels never show Jesus making such a combination of the present and future kingdom. Since this is the case, "it is exceedingly difficult to think of the kingdom in its eschatological shape as in any way growing out of the kingdom in the social sense."[55]

Having ruled out maneuvers that merely elide the eschatological problem without fundamentally engaging it, Mathews presents his own explanation for why gospel texts evince both eschatological and social understandings of the kingdom. The only justifiable starting point for one who seeks "a proper reconciliation" of the two senses of the phrase "kingdom of God" is, Mathews proposes, for the exegete first to make "a determination as to which of the two is really fundamental."[56] As he had not seen in *STJ*, here he admits that the view that the present sense of the kingdom is fundamental confronts "insuperable" obstacles, since eschatology is not incidental to the teaching of Jesus, but central.[57] If Jesus had used eschatological ideas merely by way of accommodation or as literary figures, a synthetic solution would be easy: "The eschatological pictures of the kingdom could then be treated as a poetic representation of the completion of the evolving present kingdom."[58] But "such a hypothesis is untenable," since it "involves a reversal of true exegetical method"—indeed, a decision to ignore the fact that the eschatological sense of the kingdom *prevails* in the gospels.[59] Any impartial reading of the gospels must conclude that "at the very best the passages which can be quoted in favor of the existing present kingdom are exceedingly few, while those which more naturally must be interpreted to refer to the future kingdom are all but constant."[60]

Moreover, an exegesis that aims at historical realism demands that the exegete approach the text with sensitivity to the social psychological framework within which it was written. As he notes this, Mathews delivers an indicative aside, which demonstrates that it is precisely his intent to ground social gospel exegesis in historical realism that has brought him to see the validity of the eschatological interpretation:

> If a true exegetical method demands anything, it is
> that the interpreter come to a given thought with
> the stream of historical development. The burden of

proof lies heavily upon him who gives a meaning to historical concepts which is contrary to the course of such development. Such burden of proof can be sustained in the case of certain elements of the messianic hope as taught by Jesus, notably those which concerned the office and the work of Christ himself; but, as has already appeared, the entire scheme of his teaching is so thoroughly like that which it has been shown he must have inherited, as to render the substitution of new definitions for those inherited improbable in the highest degree.[61]

On the basis of such a formulation of the exegetical task, Mathews determines that "the historico-grammatical process, if it is worth anything, demands that of the two uses of the term 'kingdom' the eschatological be chosen as fundamental."[62]

This conclusion leads to another important methodological conclusion: that is,

The practical question is therefore reversed. It is no longer one of adjusting the eschatological teachings of Jesus to his religio-sociological, but that of adjusting his references to a present kingdom to his entire eschatological scheme. Such an accommodation is by no means difficult when once it is undertaken.[63]

This conclusion neatly reverses Mathews's exegetical tactic of 1897–1902, which had been to subordinate the eschatological interpretation of the kingdom to the social. Henceforth, his theology will proceed from the recognition that the eschatological idea of the kingdom is fundamental.

But if the eschatological kingdom is fundamental, then what is the exegete to do about texts that see the kingdom as present? At the end of *MHNT*'s analysis of the kingdom in Jesus' teaching, Mathews deals with this question by identifying two meanings for sayings of Jesus "which apparently describe the present kingdom." He suggests that these sayings may refer either to those to be received into the kingdom when it appears, or to the victory of Jesus and his followers over Satan.[64] Since he is aware that critics may object that such "metaphorical" uses of the phrase "kingdom of God" presuppose inconsistency in Jesus' own understanding of the kingdom, Mathews qualifies this statement in a passage that casts important light on his continued reference to the present kingdom after 1905:

> To attempt to give to the words of Jesus any double
> definition seems very hazardous; to think of him as
> at one time speaking of the kingdom as sociological,
> and at another as apocalyptic-eschatological, is to
> raise the suspicion that he himself had no clear idea
> of the term. To say that he uses the term with a con-
> stant sense of the new kingdom which was to be es-
> tablished by God in the new age, but also in a figu-
> rative way to refer to the people who are actually to
> belong to it, is to allow him no more than a conven-
> tional freedom in his references to and use of an in-
> herited concept.[65]

These statements indicate that Mathews's post-1905 use of present-kingdom language is highly nuanced, and is not a vestigial resort
to the social interpretation of the kingdom. As a sentence immediately following demonstrates, he is willing to continue to speak of the
kingdom as present in history *only* in the discrete sense that "those
who had prepared to enter it by living a life of love, might be conceived of *proleptically* as the kingdom."[66] The sentence is one that
could easily find a place in a text of Moltmann or Metz today. It
demonstrates that, by 1905, a social gospel theologian had arrived
at a sophisticated theology of the kingdom of God that foreshadows
the thought of later political theologians.

Mathews concludes his 1905 reconsideration of the meaning
of the kingdom of God in Jesus' teaching with another explicit avowal
of the eschatological position, an avowal which further indicates
that *MHNT*'s move to eschatological realism is not a mere tactical
maneuver designed to divert criticism of the social gospel:

> Any strict definition of the kingdom of God as used
> by Jesus must be eschatological. With Jesus as with
> his contemporaries the kingdom was yet to come.
> Its appearance would be the result of no social evo-
> lution, but sudden, as the gift of God; men could not
> hasten its coming; they could only prepare for mem-
> bership in it.[67]

This conclusion consolidates an entire phase of Mathews's theological thought. From 1894 until 1925, he had been preoccupied
with the problem of discovering an adequate biblical foundation for
social gospel theology. As our examination of his work has revealed,
a central concern during this period was the question of the mean-

ing of the kingdom of God. Though critics of the social gospel have commonly held that its theologians remained in blithe ignorance of the work of the consistent eschatology school prior to World War I, a careful scrutiny of Mathews's writings supports the opposite judgment. Not only had he read J. Weiss's *Predigt Jesu* very soon after its publication, but he was keenly aware of the potentially devastating implications of the "discovery" of eschatology for social gospel theology, and was intent to devise a theological response to Weiss. In *MHNT*, Mathews's thought about the eschatological problem comes to term in his recognition that the eschatological interpretation of the kingdom is essentially correct—but "correct" in a quite specific and qualified sense, namely, that eschatology does not rob the gospels of their social-ethical import, since the "essence" of eschatology is ethical renewal.

An important historical question to be asked about Mathews's eschatological turn is whether one can correlate this turn with a shift in the exegetical authorities on whom he relies in 1905. As we have seen, *STJ* strongly evidences Mathews's dependence in the 1890s on a congeries of German liberal Protestant theologians, including Wendt. Does *MHNT* allow us to conclude with equal confidence that Mathews's eschatologically realistic exegesis presupposed a different set of mentors, one reflecting the shift that had taken place in his thought?

MHNT contains two important discussions in which Mathews outlines the critical presuppositions that underlie the study.[68] When these presuppositions are compared with those of *STJ*, one can see both continuity and significant discontinuity with the exegetical methodology of the former work. As in 1897, in 1905 Mathews still assumes that the synoptic writers employed narratives of deeds and collections of sayings of Jesus.[69] And, as in *STJ*, in *MHNT* Mathews continues to maintain that these "original materials of the gospels may be accepted as the work of the disciples of Jesus himself."[70]

However, *MHNT* surpasses the critical awareness of *STJ* in recognizing that "it is by no means to be assumed that the records contained in our gospels are verbatim reports of the words of Jesus."[71] And, whereas *STJ* had left unspecified the *terminus a quo* of the synoptics, *MHNT* specifies that these gospels reached their present form after 70 A.D. Moreover, Mathews's increasing recognition that the quest to determine the *ipsissima verba* of Jesus is fraught with profound difficulties leads *MHNT* to sharpen considerably the 1897 contention that the gospels add editorial embellishments to clearly discernible sayings of Jesus: in 1905 Mathews grants that "as they now stand, they are finished compositions in which the original material has been subjected, not only to editorial selections, but to other editorial treatment."[72]

MHNT's reconsideration of the gospel problem leads Mathews to a crucial exegetical recognition upon which the entire study turns. That is, though the original materials of the gospels may derive from the disciples of Jesus, "the synoptic gospels, as completed literary units, represent to a considerable degree the point of view of the church during the last quarter of the first century."[73] From this conclusion to the necessary deduction that "the chief interest of the synoptic writers is eschatological" is but a small step.[74]

What has led Mathews to take this step? As one compiles a list of exegetes cited by *MHNT*, one moves ineluctably to the following conclusion: in the period from 1897 to 1905, Mathews's increasing commitment to historical realism in exegesis went hand in hand with his adoption of exegetical mentors different from those on whom he had relied in *STJ*. In general, the citations in *MHNT* suggest that Mathews's exegesis has moved from a liberal to a *religionsgeschichtliche* focus. In the period following *STJ* Mathews's reading in the field of New Testament exegesis evidently kept abreast of the latest developments in German scholarship. Whereas Wendt, Beyschlag, and Edersheim preponderate in *STJ*'s footnotes, in *MHNT* Mathews most often cites J. Weiss, Bousset, Baldensperger, and Wernle. Wendt's *Lehre Jesu* receives six citations,[75] in contrast to twelve citations of J. Weiss.[76] Both Beyschlag[77] and Edersheim[78] are cited twice, while Bousset is cited fourteen times,[79] Wernle eleven times,[80] and Baldensperger four times.[81] Plainly, Mathews's increasing clarity regarding the eschatological framework of Jesus' kingdom proclamation reflects his growing penchant for that wing of liberal theology that took such historical realism as its starting point, a penchant already evident to some degree in the 1897 work.

To conclude our examination of *MHNT*'s treatment of the kingdom: Mathews's 1905 adoption of eschatological realism consolidates a fundamental transfer of emphasis in his theology. With *MHNT*, he regarded himself as having "solved" the eschatological problem that had vexed him from the start of his theological career. Having reached a satisfactory solution to this problem, he proceeded to build a constructive theology on the biblical foundation *MHNT* had elaborated. Both *MHNT*'s introduction and conclusion state that Mathews intends to use the study as an exegetical basis for a constructive theology. *MHNT* is, then, Mathews's definitive statement of social gospel exegesis. The definitiveness of the work is underscored by the fact that after 1906, when Mathews was transferred from the Divinity School's biblical department to that of systematic theology, he would never again belabor exegetical issues as in the period from 1894 to 1905.

To see *MHNT* as Mathews's definitive social gospel exegetical statement is to stress the centrality of eschatology in Mathews's theological thought in general. Far from having ignored the challenge of consistent eschatology, Mathews confronted this challenge directly and with considerable acumen in the "exegetical phase" of his career. And he took what he learned in this period into his later work, by developing a theology explicitly dependent on his eschatological turn, by building a post-1905 social gospel theology around the notion of process rather than the kingdom symbol, and by appropriating the critique of culture Protestantism that was emerging in postliberal German theology. After 1905, Mathews simply takes for granted the eschatological reading of the kingdom and, indeed, employs eschatological realism to accentuate a social gospel critique of both culture and church.

Eschatology in Mathews's Theology after 1905

In Mathews's theology soon after *MHNT*, an important theme emerges, the insistence that "it has been its eschatological message which has given the gospel its grip on human life."[82] The eschatological motif is notably in evidence in Mathews's 1907 social gospel "crisis" work, *Church and Changing Order*. Insisting that the gospel is "the good news concerning the kingdom of God," *Church and Changing Order* builds its "crisis theology" on the biblical foundation of *MHNT*, in particular on the evangelical message that the kingdom is "good news as to the possibility of salvation from sin and death, through that regenerating union with God revealed and set forth in the life, death, and resurrection of Jesus the Christ."[83] This insistence on the centrality of the kingdom message, and on the eschatological nature of the kingdom, patently enacts the exegesis of *MHNT* in theological rhetoric.

As he develops his evangelical theology in *Church and Changing Order*, Mathews proposes that the gospel alone can mediate the crisis developing in Western civilization: to be precise, only the *historical* gospel of the kingdom, rather than an attenuated modern gospel, can enable the church to meet the needs of a culture in crisis. As this synopsis of the 1907 study's central evangelical thrust suggests, a prominent theme of the book is its challenge to the church not only to preach, but to live, the eschatological gospel. Throughout *Church and Changing Order* Mathews urges that "in a profound sense the gospel must become to-day an eschatological message."[84]

Statements such as this have a critical implication for the church—namely, that it must find in the eschatological gospel a resource to enable it to avoid conformity to culture at a time in which such conformity will rob the church of its ability to meet the needs of a culture in crisis.

The claim that eschatological realism accentuates the ethical demands of the gospel on a church ministering to a world in crisis also emerges strongly in the essay "A Positive Method for an Evangelical Theology" (1909), which argues that in attempting to make the gospel pertinent to modern thinkers, a theology that wishes to be truly evangelical must beware of sloughing off eschatology. Only a gospel that remains "fundamentally messianic" can be "divinely redemptive": eschatological realism prevents evangelical theology from reducing the gospel of salvation to a mere ethic.[85] By the same token, the 1913 "The Struggle between the Natural and Spiritual Order as Described in the Gospel of John" contends that eschatology is not only the key that unlocks the significance of primitive Christianity, but also the key that opens the gospel to modern believers.[86] Here, Mathews critiques theologians of the day who, employing an unscientific homiletic apologia, advise preachers to downplay eschatology, since it is repugnant to modern sensibility. Mathews thinks that those who adopt such an apologetic "lose something of that sense of divine salvation which it is the chief virtue of chiliasm to accentuate."[87] In his view, "the messianic point of view . . . opens up the perspective of religion itself."[88]

Mathews's 1916 review of Rauschenbusch's *Christianizing the Social Order* develops similar insights. Maintaining that Rauschenbusch builds his study on an exegetically invalid understanding of the kingdom, he argues that Rauschenbusch "fails to value properly the tremendous religious and social possibilities that lie in New Testament eschatology."[89] Mathews criticizes Rauschenbusch for regarding eschatology as a manifestation of a worldview antithetical to that of the modern believer. In his estimation, this viewpoint fails to appreciate the lasting significance of eschatology for Christian faith: that is, that it is the "carrying concept of the Jewish thought for two great religious fundamentals: (1) the presence of God in history, and (2) the differences in outcome, both social and individual, between unrighteousness and righteousness."[90]

Similarly, the 1925 article "Emil Hirsch's Religion" faults Hirsch for taking a reductionistic view of the apocalyptic literature of the Jewish scriptures. Against such a tendency, Mathews proposes that "despite their literary form there is something impressive in these apocalypses"; for Mathews, they enshrine an important and irreducible aspect of Judaeo-Christian faith, the belief in the coming of the kingdom as a "great religious revolutionary hope."[91]

As the preceding citations suggest, in his work subsequent to *MHNT* Mathews does not merely insist that eschatology is fundamental to the gospel: he so insists against the tendency of an ahistorical liberalism to ignore the eschatological basis of New Testament faith. *Church and Changing Order* makes the point very plainly. In this volume, Mathews mounts a strong critique of believers who, as he thinks, are moving under the influence of modern science and philosophy to a conception of the gospel removed from that of the New Testament: "Their kingdom of God is a new social order here upon earth under historical relations."[92] In Mathews's view, while the gospel implies the salvation of society, it also stresses deliverance from sin and death.[93]

In like fashion, the 1909 entry on eschatology in Hastings's *Dictionary of the Bible* echoes *MHNT* in arguing that only "a highly subjective criticism" can deny that Jesus' notion of the kingdom was "formally eschatological."[94] Mathews urges that the "discovery" of eschatology represents a welcome corrective to the penchant of some modern Christians "to reduce Christian theology to a general morality based upon religion": "Such a situation has proved injurious to the spread of Christianity as more than a general ethical or religious system, and it is to be hoped that the new interest which is now felt in the historical study of the New Testament will reinstate eschatology in its true place."[95]

Both the 1910 *The Gospel and the Moden Man (GMM)* and the 1913 "Struggle between the Natural and Spiritual Order" develop an interesting thesis regarding eschatology. In these works Mathews argues that the history of Christianity may be viewed as a struggle between chiliastic Christians who hold the eschatological gospel in its literal sense, and "spiritualizing" Christians who reduce the eschatological content of the gospel to a depiction of the coming of divine life into the human soul.[96] Since "Struggle between the Natural and Spiritual Order" begins with a critique of contemporary believers who see Jesus as a modern teacher of social ethics, it is evident that Mathews's concern with reductionism is aimed at liberal theologians. In his judgment, theology needs to discover a "middle ground" between chiliasm and spiritualization: "viz., the recognition of the profoundly religious significance of the eschatological hope."[97] This is a contention that runs through Mathews's thought over his entire career. As the late work *Creative Christianity* asserts, for example, hope is the enucleating center of Christian faith, which sets it apart from mere religion.[98]

In addition to emphasizing eschatology as a prop for resistance to cultural reduction of the gospel, Mathews's post-1905 works develop the centrality of eschatology by insisting that all Christian doctrinal reflection after the New Testament proceeds in some sense from eschatology. In the articles outlining his sociohistorical method, Mathews contends that eschatology represents the "vertebral column of Christian doctrine."[99] Or, using a different trope, he holds that hope for the kingdom's coming was the "mold" within which the primitive church shaped its understanding of the significance of Jesus.[100] Both figures suggest the perduring significance of eschatology for Christian doctrine; just as the mold determines the shape of what is molded and the spinal column supports the skeletal structure, eschatology has given form to Christian doctrine over its whole sequence of development. While it by no means expresses the entire content of Christianity, it has, nonetheless, "always been able to fructify the dominant social minds to such an extent that the entire course of doctrinal development of Christianity might almost be described as the successive expression of the philosophical content and implications of its various elements."[101]

The sociohistorical articles further allege that the lasting significance of the eschatological hope for Christian faith has yet fully to be appreciated by theologians. While theologians have had no difficulty in recognizing that underlying New Testament or patristic formulations of the doctrines of God or Christology is a "persistent religious reality" that must be expressed in terms peculiar to each age's thought, there has yet to be a "creative theological exposition of the Christian eschatology."[102] In Mathews's view, theologians of the early twentieth century are in a unique position to make a creative exposition of the eschatological hope, both because of their increasing awareness of the indispensability of eschatology to New Testament thought, and because the "new social passion" of the age allows theologians to perceive in eschatology (hitherto either taken unreflectively in a literal sense or dismissed as archaic) a content of irreducible significance to Christianity.[103] To the extent that theologians have begun this expository task, Mathews thinks, "the religion of our modern world is already shaping up the social as well as the individual content of the eschatology of the original Gospel message."[104]

As the preceding brief thematic survey of his use of eschatology after 1905 has demonstrated, Mathews's acceptance of the eschatological interpretation of the New Testament profoundly shapes his theology subsequent to *MHNT*. In his post-1905 social gospel crisis writings, Mathews strongly insists that "the church of Jesus Christ is something more than a de-immortalized ethical culture society. The heart of the gospel is an eschatological message." [105] This claim, clearly derived from *MHNT*, is the focal point around which Mathews's social gospel theology of the pre-World War I period builds, and the assertion continues to act as a focus in Mathews's theology after he eschews the rhetorical evangelical theology of the prewar works for a more "scientific" theology in the sociohistorical theology articles, and in later book-length applications of this theology.

Given the prominence of the eschatological theme in Mathews's thought after 1905, and the explicit use of eschatology to critique liberal theology's cultural deformation of Christian faith, the charge that Mathews was a liberal Protestant theologian ignorant of the work of the eschatological school in Germany is curious. As our introductory essay has shown, such a charge was made against Mathews early in his career, and consistently sustained by later neo-orthodox critics who maintain that social gospellers ignored the eschatological turn in German theology, and built their theology around an inculturated notion of the kingdom until the postwar demise of the social gospel.

That such critiques could have been sustained for so long in the face of abundant evidence to the contrary (at least in Mathews's case) is indeed perplexing—all the more so, when one notes that sympathetic readers began to recognize the prominent role of eschatology in Mathews's thought even during his lifetime. These include G. B. Smith, who, in a 1914 AISL study course entitled "What Is Christianity?," comments on the theology of Mathews, Harnack, and Seeberg. His argument is noteworthy because it moves to a conclusion in dialectic opposition to that of critics who see Mathews as an unreflective liberal Protestant.

Smith thinks that both Harnack and Seeberg do not give positive recognition to all elements of New Testament Christianity and so retroject modern liberal notions into the gospels as the essence of New Testament faith. But, in his view, Mathews's "historical honesty" leads him to avoid such liberal stripping of archaic elements from New Testament faith.[106] Smith maintains that,

> In particular Mathews calls attention to the important place occupied by the advent hope of the early church. Harnack and Seeberg both depreciate this. Mathews allows it to have the importance which the New Testament actually gives to it.[107]

Smith appends an intriguing note to the article that contains the preceding observation. The note commends Alfred Loisy's "brilliant criticism" of Harnack—one that, it ought not to escape our attention, closely parallels that of Mathews. The suggested parallel between Mathews and Loisy opens tantalizing new vistas on Mathews's theology: Mathews the social gospeller is a fellow under the skin with Loisy the Roman Catholic modernist critic of liberal Protestantism. Both use eschatology to combat liberal reductionism; and both see the eschatological hope as the mold within which all doctrinal development takes form.

Smith is not the only scholar who recognizes the extent to which eschatological realism shapes Mathews's mature theology. In his article "Ethics and Eschatology in the Teaching of Jesus," F. C. Grant sees *MHNT* as a "pioneer work, without which, at least in this country and in Great Britain, the widespread growth of the 'eschatological interpretation' might not have taken place." [108] Noting that *MHNT* represents an important response to the work of J. Weiss, Kenneth Smith and Leonard I. Sweet's 1984 overview of Mathews's social gospel theology corroborates this thesis. [109] Another North American theologian who has seen the full import of *MHNT* is C. C. McCown, whose *The Search for the Real Jesus* observes that with the 1905 work, Mathews was already converted to the eschatological interpretation of Jesus' teachings. [110] McCown sees Mathews as a lone prophet in his defense of the eschatological interpretation of the gospels; echoing Mathews's own reservations about the style of the volume, he speculates that *MHNT* may not have received the attention it merits because it was "too bulky and too diffuse" to have been read by many scholars. [111] However, though McCown sees clearly that Mathews had made an eschatological turn by 1905, he thinks (erroneously, as our survey of the post-1905 work proves) that "the effect of that 'conversion' [i.e., Mathews's to eschatological realism] did not come to full expression for nearly a quarter of a century," presumably, with the publication of *Jesus on Social Institutions (JSI)*. [112]

Given such abundant evidence that eschatology plays a *central, formative* role in Mathews's mature theology, one must ask whether something other than historical accuracy has driven the charge that Mathews was a culture Protestant. This "something other" appears to operate independently of careful reading of Mathews's works; it is hard to understand how anyone who actually reads what he says in the period from *STJ* to *MHNT* could maintain that he was casual about the work of J. Weiss, or how anyone who reads the post-1905 writings could see Mathews as an unreflective, uncritical liberal. One suspects that the "something other" in some critiques of Mathews's theology is, quite simply, a determination to read him as a naive liberal theologian, despite his own avowals to the contrary.

Before we leave the topic of Mathews's use of eschatology after 1905, justice demands that we broach an important critical question about the thesis that Mathews abandoned the social interpretation of the kingdom of God with *MHNT*. The question is, Why does one encounter references to the kingdom as a present social reality in Mathews's writings after 1905? Do these indicate that Mathews was playing theological games with the kingdom symbol, sometimes using it to throw a sop to the postliberal Cerberus that waited at the passage social gospel theologians had to enter to gain theological credentials, and at other times speaking *entre nous* of the kingdom as present, among those already converted to the social gospel?

In regard to this question, what should perhaps be noted first is that Mathews nowhere reneges on *MHNT*'s exegesis of eschatological realism. In fact, in his only substantial exegetical discussion of eschatology after 1905, in his Hastings's *Dictionary* articles "Eschatology" and "Messiah," Mathews simply presents a précis of *MHNT*, maintaining that "the Kingdom of God, as He [i.e., Jesus] conceived of it, is formally eschatological,"[113] that "Jesus conceived of the Kingdom as the gift of God, for whose coming men were to prepare,"[114] that the *a priori* decision to deny the validity of Jesus' references to the eschatological kingdom is "a decision impossible for reasonable criticism,"[115] and that "eschatology alone forms the proper point of approach to the Pauline doctrines of justification and salvation as well as his teachings as to the resurrection."[116]

Similar unambiguous avowals of the eschatological nature of the kingdom appear as well in Mathews's theological writings after *MHNT*. For *GMM*, Jesus' teachings were "indubitably" apocalyptic.[117] And the 1910 "The Kingdom of God" states the following:

> It is of course true that Christian men and women are to transform society, and in that sense it is, of course, true that the kingdom of God is to transform society. But it is difficult to show that Jesus conceived of the kingdom as anything other than an ultimate reality that God was to introduce.[118]

In the 1930 article "Doctrines as Social Patterns," Mathews argues that "they [i.e., the first Christians] awaited neither a political reformation nor the evolution of a better social order, but an emancipating catastrophe."[119] The 1931 AISL study pamphlet *Through Jesus to God* explicates the idea even more plainly:

> There is no evidence that he [i.e., Jesus] thought that
> men would bring in the kingdom. That was to be
> done by God, who was to give it to his children when-
> ever he saw fit. They were to wait for it and prepare
> for it, but they were not to endeavor to bring it in.[120]

Finally, in the 1936 review of H. K. Booth's *The Great Galilean Returns*, Mathews observes that "forty years ago" he had seen the kingdom as a social order, but that he now sees the exegetical impossibility of such an interpretation.[121]

And yet after 1905, Mathews also continues to speak of the kingdom as a present social reality that develops through the activity of Christians in history, in sections of *Church and Changing Order*,[122] in the 1909 and 1914 social gospel study guides *The Social Gospel*[123] and *The Individual and the Social Gospel*,[124] and in articles such as "The Social Optimism of Faith in a Divine Jesus" (1914)[125] and "Present Cooperative Action by the Churches" (1917)![126]

In the case of *Church and Changing Order*, a plausible explanation is not difficult to find: the volume hobbles together material written at various moments of Mathews's career. Those chapters based on material written after 1905 carefully avoid reference to the kingdom as present; those reprinting articles published prior to 1905 preserve Mathews's pre-1905 references to the kingdom as a social order.[127] Mathews's tendency to recycle essays in later books often results in a curious hodgepodge, in which some statements constitute prima facie contradictions of others, when Mathews has altered his views or vocabulary, and has not deleted references to the issue in his recycled articles.

In its kingdom language, *Church and Changing Order* illustrates this textual problem more acutely than any other of Mathews's books. Chapter 6 exemplifies the problem: it is essentially the 1899 "The Significance of the Church to the Social Movement"; although the 1907 book is a more "scientific" presentation of social gospel themes than the 1899 article had been, Mathews reproduces the article virtually intact. And, in chapter 4, where he speaks of the kingdom of God as a present social order, he is reprinting sections of the 1900 "The Christian Church and Social Unity" without revising what it has to say about the kingdom. Consequently, he speaks of the kingdom as future in sections of the book written in 1907, while continuing to speak of it as present in chapter 4.[128]

One can, then, explain these 1907 references to the present kingdom as vestigial ones that Mathews the peripatetic loquacity, the biblical scholar with a mission, simply did not delete when he republished previous texts. But in the other post-1905 works cited, something else seems to be at work. Here, the explanation for present kingdom language may lie in the genre of all these works: all are intended to defend the social gospel or to stimulate Christian involvement in it. Can one infer that the continued use of the idea of a present kingdom in these works is *rhetorical*? Is Mathews deliberately employing present-kingdom language as a ground for his rhetorical appeal for Christian social activism? [129]

An indicative aside in *Creative Christianity* suggests that one may answer these questions affirmatively. Here, he argues that hope is the dominant motif of Christian faith. But hope presupposes imagination, he thinks, and symbols such as liberty, democracy, fraternity, and the kingdom of God activate the imagination. They do so, Mathews notes, with a power proportionate to their indeterminacy: symbols clearly defined lose their evocative power to stimulate imaginative response.[130]

Such a symbolic understanding of the function of kingdom language in social gospel rhetoric appears to underlie his continued appeal to the present kingdom in social gospel writings after 1905 aimed at a popular audience. As he maintains in the 1922 essay "The Christian Faith and the Life of the Community": "We must needs talk about the kingdom of God, although, like Paul we may very well be aware that its prospective members can more safely be addressed as those 'called to be saints' than as 'saints'." [131]

"We must needs talk about the kingdom of God": though Mathews can make such a statement relative to the need for theologians to shape the social mind of their culture, kingdom rhetoric does *not* predominate in his writings after 1905. As the preceding discussion suggests, when it does so, it does so largely in popular social gospel works, and then with a specific rhetorical function. In most of Mathews's writings after *MHNT*, a significant shift away from kingdom language occurs. Significantly, chapter 5 of *Church and Changing Order*, which is substantially the 1907 article "The Church and Social Discontent," contains only two references to the kingdom, neither this-worldly ones; in material written as the book was composed, Mathews is already moving away from a social gospel emphasis on kingdom language, to one focused on the principles of Jesus.

This shift can most accurately be described as a turn from kingdom to social process rhetoric. When Mathews articulates his theory of social process in the important sociohistorical essays of the war years and after, he transfers his focus from the kingdom of God to the social process. In most of his mature work, the penetration of the social process by Christian values displaces the present kingdom as a rhetorical center for social gospel theology, and plays the same function as the developing kingdom had in *STJ*.

If one wishes to see this shift in a nutshell, one can turn to the 1910 "The Kingdom of God," in which Mathews ruminates about a new foundation for social gospel theology after exegesis has exposed the fatuity of the social interpretation of the kingdom. Arguing that exegetes are reaching the limits of their positive knowledge of the biblical meaning of the kingdom, Mathews declares that Christian men and women must transform society, to be sure, and in this sense the kingdom is transforming society. But, he hastens to add, it is difficult to show that Jesus saw the kingdom as anything other than an eschatological event at the end of history. Since this is the case, he asserts that a social gospel theology must transfer its focus from the kingdom to the "'word' of the kingdom." [132] Mathews explicates this mysterious assertion by remarking that the entire social order must be filled with the "principles" of the gospel; this is the hope that will find its completion in the coming of the kingdom.[133]

From kingdom to social process, from Jesus' ideals to principles imbuing the process as it unfolds toward the kingdom: *in nuce*, this will be Mathews's foundational theological project for the social gospel after *MHNT*. It is a project genetically linked to the eschatological turn of *MHNT*. And it is a project that sets his course from *STJ* through the eschatological turn of *MHNT* to the new foundation of *JSI*.

From *MHNT* to *JSI*:

Eschatological Realism, Social Process, and a

New Foundation for Social Gospel Theology

As our examination of *MHNT* has suggested, in one significant respect, Mathews's turn to eschatological realism left him with a serious theological problem—to reconstruct social gospel theology on a biblical foundation radically different from that of *STJ*. After having come to a certain clarity about the exegetical problems presented to the social gospel by theologians such as J. Weiss, Mathews still lacked clarity about how to employ the kingdom symbol. Rhetorical use of the present kingdom appeared to preserve a kingdom theology he had abandoned; and language about the eschatological kingdom might be taken as an endorsement of the interim ethic. What Mathews needed was a new, less problematic, biblical foundation and theology constructed on that basis. Since *MHNT* itself intended to provide that biblical grounding, we need to turn initially to this work to see how Mathews began the task of theological reconstruction that the book itself sets for him.

MHNT *and Reconstruction of the Theology of the Social Gospel*

In two important discussions of theological reconstruction in *MHNT*'s introduction and conclusion, Mathews explains his understanding of the interplay between exegesis and constructive theology. In both, he echoes the "Gospel and Modern Man" articles by distinguishing three moments in theological reconstruction: scientific exegesis to determine the precise meaning of biblical texts; evaluation of texts to discern their permanent validity; and rephrasing this "essence" in contemporary idioms of thought.[134]

In an enlightening note to *MHNT*'s conclusion, Mathews observes that his definition of theological reconstruction implies above all that the "theologian must be a historian."[135] For Mathews, any defensible sortie into theological reconstruction of biblical data presupposes as its *sine qua non* exegesis that "judges historical facts by genuinely historical criteria."[136] It is, of course, precisely this commitment to historical accuracy that has led him to recognize with J. Weiss that "impartial comparison of New Testament literature with the contemporaneous and immediately preceding literature of Judaism shows an essential identity in the general scheme of messianic hope."[137] *MHNT* breaks even more definitively with liberal theologies that twist biblical data to ideological ends than *STJ* had done; it extends *STJ*'s critique of Kaftan's Ritschlianism by noting that Kaftan's assumption of the social interpretation of the kingdom as its "critical and exegetical norm" is "under the influence of dogmatic presuppositions as regards the kingdom of God, due to the influence of Ritschl."[138]

But a precise exegesis is hardly the endpoint of theological reconstruction. Since, in Mathews's reconstructive schema, exegetical work is always preliminary to evaluative and correlative moments, his demolition of *STJ*'s social gospel biblical foundation requires him to reframe his entire social gospel theology. Having displaced one biblical center for his theology, where does he find a new one? And where is his theology to go, once that center has been discovered?

The direction in which Mathews intends to take his reconstructed social gospel theology is evident in the chapters following his exegetical discussion of Jesus' kingdom proclamation. Having established the eschatological definition of the kingdom (and again echoing "Gospel and Modern Man"), Mathews proceeds to argue that eschatology is "a way of thinking of matters which are in no sense dependent upon the peculiar form in which they are portrayed." [139] Eschatology has two fundamental meanings, he proposes; these are "the belief that the good man must survive death, and . . . that God is bound to come to the assistance of those who trust him." [140] In Mathews's view, the first belief expresses the *individual* content of eschatology, and the second expresses eschatology's *social* content, the hope for a society in which righteousness will be supreme. [141] These hopes constitute the permanent content of New Testament eschatology for Christian faith—a content that is ethical rather than ethnic. [142]

Mathews points to the historical Jesus as an exemplar of his definition of the kingdom hope. Arguing on the basis of an assumption common in liberal theology but now largely discounted by exegetes, he maintains that the synoptic narratives of Jesus' baptism depict Jesus' breakthrough to messianic self-consciousness. [143] When he began his ministry after his baptism and temptation, why did Jesus proclaim the imminence of the eschatological kingdom and accept the identification of himself as the eschatological Christ? [144] He did so, Mathews urges, because the baptismal event enabled him to *experience* what eschatological concepts seek to convey. Thus,

> Eschatology in his teaching is essentially a recognition of immortality. The center of his teaching is not the kingdom of God, with its mingled ethnic and political connotation; it is *eternal life*—the life which, because it is like God's, persists across death into the joy of the divine life. He could teach it because he possessed it. [145]

In making this observation, Mathews appears to have two intents. The first is to ground his interpretation of eschatology in the life of Jesus. If Jesus himself can be shown to have understood the kingdom he proclaimed as the Johannine literature understands it (i.e., as eternal life), then social gospel theology can validly make the eschatological turn, while "translating" eschatology into terms meaningful to the contemporary believer, just as John "translates" the synoptics' eschatology. This intent lies behind a subsequent assertion in *MHNT* that the hope for eternal life finds its fulfillment in the historical Jesus, since the "fundamental needs and hopes" expressed by the eschatological expectation have actually been met in the life of Jesus. [146]

In the second place, Mathews intends to focus on the historical Jesus to counter the tendency of theologians such as J. Weiss to divert attention from the historical Jesus to the Christ of faith, and, in doing so, to remove Jesus' ethical teachings from the historical realm. After 1905 Mathews consistently appeals to the historical Jesus to critique those whose focus on the Christ of faith makes the gospel extrinsic to human experience.[147] That this intent underlies *MHNT*'s move from the kingdom to Jesus as proclaimer of eternal life is strongly evident in an observation following on the heels of Mathews's formulation of Jesus' kingdom preaching as the announcement of immortality: he states that "the life and resurrection and teaching of Jesus were not intended to be sources of mystery to the world. In such a case the gospel would be far enough from good news."[148]

Resistance to such "mystery" in dialectical theologies is a keynote of Mathews's late books, and with the same motivating concern. In *Christianity and Social Process* (1934), for example, he notes sarcastically that "it is no more difficult to talk about an unknown God who has been revealed apart from humanity in His Word, than it has been to argue about decrees issued by God before there was any universe and to describe a heaven which lies beyond the stars."[149] *The Church and the Christian* echoes this critique, arguing that in periods of cultural distress such as that Mathews thinks has induced dialectical theology, "apocalypse takes the place of process, submission to the unknown will of God the place of effort. God becomes almost spatially distinct from humanity, and can be reached by no human effort."[150] And, in a passage that mirrors these almost precisely, in his final book, *Is God Emeritus?*, Mathews decries the removal of God from human need, the reliance on a Word of revelation that conceals more than it discloses, and the ensuing devaluation of human effort: "The outcome [i.e., of the removal of God from the world] is logical. God has no immediate share in the direction of humanity. History is the record of demoniac power too great to be opposed by man and can be overcome only when God chooses to act."[151]

Having interpreted New Testament eschatology in relation to the historical Jesus, *MHNT* proceeds to the theology of Paul. Here, Mathews's central argument is that eschatology rather than justification by faith is the focal point of Paul's thought.[152] In passages that anticipate much Pauline exegesis later in the twentieth century, Mathews maintains that to lose sight of this focus is to diminish Pauline thought to an ethical system and to reduce the Jesus of history to a "mere social reformer or ethical poet" with no great significance for the modern world.[153] In his view all Paul's letters are addressed to those awaiting the coming kingdom; Christians of the

New Testament "as a class" expected the *parousia* to occur within their lifetime.[154] The "chief purpose" of Pauline literature is, Mathews thinks, to draw out the ethical implications of eschatological faith.[155]

To show how Paul used eschatology to arrive at ethics, Mathews rewrites the Ritschlian trope describing Christian theology as an ellipse with two foci. The allusion to the Ritschlian trope appears to be deliberate: Mathews wants to indicate how, in accepting eschatology and grounding Christian ethics in a positive evaluation of the concept, his theology moves significantly beyond liberal formulations. For Mathews, Pauline theology is an ellipse about belief in Jesus as the eschatological Christ, and the experience of the Spirit promised to believers in the eschatological Christ.[156] As Mathews notes, Paul's theology does not focus on the kingdom.[157] The implication is clear: social gospel theology has biblical warrant in Pauline and Johannine literature for disengaging eschatology from its cultural framework and diverting attention from the kingdom to the qualities of life demanded by citizenship in the kingdom.[158]

In making these theological moves, Mathews is obviously concerned to deal with consistent eschatology's central challenge to the social gospel: to discover how the ethical teaching of Jesus has significance for those not living in imminent expectation of the kingdom. It is important for him to demonstrate that Paul accepted the eschatological interpretation of the kingdom while developing an ethic with pertinence for Christians who do not live awaiting the *parousia* in their lifetime. Mathews begins this argument by noting that Paul saw the experience of the Spirit as a "first installment" of the life that will find its fullest expression in the kingdom.[159] Mathews thinks that Paul regards the Christian as *already* living under historical conditions an eternal life "built upon the historical experience of the Christ."[160] That is to say: a salvific experience of the Spirit rooted in the revelation of eternal life in Jesus is salvific in *this* world, and not only in an afterlife.

Thus, when Paul proclaims that Christians possess new life in the Spirit, he proclaims a life that is "the earthly counterpart and beginning . . . of the ideal proposed by his messianic hopes."[161] There is in Pauline theology a *functional equivalency* between the kingdom and the new life lived both within history and fully at its consummation. Within history, in "this age," Christians strive to live the life that will be theirs in the kingdom.[162] For Paul, the moral teaching of Jesus is not, then, a set of impossible-to-fulfil injunctions for those living in the interim before the *eschaton*, but the "expression of those great principles of conduct which would assure in the messianic kingdom the ideal social condition." [163] In summary, "ethical ideals were inseparable from his [i.e., Paul's] hope." [164]

Consequently, even if the goal to which the new life of believers is directed is eschatological, as the consistent eschatology school rightly finds, it is nonetheless "morally dynamic and the basis of the Christian's ethical imperative." [165] *Within history* the Christian lives by ethical ideals that will not receive fulfillment until the coming of the kingdom. New life in the Spirit finds expression that cannot be thwarted even by the mistaken apprehension that the kingdom is to arrive immediately. As Mathews notes, once such misperceptions had been removed from the forefront of the first Christians' consciousness, salvation began to root itself in and transform the historical experience of individuals and the community. [166]

As he walks step by step through Paul's adaptation of the kingdom proclamation for the first-century church, Mathews is moving toward his own goal for a reconstructed social gospel theology—a more explicit social process formulation of *STJ*'s foundational theology than had been possible in a work still so bound to the social interpretation of the kingdom. That this *is* his goal is evident in the following crucial comment ending his survey of Pauline theology:

> To trace the apostolic exposition of the ethical and social implications of this new life is, therefore, to set forth essential Paulinism. But it is also to do something far more important: it is to make easy the process by which apostolic Christianity may be accurately re-expressed in our own day. [167]

This observation follows precisely the tangent of Mathews's thought about the biblical foundation of social gospel theology subsequent to *MHNT:* the foundational argument for the social significance of Christian faith is to be transferred from a focus on the kingdom evolving in history to the new life of the believer and the community, which must receive expression in and transform the structures of society.

The concluding chapters of *MHNT*, which discuss the emergence of the church and its relationship to politics, society, and economics, illustrate such a social gospel application of essential Paulinism. Here again, the point of departure is the recognition that "so far from the eschatological kingdom of God being a secondary element in the early church, it is its great conditioning belief." [168] But Mathews believes that it would also be fair to say that the New Testament community's confidence in the imminence of

the eschatological kingdom "checked the expression of that re-
generate life which came from the believer's experience of God." [169]
Because they expected the *parousia* in their lifetime, New Testament Christians were "possessed of a conservatism in social matters amounting almost to indifference." [170]

Yet eschatological preoccupation could not entirely repress the
creative impulses of the new life of believers. Even when apostolic
Christians looked for the immediate return of the Lord, they organized
an *ekklesia* and initiated polities and offices of leadership for it. [171]
The formation of the church, an event apparently unanticipated by
Jesus, demonstrates for Mathews that eschatological Christianity
was clearly from the start "constructively social." [172]

With such postpaschal innovations as warrant for further cultural implementation of Jesus' message, Paul maintained that "Christian life must be social in order to be true to itself." [173] This is why he
so notoriously emphasized the "domestic implications" of the new
life. In making this point, Mathews offers an important aside that will
carry over into his social process theology, and confirm his social
gospel move from biblical literalism and toward cultural correlation:
he notes that many of Paul's prescriptions (that is, that the wife is to
be subject to her husband) are "essentially local and historical applications of Christianity"; to attempt to enforce such applications
today is to confine Christianity to a first-century social context and
prevent its social evolution. In a further twist on the eschatology-as-
eternal-life argument, Mathews adds that once the "check" of eschatological expectations was removed from New Testament Christianity, the "ideal element" of Paul's teaching, that which is of
permanent significance, assured that *new* social arrangements would
be developed by Christians. [174] Christians today simply presume such
arrangements, and "he would be a rare man who would today attempt to make the Pauline teaching as to Corinthian women operative in western Christendom." [175] Strip from Pauline theology its
"enswathing eschatology," and the new life of the church immediately begins to transform social institutions. [176]

Mathews parallels this argument for the New Testament's transformation of social structures with an analysis of the political stance
of the New Testament church. He contends that, to the extent that
authors such as Paul and the author of Peter's letters forbade Christian involvement in politics, their outlook was determined by the eschatological preoccupation of the apostolic community. However,
just as happened with Paul's culturally based social mandates for believers, no sooner had expectation of the immediate return of the
Lord died, than Christianity began to "remake" the political struc-

tures of the Roman empire: "The Christ did not return; Christianity could not hold itself from politics."[177]

In developing these arguments for the socially and politically transformative nature of early Christianity, Mathews makes eschatology serve his reformist bias. For example, he contends that whereas an eschatologically fixated Christianity naturally had a specific political message (that is, to honor the emperor and submit to the constituted authorities), a Christianity that seeks to work out the implications of new life beyond the New Testament period can have no specific political message. Take from the messianic hope its culturally determined elements, and one discovers a Christianity that is simultaneously politically transformative and nonspecific: "It may have political effects; it cannot have a political program."[178] What makes a government "Christian," then, is not a particular polity, but whether it develops institutions that "embody the spirit and are regulated by the principles of Jesus."[179]

One could hardly discover a more apt summary of Mathews's constructive theological project after *MHNT*. The spirit and principles of Jesus informing social institutions, the ideals of the new life working themselves out in the social process: after *MHNT* these concepts, and not the evolving kingdom, will clearly be the dominant motifs of Mathews's social gospel theology. Mathews ends the 1905 exegetical study with a strong appeal for just that type of social process interpretation he has presented in a nutshell in his survey of Pauline theology, and intends to develop in his socio-historical theological works after *MHNT*:

> Formally, therefore, the church was a group of messianists awaiting a kingdom that never came and indifferent to all customs of society except those that were evil; essentially, the church was a group of men and women endeavoring to let the new religious and ethical life that came to them from God through accepting Jesus as Christ express itself in social relations.
>
> And the life lived. Jesus was greater than the men who interpreted him, even when they interpreted him aright, and it is he and his work, and the life with God he revealed, that formed the strength of historical Christianity. The new life must needs be expressed in temporary vocabularies and concepts, but it could not be restrained by them. It conquered them—the mighty systems of an

Augustine, an Origen, a Justin, even of a Paul. And thus inevitably, because it was the social expression of a life, the church became the parent of a Christian civilization; the Christian family of the first century grew into the Christian family of today; the Christian fraternity, loyal to an imperial tyranny, became the champion of a Christian democracy that, with all its revolutionary power, even as yet has not come to its own in either politics or economics.[180]

In conclusion, *MHNT* provides a new biblical foundation for a social gospel theology both in its eschatological turn, and in its attempt to discovers a this-worldly significance in the kingdom ideals by which the believer lives. The 1905 study sees an experience of ethical renewal grounded in the historical Jesus as the organizing center of the Christian movement, an experience that must of necessity incarnate itself in and transform social institutions. Since the ideals of the kingdom point to eschatological fulfillment, they constantly move in advance of social institutions; the process of incarnation/transformation must be continuous. No structure or institution short of the *eschaton* is final or completely Christian. These insights constitute the biblical basis for Mathews's eschatologically realistic social gospel theology. As his theological attention shifts after *MHNT* from the problem of establishing a social gospel biblical foundation to that of developing a constructive theology capable of incorporating these insights, his new theological focal point will be the notion of social process.

Though the seminal insights of the process system are already present in *STJ*, and in this work Mathews can even speak of Christ as "the will of God in social process,"[181] until the social interpretation of the kingdom had been removed from the scene, there was no urgent need to articulate an explicit process theology, because discussion of the evolving kingdom could subsume the social process insights.[182] There is a clear genetic link between Mathews's 1903–5 turn to eschatological realism and the development of the social process theology. Process provides him with a theoretical structure that enables him to affirm eschatological realism while holding an ethically idealistic interpretation of the biblical foundation of Christian faith. After 1905, process language emerges in Mathews's theology as noticeably as kingdom language declines.

GMM (1910):
A Theological Companion-Piece to MHNT

At the end of *MHNT*, Mathews announces that he plans to follow the book with a constructive theological companion piece. Noting that his "Gospel and the Modern Man" articles have already sketched the outline of such a theology, he states that he will publish a book with the same title.[183] Since the book constitutes Mathews's first book-length theological exposition of a social process theology, any survey of his works that wishes to track the trajectory of thought moving between *STJ* and *JSI* needs to pay close attention to this 1910 study.

As chapter 1's overview of Mathews's work has indicated, *GMM* seeks to be an early twentieth-century "rational apologetics" for Christian faith in the wake of shattering exegesis and Darwinian theory. Unlike *Church and Changing Order*, which had addressed a popular social gospel audience, *GMM* speaks to the academy. In this work Mathews adopts a more markedly self-conscious theological manner of address than in any other of his early works. Because he writes with a certain nervousness about situating his theology vis-à-vis major theological schools of the preceding century and of his own period, a chief value of the 1910 work is that it enables us to place Mathews's social gospel theology within the theological spectrum of the period.

As a reconstructive theological statement designed to follow *MHNT*, *GMM* wants above all to link theological reconstruction to social: presuming the eschatologically realistic exegesis of *MHNT*, it seeks to develop the social import of eschatology, primarily by vindicating the creative involvement of humanity in moving the social process to its telic point.[184] Its architectonic theological concern is thus to explain why Christians ought to involve themselves in the social process, as they await the eschatological kingdom. Since this was the point at which social gospel theology would be most scrupulously examined by critical theologians, Mathews works to develop a theological rationale for such reformist activity, in order to claim academic validity for the movement.[185]

Mathews grounds his argument in a definition of religion. The main thrust of *GMM*'s thesis is that, in any culture, religion inevitably contributes to the social process, and *must* do so, if it is to be what it claims to be. Mathews defines religion as a social phenomenon that, in its ethical teaching, prefigures the evolutionary unfolding of the process, or that offers to the process ideals that will attract it to its next evolutionary stage. Religion is thus "the voluntary anticipation of the next stage of this process [i.e., specifically, of 'the entire process of history' moving toward personalization] whose goal is the perfected spiritual individual, through personal union with God."[186] Mathews's decision to anchor his social process theology in a definition of religion situates that theology vis-à-vis the liberal theology of Schleiermacher and Ritschl, who also had constructed their theologies around a definition of religion, and had interpreted Christian experience as a facet of religious experience in general.

Mathews's social gospel understanding of religion diverges from liberal Schleiermacherian-Ritschlian definitions, however, for he notes that in the continuous dialectic between nature and spirit in which humanity finds itself, religion helps to shape the social process to the ends of spirit as it anticipates the next stage of the process.[187] The observation deliberately employs the Ritschlian distinction between spirit and nature to subvert the Ritschlian formulation of religion as a facet of cultural development, by insisting that culture does not play the tune to which religion dances, but vice versa. Mathews's generic understanding of religion requires such an inbuilt critique of culture for a social gospel reason: he is en route to a social gospel theology in which the church is always moving in dialectical rejoinder to cultural developments.

Mathews's definition of religion also modifies Schleiermacher's famous definition of religion as the absolute dependence of humans on God, by maintaining that religion is "an attempt to reconcile and so make helpful the superhuman personal environment upon which mankind feels itself to be dependent."[188] In response to both Ritschl and Schleiermacher, Mathews wants to correct liberal theology's understanding of religion by emphasizing the active role of religion in culture. By enabling humanity to extend to the process its "highest ideals," religion aids in the struggle of spirit to subdue nature, Mathews believes.[189] This understanding of religion cuts out a distinct theological turf for the social gospel, one both contiguous to that of liberal theology, and distinct from it. What will separate the social gospel from its liberal forebears is its emphasis on the vital, the critical, role religion plays in the social process.

For social gospel theology, religion "looks forward to the outcome of that process and endeavors to direct mankind thither. Therein lie its task and its legitimacy."[190] Accurate definitions of religion must have, then, an eschatological component, since religion looks not to origins but to destinies: "It asks not Whence but Whither."[191] This formulation of the task of religion raises, of course, a crucial question: Is it possible to know the goal of history? To deal with this question, *GMM* appeals to the eschatologically realistic exegesis of *MHNT*, arguing that New Testament eschatology is "a pictorial presentment in terms of catastrophe of what we should call the teleology of social evolution." [192] Mathews's article on eschatology of the previous year in Hastings's *Dictionary* says almost precisely the same: "The modern equivalent of Jewish eschatology for practical purposes is that of personal (though truly social) immortality and a completion of the development of society." [193] The recurrence of this claim in Mathews's works of these years suggests that what continues to be foremost in his mind as he defends the social gospel and seeks to develop a reconstructive theology for it is the need to link eschatological realism and social activism.

In *GMM* Mathews is concerned to reinforce the identification of the *eschaton* with the goal of the social process by drawing out, even more than *MHNT* had done, the *social* content of the eschatological hope.[194] Mathews insists that New Testament eschatology was first and foremost a "politico-social hope." [195] That is, "it looked not to a theological heaven but to a social order, the kingdom of God." [196] This emphasis on the social content of the eschatological hope accounts for the appearance here of claims that sound strangely like a reassertion of the social interpretation of the kingdom—as, for example, that "not the least important among the hopes contained in eschatological programs is that of a social order, which though not to come by observation or effort, would be no less real because it was to be introduced by God." [197] Or, as *GMM* later puts the point, "the kingdom of God as a social ideal among the early Christians was eschatological, but as among the Jews it was none the less social." [198]

In making such observations, Mathews does not want to regress to a pre-1905 formulation of the kingdom teaching of Jesus. Rather, he is attempting to set forth the social content of the eschatological hope even more forcefully than he had done in *MHNT*. This intent is manifest in the following passage:

> We have already seen that, eschatological as that hope may have been, it never ceased to be social. However great the difference between the Christian conception of the kingdom of God and the Jewish ideal of the kingdom of saints to be founded at Jerusalem, they are alike in the belief that the final consummation of the deliverance of the individual will be in his fullness of life in an ideal society within which God is supreme.[199]

While emphasizing the social implications of the kingdom hope, this formulation preserves the futurity of the kingdom expectation. Though the coming of the kingdom will be the eschatological fulfillment of what has begun in history through human activity, the consummation of social evolution will be accomplished through divine activity alone. In speaking of the eschatological hope as social, Mathews is referring to a proleptic effect of the final kingdom on history.

Since eschatology contains the hope for an ideal social order, Mathews thinks that it may not be ignored by a church seeking to make common cause with secular social reformers. He asks: "Why go back thus to the New Testament and seek to recover the primitive eschatological gospel?"[200] His answer is revealing: Though "the gospel is not identical with Christianity," only those Christian groups that have maintained continuity with the primitive eschatological gospel are "of commanding significance" in the modern world.[201] In Mathews's judgment, "the religion of the future must be evangelical or it will be socially powerless."[202]

Furthermore, the "fundamental beliefs" implied by the eschatological hope—namely, the expectation of a future divinely established social order, the belief in personal immortality, and the conviction of the inevitableness of reward or punishment—cannot be safely discounted by the church, Mathews thinks. If the church overlooks these fundamental beliefs by ignoring eschatology, then it is in danger of losing the ethical impulse that drives its encounter with culture and provides the church with a transformative message for culture:

> Paradoxical as it may seem, eschatology in these equivalents brings the gospel into closest touch with the thought of the modern world. Any man who, in the spirit of the New Testament, would attempt scientifically to minister to our day must embody it in his message. He cannot omit the effects of God's presence and activity in social evolution, the future of the individual, the triumph of righteousness and the spiritual order.[203]

What seems to lie behind this assertion is a certain nervousness about *MHNT*'s claim that eschatology has ethical content. In the period between *MHNT* and *GMM*, Mathews appears to have become aware of a potentially devastating critique of his interpretation of eschatology in 1905. This is the charge that his interpretation represents precisely that reductionism he thought he was combating in retrieving eschatology and translating its fundamental significance into modern terms.

With its eye clearly turned to critiques of social gospel readings of eschatology, *GMM* carefully exegetes the claim that eschatology has ethical content. Mathews's 1910 work does this by adopting a strong defensive posture against such critiques. Mathews's defensive posture is evident, for example, in *GMM*'s claim that eschatology is "part of the content of the gospel." [204] The 1910 volume also argues that, even though Jesus' teachings were "indubitably apocalyptic," apocalyptic represents, on the one hand, "not the content, but the clothing of his message." Yet, on the other hand, the modern interpreter must be slow to draw a precise line between what is to be taken literally and what figuratively in apocalyptic discourse—although it must be noted that the Jewish scriptures demonstrate that authors often employed symbolic discourse that was never intended to be taken as an end in itself, but was meant to refer to realities beyond itself.[205]

GMM's cautious response to critics of social gospel exegesis concludes with the insistence that, even if the New Testament does present eschatology in culturally limited apocalyptic ideograms, "eschatology must not be banished with its pictures." [206] In saying this, Mathews is once again placing his theology in relation to that of liberal theologians such as Ritschl, Harnack, and Kaftan. His concern with liberal reductions of the eschatological content of the gospels is apparent in Mathews's insistence that eschatology has an irreducible content for Christian faith. As Mathews mounts this insistence, he notes that he does so over against those contemporary believers who think that the attempt to separate apocalyptic content from its form implies that New Testament eschatology cannot be retrieved by Christians today, because it reflects a worldview incomprehensible to modern believers. Against such a view, Mathews concludes the following:

> Eschatology, it is true, as represented in the Jewish apocalypses is a bizarre mixture of symbols, but he is a superficial student of the ancient world who can see in these apocalypses nothing that reaches into the depths of religious faith. When one ceases to look at it in its broad lines, eschatology at once appears to have been something more than an iridescent dream.[207]

For Christians who wish to contribute to the social process, eschatology illuminates the fundamental meaning of the gospel as "a message of divine redemption." [208] It is the means by which the ancient world envisaged God's accomplishment of the divine redemptive purpose in history.[209] Moreover, the synoptic gospels illuminate the fundamental significance of the evangelical message by showing that salvation has already entered history and demonstrated its efficacy in the historical Jesus. The gospel is most precisely, then, "a message of personal and social salvation revealed and wrought through Jesus by God"; it is a "message of individual and social salvation through the spiritual inworking of a God who is at once love and law, revealed in and guaranteed by the experience of the historical Jesus." [210]

GMM thus strikingly accentuates MHNT's thesis that the historical Jesus constitutes (with the experience of the Spirit) the focal point of the good news of salvation.[211] How may believers discern the goal of the social process? Mathews suggests that they look to Jesus: "The free spirit is he whose impulses are controlled and directed by an ideal that is the very anticipation in history of humanity's goal. And that is the very paraphrase of Christian faith. For that ideal is Christ." [212]

For GMM there is an indissoluble bond between the historical Jesus as the revelation of the meaning of humanity, and the eschatological future of humanity. Jesus is the future of humanity, the telic point to which all social evolution moves, "the embodiment of the ideal life," "the proclamation of the conditions under which this life is to be lived in an evil world," "the type of that kingdom which was to come," "the exposition in terms of an historical situation of those timeless values that shall characterize the kingdom of God." [213] In the conflict between nature and spirit in which believers find themselves, they may have confidence in the triumph of spirit, precisely because in Jesus this triumph has already occurred:

> In a sense almost startlingly true, Jesus is a second Adam. As the first man marked the rise of the new type of individual above the brute, so Jesus reveals the completion of the next step ahead in the process of the development of the spiritual individual. The a priori probability that there should develop some life through its identity with the End of the spiritual order made strong enough to conquer the conditions set by our physical limitations, is met by the message that such a life has appeared. The a priori probability meets the historical.[214]

GMM's reading of the historical Jesus thus makes a theological advance on the exegesis of *MHNT* by insisting that the historical Jesus is not only the historical anchorhold for the believer's new life of the Spirit, but also a revelation of the ideal life of the kingdom to which the believer aspires.[215] In *GMM* Mathews puts this insight to an interesting theological use. He argues that because the ideals of the gospel have actually received full expression in his human life, the life of Jesus demonstrates the pertinence of these ideals for the human situation: "The gospel includes moral and social ideals which are more than visionary because they have been incarnated in an actual life."[216]

This theological reading of the historical Jesus patently rises out of *GMM*'s predominant concern to justify Christian contributions to the social process, and to do so on grounds that will be convincing to academic theologians. To focus this concern on the historical Jesus is inevitably to focus as well on the question of the applicability of Jesus' teaching to contemporary society. Such a focus raises questions about the relationship of *GMM*'s ethically idealistic interpretation of the New Testament to theologians such as Schweitzer.[217] Though Schweitzer is never named in the study, Mathews deals very explicitly with his *ad interim* thesis:

> There is also the rising school of radicals who believe that the gospel's ideals were not intended for the historically developing social order, but were intended to serve *ad interim* during the bitter period when the followers of Christ awaited his return to establish his new kingdom.[218]

GMM attacks this thesis for depending on the assumption that the catastrophic inauguration of the kingdom is an essential element in Jesus' thought. Though he does not wish to deny that Jesus expected the coming of the kingdom through catastrophe (and openly avows this position at one point in *GMM*),[219] in Mathews's view this is not the "permanent" element of Jesus' kingdom proclamation.[220] Eternal life, the new life of the believer that begins in the present age and reaches its culmination in the kingdom, is that element:

> Both Paul and Jesus, but particularly the latter, looked across the great chasm which was to separate the one age from the other and centered attention upon the quality of life which, beginning in the present age, would reach fullest element in the coming age.

> Such ideals may be criticized as too high for the so-
> cial order as we know it, but they cannot fairly be
> criticised as not intended for the present age.[221]

On the basis of such an interpretation of the relationship between the eschaton and the present order, Mathews advances the
following thesis to counter the *ad interim* thesis: he holds that though
the gospel's ideals always move in advance of any attempt to realize
them in a given historical situation, they are nonetheless meant to
be applied in history. In his estimation "no religious message can
deserve acceptance that promises only an endless suffering born of
ideals perpetually maladjusted to social evolution."[222] To deny that
the ideals of a religion are pertinent to the social process is, Mathews
thinks, to deny that the religion serves human needs; with regard to
Christianity, to suppose that gospel ideals are beyond realization is
to assume that the gospel is not fitted to humanity.[223]

If Christian ideals are pertinent to the social process, then the
contemporary believer must seek to interject these ideals into the social process, just as the primitive church did when it began to "so-
cialize" the ideals of the gospel even while eschatological expectation
restrained this attempt—for "the ethics of the gospel is its religion
coming to self-realization."[224] In a theological application of the crisis rhetoric of *Church and Changing Order*, *GMM* insists that the demand of the gospel to be incarnated in the lives of believers and the
world around them is even more acute in a world in which the forces
that are making the future clearly require regeneration. In such a
world, the church's vocation to serve the kingdom appears in sharper
relief than ever before: "Only as the church is a servant of the kingdom has it a right to exist. To doubt that God is working in extra-ec-
clesiastical efforts at social betterment is to come dangerously near
the sin against the Holy Spirit."[225]

"Only as the church is a servant of the kingdom has it a right
to exist": on *MHNT*'s biblical foundation, *GMM* has begun to develop a social process theology with several distinctive features. In
the first place, the 1910 volume locates Mathews's social gospel theology in critical response to liberal theology, and demonstrates that
he wishes to employ central ideas of liberal theology to move it to a
critique of culture it significantly lacks, and to action on the basis of
that critique. In addition, *GMM* shows that when Mathews claims to
have accepted the eschatological interpretation of the kingdom while
divesting that interpretation of what he sees as its "ethnic" content,
he does not intend to strip eschatology of its permanent significance
for the church. And finally, it reveals that Mathews's appeal to the

historical Jesus is his attempt to find a bridge between the Jesus of history and the social process of today. The foundational theological claim made by *GMM* is that believers must focus on a Jesus who exemplifies the efficacy of the gospel ideals in his own life, and who thus illustrates the pertinence of those ideals for the social process. It is this Jesus, and this proclamation of the eschatological kingdom, that *GMM* intends to foreground for social gospel theology, a theology that will receive its fullest expression in *JSI*.

SIH (1916) and the Philosophical Foundations of Social Process Theology

While both *MHNT* and *GMM* make abundantly clear Mathews's intent to build an eschatologically realistic social gospel theology around the notion of social process, neither work provides a philosophical explication of the notion. Both volumes employ the phrase and analogues of it as though readers already know what it means. However, although the concept was "in the air" in early sociology and the social gospel movement, in order to develop a new social gospel foundation that would effectively harness the eschatological turn of *MHNT* and yoke it to a social process theology, Mathews had to think more carefully about the precise meaning of "social process." He does so in the 1916 lectures entitled *The Spiritual Interpretation of History*. Since the lectures represent Mathew's most exacting philosophical statement of social process, they deserve scrutiny as another important roadmark along the way from *STJ*'s foundational theology to *JSI*'s.

In keeping with its intent to vindicate idealistic interpretations of history against critics who pointed to the First World War as a demonstration of the untenability of liberal bourgeois reformers' belief in progress, *SIH* has a strongly apologetic intent. To interpret this study accurately, one must keep this intent in mind. In *SIH*, by defending a philosophy of history which holds that society evolves under the impulse of ideals, Mathews is arguing against those who attack a *specific* idea of process—namely, the idea that humanity is responsible for the social process, a process that he never believed to be automatic, as the process of natural evolution has sometimes been thought to be. As Mathews was to observe in his 1935 work *Creative Christianity*, the 1935 volume extends *SIH*'s argument that the tendencies of history generally indicate progress toward a telic point, but "such progress is not blind but dependent upon the intelligently directed cooperation of various elements in a social situation." [226] *SIH* has a decisive social gospel apologetic purpose, then—

to defend idealistic philosophies of history because they support the social process theology Mathews wants to employ in his new social gospel foundation.

SIH mounts its defense of idealistic readings of history by asserting that natural and social evolution are both continuous and discontinuous with each other.[227] The evolutionary process is, Mathews argues, a continuum moving from matter to spirit: the tendency of process "sets" from monism to multiplicity, from simple forms to greater complexity, from impersonality to personality.[228] With the emergence of humanity on this evolutionary continuum, a creative "plus element" is added to the process; when spirit evolves from nature, evolution becomes self-conscious. With this self-consciousness comes the ability of an evolutionary product, human beings, to contribute to the shaping of the natural process to spiritual ends.[229] Though humans emerged out of a material base and are therefore continuous with (and to this extent determined by) material factors, they also interact creatively with their material environment, molding it to specifically human ends.[230]

With the evolutionary emergence of humanity comes society. Just as humanity itself is matter-reaching-to-spirit on the evolutionary continuum, the social process within the natural is also continuous and discontinuous with the process of material evolution. In granting the "materialistic" determinism of society, Mathews wants to acknowledge the validity of critiques of idealism that see social evolution as determined by material factors including environment, geography, climate, or economic needs.[231] Yet, since the social process is a human construction and thus a manifestation of spirit, societies respond to such material determinants in creative ways. If one is able to grant this in any sense at all, Mathews thinks, one must also grant that the social process moves to and can be guided to spiritual ends.[232]

Mathews seeks to corroborate this philosophical claim about the social process with a historical case. History itself, he claims, provides evidence of the movement of the social process toward spiritual ends. If one looks over the broad sweep of human history, one can discern certain clear "tendencies" suggesting that the social process is evolving in a telic direction. These include the gradual substitution of moral for physical force and the growing recognition of the worth of the individual.[233] But such telic tendencies are not to be equated with any given culture or cultural development. As Mathews notes, the specification of tendencies in history requires a broad perspective permitting a multiplicity of viewpoints; to attempt to identify telic directions in history is also to strive to account for the entire complexity of social development at a global level over the course of human history.[234] In asserting this, Mathews once again echoes Small the sociologist, who also wants to avoid making the sociological attempt to specify the *telos* of history so culture-specific that history's goal appears to be confined to any given culture.[235]

As he develops *SIH*'s historical case for telic tendencies in the social process, Mathews argues that when one moves from the macroscopic perspective that attempts to isolate tendencies in the global social process to the microscopic level of individual cultures, one can easily discern the influence of material factors such as economic interest in the development of particular cultures or particular cultural institutions and events (e.g., the rise of Christianity in the Roman Empire, the Reformation, the American Revolution).[236] In saying this, Mathews evidently intends both to accede to "materialistic" interpretations of history and to maintain that such "correct" interpretations are nonetheless incomplete ones.[237] They do not go far enough; they do not account for the complexity of cultural development when one looks at history from the macroscopic vantage point. These theories do not recognize the creative "plus-element" of spirit in history.

In both endorsing and critiquing the materialist reading of history, Mathews appears to have a motive that goes beyond merely correcting this reading. He also wants to offset simplistic assumptions that one can either easily isolate the tendencies of history, or, on their basis, effortlessly forecast history's course. To the extent that one can identify them, the tendencies of history are never a precise forecast of future historical developments, but rather simply indicate that history is moving in a telic direction.[238] He puts the point tersely: "Teleology . . . must not be too precise"[239]—an enigmatic statement which seems to mean that, in looking over the sweep of history and discerning tendencies, one does not discover specific goals, but merely an indication that history has a spiritual goal. Indeed, Mathews wants to caution against any pseudo-idealistic reading of history that finds it easy to identify *any* goal as the *telos* of history:

> Here is indeed a danger. At the door of every one who believes in the presence of spiritual forces in human life there always crouches the temptation to see a destination, and estimate the progress of human life by sighting across it to this destination. But who of us is wise enough to know the destination of history? We may not with the pessimism which finds such beautiful expression in William

> Vaughn Moody's *Gloucester Moors*, deny a port be-
> yond the mists of the present, but when a historian
> dogmatizes as to the precise location and organiza-
> tion of a Utopia, he is experimenting as a prophet
> and must stand examination as to the source of his
> inspiration.[240]

This passage has crucial significance for Christian reformers. Since both Small and Mathews had been vexed in the 1890s by works such as Herron's *The New Redemption* and *The Christian State*, which identified particular governmental and economic polities as "Christian" ones, when *SIH* cautions against the effort to find the goal of history in particular cultural developments, it is also implicitly arguing against the social gospel quest to find the ideal Christian society in given cultures and their institutions. In Mathews's view, it is not just that reformers cannot discover in the teaching of Jesus specifications for the political or economic organization of society; the tendencies of the social process as well lack such information. They point to a *telos* that may not be specified, toward which we are in process, and of which we have only general indications enabling us to chart our course:

> It is the sense of direction that gives the *élan vital*, to
> use Bergson's almost too happy term, its spiritual
> value. So much we can see clearly and positively.
> Further we must "faintly trust the larger hope" thrust
> upon us by the process of human social life.
>   . . . As we stand on the bow of some great steamer
> hustling itself across a trackless ocean, we feel only
> the rush of change, the toss of waves and the buffet-
> ing of winds. But as we stand on the stern of the ves-
> sel we see the wake, boiling out even as we watch,
> stretch unswervingly behind us. Then we know that
> we are held to a course. We cannot see our port, but
> we know we are going some-whither because we
> have come some-whence.[241]

The passage is poetic and moving. Its evocative power is such that it almost causes one to forget that Mathews himself often comes dangerously close to identifying United States democracy with the *telos* of the social process—as we have seen, he does so even in *MHNT*, where this near-identification is in ironic contrast to the book's own previous assertions that Christianity is never bound to any cultural development, but moves to an eschatological goal that transcends all such developments.

At its best, in its avowed intent, Mathews's theory of social process accents change, flux, the necessity for constant experimentation, for a multiplicity of perspectives as the reformer seeks to discern the movement of the social process and contribute to that movement.[242] Mathews's social process system thus has an inbuilt critical norm that precludes the absolutization of any culture or cultural development. For Mathews, Christian reformism must of necessity seek to implement a variety of programmatic departures as social structures evolve to the absolute spiritual goal of social evolution. This point—that all social development occurs under an eschatological proviso that prohibits the politically engaged Christian from concluding that the kingdom has come definitively in history—is one that has been made with even greater acuity by contemporary political theologians such as Moltmann and Metz. Its appearance in Mathews's theology suggests once again to what an extent his social gospel theology has affinities with political theology, ones that, unfortunately, remain conspicuously unexplored in contemporary critiques of social gospel theology. In our next chapter's examination of *JSI*, we shall return to this point as we ask how Mathews incorporated the social process philosophical foundation of *JSI* into his final foundational statement of social gospel theology.

CHAPTER FOUR

JESUS ON SOCIAL INSTITUTIONS

A Revised Foundation for Social Gospel Theology

The revised edition of *STJ*, published in 1928 as *JSI*, represents the culmination of Mathews's long reflection about the foundations of social gospel theology. As we have seen, that process of theological reflection involved two moments. From 1897 to 1905, the question of eschatology occupied Mathews's attention. The drive to exegetical accuracy that he had built into the search for a social gospel foundation required that he wrestle with the challenge of consistent eschatology. Since this challenge could not be dismissed out of hand if one wanted to be scrupulously honest about the historical background of New Testament literature, a way had to be found around the impasse consistent eschatology appeared to create for the social gospel. In the period from 1903 to 1905, Mathews found that way, and *MHNT* describes it in detail. It involves a simultaneous acceptance of the eschatological interpretation of the kingdom (with a consequent abandonment of the social interpretation), and a move to an ethically idealistic reading of the eschatological kingdom. This is the first moment in Mathews's revision of his initial foundation for social gospel theology in *STJ*.

But revision of the exegetical foundation for social gospel theology also required a reframing of the theological framework that the 1897 work had built on that foundation. Though *STJ* anticipates Mathews's subsequent social process theology by speaking of the kingdom's ideals unfolding in the social process over the course of history, it does so by accenting the kingdom itself. To abandon this theology of the kingdom-coming-in-history, as Mathews had done in 1905, is to displace the traditional theological center for social gospel theology.

After 1905, the theological question that primarily occupied Mathews's attention was this: If the kingdom of God is not to be the theological focus of a foundational theology for the social gospel, then what *is* to be that focus? *MHNT* begins to answer that question, and prefigures the post-1905 work, by sketching the outlines of a new theology of social process that was to receive theoretical expression in *GMM*, in the World War I socio-historical theology articles, and in *SIH*. This theology of social process sees society moving to a *telos* that Christian faith names as the kingdom of God, and that proleptically draws the social process to itself via kingdom ideals that intersect with telic tendencies in the process itself. The kingdom is thus not *in* history: it is the eschatological endpoint of history, to be established by God alone at the end of history. Yet it *affects* history by reaching from the future into the present and pulling social evolution toward itself, and by acting as a critical norm against which both social and ecclesial developments are to be measured. These social process insights constitute the second moment in Mathews's revised foundation for social gospel theology.

Because *JSI* appropriates these two moments as it seeks to build a new social gospel foundation, a comparison of *JSI* with *STJ* that is closely attuned to the development of Mathews's thought between these two works reveals how, at a foundational level, a social gospel theologian dealt with the problems posed by the eschatological turn in German theology at the end of the nineteenth century. Such a comparative study provides us with important information about how one social gospel theologian sought to come to terms with the eschatological interpretation of the New Testament, and to develop theological legitimation for Christian reformism in light of eschatological readings of the kingdom symbol.[1]

STJ and JSI:

A Textual Comparison

If one wishes to discover how Mathews's 1928 life of Jesus alters the theology of the 1897 work, an obvious first step would be to compare the two texts. Does *JSI* reproduce portions of *STJ*? If it does so, does it make significant revisions of the former text, particularly in the area of the theology of the kingdom? Are any portions of the 1928 text new, and if so, do these new sections illuminate Mathews's revision of his initial foundation for social gospel theology? Questions such as these provide the point of departure for a close comparative study of the texts of the two lives of Jesus, and of their two formulations of social gospel theology.

As a preliminary to such textual comparison, one might profitably note the difference in the two studies' titles. The 1897 title is a telling indicator of where Mathews's understanding of social gospel theology was at the beginning of his theological career: at this point, he considered it essential to come to an accurate statement of Jesus' social teachings. Not only did he consider this essential, but as *STJ* itself indicates, he thought it possible for the exegete to arrive rather easily at such a cumulative picture of Jesus' teaching. Since the kingdom was the center of all Jesus' teaching, Mathews was compelled to center his social gospel theology on Jesus' kingdom teaching. A byproduct of such a focus was that his first life of Jesus would have to struggle with *exegetical* questions: to isolate the teaching of Jesus required careful consideration of such issues as the hermeneutics of gospel interpretation, the dating and process of composition of the gospels, and the relationship between the final text and the teaching of Jesus it presumably presupposes. Mathews evidently did not consider this exegetical consideration to be misplaced, since it was for their lack of attention to scientific exegesis that he faulted other social gospel studies of the period.

By contrast, the 1928 study purports to study the significance of Jesus for social institutions. The difference in focus indicated in the change of titles is not without importance. As a perusal of the material new to the *JSI* text reveals, in contrast to *STJ*'s intent to ground social gospel theology in a synthetic appraisal of Jesus' teaching (in particular, in the kingdom proclamation), in *JSI* Mathews focuses on the "Jesus of history and in history" as the constant nucleus for the movement that seeks to implement his ideals and example in the social process. Mathews's concern in 1928 is less precisely exegetical than it had been in 1897. As the chapters unique to the 1928 study suggest, social process theology, rather than exegesis of the gospels, predominates in Mathews's concern in *JSI*. These chapters largely lack the abundant scriptural citations found in the 1897 study.

Textual comparison of the two studies reveals another important shift. *JSI* contains five chapters that had not appeared in *STJ*. These are entitled "The Revolutionary Spirit in the Time of Jesus" (chapter 1), "Jesus and the Revolutionary Spirit" (chapter 2), "Jesus on Social Attitudes" (chapter 3), "Jesus and the Church" (chapter 8),[2] and "The Social Gospel of Jesus" (chapter 9).[3] Chapters 4 through 7 draw (with revisions and emendations) from *STJ*'s chapters on Jesus' teaching as to the family, wealth, the state, social life, and the forces of human progress.[4] What *JSI* deletes from the 1897 text is extremely significant: the two chapters of *STJ* that had argued for the social interpretation of the kingdom do not reappear in the 1928 study.

Moreover, the titles of those chapters added to the 1928 volume reinforce the judgment that Mathews's center of concern has shifted in 1928 from the kingdom to the effect of Jesus on the social process. As these titles indicate, in *JSI* Mathews will ground social gospel theology in a social psychological study of the gospels that sees Jesus reflecting a revolutionary messianism strongly present in late Palestinian Judaism. In *JSI*, rather than focusing on how Jesus proclaimed the kingdom of God, Mathews will build his theology around the notion that Jesus appropriated the messianism of his culture only to "sublimate" his followers' revolutionary expectations, and so inculcate in them attitudes that would inevitably have a transforming effect on social institutions.[5]

Two final noteworthy contrasts reveal themselves when one compares the text of *JSI* carefully with that of *STJ*. In the first place, to several of the 1928 chapters that employ material from the 1897 study, *JSI* appends important considerations of topics not considered by *STJ*. In its chapter on the family, for example, *JSI* includes a discussion of whether legislation ought to attempt to enforce Jesus' ideal regarding marriage as a norm for society.[6] Here, Mathews argues that Jesus' ideal of indissoluble marriage, with its concomitant discountenance of divorce, was intended for his followers and not society at large. Consequently, legislation regarding the family and divorce ought realistically to attempt to mitigate the effects of social injustices, rather than to impose an ideal that, if legislated, might actually have pernicious effects on some marriages.

In addition, *JSI*'s chapter on the state incorporates a discussion of the relationship between modern warfare and Jesus' ideal of nonresistance to violence, as well as a consideration of whether the state can be considered a "moral integer."[7] Both concerns arise in part out of Mathews's response to critiques of the social gospel in the postwar years. In this regard, *JSI*'s conclusions regarding war and peace are interesting. Paralleling the line of thought he follows in his consideration of divorce, Mathews argues that Jesus' "absolute ideal" of pacifism must be implemented in concrete historical situations by means of an "intelligent balancing of possible goods."[8] Both in the added section on divorce and in that on pacifism, Mathews exhibits an increasing (a neo-orthodox) awareness that while Christian ideals may represent goals for Christian behavior, these ideals may not be useful as organizing principles for a pluralistic society. As Kenneth Cauthen's introduction to the 1970 Fortress Press edition of *JSI* notes, Mathews's reflections in these new sections of the study display a note of realism not evident in *STJ*—a note that surely reflects the sharpening of his ideas in the social gospel's interchanges with neo-orthodoxy in the postwar period.[9]

Finally, a textual comparison of Mathews's 1897 and 1928 social gospel foundational statements uncovers another interesting difference in the two works. This is that the 1928 study addresses a somewhat different audience than that addressed by the 1897 work. Whereas *STJ* is extensively documented both with gospel citations and references to recent Continental exegetical studies, those chapters in which *JSI* innovates on the *STJ* text have relatively few footnotes. In particular, these chapters have almost no citations of volumes in languages other than English; if foreign-language studies are cited, reference is usually made to an English translation.[10] This, and the fact that the new portions of *JSI* are written in a more accessible and popular style than that used in *STJ*, lead one to suppose that Mathews is seeking a wider audience for *JSI* than he had done in 1897. *JSI* is addressed less to the exegete or theologian than to the ordinary Christian concerned to discover the social implications of the gospels—though, ironically, the 1897 work appears to have had much more popular influence than the 1928 one, which was largely overlooked.

THE BIBLICAL FOUNDATION:

Jesus and the Kingdom

Jesus and Revolutionary Messianism

The first three chapters of *JSI*, which replace *STJ*'s introductory chapter and those on man and society, present Mathews's revised biblical basis for Christian reformism. In these chapters Mathews's thesis is that Jesus "corrected" the dynamic idealism of his followers, most of whom were drawn from circles of revolutionary messianists in late Palestinian Judaism. Continuing to employ *STJ*'s liberal theological assumption that the gospel texts provide us with access to Jesus' inner life, Mathews argues that Jesus' experience of God as father acted as a "censor" of the revolutionary aspirations of his followers; when the revolutionary hope was refracted through the medium of Jesus' inner experience, it was "reshaped" or "sanctified."[11] Thus, the "timeless elements" or "timeless ideal" of Jesus' kingdom proclamation are not those that derive merely from the historical context of Jesus' ministry, or from his expectation of the imminent coming of the kingdom; rather, these elements—the belief that God is love and that love is a practicable basis for human society—must be extrapolated from their peculiar historical setting.[12] It is these, and not the historical accidentals in which they were clothed in Jesus' proclamation, that constitute his real legacy to Christianity, with his life and example as their ground.

As should be apparent, this line of argument develops Mathews's turn-of-the-century insight that the social psychological phenomenon of messianic expectation is the proper point of departure for interpreting Jesus and his teaching. Indeed, Mathews explicitly acknowledges the seminal importance of this insight in his preface to the 1928 study: he says that "this little book" is the outcome of his conviction (derived from his study of the French revolution) that the "study of Jesus as a factor in the development of civilization" must adopt a social psychological approach.[13] Consequently, as in *MHNT*, and building on his history of the revolution in France, in the first chapter of *JSI* Mathews centers his case around the claim that the "abiding significance" of Jesus was "determined" by the revolutionary messianism prevalent in the late Palestinian Jewish culture in which Jesus came to maturity:

> For without leading revolt, he was to live and teach
> in the atmosphere of revolution, use the language of
> revolution, make the revolutionary spirit the in-
> strument of his message, and organize a movement
> composed of men who awaited a divinely given new
> age. [14]

As this sentence suggests, in 1928 Mathews places greater emphasis than he had done in 1897 on the *revolutionary* implications of the messianic hope. Mathews urges that if one wishes to understand Jewish messianism, one must be a student of revolutions. As he notes, all revolutions spring from the same nexus of social concerns and discontent: class consciousness; a sense of political, economic, and social inequality; the desire for revenge; and enthusiasm for certain abstract ideals.[15] Such social factors were clearly present in the world into which Jesus was born, in Mathews's view.[16]

Mathews adds a next stage to his argument for interpreting Jesus' social significance via revolutionary messianism by maintaining that in late Palestinian Judaism the revolutionary hope had a "code-language," that of apocalyptic. Though apocalyptic literature was "deeply religious," it was as well, he thinks, political. Indeed, politics and not theology predominated in the apocalyptic outlook: apocalyptic is best characterized as a literary presentation of the "interplay of transcendental and political conceptions."[17] Clearly, this way of framing his argument is similar to the tactic he had employed in both *MHNT* and *GMM*; as in these studies, in accentuating the apocalyptic elements of Jesus' kingdom proclamation, Mathews is giving the social gospel foundation to consistent eschatology with one hand, while planning to pull it away with the other, as he argues that apocalyptic is a literary form in which a permanent and non-culturally determined message is encoded. Consequently, drawing on his argument for the social content of the kingdom hope in *GMM*, in *JSI* Mathews maintains that an underlying constituent meaning of Jewish apocalyptic was the hope for the establishment of a "social order in which God's will is perfectly done"—that is, the kingdom of God.[18] The kingdom expectation was not the hope for an etherealized heaven, but for a concrete kingdom.[19]

Though this statement would appear to indicate that the apocalyptic kingdom was merely a cultural phenomenon, a politically charged expectation that presupposed the cultural context of Jewish oppression by the Romans at the time of Jesus, in making the claim Mathews is actually inveighing against such a cultural definition of the kingdom proclamation. As he notes, even if the revolutionary messianism of Jesus' contemporaries was imbued with concrete, culturally determined political expectations, it nevertheless had an idealistic content separable from its cultural wrappings.[20] To say that the kingdom expectation was a hope for an earthly kingdom is implicitly to maintain that within messianism were "human values" that needed to be reinterpreted: "To accomplish this proved to be the task and opportunity of Jesus."[21] In a suggestive formula that runs through a number of Mathews's late works, Mathews concludes that in proclaiming the kingdom of God, Jesus became the leader of a "band of hope"—a hope for a new heaven *and* a new earth; a hope for a world transformed by his ministry and that of his followers.[22]

In speaking of Jesus as leader of a band of hope, Mathews intends to develop the revolutionary implications of messianism even further than he had done in previous writings. In contrast to the line of interpretation he had followed in *MHNT*, in which he had rather consistently downplayed the revolutionary implications of Jesus' kingdom proclamation even as he had set that proclamation against a revolutionary background, in *JSI* Mathews stresses that Jesus' ministry had strong revolutionary overtones. In chapter 2, he puts the point very sharply and precisely: he asserts that Jesus actually *joined* a group under the sway of a revolutionary psychology.[23] In Mathews's view, it would not be far from the mark to conclude that Jesus forged his own understanding of his messianic mission within a cultural context in which class strife predominated and fomented revolutionary discontent.[24]

Mathews applies the insight to John the Baptist, who, if the synoptic gospels are to be believed, had a seminal influence on Jesus's ministry: he supposes that John's followers came generally from the "crowds of the less privileged."[25] In Mathews's view the Baptist was thus the "center of a mass movement" that looked to divine deliverance as a means of righting social wrongs.[26] In saying this, Mathews is evidently attempting to build a hermeneutical bridge between John's revolutionary messianism and that of Jesus: by transferring the emphasis of revolutionary messianism from political rebellion to divine deliverance, even as he maintains the political basis of Jesus' ministry, Mathews is casting about for a definition of revolution that will allow Jesus' kingdom proclamation to have revolutionary meanings, without being explicitly revolutionary in intent (that is, in a political sense).

As he moves to this conclusion, Mathews adds another rung to the ladder of his argument by contending that, among all the revolutionary programs of the period, Jesus saw John's as "the expression of reality."[27] In joining John's movement, Jesus was so aware that he was associating himself with a revolutionary band, Mathews thinks, that he foresaw the price he would have to pay for taking such a step.[28] This claim provides a basis for Mathews's argument that Jesus assumed, then apotheosized, the revolutionary hope of his culture. If Jesus joined a group expecting revolution through the apocalyptic intervention of God, then he would naturally have drawn together disciples such as John himself had. Mathews assumes that Jesus' followers were primarily from the underprivileged classes—an assumption that on the face of it contradicts *STJ*'s assertion (reproduced in *JSI*'s chapter on Jesus' view of wealth) that "it is a mistake to think of early Christians as altogether from the poorest classes."[29] Indeed, Mathews appears so intent to stress the revolutionary aspect of Jesus' ministry that he characterizes Jesus, provocatively, as an "agitator," one who was the "center of popular agitation" and who deliberately employed tactics of "systematized propaganda."[30] He can even go so far as to say that the *ekklesia* itself had its origin in the revolutionary band that Jesus called together in imitation of John.[31]

Again and again, and far more emphatically than he had done in any of his previous social gospel foundational works, throughout *JSI* Mathews stresses Jesus' identification with the oppressed, the *am-ha-aretz*, the poor, the hungry, the weak, and the lowly. In short, he concludes, "Jesus is out of perspective when placed against any other background than this attitude [i.e., of identification with the oppressed]."[32] Jesus did not turn to the poor with "smug confidence in a prosperity-giving providence"; rather, he saw them as they saw themselves, and consequently he suffered the fate of the prophets.[33] Ultimately, in the death he died, Jesus was, Mathews thinks, a victim of the fear and resentments of the "privileged classes."[34]

This emphasis on the revolutionary associations of Jesus' ministry and in particular of his death is one that is characteristic of Mathews's writings on the life of Jesus in the 1920s and 1930s, after the turn to the eschatological kingdom had been consolidated in his early-twentieth-century works. The motif emerges as early as 1920 in the article "The Deity of Christ and Social Reconstruction." Here, a factor motivating the appearance of this stress in Mathews's theology seems to be his concern to defend the social gospel against the charge that it had made the gospel captive to culture. In response to such charges, in "Deity of Christ" Mathews accentuates the countercultural implications of Jesus' life and ministry by insisting that Jesus died the victim of those who wished to perpetuate their privilege at the expense of the underprivileged.[35] In one of those sometimes enchanting, sometimes maddening, jingoistic formulas that crop up at various places in his writings, Mathews caps this 1928 argument for the revolutionary meaning of Jesus' kingdom message by asserting that "he rebuked the classes, but he joined the masses." [36]

The same stress is found in a discussion of Jesus' ministry and death in the article "The Early Followers of Jesus and His 'Way'" (1926). Here, Mathews argues that Jesus preached to "eager, reckless, revolutionary masses," and, while he clearly discountenanced the particular political expectations of his hearers, he was put to death because his kingdom preaching and organization of a group of followers suggested to those in power "revolutionary developments." [37] The volume *Atonement and Social Process* (1930) continues the discussion by holding that Jesus' followers were "Jewish radicals" who were "full of the revolutionary spirit." [38] It was this radical spirit that dismayed those who sought to silence Jesus and dismantle the movement he had begun: those responsible for Jesus' execution were, in the view of *Atonement and Social Process*, "representatives of progress" dominated by the "will to command and the will to power." [39] The book encapsulates this political interpretation of the crucifixion of Jesus with a particularly fine statement of the significance of Jesus' death: "What it [i.e., the execution of Jesus] really sets forth is how a society bent upon maintaining privileges brings suffering to such of its individual members as question the permanence of the *status quo.*" [40]

A similar line of thought is to be found in Mathews's contribution to the AISL study pamphlet *Through Jesus to God* (1931). In his essay entitled "Jesus' Experience of God in His Contact with the Political Conditions of His People," Mathews obviously wishes to stress, against neo-orthodox critiques of the social gospel, that Jesus' death had a strong sociopolitical motivation and significance. Consequently, the essay reads the crucifixion as a demonstration that a simplistic love ethic that neglects the call for social justice is an inadequate foundation for building a really effective Christian social ethic. In the view of this essay, when one looks at Jesus on the cross, one must conclude that any attempt to implement Christian ideals in the social process demands sober realism. [41]

This train of thought culminates in an assertion of *Is God Emeritus?* (1940), which echoes Mathews's 1920 observation that, as a result of his empathetic identification with the "poor and outcast," Jesus died "a victim to the enmity of those who would perpetuate their privileges at the expense of the underprivileged." [42] In his theological swan-song, Mathews more strikingly accentuates the political motif in Jesus' life and ministry than he had done in any previous work: "He was poor, despised, forsaken. The common people, the poor, the criminal, were his followers. He spoke his blessing to the hungry, the sorrowful, the poor. He himself partook in the struggle of these depressed classes. He gave personal value to the despised masses. He took upon himself the form of a servant and died the death of a criminal."[43] Clearly, this is the conclusion toward which *JSI* itself is moving. This strong political interpretation of Jesus' death is one of the novel features of *JSI*, one that recapitulates an insistence that emerges in Mathews's thought in the 1920s, and prefigures strands of his later theology as he continues his dialogue with neo-orthodoxy to the end of his career. In accepting the eschatological reading of the kingdom, Mathews has moved to a basis for social gospel theology that can read the gospels from a sharper and more explicitly radical political standpoint than his 1897 foundation had permitted.

The Kingdom of God Revisited

To speak of Jesus' life and death in political terms is also inevitably to raise anew the question of the exegetical meaning of the kingdom. In *JSI* Mathews once again broaches this exegetical issue, but this time from a new angle of approach, that of Jesus' response to the revolutionary expectations of his hearers. In contrast to the stance he had taken in *STJ*, in *JSI* Mathews openly declares that, with his contemporaries, Jesus expected the establishment of the eschatological kingdom as a gift of God within his lifetime.[44] The sentence asserting this has a footnote that provides a virtual compendium of the authorities on which Mathews bases his revised exegetical foundation for social gospel theology: the note recommends *MHNT*, Schweitzer's *The Quest of the Historical Jesus*, and J. Weiss's *Predigt Jesu*.[45] If no other evidence were needed for deducing that *MHNT* represents a definitive turn to eschatological realism in Mathews's thought, the list of exegetical authorities cited alongside the 1905 work in this note would suffice. Moreover, capitulating even more decisively than he had done in 1905 to the eschatological interpretation of the kingdom, in *JSI* Mathews adds to his contention that Jesus expected the kingdom to come in his lifetime an important qualification, namely, that Jesus did not expect the kingdom to be brought in by human effort. God alone would establish God's reign at the end of history.[46]

If one grants this, one must also grant, Mathews thinks, that Jesus did not seek to *found* the kingdom, but rather to *prepare* men and women to enter it. *JSI* again explicitly repudiates the social interpretation of the kingdom, but with an interesting twist. Here,

Mathews contrasts Jesus' view of the kingdom as the eschatological gift of God with the view of those who promote reform programs in the expectation that these will yield utopian societies; in Mathews's view, among such utopian programs are ones promoted by those who subject the individual to society in the name of a higher good, or who subject the individual to the military establishment, or who establish industries in which profit is expected to generate a good society, even when no provision is made for the welfare of the worker.[47] What is wrong with such utopian schemes is what is wrong with the social interpretation of the kingdom: all seek to take short cuts to happiness that appeal particularly to the discontented who look for "romantic" solutions to their problems.[48] An eschatological reading of Jesus' kingdom proclamation prevents such utopian-romantic interpretations of the kingdom, Mathews suggests, because in pointing to a kingdom to be established by divine action at the end of history, it makes all historical developments provisional.

Thus, even though one may plead certain sayings of Jesus on behalf of a social interpretation of the kingdom (e.g., Mt. 13:33, Lk. 13:20–21 and 17:20, Mk. 4:26–29), a "fair interpretation" of these sayings "finds in them a reference not to progress but to eschatological outcome."[49] In *JSI* Mathews admits that *STJ* used these sayings to support a social interpretation of the kingdom, but he now holds flatly that such an interpretation is impossible to support exegetically.[50] However, employing the argument he had sketched in *MHNT*, he quickly adds that to discount the social interpretation of the kingdom is *not* to say that the teaching of Jesus is without pertinence for the social order:

> That a better social order will arise by the following of the teaching of Jesus is of course the point of my contention, but it is one thing to say that Jesus meant this when the term "kingdom of God" is used and another to say (more accurately) that social institutions will be improved as the human material that goes into them enables them to be improved.[51]

Since the eschatological turn is always in danger of undercutting interpretations of the kingdom that have social-ethical implications even when they are not social interpretations, in *JSI* as in *MHNT*, Mathews is eager to qualify his argument against the social reading of the kingdom by noting how the eschatological kingdom affects society. In 1928 he does so by building on his contention that Jesus' kingdom preaching employs concepts derived from revolutionary messianism. Mathews argues that even if Jesus did clearly share in his followers' expectations of the imminent arrival of the eschatological kingdom, he nonetheless "reshaped the revolutionary hopes in the crucible of his own individuality." [52] Jesus' relationship to revolutionary messianism was thus dialectic: not only was his understanding of the kingdom determined by the eschatological hope as it was found in the culture of his day, but Jesus also took the revolutionary hope and made it into something entirely new.

In *JSI* Mathews reinforces this thesis, which unmistakably harks back to *MHNT*, with an argument derived from *SIH*. He maintains that the individual is both determined by and an independent creative factor reacting on his or her environment.[53] Jesus was for Mathews one of those "creative spirits" of history who have the unique capacity to rise above the circumstances of their historical situation, and who thereby become makers of history.[54] Thus, though Jesus "shared in and started with" the revolutionary hopes of his followers, he also perceived and set forth the "true nature" of the kingdom hope—that is, that God is love, and love will ultimately triumph in human affairs.[55]

As in *GMM*, in *JSI* Mathews presents Jesus as a "type of the kingdom to be announced," "the embodiment of its true character," and "the revealer of the way by which it was to be entered." [56] This presentation of Jesus as a paradigm of the life of the kingdom depends on a presupposition Mathews had first articulated in *MHNT*, which is crucial to *JSI*'s thesis that Jesus reshaped the revolutionary hope. That is, Jesus' kingdom teachings were "the vocalizing of his experience." [57] Following the lead of liberal theologians of the nineteenth century who built their Christologies around assumptions about the inner life of Jesus, Mathews asks why Jesus stressed love of God as the true nature of the kingdom hope, and love of neighbor as a basis for society. He did so, Mathews argues, because his unique experience of God as father had enabled him to perceive the real significance of the revolutionary expectations of his followers: "All elements in the hopes of his times that were inconsistent with this filial experience he rejected." [58]

If love of God and neighbor constitutes the essence of Jesus' inner life and therefore of his kingdom proclamation, then we have strong warrant for concluding that the basic attitude Jesus sought to inculcate in his disciples was one of absolute faith in the goodwill of God.[59] Only on that basis could the kingdom come proleptically within them, and could the love it represented then manifest itself in social conditions. Jesus could urge his followers to develop such an attitude of total faith because this absolute faith in God's goodwill was "central in his own experience," [60] and therefore validated by his life and ministry. Mathews thus grounds his appeal to love as a practicable basis for the good society in the character of God, as revealed by the life and teaching of Jesus: "In the character of God lies the justification of goodwill and love on the part of those awaiting the kingdom." [61]

Obviously, this argument draws heavily on *GMM*'s insight that the historical Jesus is the constant focal point of the Christian movement, the reference point to which Christians throughout history must look as they seek to implement this movement's ideals in the social process. In *JSI* Mathews expresses the idea very succinctly: he argues that the "central principle" of the Christian movement is "that of loyalty to the ideals of its founder." [62] Saying this allows him to move even more decisively from the social gospel foundation he had established in 1897, in which the teachings of Jesus are central, and the social gospel is always susceptible to revision as exegetes deal with those teachings in new ways. To move away from such a teachings-centered foundation and to loyalty to Jesus as the biblical center of social gospel theology, in *JSI* Mathews maintains that the "real social influence" of Jesus does not lie in his teachings or sayings, but rather in those men and women who "endeavor to express in social relations and institutions the attitudes which he himself taught and embodied." [63]

What Mathews means when he speaks of the social influence of Jesus, embodied in those loyal to him, is even more evident in a subsequent striking formulation of the significance of the historical Jesus for the believer: namely, that "the one real Jesus is the Jesus *of* history and the Jesus *in* history. And he is more than the Jesus of the gospels." [64] To perceive the full import of this claim, one must give some attention to the fact that Mathews links the Jesus *of* history and the Jesus *in* history, the historical Jesus and the import that Jesus has had on generations of Christians. *JSI*'s linkage of the two does not introduce some novel element into Mathews's Christological thought; this linkage is characteristic of his thought about Jesus from very early in his career. In writings dealing explicitly with the place of the historical Jesus in the life of the believer, Mathews often equates the Jesus of history with the Jesus in history. He argues from the perceived effect of Jesus on men and women and social institutions throughout history, to the deduction that the historical Jesus was a revelation of the saving power of God in history. [65] The historical Jesus is for Mathews the Jesus who has had a transformative influence on the social process; when one traces the course of that influence backward in the social process to its originating point, one must conclude, Mathews believes, that in the man Jesus, God "actually entered human life as a Saviour." [66]

This social process argument for discovering in the historical Jesus the revelation of a God who has entered history salvifically, and whose saving presence in the process can be demonstrated by the effect of this presence over the course of history, predates Mathews's full-blown sociohistorical theological system. In the 1900 editorial "The Reality and Simplicity of Jesus," for example, he develops a thesis about the historical Jesus that clearly underlies what he has to say about the historical Jesus in *JSI*. Mathews maintains that, despite its insistence that Jesus was fully human, popular evangelical Christology is essentially docetic, in that it persistently refuses to allow him any true place in the great chain of cause and effect that makes humanity human. In Mathews's view, popular piety often views Jesus as an "extra-legal irruption into history." [67] In the docetic theology of many Christians, Jesus is "ex-territorialized from humanity," Mathews thinks. [68]

Implicit in Mathews's attempt to develop a process method for equating the Jesus of history with the Jesus in history is the assumption that the basic imperative of Christian discipleship is *imitatio Christi*. Mathews sees the believer as called within his or her discrete historical situation to imitate the Jesus who constantly remains the focal point of the Christian movement. Since the disciple lives in historical circumstances radically different from those of the master, such imitation can never take the form of slavish fidelity to Jesus' example. Rather, the disciple must seek to implement his attitudes, ideals, or "spirit" in the changing circumstances of history. Mathews develops such a notion of discipleship in the 1905 article "Imitation of Jesus," where he asserts that "to place Jesus in the world is to emphasize the freedom of his spirit. Paradoxical as it sounds, he who would be most like Jesus will be most unlike him." [69]

While the insight contained in these aphoristic formulations of the task of the disciple is by no means alien to *STJ*'s foundation for social gospel theology, it does advance on that foundation in one significant respect. Insofar as it explicitly departs from fidelity to the teaching of Jesus for loyalty to him as the center of a movement unfolding in always new ways over the course of history, it privileges continuous development and not repristination. As chapter 1 has noted, when Mathews comments on both *MHNT* and *GMM* in *NFO*, he observes that his early works presumed an indirect Ritschlianism, in which post–New Testament developments must always be checked against New Testament evidence, as if the New Testament is a norm against which all later developments are to be judged lacking. As he suggests, to use the Christian scriptures in this way is to imply that all development of doctrine or ecclesial structures represent a lapse from the presumably pristine origins of Christianity; to assume this is to diminish the significance of and necessity for development of Christian faith-expressions and institutions after the New Testament period.[70] In moving to a more tempered judgment about the value of post-New Testament development, the social gospel foundation of *JSI*, clearly incorporates the process theology of the post-*MHNT* period, which transfers the focus of social gospel theology from the social teachings of Jesus to Jesus in social process. As the 1928 study concludes, "[the historical Jesus] has been built into history as an influence rather than a biography."[71]

Since an obvious counter to this process reading of the historical Jesus is Schweitzer's objection that, expecting the *eschaton* in his lifetime, Jesus taught an ethic for those awaiting the imminent arrival of the kingdom, and not an ethic for later generations of Christians, *JSI* needs to supplement this process theology with an exegetical argument for the permanent validity of Jesus' kingdom message of love. It does so by implementing the biblical foundation established by *MHNT* and replicated in *GMM*. In *JSI*, Mathews reiterates the contention of both these studies that Jesus' ethical teaching is not entirely determined by the expectation of the arrival of the kingdom in his lifetime.[72] In Mathews's estimation, "we may, perhaps, find in his teaching interim *mores* but not an interim ideal."[73] Once again: in saying this Mathews thinks himself to be accepting the eschatological interpretation of the kingdom, without endorsing what he sees as an illicit attempt on the part of that interpretation to confine the significance of Jesus' kingdom proclamation to a culturally determined understanding of the kingdom that has no pertinence for Christians after the early New Testament period.

As in previous works dealing with this topic, in *JSI* Mathews builds into his social gospel foundation a fundamental distinction between interim *mores* in Jesus' teaching, and an ideal that transcends the historical context of the hope for the speedy establishment of the kingdom. The theme recurs in the study with a frequency which suggests that the desire to refute the *ad interim* thesis is one of the major underlying preoccupations of *JSI*. Against this thesis, Mathews argues strongly that the belief the kingdom would arrive in his lifetime was "not the cause of his [i.e., Jesus'] teaching that God is love and that love is a practicable basis upon which to build human life."[74] In fact, the effect of Jesus' expectation that the kingdom would come in his lifetime was precisely opposite to what

Schweitzer thinks, Mathews submits: insofar as the early Christian community awaited the end of time and found itself mistaken in its assumption that this end was near, it *had* to focus on the "timeless elements" of Jesus' teaching.[75] To have one's hopes shattered is not necessarily to abandon the message on which hope rested; it may be to sift that message to discover what has more lasting significance than that in which one fallaciously placed one's entire hope. The anticipation of Jesus and his first disciples that the arrival of the new age was imminent, then, was merely an aspect of the historical situation that conditioned but did not determine Jesus' basic kingdom message, in Mathews's view. In that announcement, "a timeless ideal was set forth as unaffected by time."[76]

Since the point was one obviously so central to the foundation of a social gospel theology under attack by neo-orthodox theology, in *JSI* Mathews further sharpens this distinction between the form of Jesus' kingdom proclamation (that is, the expectation of the *eschaton* in his lifetime) and its content (that is, the timeless ideal of love grounded in the character of God).[77] He proposes that Jesus' "indifference" to what he calls moral opportunism (that is, to specifying moral teaching for a particular historical situation) does indeed derive from his belief in the speedy coming of the kingdom; but (vs. Schweitzer) this indifference "unexpectedly" appears to be of tremendous importance to the contemporary believer. It is important in the following sense: because he believed that the kingdom would come imminently, not only was Jesus unconcerned about the specification of concrete ethical principles for such social institutions as marriage; but his ethical thought had another center entirely—this was an "absolute ideal," and it is toward that ideal and not to specific ethical goals that believers are to direct their lives of discipleship.[78]

In postulating such an interpretation of Jesus' interim ethic, Mathews has hit on what he thinks to be a clever exegetical ploy for distinguishing between the historical situation in which Jesus proclaimed the kingdom and the timeless ideal implicit in the kingdom proclamation. This ploy is obviously designed to reinforce his constant insistence, from *STJ* on, that Jesus' teaching does not contain a political or economic program. In *JSI*'s chapter on Jesus' attitude to wealth, Mathews adds to the text of *STJ* a consideration of the relationship between Jesus' attitude to wealth and the interim ethic. In this gloss on his original social gospel exegetical foundation, he maintains that if Jesus' ethical ideal is to have influence in the economic sphere, we must "eliminate" from his teaching elements that obviously derive from the expectation of the imminent arrival of the *eschaton*. These include the incitement of his followers to give away possessions as a prerequisite to entering the kingdom, and the command to sell what one has and give it to the poor. As in all his previous considerations of the topic, Mathews concludes that Jesus in fact had no economic philosophy or program.[79]

The disciple of Jesus who seeks, therefore, to apply Jesus' teachings to the social, economic, or political sphere must distinguish between Jesus' "central message" and the "occasional application" that Jesus made of his ideal in his particular historical circumstances.[80] Jesus' ideal was "unaffected and uncaused by his belief in the immediacy of the kingdom."[81] Far from intending to stipulate how his followers ought to implement his ideal, Jesus was actually concerned to describe "an absolute moral attitude as found in the will of God": "Facing eternity, he taught men to embody the basic character of God."[82]

As these observations indicate, in his 1928 revisions of *STJ*'s chapters on Jesus' "economic," "social," and "political" teaching, Mathews is intent to preserve *STJ*'s seminal insight that Jesus' social teaching is not some *reductio ad absurdum* of the gospel text— namely, a reduction to a literalism that keeps Christianity captive to socio-economic conditions it has long since outgrown. But he is intent to preserve this insight with a post-*MHNT* awareness that Jesus did not present his followers with a constitution for a social kingdom whose basic precepts they were to fill in as they followed him, as *STJ* had claimed. In his 1928 biblical foundation for social gospel theology, Mathews continues to be acutely and critically aware that another important move must take place in a social gospel exegesis that hopes to compel scholarly assent—a theological move away from kingdom language to some other theological language which recognizes that the kingdom is not evolving in history, even in the form of ideals implicit in the kingdom message. As at the end of *MHNT* and in subsequent works such as *GMM* and *SIH*, that theological language is process language.

THE THEOLOGICAL FOUNDATION:

Social Process

As one works one's way through his social process writings, one comes to the conclusion that in all Mathews wrote about social process, the theological "system" he developed was never rigid or fixed, but fluid. It tended to move in new directions as the focus of his theological attention shifted from one problem to another, one topic to the next. Indeed, to describe Mathews's social process thought as systematic is probably misleading. This thought proceeds from an unsystematized principle so inchoate, unformulated, and well-nigh unreflective in early North American sociology that it operates more as a guiding ideological principle of that early discipline, than as the starting point of a system of analysis. In the sociology of both Ward and Small, one finds a fundamental underlying assumption that is hardly ever treated as an object of sociological inquiry per se, but is simply taken for granted: this is that society evolves as does the natural world, and that social (and religious) institutions can contribute to the process of social evolution by bringing idealistic impulses to bear on the process. This assumption is the guiding insight of Mathews's social process thought as well, but it hardly ever receives explicit theoretical articulation *as a system* in his thought. The ways in which he "systematized" this insight varied widely throughout his theological career.

In *JSI*, for example, Mathews places far less emphasis than in works such as *GMM* and *SIH* on the role of Christian *ideals* in the social process. *JSI* prefers to speak rather of the germinative influence of Christian *attitudes* in social evolution. This transfer of emphasis from ideals to attitude is not without significance. Indeed, it is key to *JSI*'s shift from a social-teachings foundation for social gospel theology to a loyalty-to-Jesus foundation. To appreciate the point, one must bear in mind that social process is analogical language: it takes a metaphor from the realm of biological evolution and applies it to social phenomena. This metaphor enables one to conceive of social evolution in two different ways. On the one hand, one can speak of social institutions evolving *from* germinative principles; and on the other hand, one can emphasize that they evolve *to* telic points. As we have seen, Mathews's social process thought makes use of both schemata. He can at times speak of social evolution as the "working out" of germinative insights, attitudes, or ideals in history. Or, he can seek to justify Christian reformism by referring to Christian participation in the social movement as a "seeding" of the social process with Christian principles, principles that will work themselves out over the course of history and precipitate new structures and institutions.

Alternatively, Mathews often regards ideals as telic points toward which social evolution moves. As we have seen, this viewpoint runs through many of the early writings about social process, and is implicit in, though never made explicit by, *STJ*. A formula that appears frequently in early social process writings is that ideals "draw" the process to themselves. The article "The Spiritual Challenge to

Democracy" (1917) contains a particularly clear statement of this way of envisaging the role of ideals in the social process:

> For history is not composed of abstractions; it is made of the activities of men. Ideals work only as they draw to themselves and govern the practical efforts of concrete human lives in which they are embodied. Social evolution does not leap into Utopias. It must walk toward them. When in the progress of history ideals are partially embodied in human institutions which preserve the more spiritual values, their significance is to be judged by the general direction of social movements and by the power of men to protect their imperfectly idealistic achievements.[83]

The term "ideal" has a certain equivocalness in Mathews's social process thought, then. When he focuses on the *telos* of history, he sees the ideal as that toward which social evolution is moving. But when he thinks of the originating principles out of which social evolution moves, he can speak of the ideal as the "germ" that has vitalized the social process. The study *The Validity of American Ideals* (1922) captures the latter sense in a lucid formulation: it notes that ideals are "developed expressions of germinative hopes and faiths that gave our history inner self-direction."[84] It is perhaps not accidental that this statement occurs in one of those studies (akin to *SIH*) in which Mathews is seeking to validate the role of idealistic reformers in shaping the structures of society, in a period in which many influential Western thinkers felt betrayed by such idealism. Clearly, in speaking of ideals as the germ of the process, Mathews wants to emphasize that ideals must embody themselves in the activities of men and women, if they are to have any significance for the world here and now. As "The Spiritual Challenge to Democracy" insists, "Every ideal must work itself out through flesh and blood into social movements, institutions, and the organization of the interests and activities of real people."[85] The ideal as germ rather than as *telos* of history is something that must inevitably grow to a higher "biological" state in the evolutionary process of society.

This tangent of thought certainly gives rise to *JSI*'s transfer of emphasis from ideals to attitudes, from the social teaching of Jesus to loyalty to Jesus. Though *JSI* seldom speaks of ideals as the germinative principles of social evolution, in emphasizing the formative influence of Jesus on his disciples' attitudes, the 1928 study wants to say something very similar to what essays such as "The Spiritual Challenge of Democracy" say regarding ideals. It is because he wants to free Jesus' kingdom message to penetrate the social process in the lives of his disciples that Mathews shies away from the term "ideal." As in *STJ*, he paves the way for such an interpretation of Jesus' teaching by arguing that Jesus provided his disciples with no "social directions."[86] Rather, in all his teaching Jesus was primarily concerned to set forth "the quality of life which must be possessed by those who would enter the kingdom of God."[87] Consequently, those who turn to Jesus' teaching for specific directives will be disappointed—another move of *STJ* incorporated into the argument of *JSI*.

However—and here *JSI* begins to turn definitively from *STJ*'s implicit social process formulation of Jesus' teaching as ideals—in *JSI* Mathews's post-1905 awareness of the eschatological intent of Jesus' kingdom proclamation leads him, in his chapter on Jesus and the church, to argue that honesty compels us to admit that Jesus' teaching is "as yet impracticable" as a legislative direction for social life.[88] Though Christians may hope that "the kingdoms of this world may become the kingdoms of their God and of his Christ," such "myopic optimism" appears fatuous in light of what history has demonstrated the real nature of humanity to be.[89] Even if we could arrive at a *mishna* of Jesus' sayings, that *mishna* would be "far less practicable" than those of the rabbis, for "Jesus was a champion of an absolute timeless ideal."[90]

In formulating the kingdom proclamation of Jesus as a timeless ideal, Mathews is acutely aware that an eschatologically realistic social gospel theology must avoid a certain chasm that yawns between ideals and history. To speak of the timeless ideal of Jesus' kingdom teaching is to open the door to the dangerous inference that social gospel theology so removes the "ideals" of Jesus from history that they are extrinsic to the concerns of this world. It is precisely this suggestion that Mathews combats as he confronts the theology of the consistent eschatology school. If his statement that Jesus championed a timeless ideal is not to be read as an observation about the inapplicability of Jesus' teaching to the social process, then, he must find a way to speak of that teaching as the germinative principle of Christian reformist involvement *in* history, rather than an ideal to be attained only *at the end* of history. He finds this by speaking less of ideals and more of the attitudes that loyalty to Jesus produces in his followers.

As he argues, if we grant that Jesus was preoccupied with an absolute timeless ideal, it is fallacious to assume that Jesus had a political, economic, or social program. Thus, if one seeks the economic (or social, or political) pertinence of Jesus' teaching, one must not comb the gospels for maxims to apply to economic life: "The question . . . whether Jesus has any meaning for an economically developing social order is not to be answered by erecting epigrams into laws." [91] There is, in fact, "no more justification in making one saying of Jesus the center of a Christian legalism than another. . . . A saying of Jesus can be used safely only as it is interpreted as an epigrammatic emphasis of his fundamental position." [92] And what is this fundamental position? It is for Mathews that disciples of the coming kingdom must seek to embody in all their social relationships the attitude of love, or goodwill. [93]

In the final analysis, "it is his elevation of love that gives Jesus his place as a social teacher": this is the linchpin of Mathews's 1928 theological foundation for social gospel theology, and for his argument that the significance of Jesus to the social process lies less in ideals transmitted to his followers, than in the attitudes loyalty to him inculcates in them throughout history. [94] Mathews seeks to justify this fundamental tenet of his revised foundation by maintaining that attitudes *derive* from ideals: "An attitude as distinguished from an ideal belongs in the realm of motive and mind-sets rather than in the realm of specific duties. One discovers his attitude by facing some task or ideal or goal." [95] In arguing that, under the influence of his expectation of the immediate arrival of the eschatological kingdom, Jesus focused constantly on the absolute ideal of the love or goodwill of God, and in viewing attitudes as attempts to embody absolute ideals in historical circumstances, Mathews stands the Schweitzerian *ad interim* thesis on its head. He does so by regarding all Jesus' social teaching as, at base, the injunction to embody those transformative social attitudes that spring from a focus on the absolute ideal of the character of God.

Mathews's continuing and predominant intent in *JSI* (as in *MHNT* and *GMM*) to move beyond the ideal-historical quandary that consistent eschatology appeared to pose for social gospel theology is further evident in a passage glossing the preceding one, in which he observes that,

> [t]o unify action in accordance with an ideal that is social, and to develop the attitude of response to the ideal which shall remain constant and unifying in the midst of the variety of life, is the center of Jesus' method of teaching. His ideal is the character of God as Father; his dominant attitude is goodwill or love. [96]

Mathews has something quite specific in mind as he further specifies the distinction between ideals and attitudes in this passage, and as he relates this distinction to Jesus' teaching. What he has in mind is the question that had vexed him from the beginning of his theological career and had been central to his concern in *STJ*, namely, in what sense is it possible for social gospel theology to call Jesus a social reformer? As the preceding passage suggests, the turn to eschatological realism incorporated by *JSI* permits him to approach the problem quite differently than in 1897.

In 1928, Mathews grants that Jesus' thought was dominated by the absolute ideal of the character of God. Since this was the case, to regard Jesus as a social reformer or social legislator is to misperceive his significance: "He was not concerned with telling people how to proceed toward an ideal; he set forth in unqualified fashion the quality of life which the ideal demanded." [97] If the kingdom of God is an absolute ideal, one rooted in the character of God as the absolute goal toward which Christian life moves, then the attitude of goodwill is also absolute. Indeed, in partaking of the kingdom ideal, goodwill is not only an attitude, but is itself an ideal: "The goodwill of God is not to be identified with social evolution, but is an absolute ideal." [98] For *JSI*, the kingdom is the absolute goal of social evolution, which can never be perfectly realized in any Christian attitudes over the course of history: just as circles and hyperbolae are only approximate illustrations of absolute figures that the geometrician can describe in theory, so "human conduct is only an imperfect embodiment of the absolute ideal. Its value is determined by the approach which it makes to that ideal." [99]

Even if one *can* isolate in the gospel text specific social teachings regarding life in the kingdom, then, these ought not to be regarded as "forecasts of a social process," but rather as "the expression of what would be true in case the attitude of love were realized." [100] As is evident, in his 1928 work, Mathews employs his post-1905 recognition of the eschatological nature of the kingdom as a safeguard against the identification of particular cultural developments with the absolute will of God. [101] In fact, his distinction between the character of God as the absolute ideal of Christian discipleship and those historically conditioned attitudes by which the disciple tries to embody that character, allows him to make the point even more carefully than he had done in his previous process theology works. In *JSI*, Mathews clearly intends to expunge from the social gospel any assumption that the specific reform program Christians enact as they seek to realize the character of God in their attitudes *is* the kingdom of God, the absolute ideal toward which

historical developments move. To speak of Jesus' teaching as elic-
iting attitudes is, for Mathews, to speak of attitudes that always
move toward a goal which they never perfectly attain.

However, to grant the provisionality of all attempts of Christians
to move toward the *telos* of history is not to concede that the kingdom is void of social content. As we have seen, throughout *JSI* Mathews is keenly concerned to relate the absolute goal of history to the
historical process by insisting that the ideal kingdom reaches back
into history via the attitudes of Jesus' disciples. Thus, as he argues
against the equation of any historical structure with the eschatological kingdom, Mathews also maintains that the attitude of goodwill which Jesus enjoined his followers to adopt has a social content. This insistence on the social content of goodwill clearly builds
on *GMM*'s notion that the kingdom hope is both eschatological and
full of social import. This argument is basic to the social gospel foundation constructed by *JSI*, and is in evidence throughout the work—
as, for instance, when Mathews contends that Jesus' teaching is a
refinement of the dynamic idealism inherent in revolutionary messianism. When he makes this claim, he urges that, though Jesus did
not delineate a set of social obligations for his followers, his subli-
mation of the revolutionary hope nonetheless has social implications, for "he transformed the revolutionary spirit into a new moral
attitude pregnant with social implications."[102]

JSI continuously reinforces the social implications of Jesus'
teaching by insisting that social institutions may invariably be traced
to attitudes. Attitudes are the germinative principles from which all
social development proceeds; as they work themselves out through
human activity in the social process, institutions result. *JSI*'s chapter on Jesus' social attitudes puts the point this way: in evoking a
social attitude in his followers, Jesus was laying a foundation for social institutions, "for they are the all but inevitable precipitate of
attitudes."[103] As should be apparent, this strategy to salvage the social significance of the eschatological kingdom after one has granted
that Jesus never thought of the kingdom as this-worldly presumes the
insight of *MHNT* that, while eschatological expectation inhibited
Christian social developments, the new life of the primitive Christian community nonetheless immediately reacted on its social environment to produce new social institutions.

In *JSI*'s chapter on Jesus on social attitudes, Mathews applies to
the love ethic the notion that social attitudes give rise to social institutions. He argues that "love as Jesus sets it forth may . . . be described as an urge to social cooperation in which the cooperating par-
ties treat each other as persons."[104] Furthermore, Mathews thinks,

when this urge to social cooperation expresses itself in human actions, institutions are born, in a process analogous to that by which attitudes produce social realities:

> But when men undertake to express the attitude of coordination in group action social institutions emerge, for institutions are one of the means which preserve and socialize attitudes. By them values are passed on from generation to generation. They are indispensable in proportion as they enable group action to favor the personal worth of individuals.[105]

For Mathews, in the last analysis, love *is* an attitude; as do other attitudes, it enfleshes itself in the social process. As with other attitudes, "love must beget institutions of social value."[106]

This linking of the love ethic to other social attitudes provides Mathews with yet another process argument for the tentativeness of all social institutions short of the eschatological kingdom. Noting that "the attitudes which an institution organizes and preserves precede the institution itself," Mathews asserts that one may ascertain the value of a given institution by considering the extent to which it preserves attitudes that foster personal values in the midst of an ever more complicated social order.[107] In saying this, Mathews is implying that from a process perspective, an attitude such as love continuously precedes every attempt to realize it in institutional structures: no institutional attempt to embody love ever exhausts the content of the love ethic. In Mathews's view, institutions must be perpetually restructured not only in light of the eschatological proviso that the kingdom of God presents to history, but also in light of the Christian love ethic.

Conversely, the love ethic does not dictate the particular forms that an institution or social structure must develop or employ as it seeks to realize the attitude of love. Thus,

> The attitude of goodwill, upon which he [i.e., the believer] relies because of its accord with the goodwill of God, will find different expressions in different economic situations. . . . Its expression will differ in accordance with men's perception of particular needs.[108]

JSI develops this notion that the love ethic does not include particular directives for its realization by distinguishing between the *attitude* of love and the *technique* by which love is applied. In the chapter on Jesus and the church, for example, Mathews observes that "sooner or later goodwill becomes a problem of social technique, and such technique is a matter of science rather than motive." [109] The transfer of emphasis this statement assumes—from motive to science—assumes that mere goodwill is not enough to create effective social reform. What is needed as well is technique. That is, truly viable reform of society cannot prescind from such "scientific" considerations as whether a proposed reform will be workable and produce desirable results. At this point, Mathews's thought clearly remains in continuity with the sociology of Small, but in an eschatologically realistic way not in evidence in *STJ*. In *JSI*, the reformer needs to engage in scientific analysis of society precisely because no attempt to realize the love ethic will ever be automatically successful.

The discussion of the Christian approach to war, in the chapter on the state which, as indicated previously, adds new material to the text drawn from *STJ*, provides a telling case study of what Mathews means when he asserts that goodwill sooner or later becomes a problem of social technique. In this section of *JSI*, as he notes that the supreme duty of humanity is from a Christian standpoint to embody the principle of love in social groupings, Mathews argues that the motives and attitudes that a Christian derives from his or her experience of discipleship must be normative in the political realm as in all other social groupings. [110] Yet he grants that moving from such a general and absolute principle to specific applications is never simple or automatic—and this is particularly the case when the principle of love is applied to the problem of war. [111]

Drawing on insights he had developed in his reflections on this topic in the World War I period, Mathews characterizes pacifism as an attempt to apply "the absolute ideal of Jesus" to human affairs, an attempt that overlooks the necessity for adaptation of this absolute ideal to particular circumstances. [112] It is at this point in the text that Mathews presses the argument mentioned above, that there is no more justification for raising one saying of Jesus (e.g., the injunction to turn the other cheek or not to resist evil) to the center of a "Christian legalism" than another (e.g., the encouragement of the disciples to buy swords [Lk. 22:35–38]). [113]

More explicitly than he had done in those World War I writings tinged with war hysteria, in *JSI* Mathews grants that beyond question "war as an institution is opposed to the spirit of Jesus." [114] Yet, on the other hand, he continues to want to maintain regarding violence that "the attitude of goodwill does not determine the technique by which goodwill must be expressed." [115] Though in his view the ultimate goal of any reform movement that seeks to address this issue from the Christian standpoint must be to "Christianize" politics (and thus abolish war), when faced with a concrete decision about a particular war, the believer must consider whether the good possibly to be attained by the war appears to outweigh the evil of engaging in violence. The application of the absolute ideal of Jesus to the specific circumstances of a historical situation of conflict thus demands "an intelligent balancing of possible goods."[116] As Kenneth Cauthen's introduction to the 1970 edition of *JSI* points out, without using the precise terminology of the classic just-war theory, Mathews's argument here closely parallels this theory.[117]

JSI's consideration of the ethical problems posed by war highlights how the 1928 study is both in continuity and discontinuity with *STJ*'s foundational theology. Because the 1897 work sought to build a social gospel theology around the social teaching of Jesus, and in particular around the kingdom of God evolving in history, it could not come to such a precise formulation of the relationship between gospel texts (and the ideals they enshrine) and particular social issues. Though Mathews was indeed critically aware in *STJ* that neither scriptural verses nor Christian ideals automatically yield reform programs (it was that assumption in Herron's theology that he wished to overturn in his own social gospel foundation), his fixation on the social kingdom prevented him from seeing as clearly as he would later that every attempt of Christians to Christianize the social process is fraught with irony and effects that often betray the very ideals Christians think themselves to be serving.

The turn to the eschatological reading of the kingdom, and the subsequent development of an explicit social process theology, allows *JSI* to move social gospel analysis of the relationship between Christian idealism and particular historical problems in a new and fruitful direction. In the 1928 work, Mathews remains in continuity with *STJ* as he combats the notion that the scriptures mechanically produce reform programs. But he does so with the added assumption that the gospels do not ineluctably create viable Christian reform programs, because all such programs are provisional and imperfect attempts to realize ideals that move ahead of social development, and of the kingdom that will not come until history's completion. As the preceding discussion of war indicates, this assumption allows *JSI* to continue *STJ*'s insistence that Christian idealism *is* a sound basis for social gospel theology, while simultaneously rejecting any idealism that naively presumes to know what is *the* "Christian" agenda for society. Mathews's second foundation for social gospel theology echoes his social process theological works as it undercuts any attempt to identify a particular cultural development with the will of God, as though the Christian reformer has direct access to God's will in scripture or anywhere else.

JSI AS A SOCIAL GOSPEL

FOUNDATIONAL STATEMENT:

An Assessment

As our examination of *JSI* indicates, in Mathews's 1928 revision of his first foundation for social gospel theology, a significant transfer of emphasis occurs—one reflecting important aspects of his thought about the foundational question in the intervening period. In 1897, Mathews urged that, since there are numerous points of contact between the kingdom unfolding within history and the evolution of society, Christians may validly make common cause with secular social reformers. But the 1897–1905 turn to eschatological realism undercuts such an appeal to the social interpretation of the kingdom, and calls for a new basis for social gospel theology. *JSI* creates that basis by incorporating into the foundation of social gospel theology the eschatological realism of works such as *MHNT,* and the subsequent genetically related social process theology of studies such as *GMM* and *SIH.*

For *JSI,* the kingdom of God is removed from the center of social gospel theology's stage. Where *STJ* focuses social gospel theology on the this-worldly growth of the kingdom of God, *JSI* concentrates instead on the germinative influence of Christian attitudes on the social process. These attitudes spring from the constant encounter of the believing community throughout history with the Jesus of history and in history. In this encounter, Christians imbibe the central ideal of conformity to the character of God that Jesus himself promoted and by which he lived and shaped his attitudes. Above all, the social gospel consists of the implementation in social situations of that love which was preeminent in Jesus' own understanding of God and of moral obligation.

Since *JSI* makes the love ethic central to its argument for a revised social gospel theological foundation, theological assessment of the study must inevitably examine its use of the love ethic. This focus will broach entirely different critical questions than those we raised about *STJ.* Because the kingdom symbol predominates in Mathews's initial foundational statement of social gospel theology, our critical concern there had necessarily to engage critiques of social gospel theology that charge the movement with misunderstanding and misusing the kingdom of God concept. But that critique hardly extends to *JSI*. With regard to the 1928 work, one may perhaps quibble about whether Mathews turns eschatology into what it was never intended to be, into an essence void of cultural references and adapted to a cultural Christianity. But, even if one finds his interpretation of eschatology in *JSI* unsatisfactory (a question I shall consider in detail in the following chapter), one must also grant that in his theology after 1903 Mathews *intends* to accept eschatology and to find in it a basis for a countercultural reading of the gospel.

Critical assessments of *JSI* must deal with an entirely different critique of social gospel theology. This is the claim that the social gospel speaks of love to the exclusion of justice. Critics who follow this line of attack maintain that the social gospel use of the love ethic neglects the demands of justice, and in doing so, provides an ideological gloss for structural injustices that do not yield to vaporous sentiments of goodwill, but require structural change. The critical question that must be asked above all about the foundational theology of *JSI* is this, then: when Mathews enshrines love as the center of the social gospel theology of *JSI*, when he claims that "it is his elevation of love that gives Jesus his place as a social teacher," is he guilty of such ideological use of the love ethic? To put the point differently, in terms of the broad sweep of Mathews's thought after *STJ*, is the social gospel foundation of *JSI* as indebted to liberal theology as that of *STJ*? Does the turn to eschatological realism and social process theology in Mathews's thought after 1897 really do anything different to his social gospel foundation? Or does the substantial textual continuity to be found between *STJ* and *JSI* suggest that, after all, *JSI* merely adds a soupçon of eschatological spice to an otherwise unaltered social gospel theology originally offered in *STJ*?

Implicit in critiques of the social gospel's love ethic is the suspicion that this theology speaks of love in such airy ways as to remove love from the real world, or as to imply that love automatically and rather magically creates social change, in the absence of rigorous analysis of social conditions and the structural causes of social problems. If this is the central objection to the social gospel's appeal to love, then one can respond immediately to this critique by noting that Mathews's use of the love ethic in *JSI* is far more complex and nuanced than such critiques imply was the case in social gospel theology. In *JSI* "love" is a blanket concept that refers both to an attitude or affect driving the social reformer, and to a set of second-level decisions about how best to implement the attitude of love in given concrete situations. Mathews argues that love has a social content, and that the attitude of love must be distinguished from the technique by which love is enacted in a given situation. When these insights are applied to the question of war, the qualified and postliberal nature of Mathews's love ethic is striking. It would not be far from the mark to say that Mathews's insistence on applying love in historical circumstances, and on analyzing social problems and deciding on proper technique as one does so, stretches the love ethic to include the demands of justice.

Such a stretching of the love ethic is hardly unique to *JSI*. It is a leading feature of many of Mathews's later works. In studies such as *Christianity and Social Process* and *Creative Christianity*, he explicitly broadens the love ethic to allow consideration of matters that ought perhaps properly to be treated under the rubric of justice. In the former work, for example, Mathews notes that his previous books too often assumed that the individual who acts singly and under the impulse of love can effectively change society. In his view, the socioeconomic and political realities of the Western world after World War I expose the fallacy of such a "Christian individualism," and, implicitly, of a naive love ethic. In *Christianity and Social Process*, Mathews expands the love-centered social gospel analysis of his previous work by treating the issue of group (as distinguished from individual) morality—an issue that clearly raises the question of the relationship between love and justice.[118]

The 1934 volume argues that moral precepts such as the Golden Rule apply equally to individuals and to groups, including nations. Mathews builds the argument by insisting that attitudes are to be distinguished from techniques. If one uses this distinction to approach the problem of whether a society can be expected to be loving, one can justifiably apply the love ethic to groups as well as individuals, because love is always an ideal, rather than a technique by which that ideal is to be applied. A love ethic analysis of the ethical situation of a corporate entity such as a nation thus implies structural analysis that raises questions of justice; in asking how we may "use" love via various reform techniques, we are also asking what is the just thing to do in this situation.[119] In pressing this argument for the viability of the social gospel's love ethic as applied to society, and in stretching this ethic to include justice, Mathews is patently responding to Niebuhr's critique of the love ethic in his *Moral Man and Immoral Society*.[120] Though he wishes to salvage the love ethic in face of Niebuhr's critique, he also accepts some of the premises of Niebuhr's argument—in particular, the contention that it is utterly naive for Christian reformers to think love will automatically yield structural changes that can more effectively be realized through attempts to seek justice.[121] In addition, Mathews argues that love is a practicable basis for society; such an argument is very characteristic of Mathews's later work, and derives from the defense of the social gospel against neo-orthodox critique.

In *Christianity and Social Process*, Mathews applies the preceding argument in a novel way to the doctrine of the atonement. In particular, he argues against the moral influence theory of the atonement on the grounds that this theory is "sentimental" and does not adequately coordinate God's love with God's justice. Once again, here Mathews telescopes justice into love, by maintaining that, while the love of God is the indispensable center of all Christian doctrines of the atonement, love is more than sentimentalized goodwill. In his view, love (including the love of God) always implies "action looking toward the welfare of others." [122] If one reads this critique of the moral influence theory in light of *JSI*'s defense of the love ethic (which *Christianity and Social Process* explicitly echoes) and of both studies' attempt to expand this ethic by resorting to the distinction between attitudes and technique, the clear implication of Mathews's evaluation of the moral influence understanding of the atonement is that, properly understood, love *includes* the demands of justice.

Creative Christianity stretches the love ethic to its breaking point. In this study, Mathews argues (rather oxymoronically) that the love ethic permits even hatred, albeit a sublimated hatred that seeks to channel its dark energies in constructive directions.[123] As may be evident, this contention dovetails with the pragmatist justifications of World War I by both Mathews (and John Dewey) examined in chapter 1. In doing so, it raises disquieting questions about the later Mathews's appeal to the love ethic, and in particular about the foundation for social gospel theology developed by *JSI*.

If the love ethic can be pushed to such a limit, is it in the final analysis the most effective way to speak about Christian ethical response to social institutions? Even when Mathews subsumes justice concerns under the category of love, does he neglect to face adequately the radical demands that justice makes on the structures of any society; does he fail to understand that rhetoric about Christian love can mask Christian indifference to the clamor for justice on the part of those whose lives the socioeconomic or political structures of a society impact unjustly?[124] In my view, these questions must be answered affirmatively. The later Mathews's stretching of the love ethic reveals a fundamental weakness in the social gospel's use of the love ethic. Mathews's later theology (including *JSI*) would have benefited from a more careful consideration of the theme of justice, as a balance to its preponderant concern with love. If love cannot answer all questions about what constitutes ethical behavior in a given situation—as Mathews himself admits—then a balanced Christian social ethic needs another category of analysis to answer those questions. Though nuanced, Mathews's love ethic needs the category of justice as a foil.

But any assessment of the social gospel foundational theology of *JSI* that ends on this critical note would be unbalanced. Mathews's 1928 life of Jesus does indeed make an important positive contribution to social gospel theology, and this contribution is most evident when one compares the foundational theology developed by the 1897 and 1928 lives of Jesus, in light of the unfolding of Mathews's thought in the years intervening between these two works. When one makes such a comparison, one discovers that *JSI* teases out of *STJ* themes that were implicit in but undeveloped by the first foundational statement, that emerged in Mathews's theology soon after *STJ*, and that place social gospel theology on a very different footing than the 1897 life of Jesus had.

Throughout the preceding chapter, I argued that the turn to eschatological realism after 1897 and the adoption of a social process framework for doing theology revise very significantly how Mathews views the relationship between the New Testament and contemporary Christians. We have seen how both turns are implicit in *STJ*'s theology and how they became explicit in works subsequent to *STJ*. We have carefully tracked the development of Mathews's thought about both the eschatological kingdom of God and social process in these studies, and have seen how *JSI* incorporates the various facets of Mathews's theology from 1897 to 1928. Such a microscopic examination of the development of Mathews's thought between the two lives of Jesus is necessary, if we are to discover precisely how the second life advances on the first. But it also presents a certain danger, that of becoming so involved in the details of Mathews's reflections about eschatology or social process that we cannot glimpse the larger picture, the fundamental significance of the turns his social gospel theology of 1928 incorporates. In order to see that significance, we have to step back somewhat and try to see how *JSI* revises *STJ* at a *fundamental* level, and not in this detail or that.

For one who seeks to apply such a large perspective to the sweep of Mathews's thought over the course of his career, his intellectual autobiography is an invaluable aid. In an illuminating passage, *NFO* comments on Mathews's work from the late nineteenth century to 1936. The passage reveals much about how he considered late works such as *JSI* to have critiqued and surpassed the theology of early studies such as *STJ*. It notes that Mathews's immature theology failed to perceive the social significance of the historical development of Christianity, as distinct from New Testament literature. He attributes his shortsightedness in this regard to the Rankean view of history his early works adopt: these studies see history as "a presentation of facts." [125]

As he says this, he also observes in passing that *MHNT* was the first of his studies to recognize that the thought of Jesus and the apostles presupposed the Jewish cultural context in which they lived; yet he thinks his 1905 volume failed to work out the full implications of this historical insight. Even after he was transferred from the Divinity School's New Testament department to its theology department in 1906, he still employed a method of "indirect" Ritschlianism which assumed that theology ought to extract from the New Testament the "content of the gospel," and then translate that content into contemporary terms. What such a method lacked was an appreciation for the development of Christian thought from the New Testament period to the present, an appreciation for Christianity itself as a religious movement embodying the fundamental affirmations of Christian faith as the church grew within the social process of Western culture.[126]

In Mathews's judgment, *GMM* continued to employ such a perspective of indirect Ritschlianism, so that the "total effect" of the 1910 study was to provide a "restatement of evangelicalism as if there had not been any contribution to Christianity from the days of the New Testament." [127] When one reads this statement with the two lives of Jesus in mind, an elemental recognition of great importance regarding Mathews's social gospel theology leaps out. This is that Mathews sees his later work (e.g., *JSI*) as having advanced on his earlier (e.g., *STJ*) in one crucial respect—in how it treats the relationship between the foundational testimony of the New Testament and all that developed from that foundational testimony. Or, to put the point in terms of Loisy's important Roman Catholic modernist critique of Harnack's liberal Protestant theology: Mathews thinks that his theology after *GMM* envisages the relationship between the Christian church and Jesus' proclamation of the kingdom of God in entirely different terms—in precisely *postliberal* terms—than from those his earlier theology had employed. His fledgling theology ties the church to the New Testament in a way that implicitly makes all post-New Testament development secondary to the New Testament itself. But the social process perspective incorporated by his mature thought enables him to valorize the constant development of Christian faith, even when that development does not replicate New Testament structures or norms.

This insight opens up the *fundamental significance* of the shift in Mathews's theology between 1897 and 1928. As *NFO* suggests, Mathews clearly understood the two social gospel foundations to depend on different theological understandings of history. Whereas *STJ* sees history as "a presentation of facts," and the gospel as an irreducible "content" to be communicated to the contemporary church and world in thought categories drawn from that world, *JSI* accents constant historical development, and sees the believer as living within a "Christian" social process that unfolds simultaneously with and in ongoing relation to the broader social process. The two visions of history and the relationship of the believer to history are not antithetical. But they involve very different allocations of emphasis that have markedly divergent theological implications.

If one asks about the fundamental meaning of the shift in Mathews's social gospel thought from *STJ* to *JSI* after examining *NFO*'s discussion of the different understandings of history employed by Mathews's early and late works, one must conclude that the social gospel foundational theology proposed by *JSI* advances on that of *STJ* (precisely in this regard: to an extent surpassing the 1897 study, the 1928 life of Jesus places the socially engaged believer *within history*. For a social gospel theology that adopts the theological perspective of *JSI*, an important theological door forever closes: no longer can Christian reformers look back to the New Testament for some pristine mandate for Christian activism that is to be translated into contemporary terms and enacted in the contemporary world; no longer can they live outside history as those who have answers exceeding answers offered by history itself to secular reformers. In *JSI*, social gospellers are within history and the process of history *with* these reformers; in their struggle to be loyal to Jesus, they seek to understand the vagaries of history just as earnestly as do those who come to social reform with other loyalties.

The re-accenting of social gospel theology represented by this retrieval of the category of historical development, with its reappraisal of all post–New Testament Christian development, uncannily echoes the insights of Loisy. As we have seen, Mathews's colleague G. B. Smith recognizes that there are affinities between Mathews's theology and that of Loisy. As he notes these affinities, Smith also critiques *GMM* by focusing on the shortcomings of its Ritschlian use of the New Testament to invalidate all subsequent theological development, and encourages Mathews to pay closer attention to the developmental theology of theologians such as Loisy. The parallels between Smith's critique of *GMM* (and, implicitly, of all Mathews's early theology) and *NFO*'s are striking. What is to be made of Mathews's own recognition that his theology underwent a major shift after *GMM*, as he developed his social process theology—a shift that exactly parallels the turn Smith calls for in Mathews's theology? What are we to make of this shift from a Ritschlian base for social gospel theology to a modernist one?

If *STJ* is a foundational statement of social gospel theology that emphasizes themes central to some branches of liberal Protestant theology at the end of the nineteenth century, *JSI* is one that appropriates insights akin to those of European modernist theology in critical response to such liberal theology. Since this is the case, and one can show that it is through a painstaking examination of Mathews's work from *STJ* to *JSI*, one must conclude the following about Mathews's search for a theological foundation for social gospel theology: to limit one's analysis of this search to a discussion of its relationship to liberal Protestant theology (as critics of the social gospel have tended to do) narrows one's optic in a way that prohibits one's seeing important and neglected parallels between social gospel theology and *postliberal* theology.

In particular, if one adopts a polemical hermeneutic that seeks to collapse social gospel theology into the liberal project, one ignores the development of that theology toward a quite different theological future, the future opened for Christian theology by those who responded dialectically to liberal theology. The social gospel theology of Shailer Mathews indubitably mirrors nineteenth-century liberal theology. But it also incontrovertibly looks ahead to twentieth-century European Roman Catholic modernist theology, and through the eschatological turn made by modernist theology, to political and liberation theologies later in the century. If Mathews's theology, and that of other social gospellers, have any compelling pertinence for theologians today, that pertinence lies not in the ways in which social gospel theology reflects liberal theology, but in how it prefigures political and liberation theology. It is to this still unexplored, but promising, field of inquiry that future research into social gospel theology needs to direct itself.

AFTERWORD

THE SOCIAL GOSPEL'S

CONTINUING PERTINENCE

The social gospel, which powerfully shaped North American Christian thought in the latter half of the nineteenth century and the first part of the twentieth, and still moves like a subterraneous stream through the repressed memories of American theology: what is one to make of this diffuse, exuberant, at times naive and at other times remarkably prescient, theological movement? If the case of Shailer Mathews suggests anything, it suggests that social gospel theology continues to be pertinent, worthy of retrieval.

This is not to say that *all* social gospel theology is retrievable. As Roger Haight has noted, even for those who see continuing pertinence in it, the social gospel movement is an unrepeatable moment in American religious history.[1] The cultural and theological circumstances in which this movement came to life no longer exist. Some aspects of its thought are clearly dated. The innocence that permitted Americans to presume that history was marching ineluctably toward a North American democratic utopia has been irretrievably shattered first by the war to end all wars, and then later in the century by another world war, followed by the watershed events of the

civil rights movement and the Vietnam War.[2] It was American innocence that allowed social gospellers, in their unguarded moments,
to speak so confidently about progress, and to believe that the kingdom of God was being built in this world, as Western culture moved
in "progressive" directions. To the extent that social gospel theology enfolds nineteenth-century liberal optimism and belief in progress,
it is a dated phenomenon, and can have no more than historical interest for Christian theologians of the latter half of the twentieth
century.

But, as our close reading of Mathews's attempt to find an eschatologically realistic foundation for social gospel theology has
demonstrated, stories about social gospel liberalism and progressivism are not the whole story. In several important respects, Mathews's social gospel theology prefigured key developments of Christian theology later in the century. As does Rauschenbusch's,
Mathews's theology breaks the mold of individualism that had contained (and constrained) Christian theology, and in particular its soteriological outlook, for some centuries prior to the social gospel
period.[3]

As we have seen, Mathews thinks that, from the time of the
confessional statements of the sixteenth century up to the twentieth,
the soteriology of Protestant orthodoxy was overwhelmingly individualistic. He argues that a significant consequence of the rise of
sociology as an academic discipline and of Christian theologians'
adoption of tools of social analysis has been to correct the individualistic anthropology underlying this soteriology. Sociology teaches
theologians to see the human being as a *social* being, one shaped in
manifold ways by his or her social environment. The sociological
perspective enables one to see that, in order to speak effectively of the
salvation of individuals, one must also speak of salvation of the social environment of individuals. This insight paves the way for another: sin can make its home not only in the hearts of individuals, but
in social structures as well. The doctrine of social sin, which finds its
most eloquent expression in Rauschenbusch's notion of the kingdom of evil, is an outstanding contribution of the social gospel movement to Christian theology as a whole—one whose implications are
still being explored by theologians.

Though Mathews does not speak so clearly or so often about
social sin as Rauschenbusch does, his socio-historical theology adds
something of consequence to the discussion. This is an analysis of the
reasons for the persistence of individualistic preoccupations in Christian theology long after the cultural conditions that gave rise to six-
teenth-century confessionalism have disappeared. This analysis oc-

curs chiefly in the article "Theology and the Social Mind," but is echoed elsewhere in Mathews's writings.

As we have noted, in his classic 1915 article Mathews identifies six creative social minds in the history of Western Christianity: Semitic and Hellenistic monarchial, imperialistic, feudal, national, and bourgeois. In Mathews's view, a new social mind is making the future in the early twentieth century; he calls this social mind scientific-democratic. Mathews thinks that the development of bourgeois capitalism in the early modern period (that is, the period in which the creeds foundational to Protestant orthodoxy were written) required a formulation of Christian faith different from that which had governed the social mind of the national period.

Mathews's analysis of the bourgeois capitalist social mind is incisive. Though he credits this social mind with having stimulated reform movements such as abolitionism, in his view, the bourgeois mind has come to be "under the spell of the 'Will to Get'."[4] He sees bourgeois capitalistic Christianity as excessively preoccupied with the salvation of individuals after death, and resistant to understanding the implications of the Christian message of salvation for the social order.[5] This other-worldly preoccupation allows "the self-centered community to find satisfaction for its religious needs in the extension of commercial principles to religion."[6] The piety of bourgeois Christianity has "commercialized" the atonement, Mathews thinks—to such an extent that it can sing hymns with titles like "Jesus Paid It All," titles which imply that the atonement was akin to an economic transaction between God the Father and Jesus.[7]

Since Mathews thinks that Christianity in the twentieth century should be discarding the social mind of bourgeois capitalism for scientific democracy, he argues that returning to this old-time religion is unfeasible. Though he grants that large numbers of North American Christians desire such retrogression, he maintains that what the church might gain (e.g., a reawakening of individualistic moral fervor) by resisting the formative social mind of the early twentieth century would be far outweighed by what it would lose in the area of social ethics: "For the very men who were most loyal to the commercialized atonement were the men who were indifferent to the needs of tenants and employees, the dangers of industrialized childhood and womanhood."[8] In Mathews's judgment, a Christianity emerging from the bourgeois capitalistic social mind must disengage itself from the domination of capitalism, in order to meet the challenge of the social mind making the future.

Mathews argues that, in the twentieth century, capitalism and democracy have entered into a battle for control of the social mind,

and thus the social process, of Western culture. In his view, capitalism has "frankly undertaken the worship of Mammon," and its religious interests are thus "in the very nature of the case allied with
those of imperialism and supramundane salvation."[9] As a consequence, capitalism has become religiously sterile: "It can no more
invent a theology than the feudal knight or the Roman Empire could
invent a theology."[10]

The roots of the battle between capitalism and democracy lie,
Mathews believes, in the tendency of the late nineteenth-century
corporation to become "an impersonal person," a being with a life
of its own, as it were, a life not constrained or controlled even by the
corporation manager.[11] Once capitalism made its transition into this
phase, "in the economic world persons with political rights and legal
freedom were treated impersonally."[12]

In a passage reminiscent of Marx's *Das Kapital*, Mathews argues that the emergence of the corporation as an impersonal person
is an entirely unprecedented phenomenon. Slavery, feudalism, early
industrialism—all undeniably treated the worker as an object, but
nonetheless all also engaged owner and worker in a personal relationship. In Mathews's view, late capitalism has succeeded in establishing in economic life an impersonality that does not even recognize
the feudal obligation of the lord to protect the serf. He thinks that such
impersonality is particularly characteristic of late capitalism in the
United States.[13]

The result of such developments is, rather predictably, class
strife. For Mathews, such strife must force democracy to move beyond
its preoccupation with the "personal" rights of individuals to an economic analysis of society and a concern for economic rights. The
hope of Western societies lies, Mathews judges, in a democratic consciousness that can develop a "passion for justice."[14] Only a democratic social mind characterized by "justice-giving, service, and social
solidarity" can overcome impersonal capitalism.[15]

This sociohistorical analysis is a remarkable contribution to
Christian social ethics, one still worthy of attention. It offers a cogent explanation for why large sectors of American Christianity continue to be fixated on individualistic understandings of salvation:
the fixation is based in resistance to the creative social mind of the
day; and this resistance is fueled by economic self-interest. If Mathews is correct, despite their protestations to the contrary, defend-
ers of "orthodoxy" and tradition who reflect the interests of the
owning classes are often not defending orthodoxy *tout court*; they are
defending social arrangements that accord them power and privilege, against attempts of some of their co-religionists to come to

terms with cultural forces that promise to build a very different future. In Mathews's view, the penchant of some North American Christians for the orthodoxy of a previous cultural moment is more than a theological penchant: it is quintessentially a socioeconomic one.

Mathews develops this notion in writings other than "Theology and the Social Mind." In the volume *Creative Christianity*, for example, he insists that North American Christians have made the gospel captive to capitalist interests, and have made the church "the property of the middle class whose fortunes rise and fall with those of capitalism." [16] *Christianity and Social Process* adds theoretical substance to this observation by maintaining that Christian moral perceptions not uncommonly lag behind the unfolding social process. Here, Mathews argues that, prior to the development of industry, capitalism was characterized by master-slave relationships. With the emergence of industrial technology, the serf and slave became the wage earner. Yet even after this development, the ethical analysis of Christian churches still tended to view the laborer as a commodity and the employer as a master. [17]

This tendency to view the owner-worker relationship as a master-slave relationship was far from being eradicated in early twentieth-century North American Christianity, Mathews thought. Though consciousness of the moral implications of industrial capitalism had developed among Christian socialists, the church of the day still largely attempted to deal with the moral quandaries the economic sphere presented to the church by inculcating moral sensitivity in individuals and encouraging philanthropy, rather than by calling for the transformation of the structures of society. [18]

As this analysis of the economically based resistance of twentieth-century North American Christianity to structural critique of capitalism indicates, the social gospel continues to be pertinent not only because it has added to our theological discourse such useful concepts as social sin, but because its prophetic critique of North American culture remains, in some respects, quite compelling. A primary contribution of the social gospel to North American Christianity—one still insufficiently appreciated—is its theological application of social analysis. The social gospel's critique of American culture demands respect not merely because it appeals to biblical prophetic warrants, but because it is grounded in social scientific analysis of culture. As Klaus Jürgen Jähn has argued, it is the sociological basis of social gospel theology that makes this North American movement a particularly valuable counterpart to European Christian theology, since European theology often lacks such a basis. [19]

Our study of Mathews's reflection about the foundations of social gospel theology has shown to what an extent this reflection presupposes a sociological matrix. Studies of the origins of the social gospel that have emphasized the large indebtedness of this movement to European liberal Protestant theology have done scholars a disservice, insofar as they have drawn our attention away from what may have been much more decisive: the movement's North American roots, and in particular its close relationship to sociology in the emerging years of that discipline. As we have seen, this relationship is clearly predominant in Mathews's first attempt to find a foundation for social gospel theology. And, as the preceding analysis of the struggle between the bourgeois-capitalistic and scientific-democratic social minds illustrates, it continues to be predominant in Mathews's later social process theology.

With its theological enshrinement of social analysis, the social gospel movement becomes part of the wave of the future of twentieth-century North American theology. Its careful reading of sociological works; its creative use of sociology to explore the meaning of theological concepts such as salvation; its use of social analysis to develop pastoral strategies: all these aspects of social gospel thought remain viable, and demonstrate that the movement was something more than European liberal Protestant theology in American garb, something that deserves to be remembered in a living way after liberal theology has been buried. If in nothing else, our persisting debt to the social gospel movement, and its persisting influence on North American Christianity, are evident in this fact alone: since the movement's heyday, it is unthinkable that the academic training of ministers would overlook sociology. After the social gospel movement, most North American Christian churches simply presuppose that ministers need to have some familiarity with sociological concepts, and to employ tools of social analysis in their pastoral work.[20]

A social anthropology and soteriology, and the use of social analysis in prophetic critique of North American culture: an examination of Mathews's foundational theology indicates that these aspects of social gospel theology clearly command attention today, in a period of renewed theological concern with the sociopolitical implications of faith. But these are not the only facets of social gospel theology that deserve notice at the present time. As our reading of Mathews's social gospel foundational theology has also shown, it is his kingdom theology, and the philosophy of history that it incorporates, that notably merit continued scrutiny, in light of present theological developments.

As we have seen, both supporters and critics recognize that kingdom theology is nodal to all social gospel theology. To the extent that its kingdom theology stands, the social gospel as a whole may stand. To the extent that its kingdom theology is exegetically and theologically indefensible, the social gospel itself will be indefensible. In this regard, Mathews's case is critically important, then, because it suggests that the social gospel's kingdom theology (with its attendant philosophy of history) may be both its most valuable contribution to Christian theology in the twentieth century, and its least understood facet.

Above all, a close reading of Mathews's attempt to discover a theologically adequate foundation for the social gospel demonstrates that social gospel kingdom theology is far from being what critics have often maintained. Mathews's kingdom theology is *not* naive nineteenth-century progressivism decked out in biblical symbols—at least, not after 1905.[21] Nor, after 1905, was Mathews's theology of the kingdom a this-worldly one. As our close reading of his texts has indicated, Mathews is actually one of the first North American theologians to respond to the work of J. Weiss. In pieces published during the decade following Weiss's *Predigt Jesu vom Reich Gottes*, Mathews considers Weiss's work very carefully, and by 1905—years before critics of the social gospel claim that social gospellers became aware of consistent eschatology—he grants the substantial accuracy of the eschatological reading of the kingdom symbol.

Mathews's post-1905 kingdom theology is an attempt to confront the eschatological interpretation of the kingdom forthrightly, and to build a theological foundation on its basis. With *MHNT*, Mathews not only abandons the social interpretation of the kingdom; he also reinterprets the kingdom symbol and begins to develop a foundational theology for the social gospel that presumes the eschatological understanding of the kingdom. Thereafter, he constructs a social process theology in which eschatology plays a central role; and he uses eschatology as a norm by which liberal theologies' collapse of faith to culture can be critiqued. Mathews's eschatologically realistic social process theology both accedes to the eschatological reading of the kingdom, and maintains a strong social ethic in the face of exegetical findings that threatened to erode the foundations of any social ethic based on the kingdom symbol. To put the point baldly, Mathews's social process theology is inexplicable without reference to eschatology.

When one attends to the eschatological strands in Mathews's social process thought, one can only conclude that something is seriously awry with the charge that the social gospel ignored or combated consistent eschatology, and that, as a result, it identified faith with culture, as liberal theology is said to have done. As we have seen, Mathews's theology of social process has built-in critical norms that preclude the identification of particular cultural developments with the eschatological fulfillment of history. Though Mathews's de facto identification of democracy with the kingdom of God during the World War I period comes perilously close to culture Protestantism, his own social process theology challenges such an identification, as it maintains that the social order is continuously susceptible to critique in light of the ideals and the kingdom proclamation of the gospels.

This countercultural emphasis in Mathews's social process theology clearly derives from his thesis that the social content of eschatology must be developed by contemporary theologians, from his notion of eschatology as the vertebral column or mold of Christian doctrine, and from his formulation of doctrinal development as the interchange between proponents and opponents of eschatology. Anyone who charges Mathews with having ignored consistent eschatology must deal with the strong eschatological current in his post-*MHNT* theological thought, and with the explicit critique of culture (and cultural adaptation of faith) that emerges on its basis.

In order to assess his social process theology, one must appreciate the fundamental problematic that Mathews faced as he sought to develop a foundation for social gospel theology. As our study of the two lives of Jesus has shown, at its most fundamental level, this problem was to relate the eschatological kingdom of God to history. For *all* social gospel theology that sought to be exegetically sound, this central problem presented a twofold challenge: first, some way had to be found to interpret the kingdom symbol, to make it speak to contemporary Christians; and second, the relevance of the eschatological kingdom to the historical process, to all that develops in history before the final establishment of the kingdom, has to be explained.

In his social process theology, Mathews is searching for a way to think about history that sees history proceeding to the kingdom of God, but that is not evolutionary or progressivist in the traditional sense.[22] As a social gospeller, he is committed to the belief that history moves in a telic direction. He is committed to such a belief on biblical grounds, because his theology appeals to the biblical revelation of a God who directs the course of history, and on theological grounds, because he thinks that abandoning belief in history's telic direction will undermine the social ethic of the social gospel. His quarrel with neo-orthodox theology has to do with this theology's stress

on alterity, a stress that Mathews regards as inimical to a strong social ethic. He argues that a God who is totally other, and who speaks
to the world a Word that is merely dialectic, is a God who appears to
be totally extrinsic to the concerns of this world. This God is "ex-territorialized" from history. For Mathews, the fundamental problem
with dialectic theology is that its alterity represents a diversion from
history, and thus from a social ethic that would urge believers to be
involved in action to change the world.[23]

To relegate the eschatological kingdom to the end of history—
in the sense that the kingdom is seen as some apocalyptic event
alien to all history preceding its coming—is, then, in Mathews's
view, to undermine a Christian social ethic. On the other hand, Jesus'
kingdom proclamation *was* clearly eschatological. Having accepted
this, Mathews was faced with the problem of developing a philosophy of history in which history moves toward the eschatological
kingdom, but all historical developments only approach, without
perfectly realizing, the eschatological goal of history. In addition,
this philosophy of history would have to skirt naturalistic models of
evolution that see the movement of history as ineluctable progress
to higher and higher stages of development.

Though Mathews was obviously thinking about this problem as
he transferred the emphasis of his foundational theology from the
kingdom evolving in history to the proleptic effect of the kingdom on
the social process, he never thought systematically about the philosophy of history that underlies his mature foundation for social
gospel theology. As we have seen, the closest he comes to such a
systematic presentation is the 1916 volume *Spiritual Interpretation
of History*, where he speaks of tendencies in history that point to
this *telos* without providing specific, culturally determined information about how to realize it. This defense of idealistic interpretations of history seeks to preserve the idea of progress in the face of
growing criticism of idealistic philosophies, and to create critical
norms that prevent the identification of particular cultural developments with the ideal to which the historical process is moving. For
Mathews, the notion of process is the solution to the fundamental
problematic faced by an eschatologically realistic social gospel foundational theology: it permits social gospellers to read history in a
progressivist way, but without idolizing cultural developments, or assuming that history will automatically move in a progressive direction. Mathews's mature kingdom theology of *JSI* is built around the
eschatological kingdom and this implicit, unsystematized social
process philosophy of history.

ASSESSING MATHEWS'S KINGDOM

THEOLOGY IN LIGHT OF POLITICAL

AND LIBERATION THEOLOGY

If one wishes to retrieve Mathews's kingdom theology critically, one can do so most fruitfully, in my view, by critiquing his social process understanding of history, and not his exegetical handling
of the kingdom symbol.[24] Once he had recognized the untenability of
his 1897 reading of this symbol, Mathews dealt with the exegetical
challenges to social gospel kingdom theology with conspicuous success. Though the exegesis of MHNT may be dated in many respects,
in its central thrust it remains tenable. In this foundational work,
Mathews effectively demonstrates that eschatological presuppositions are not peripheral to, but formative for, the entire New Testament canon. His attempt both to respect the original biblical significance of the kingdom concept and to make sense of that significance
in light of present experience is theologically sound. A close reading
of his reflections about the problem of eschatology in the 1897–1905
period, and of his endeavor to construct an eschatologically realistic
theology after that, shows that attempts to discredit social gospel
theology on the grounds that its exegesis ignored or mishandled the
kingdom symbol after the eschatological turn in German theology
are quite simply beside the point, at least in Mathews's case.

One may quibble about this or that facet of Mathews's exegesis.
But one cannot validly maintain that, in accepting the eschatological
reading of the kingdom of God, Mathews intended to co-opt consistent eschatology to a liberalism that voided the eschatology of the
gospels of its perduring significance for Christian believers. Both
MHNT and works published after 1905 explicitly avow Mathews's intent not to diminish the significance of eschatology via a reductionistic interpretation that betrays its essence as it "translates" this
essence into contemporary terms, but precisely to disclose the central significance of eschatology for Christian belief. In this intent,
and in the way in which he deals with eschatology in MHNT and
JSI, Mathews has been substantially vindicated by later Christian
theology.

In seeking a via media between a crude literalism that makes the
gospels captive to the cultural context in which they were written, and
a glib liberalism that prescinds from the cultural context of New Testament faith as it "adapts" that faith to a modern context, Mathews

reveals himself to have been a rather sophisticated theologian—in F. C. Grant's view, more sophisticated than those consistent eschatologists whose defense of eschatology cannot demonstrate how it has anything to do with a cultural context different from that in which biblical texts were composed.[25] Grant thinks that Mathews successfully negotiates the two-horned dilemma that confronts those who see only two possibilities facing anyone who accepts the eschatological nature of the kingdom: either illicitly to modernize this biblical symbol; or to relegate it forever to the obscurity of its original cultural context.[26]

At the time in which Mathews was developing his mature kingdom theology, his intent both to respect the original meaning of the eschatological kingdom and to retrieve that meaning for contemporary Christianity appears to have escaped the notice of critics. As often happens in a period of polemical exchange (in particular, when children are distancing themselves from parents whose visage they uncannily mirror), the choices confronting theologians after J. Weiss and Schweitzer may have seemed more stark than they actually were, either-or options for one path or another. But when Mathews's interpretation of the kingdom symbol is read after the brouhaha has died down and new movements have come onto the theological scene, it appears in an altogether different light. What Mathews was seeking to do with the kingdom symbol sounds uncannily akin to what Schweitzer himself, in 1946, described as the task confronting theologians in the mid-twentieth century:

> Belief in the Kingdom of God now takes a new lease of life. It no longer looks for its coming, self-determined, as an eschatological cosmic event, but regards it as something ethical and spiritual, not bound up with the last things, but to be realized with the cooperation of men. . . . Mankind to-day must either realize the Kingdom of God or perish. The very tragedy of our present situation compels us to devote ourselves in faith to its realization.[27]

Objections to Mathews's exegesis on the ground that its attempt to interpret the biblical symbol of the kingdom represents a modernization of this symbol are, in my view, quibbling objections. What Mathews did with the kingdom symbol is what Christian theologians have *had* to do after Weiss and Schweitzer: to correlate a concept rooted in a culture radically different from our own with contemporary thought patterns.

In my judgment, Mathews's kingdom theology falters not at an exegetical level, but at the level of its implicit philosophy of history. Here, Mathews's underlying intent—to maintain an idealistic reading of history while avoiding the pitfalls of naive progressism— is unimpeachable. As we have seen, in some important respects, Mathews's social process theology prefigures such important contemporary political-liberation notions as the proleptic effect of the *eschaton* on history, and the "eschatological proviso" under which all historical institutions live. But I wish to argue that the price social gospel theology pays for this critical defense of idealistic readings of history is too steep. Even as it seeks to skirt some negative implications of the evolutionist model it adopts, Mathews's philosophy of history still borrows heavily from key presuppositions of that model, and is thus susceptible to a number of compelling critiques of evolutionary thinking that have been articulated in the twentieth century.

Critics of process theologies have argued that even when these theologies attempt to mitigate the heartless implications of naturalistic models of evolution by speaking of God's redemption of the unmerited suffering of creatures in the evolutionary process, they sometimes exhibit a certain heartlessness.[28]

In Darwinian natural or Spencerian social evolution, heartlessness is a built-in function of the evolutionary process: higher stages of development can be reached only when lower ones have been transcended. If this transcendence demands the sacrifice of the flawed or the weak, then that is the unfortunate cost of evolutionary development.

Process theology explicitly repudiates such heartless models of evolution, of course. In fact, as we have seen, the desire to critique Spencerian determinism is a motivating factor in Small, Ely, and Mathews's development of a sociologically astute social gospel theology. In challenging social appropriations of Darwinian natural evolution, social gospellers wanted to defend human direction of the social process, and to combat the assumption that attempts to ameliorate undesirable social conditions (such as efforts to eradicate poverty) represented meddlesome interference with the mechanisms of a "natural" process that would otherwise inevitably produce desirable results.

Yet, even as it opposes the heartless model of social evolution and seeks to develop a nonheartless alternative, the social process thinking of Small, Ely, and Mathews partakes strongly of some of the problematic suppositions of this model. Social process imports into sociological thinking a metaphor that is fundamentally scientific; it applies to the social sphere a paradigm drawn from the natural sciences. Small's stress on the scientific nature of sociology has been stringently criticized by a number of scholars, including Herman and Julia R. Schwendinger. In their view, Small's insistence on the empirical basis of social science, and his demand that researchers continuously expand their data base and broaden their perspective, derive not only from his concern to give the discipline academic validity. This insistence arises as well from his belief that sociologists should be something like technicians for whom society is a laboratory. The Schwendingers see Small's prescriptions for early sociology as essentially technocratic: He views the sociologist as a scientist, who in the hope of effecting reform, applies technical rationality to social conditions through "experiments" on these conditions.[29]

This critique reflects classic critiques of Chicago school sociology by Thorstein Veblen and C. Wright Mills, who argue that the "scientific" bias of Chicago sociology has, from its inception, had a decidedly conservative application.[30] Though I have insisted throughout this study that there is another, retrievable side to the social process thought of Small and Mathews—one incisively aware of the shortcomings of North American culture—I think that the critique of Veblen, Mills, and the Schwendingers must be engaged, if one wishes to retrieve Mathews's kingdom theology critically. It must be engaged because it asks important questions about what happens when a philosophy of history relies so largely on a quasi-scientific paradigm such as that of process.[31] In doing so, does it make itself susceptible to some of the heartlessness of its parent paradigm, even when it critiques heartless evolutionism? And when social scientists are social reformers, as were Small and Mathews, do they run the risk of dulling the edge of their critical perceptions about the society they seek to reform, when they turn to natural science for explanation of themselves?

In my view, what is most fundamentally problematic about the reliance of Small and Mathews's social process thought on a scientific self-understanding is its dependence on technical-instrumental reason. When reformers use instrumental reason to define the "tendency" of the social process, or to discern history's goal, they too often provide a quasi-scientific rationale for that which ought not to be rationalized in history. Instrumental reason is too easily tempted to see inexplicable suffering as what must be subsumed by the process in its movement toward the goal of history. Because it can ultimately explain everything—justify everything—from the vantage point of history's goal (a goal that it knows rather too confidently), instrumental reason is unable to recognize that history contains incomprehensible aporias, aporias created by what is *not* rational or explainable. Instrumental rationality lacks the rhetorical power to challenge what ought not to occur in the social process. In the final analysis, a significant deficiency of social process thought is that it simply does not have an adequate language to speak about the aporias that occur in history when people are subjected by others to cruel, unmerited suffering; like all technical-instrumental systems of language, it is a language that is tone-deaf in face of the demonic aspects of history. Its vocabulary for the negative, the *nonprocessive*, nature of history, is insufficient.

Because it does not have such a vocabulary, social process thought also often lacks the will to stand against those who inflict unmerited suffering on others. Kingdom theologies that seek to understand the relationship between the *eschaton* and the present by means of social process philosophies of history undercut their critique of culture, because they do not have adequate vantage points from which to critique the "enlightened" and "progressive" sectors of society—sectors that have, after all, not always been conspicuously noteworthy for their resistance to barbarism in the twentieth century. Social process thought too easily apotheosizes the values and ideas of its practitioners as enlightenment or progress. In doing so, it loses the ability to ask why this practice or that way of doing things is so self-evidently the goal of social development. Who is to say that the goal for which we strive today will not be the goal that a subsequent generation defines as barbaric?

Mathews's social gospel kingdom theology is preeminently retrievable, then, but retrievals of this theology need to approach it via Max Horkheimer and Theodor Adorno's dialectic critique of Western culture's instrumentalization of Enlightenment reason (and its suppression of the liberative function of reason), and Michel Foucault and Jean-François Lyotard's hermeneutic of suspicion about "enlightened" societies' penchant to rationalize the status quo, as if it is given and unquestionable, while marginalizing alternative imaginations of social reality, as if they are unthinkable and irrational.[32] To say this is also to say that the social gospel's kingdom theology is an unfinished project: in its basic thrust and intent, it is theologically sound; in its exegesis, it is also defensible; but in its philosophy of history, it must move through dialectic critiques of the Enlightenment, in order to be compelling today.[33]

As political and liberation theologies have done: in their employment of the kingdom symbol, these theologies are in significant continuity with social gospel theology, and thus demonstrate its continuing viability. But in their use of hermeneutics of suspicion about

progressive philosophies of history, these theologies move the kingdom theology of the social gospel in a new direction, and thus demonstrate that the project of social gospel kingdom theology is also unfinished. If one looks back at the broad sweep of twentieth-century
Christian theology through the optic of kingdom theology, one might
conclude the following: in its intent to ground a politically engaged
Christian theology in the kingdom symbol, social gospel theology
set the course for subsequent political theologies. This intent is theologically valid, and to the extent that critiques of social gospel theology combat that intent, they misunderstand what social gospel theology is about; with its emphasis on the alterity of God and the divine
Word, the dialectic response of neo-orthodoxy to social gospel theology
did not adequately deal with the problem of relating the eschatological kingdom to history; but this dialectical response was warranted,
insofar as it exposes the fatuity of the social gospel's appeal to liberal
progressivist notions of history. Contemporary political and liberation
theologies inherit the kingdom theology of the social gospel through
the dialectic moment of neo-orthodoxy. As dialectic heirs of social
gospel kingdom theology, these theologies have the task of explain-
ing the relationship between history and the *eschaton* in nonevolu-
tionary ways.[34]

In the final portion of this essay, I want to comment briefly on
the work of three political or liberation theologians, to show how
their theology both remains in continuity with social gospel kingdom theology, and how it continues the unfinished task of grounding
kingdom theology in nonprogressive philosophies of history. The
theologians on whom I wish to focus are Moltmann, Metz, and Gutiérrez. My point is not to claim that any of these theologians writes
with explicit awareness of connections between his theology and
that of the social gospel; none in fact acknowledges such connections.[35] The point is to show that, even in the absence of such explicit connections, there is nonetheless demonstrable continuity between the kingdom theology of the social gospel and these theologians'
political or liberation theologies—but continuity that moves in a different direction than that of the social gospel's evolutionary view of
history.

The continuity between Mathews's kingdom theology and contemporary political or liberation theologies is particularly evident in
these theologies' appeal to eschatology. As Mathews had done, Moltmann, Metz, and Gutiérrez all note the central, formative role of eschatology in Christian theology; each echoes Mathews in using eschatology to critique cultural adaptation of faith, and to urge believers
to enact their faith in the economic and political spheres.

Among contemporary Christian theologians, perhaps none has so forcefully stated the case for the pivotal function of eschatology in Christian faith as has Moltmann. In his *Theology of Hope*, Moltmann maintains that "the eschatological is not one element *of* Christianity, but it is the medium of Christian faith as such, the key in which everything in it is set, the glow that suffuses everything here in the dawn of an expected new day."[36] In Moltmann's view, the discovery of the central significance of eschatology for Jesus' preaching and for the faith of the first Christians is one of the most important events of recent theology, one that breaks the foundations of scientific theology and culturally adapted expressions of piety.[37] For Moltmann as for Mathews, this discovery is one with a critical edge for the church itself: it calls for the church to critique its alliance with the powers-that-be in this world, to live by an eschatological orientation that draws it continuously beyond adaptation and compromise.[38]

For Metz, as for Mathews and Moltmann, the eschatological turn represents an "apocalyptic sting" for those who have made Christian hope a purely interior, purely private hope, rather than a mandate for solidarity with history's victims.[39] As Metz argues in his volume *Faith in History and Society*, the discovery of eschatology is turned against such privatization of faith: this discovery militates against all "anthropological reductions" that dehistoricize the human subject, as they explore the implications of faith for the individual, without developing those implications for history and society.[40] For Metz, privatized understandings of faith are part and parcel of the alliance Western Christian churches have made with the culture that proceeds from technical-instrumental appropriations of the Enlightenment. But eschatology undercuts this alliance: "God's eschatological history of freedom . . . cannot be absorbed into the ideal of man's coming of age that is contained in the middle-class history of the Enlightenment or into the apotheosis of the history of liberation by revolution."[41] In Metz's reading of eschatology, the church lives under an eschatological proviso that operates as a double-edged sword: on the one hand, this proviso prohibits the church's idolization of any ideological system over the course of history; but on the other hand, it also continuously orients it to a praxis of solidarity with the victims of history.[42]

As do social gospel and political theologians, Gutiérrez also constructs a politically engaged theology around an eschatological core. With Mathews, Moltmann, and Metz, Gutiérrez notes that the rediscovery of eschatology at the turn of the twentieth century revolutionized Christian theology by showing that "eschatology is . . .

not just one more element of Christianity, but the very key to understanding the Christian faith." [43] In addition, as with the other theologians we are considering, Gutiérrez views the "current eschatological perspective" as a ground for believers' involvement in the sociopolitical activities. Gutiérrez argues against the use of eschatology by dialectic theologians to encourage Christian disengagement from the world: in his view, "not only is it [i.e., eschatology] not an escape from history, but also it has clear and strong implications for the political sphere, for social praxis." [44] In Gutiérrez's theology, eschatology implies a "tension toward the future" in which "the attraction of 'what is to come' is the driving force of history." [45]

As this all-too-brief summary of the appeal of several representative contemporary political and liberation theologians to eschatology indicates, in their recognition of the nodal function of eschatology for Christian faith, political and liberation theology is in significant continuity with social gospel theology. In emphasizing the formative function of eschatology for Christian theology, Mathews presciently anticipates Moltmann, Metz, and Gutiérrez. And in using eschatology as a ground for a critical, politically engaged theology, Mathews anticipates important aspects of political and liberation theologies today. In its handling of the question of eschatology, the social gospel theology of Mathews strikingly prefigures political and liberation theology, in several key ways.

But in their treatment of the question of the relationship of the *eschaton* to history, Moltmann, Metz, and Gutiérrez part company with Mathews. To be specific, each seeks a philosophy of history that accentuates the effects of the future on the present, without understanding the relationship between the present and the future in evolutionary terms.

As had Mathews, Moltmann recognizes that to face the eschatological reading of the Christian scriptures squarely is also to face the question of how to relate the eschatological kingdom of God to present history. Consequently, *Theology of Hope* devotes considerable attention to developing a philosophy of history adequate to this eschatological interpretation of the gospels. Significantly, however, Moltmann does not locate the fundamental significance of history in progress or social process toward the *eschaton*, but in hope. For Moltmann, hope is a mediating concept: hope moves between historical developments and the eschatological consummation of history; it "embraces both the object hoped for and also the hope inspired by it." [46]

Hope must mediate between history and the *eschaton*, Moltmann thinks, because, as we have come increasingly to recognize in the twentieth century, if history means anything at all, it clearly does not mean progress toward an ideal, but crisis.[47] If the present century indicates anything about history's meaning, it indicates that it is no longer possible to conceive of history as inevitable movement upward and forward. As a message of hope, eschatology cannot be a blessing of history, then, not an announcement that everything that occurs in history will receive fulfillment in the kingdom of God.[48] From the standpoint of a philosophy of history that takes crisis as its norm, the relationship between history and *eschaton* is dialectic: God's kingdom annihilates history, as much as it fulfills it.[49]

But a *purely* dialectic message cannot be a message of hope. If all the church has to preach to history is a message of annihilation, it has no gospel, no good news, for those caught in the dilemma of historical existence. As a mediating concept, hope both looks to the end of history, and seeks to elicit within history a sense of promise:

> Christian eschatology . . . is the language of promises.
> It understands history as the reality instituted by
> promise. In the light of the present promise and hope,
> the as yet unrealized future of the promise stands
> in contradiction to given reality. The historic char-
> acter of reality is experienced in this contradiction,
> in the front line between the present and the
> promised future.[50]

In pointing the world to a future that both consummates and annihilates it, hope calls upon the world to "read" within present reality its ultimate destiny.[51] Through hope, the *eschaton* thus has a proleptic effect on present history; the future enters the present via this effect, and moves the present toward itself.[52]

Moltmann breaks decisively with processive understandings of history because, even when they seek to critique naive progressivism, these philosophies of history still absorb something of the dangerous fatuity of progressivism. They are conspicuously unable to incorporate the sense of crisis that must be fundamental to any viable philosophy of history in the twentieth century. Because they are unable to incorporate this sense, they prematurely pronounce a blessing on what ought not to be blessed; they allow history to buy the *eschaton* at too cheap a price.

To a great extent, Moltmann's philosophy of history and of hope reflects the thought of Ernst Bloch.[53] A key concern of Bloch's master-work, *The Principle of Hope,* is to relate the present to the absolute future—the Novum that both fulfills and supersedes all historical development—without resorting to the concept of progress. As Bloch notes, the fundamental problem with this concept is that it has been too susceptible to technological appropriations in modern Western culture; these appropriations "always made progress appear too cheap, too linear; just as today, presented in isolation and with social change left out, they are delusions or means of deception."[54] In Bloch's view, hope that is worth its salt does not bless history as readily as progressivist ideologies do. Hope must always refuse to apotheosize the present, because its sense of the future implicit in the present does not permit it to see the present as history's fulfillment:

> Hence hope makes us mistrustful—justly and with precision, in fact with the highest kind of conscience: that of the goal—of every realization that offers itself all too plumply; apotheoses are also always flat and decorative to a consciousness that does not esteem Kierkegaard's abstract radicalisms.[55]

For Bloch as for Moltmann, then, hope is "the mediated Novum"; it plays a mediating function between the possible future and the present and unfinished past, by discerning within history "concrete movements toward perfection," while refusing to collapse history into its goal.[56] As Bloch's essay on process thinking in his volume *A Philosophy of the Future* argues, hope views world history as a "real experiment . . . aimed toward a possible just and proper world."[57] As mediation, hope envisages movement in history that is not unilinear (as the concept of progress would imply), but polyrhythmic and polyphonic.[58]

In Metz's theology, one can discern a similar attempt to ground an eschatologically realistic theology in a nonprocessive philosophy of history. But where Moltmann's political theology grounds itself in a philosophy of history reflecting the thought of Bloch, Metz's theology echoes the critical theory of Horkheimer and Adorno. In critiquing the privatized understandings of faith that have come to predominate in many forms of post-Enlightenment Western Christianity, Metz is repudiating the theological reduction of Enlightenment reason to instrumental reason, and (with Horkheimer and Adorno) calling for the retrieval of the liberative function of reason. It is this dialectic retrieval of Enlightenment reason that informs his critique of linear understandings of history:

> Whenever the history of freedom takes place without reference to this memory of the eschatological

> reservation, it always seems to fall a victim to the
> compulsive need to substitute a worldly subject for
> the whole history of freedom and this always moves
> in the direction of a totalitarian control of men by
> men. In the end, a history of freedom which has lost
> this eschatological memory can only be interpreted
> as a non-dialectical and to some extent abstract his-
> tory of emancipation in which the new conflicts and
> disasters of the freedom gained are ignored and the
> idea of coming of age . . . threatens to sink to the
> level of a commonplace idea of pure survival or cun-
> ning animal adaptation.[59]

This rejection of instrumental reductions of reason and appeal to liberative reason place Metz's theology on a very different philosophical basis than that of Mathews. As does Moltmann's theology, it represents a repudiation of evolutionary progressivist readings of history.[60]

Metz and Moltmann are both European political theologians
who are thinking through the problem of history's relation to the *eschaton* in terms that reflect the preoccupations of contemporary European philosophy. The liberation theology of Gutiérrez proceeds
from an entirely different cultural and philosophical matrix, that of
the so-called Third World. Writing from such a context, Gutiérrez
moves the discussion of eschatology and history in a new direction.
He does so by reframing this discussion around the socioeconomic
concept of development. In an admirably succinct summary of recent Roman Catholic magisterial consideration of the relationship
between temporal progress and the kingdom of God, Gutiérrez argues that magisterial documents generally affirm that temporal
progress (or human development) is related to the kingdom's growth
within history, but the two are not synonymous.[61] In Gutiérrez's
view, these documents open the door to further discussion—precisely, for attempts such as his own endeavor to transfer the emphasis of a praxis-oriented theology of history from the concept of development to that of liberation.

As Gutiérrez notes, the Vatican II document *Gaudium et spes*
deals with the relationship between history and the *eschaton* by making two general affirmations: there is a close relationship between
temporal progress and the growth of the kingdom; but these two
processes are distinct, and may not be identified with one another.[62]
The papal encyclical *Populorum progressio* adds to this analysis another concept, that of integral development. The term "development"
borrows from scholarly discussion of the political and economic de-

velopment of Third World countries. But whereas, in its usual usage, the term envisages something that First World nations do for Third World nations, the concept "integral development" employs the term "development" to refer to theological concern for the *total* salvation of human beings—a salvation that embraces not merely their private, interior life, but their socioeconomic circumstances as well. In *Populorum progressio*, integral development is a way of speaking about salvation in nonprivatistic, politically engaged, terms.[63]

Gutiérrez moves through the door these magisterial documents open by distinguishing between development and liberation. In his view, the term "development" is tainted with associations that make it inadequate to explain the relationship between history and the kingdom. In particular, the term owes too much to progressivist philosophies of history; this is evident above all in its tendency to disguise the conflictual nature of history's movement.[64] The term "liberation," on the other hand, enables one to speak of history's non-progressive, conflict-ridden movement toward the kingdom; this term recognizes that movement toward the *eschaton* is not automatic or something to be engineered by technocrats, but will necessitate a praxis that moves through the real history of real human beings, including history's conflicts. In Gutiérrez's use, liberation refers to a movement that both affects the historical process, and is not co-extensive with it, because it recognizes that no historical event fully realizes the kingdom of God that is to come as God's gift at the end of history:

> Temporal progress—or, to avoid this aseptic term, human liberation—and the growth of the Kingdom both are directed toward complete communion of human beings with God and among themselves. They have the same goal, but they do not follow parallel roads, not even convergent ones. The growth of the Kingdom is a process which occurs historically *in* liberation, insofar as liberation means a greater human fulfillment. . . . Without liberating historical events, there would be no growth of the Kingdom. But the process of liberation will not have conquered the very roots of human oppression and exploitation without the coming of the Kingdom, which is above all a gift.[65]

What is remarkable in this analysis of liberation is how it continues social gospel and political theologies' discussion of history's relationship to the *eschaton*, but on an entirely new philosophical basis.

The same concerns are present: the need, after the eschatological turn, to relate history to the kingdom of God without identifying historical developments with the eschatological fulfillment of history.[66] But what is new in Gutiérrez's critique of the concept of development is how it appeals to a socioeconomic concept, liberation, as it critiques another socioeconomic concept. This move enables Gutiérrez to build a kingdom theology around a philosophy of history that avoids progressivism, while rooting theological reflection more decisively in human experience—experience as socioeconomic experience—than is the case with European political theology.

As this cursory perusal of three preeminent political and liberation theologians demonstrates, the kingdom theology of Mathews is part of an important current that runs through twentieth-century Christian theology. With such postliberal critics of liberal theology as the Roman Catholic modernist Loisy, Mathews's theology makes the eschatological turn to a critique of liberal theology's collapse of faith into culture. In this respect, it anticipates the very critique that would be pressed by dialectical theologians against the social gospel. But, in its attempt to discover some basis for seeing the *eschaton* as proleptically affecting history, while adopting a stance of eschatological realism, Mathews's kingdom theology also avoids what may have been dialectical theology's diversion from the mainstream of twentieth-century theological reflection, insofar as this theology did not adequately deal with the relationship between eschatology and history. In this respect, if not in the philosophy of history that it implicitly endorses, Mathews's kingdom theology clearly moves toward contemporary political and liberation theologies. If the social gospel is critically retrievable, if it still merits attention as an indigenous North American basis for a North American political/liberation theology, then in the final analysis, any contemporary attempt to appraise social gospel theology and discover its significance for Christianity today must do more than analyze its roots in the liberal theology of the nineteenth century: it must also recognize its affinities with political and liberation theology. Therein lies its continuing importance for theologians as the twentieth century nears its end.

NOTES

INTRODUCTION

1. As Donald K. Gorrell notes, the term "social gospel" had numerous analogues in the movement's writings; these include "social Christianity" and "the social movement in Christianity" (*The Age of Social Responsibility: The Social Gospel in the Progressive Era, 1900–1920* [Macon, Ga.: Mercer University Press, 1988], p. 4). See also Robert T. Handy, ed., *The Social Gospel in America: Gladden, Ely, and Rauschenbusch* (New York: Oxford University Press, 1966), p. 4. For the sake of simplicity, I use the designation "social gospel" throughout, except where a source I am citing uses another term.

2. Ronald C. White Jr. and C. Howard Hopkins, eds., *The Social Gospel: Religion and Reform in Changing America* (Philadelphia: Temple University Press, 1976), p. xi.

3. See Charles Strain, "Walter Rauschenbusch: A Resource for Public Theology," *Union Seminary Quarterly Review* 34 (1978): 23–34; David Nelson Duke, "Theology Converses with the Biographical Narrative of W. Rauschenbusch," *Perspectives in Religious Studies* 18 (1991): 143–58; Winthrop Hudson, ed., *Walter Rauschenbusch: Selected Writings* (New York: Paulist, 1984); Klaus Jürgen Jähn, *Rauschenbusch: The Formative Years* (Valley Forge, Pa.: Judson, 1974); Carl E. Johnson, "The New Present and the New Past: Some Timely Reflections on the Rauschenbusch Legacy," *Perspectives in Religious Studies* 14 (1987): 131–45; Philip Lemasters, "Theological Ethics and the Kingdom of God: A Comparative Study of Walter

Rauschenbusch and Gustavo Gutiérrez," in *Church Divinity 1987*, ed. John H. Morgan (Bristol, Ind.: Wyndham Hall, 1987), pp. 102–18; Alistair Mason, "Re-Review: Walter Rauschenbusch's *Christianity and the Social Crisis*," *Modern Churchman* n.s. 30.1 (1988): 46–49; Paul Minus, *Walter Rauschenbusch* (New York: Macmillan, 1988); and Gary Scott Smith, "To Reconstruct the World: Walter Rauschenbusch and Social Change," *Fides et Historia* 23 (1991): 40–61.

4. John C. Bennett, *The Radical Imperative: From Theology to Social Ethics* (Philadelphia: Westminster, 1975), pp. 105–6; and "The Social Gospel Today," in *Social Gospel: Religion and Reform*, pp. 292–93.

5. See Howland Sanks, "Liberation Theology and the Social Gospel: Variations on a Theme," *Theological Studies* 4 (1980): 668–82.

6. Roger Haight and John Langan, "Recent Catholic Social and Ethical Teaching in Light of the Social Gospel," *Journal of Religious Ethics* (hereafter *JRE*) 18 (1990): 103–28. In this theme issue of *JRE*, which focuses on the ethics of the social gospel, see also Reinhard L. Hütter, "The Church: Midwife of History or Witness of the Eschaton?" pp. 27–54, which views Rauschenbusch as "a prefiguration of modern political theology" (p. 48); and Susan Lindley, "'Neglected Voices' and *Praxis* in the Social Gospel," pp. 75–101, who call for the rediscovery of the concept of *praxis* as a key to understanding the theology of the social gospel.

7. Gary J. Dorrien, *Reconstructing the Common Good: Theology and the Social Order* (Maryknoll, N.Y.: Orbis, 1990), p. 17. See also Dorrien, "Liberal Socialism and the Legacy of the Social Gospel," *Cross Currents* 39 (1989): 340–41.

8. *Reconstructing the Common Good*, p. 17. For another recent reappraisal of social gospel theology in light of contemporary liberationist concerns, see John C. Cort, *Christian Socialism* (Maryknoll, N.Y.: Orbis, 1988), pp. 226–65.

9. Diane Yeager, "Introduction," *JRE* 18 (1990): 4. See *The Rise of the Social Gospel in American Protestantism, 1865–1915* (New Haven, Conn.: Yale University Press, 1940). The claim of theologians such as James Gustafson that Rauschenbusch subordinated faith to social activism seems to be grounded in the belief that social gospel theology was a primarily adaptive, rather than creative, theological movement: for this claim, see Gustafson's "From Scripture to Social Policy and Social Action," *Andover Newton Quarterly* 61 (1969): 161.

10. Yeager, "Introduction," pp. 4–5. The term "liberal Protestantism" refers to a broadly defined theological movement that had its heyday in the nineteenth century. The German theologian Friedrich Schleiermacher (1768–1834) is commonly regarded as the seminal figure of the movement. A predominant concern of Schleiermacher's theology is to find bridges between modern culture (increasingly affected by the secularizing tendencies of the Enlightenment) and religious faith. Schleiermacher's 1799 *Religion: Speeches to Its Cultured Despisers* was a foundational work for the liberal

Protestant movement. This, and Schleiermacher's later works, including *Christian Faith* (1821–22), argued that human beings have an innate capacity for religious feeling, which finds its expression in various cultures in religious forms appropriate to those cultures.

The liberal Protestant movement reached its culmination in the theology of Albrecht Ritschl (1822–89), whose *The Christian Doctrine of Justification and Reconciliation* (1870–74) provided a systematic statement of the major themes of liberal Protestant theology. In the view of neo-orthodox critics of the movement, including Swiss theologian Karl Barth and American theologians Reinhold and H. Richard Niebuhr (see note 35, below), the anti-dogmatism Ritschl exhibited in this work, and Ritschl's tendency to seek rapprochement between religion and culture, ultimately so inculturate Christian faith that believers lose any vantage point from which to challenge culture. For Barth and other critics of liberal Protestantism, the willingness with which many major liberal theologians in Germany endorsed the First World War was a watershed moment in which the inculturation of Christian theology in the liberal project became undeniably apparent.

11. Ibid., p. 5.

12. Ibid. For an argument on behalf of retrieving still-useful aspects of Rauschenbusch's kingdom theology in politically engaged Christian movements today, see William Crowell Trench, "The Social Gospel and the City: Implications for Theological Reconstruction in the Work of Washington Gladden, Josiah Strong, and Walter Rauschenbusch," unpubl. Ph.D. diss. (Boston University, 1986), pp. 320–25, 421–22.

13. In addition to the articles by Hütter, Lindley, and Haight and Langan cited above, the *JRE* theme issue on social gospel ethics contains the following: Christopher Lasch, "Religious Contributions to Social Movements: Walter Rauschenbusch, the Social Gospel, and Its Critics," pp. 7–25; and Grace C. Long, "The Ethics of Francis Greenwood Peabody: A Centenary of Christian Social Ethics," pp. 55–73.

14. For a classic statement of this theme, see Willem A. Visser't Hooft, *The Background of the Social Gospel in America* (Haarlem, The Netherlands: H. D. Tjeenk Willink and Zoon, 1928; repr. St. Louis, Mo.: Bethany, 1963), p. 186.

15. See James Dombrowski, *The Early Days of Christian Socialism* (New York: Columbia University Press, 1936), esp. pp. 20–21.

16. See Bennett, *Radical Imperative*, pp. 119–21, and "The Social Gospel Today," p. 288; Christopher Lasch, *Haven in a Heartless World* (New York: Basic Books, 1977), p. 8; Janet Forsythe Fishburn, *The Fatherhood of God and the Victorian Family: The Social Gospel in America* (Philadelphia: Fortress, 1981); and Martin E. Marty, *Modern American Religion*, vol. 1: *The Irony of It All, 1893–1919* (Chicago: University of Chicago Press, 1986), pp. 291–94. For other statements of these charges, see Glenn R. Bucher, "Social Gospel Christianity and Racism," *Union Seminary Quarterly Review* 27 (1973): 146–57; Thomas J. Gossett, *Race: The History of an Idea in America*

(Dallas: Southern Methodist University Press, 1963), p. 177; and Visser't Hooft, *Background of Social Gospel*, pp. 52–53, 65.

17. For an important pioneering attempt to recognize the complexity of the social gospel's response to racism, see Robert T. Handy, "The Social Gospel in Historical Perspective," *Andover Newton Quarterly* 9 (1964): 177–78.

18. White and Hopkins, *Social Gospel: Religion and Reform*, pp. 103–7, 109–13, 122–23, and 123–26.

19. On White and Hopkins, *Social Gospel: Religion and Reform*, as the source for the phrase "neglected voices," see Lindley, "'Neglected Voices'," p. 76.

20. See Fishburn, *Fatherhood of God*, pp. 22–23, 26, 95–96, 118–19, 123–26, 165.

21. Fishburn, "The Methodist Social Gospel and Woman Suffrage," *Drew Gateway* 54 (1984): 85–104; esp. 104.

22. Shailer Mathews, *The Individual and the Social Gospel* (New York: Missionary Education Movement of the U.S. and Canada, 1914), pp. 29–30. See William D. Lindsey, "The Social Gospel and Feminism," *American Journal of Theology and Philosophy* 13 (1992): 194–210.

23. For a recent judicious statement of the historiographical problems that must be confronted by those who seek to evaluate Rauschenbusch's response to the women's movement, which argues that Rauschenbusch was ambivalent about the movement, rather than opposed to it, see Dorrien, *Reconstructing the Common Good*, p. 183n.74.

24. Jean Miller Schmidt, *Souls or the Social Order* (Brooklyn, N.Y.: Carlson, 1991), pp. xvii–xxxiii.

25. Arthur M. Schlesinger, "A Critical Period in American Religion, 1875–1900," *Proceedings of the Masschusetts Historical Society* 64 (1931–32): 523–47.

26. Ralph E. Luker, *The Social Gospel in Black and White: American Racial Reform, 1885–1912* (Chapel Hill: University of North Carolina Press, 1991), pp. 5–6. Among the reasons that the response of the social gospel movement to race may have been oversimplified in previous studies of the movement is that few previous studies have focused on the *Southern* contributions to the movement: on this, see John Lee Eighmy, *Churches in Cultural Captivity: A History of the Social Attitudes of Southern Baptists* (Knoxville: University of Tennessee Press, 1972), esp. pp. 61–71; and White and Hopkins, *Social Gospel*, pp. 80–97.

27. See Luker, *Social Gospel in Black and White*, p. 176.

28. For Martin Luther King's acknowledgment of social gospel influence, and in particular Rauschenbusch's influence, on his thought, see *A Testament of Hope: The Essential Writings of Martin Luther King, Jr.*, ed. James M. Washington (San Francisco: Harper & Row, 1986), pp. 37–38.

29. Lindley, "'Neglected Voices'," pp. 75–76.

30. Reinhold Niebuhr, "Intellectual Autobiography," in *Reinhold Niebuhr: His Religious, Social, and Political Thought*, ed. Charles Kegley and Robert Bretall (New York: Macmillan, 1956), p. 13.

31. See *Moral Man and Immoral Society* (New York: Scribner's, 1932), pp. xv, xix–xx, 71–82; and *An Interpretation of Christian Ethics* (New York: Harper and Brothers, 1935), pp. 169–71. For a succinct critique of Rauschenbusch as a culture Protestant, see Niebuhr's "Walter Rauschenbusch in Historical Perspective," *Religion in Life* 27 (1958): 528, 530–35.

32. H. Richard Niebuhr, *The Kingdom of God in America* (Chicago: Willett, Clark, 1937), pp. 183–84. See also Waldo Beach and Niebuhr, *Christian Ethics* (New York: Ronald, 1955), pp. 445–48.

33. See "The Attack upon the Social Gospel," *Religion in Life* 5 (Spring 1936): 176–81 (repr. in White and Hopkins, *Social Gospel: Religion and Reform*, pp. 263–91).

34. H. Richard Niebuhr, *Kingdom of God in America*, pp. 183–84.

35. White and Hopkins, *Social Gospel: Religion and Reform*, p. 259. As note 10, above, indicates, neo-orthodox theology grew out of a critical response to nineteenth-century liberal Protestant theology, and, in particular, to what critics of liberalism regarded as this theological movement's tendency to inculturate Christian faith. In 1919, after leading liberal theologians in Germany had given their blessing to the First World War, Swiss theologian Karl Barth (1886–1968) published a devastating critique of liberal theology entitled *Der Römerbrief*, in which he argued that liberal theology made a fatal mistake in seeking to reconcile Christian revelation with secular culture. In Barth's view, the Word that God speaks to the world is a totally other Word, one that subjects the world to radical critique, and that cannot be appropriated by culture.

Barth's crisis or dialectic theology initiated a neo-orthodox theological movement in both Europe and North America. In North America, the chief representatives of this movement were the brothers Niebuhr. In works such as *Moral Man and Immoral Society* (1932) and *The Nature and Destiny of Man* (1941–43), Reinhold Niebuhr (1892–1971) argued that liberal Protestant theology had fundamentally betrayed biblical revelation by assuming that God's kingdom could be built within history, and that history was progressing toward the kingdom of God. In Niebuhr's view, such liberal optimism ignored the radical tendency of human nature and human institutions to evil, and thus overlooked the need of a dialectic response to culture that envisaged struggle by and persecution of those seeking to transform culture. Reinhold Niebuhr's critique of liberal thought was echoed in the work of his brother H. Richard Niebuhr (1894–1962), whose 1937 *The Kingdom of God in America* mounts a particularly sharp attack on the progressivist philosophy of history that underlies the liberal schema.

36. Lasch, "Religious Contributions to Social Movements," p. 7.

37. Dorrien, *Reconstructing Common Good*, p. 16. See also Bennett, *Radical Imperative*, p. 18; and Martin A. Marty, *Modern American Religion*, vol. 2: *The Noise of Conflict, 1919–1941* (Chicago: University of Chicago Press, 1991), pp. 318–27.

38. Harry Antonides, *Stones for Bread: The Social Gospel and Its Contemporary Legacy* (Jordan Station, Canada: Paideia, 1985), p. 192.

39. For other recent appeals to the received tradition about social gospel theology that do not substantially engage new historiographical findings about it, see Ramsay Cook, *The Regenerators: Social Criticism in Late Victorian English Canada* (Toronto: University of Toronto Press, 1985); Susan Curtis, *A Consuming Faith: The Social Gospel and Modern American Culture* (Baltimore: Johns Hopkins University Press, 1991); and P. Travis Kroeker, "Theology, Ethics, and Social Theory: The Social Gospel Quest for a Public Morality," *Studies in Religion/Sciences religieuses* 20.2 (1991): 181–98.

40. Visser't Hooft, *Background of Social Gospel*, pp. 41, 169.

41. Ibid., p. 50.

42. Ibid., pp. 46–47.

43. Bennett, "Social Gospel Today," pp. 287–88.

44. Kroeker, "Theology, Ethics, and Social Theory," pp. 194, 196–98.

45. For recent arguments on behalf of a post-neo-orthodox retrieval of social gospel theology that returns to the sources with a more sympathetic hermeneutic, see White and Hopkins, *Social Gospel*, pp. xi–xii; and Roger Haight, "The Mission of the Church in the Social Gospel," *Theological Studies* 49 (1988): 477–97.

46. Sidney Ahlstrom, *A Religious History of the American People* (New Haven, Conn.: Yale University Press, 1972), p. 777.

47. The phrase is Mathews's self-designation in his autobiography, *New Faith for Old* (New York: Macmillan, 1936), p. 83.

48. Leander Keck, "Foreword to the Lives of Jesus Series," in Shailer Mathews, *Jesus on Social Institutions* (Philadelphia: Fortress, 1970), p. vii. For a similar appeal for a contemporary retrieval of Mathews, and a recognition of the partiality of most previous studies of his theology, see Robert Wesley Clark, "The Contribution of Shailer Mathews to the Social Movement in American Protestantism," unpubl. Ph.D. diss. (Southern Baptist Theological Seminary, New Orleans, 1960), p. 6.

49. Henry J. Cadbury, *The Peril of Modernizing Jesus* (New York: Macmillan, 1937), pp. 89, 93, 202n.1.

50. H. Richard Niebuhr, *Christ and Culture* (New York: Harper & Row, 1951), p. 101.

51. Visser't Hooft, *Background of Social Gospel*, pp. 46–7, 56; and Beach and Niebuhr, *Christian Ethics*, pp. 445–8. See also John C. Bennett, "The Social Interpretation of Christianity," in *The Church through Half a*

Century: Essays in Honor of William Adams Brown (New York: Scribner's, 1936), pp. 114–20.

52. Norman Perrin, *The Kingdom of God in the Teaching of Jesus* (London: Student Christian Movement [SCM], 1963), pp. 37, 47–49, 55.

53. Amos Wilder, *Kerygma, Eschatology, and Social Ethics* (Philadelphia: Fortress, 1965), p. 5.

54. John Macquarrie, *Twentieth-Century Religious Thought* (London: SCM, 1963), p. 165.

55. R. K. O. White, *Christian Ethics* (Atlanta, Ga.: John Knox, 1981), pp. 295–96.

56. See, for example, Bennett, "Social Interpretation of Christianity," which maintains that the "last generation" of social gospellers (i.e., Rauschenbusch and Mathews) did not face the problem of the apocalyptic conception of the kingdom of God: pp. 117–18, 131. For a more recent statement of this claim, see Johnson, "New Present and New Past," pp. 135, 144.

57. Richard H. Hiers and David Larrimore Holland, "Introduction," in Johannes Weiss, *Jesus' Proclamation of the Kingdom of God,* trans. and ed. Hiers and Holland (New York: Fortress, 1971), p. 2. For a recent (and somewhat unnuanced) claim that "Rauschenbusch rejected the conclusions of contemporary biblical studies regarding Jesus as an apocalyptic, eschatological figure," see Lemasters, "Theological Ethics and Kingdom of God," p. 112. For a more balanced assessment of Rauschenbusch's response to the eschatological school of German biblical scholarship, which retrieves significant aspects of Rauschenbusch's kingdom theology, see Max Stackhouse, "The Continuing Importance of Walter Rauschenbusch," in Rauschenbusch, *The Righteousness of the Kingdom,* ed. Stackhouse (Nashville, Tenn.: Abingdon, 1968), pp. 13–59.

58. Hiers and Holland, "Introduction," p. 35.

59. Ibid. The ability of the received interpretation to skew even sympathetic appraisals of Mathews's theology is evident in Kenneth Smith's claim that Mathews discovered the work of Weiss "shortly after he completed" *Social Teaching of Jesus:* see "Shailer Mathews: Theologian of Social Process," unpubl. Ph.D. diss. (Duke University, 1959), p. 178n.30. Despite the several explicit references Mathews makes to Weiss in the period 1895–1905, Smith argues that Mathews did not mention his post–1897 discovery of Weiss until he wrote his 1928 *Jesus on Social Institutions* (p. 35n.5).

A 1976 article Smith co-authored with Leonard Sweet partly corrects this mistake. The article notes that Mathews's 1905 *Messianic Hope in the New Testament* is a significant response to Weiss. However, it repeats the contention that Mathews discovered Weiss only "shortly after" he wrote *Social Teaching of Jesus:* "Shailer Mathews: A Chapter in the Social Gospel Movement," *Foundations* 19 (1976): 153.

60. Ibid., p. 36.

61. Robert Funk, "The Watershed of the American Biblical Tradition: The Chicago school, First Phase, 1892–1920," *Journal of Biblical Literature* 95 (1976): 4. A still useful survey of the main themes of American exegesis up to the middle of the twentieth century is Amos Wilder, "Biblical Hermeneutic and American Scholarship," in *Neutestamentliche Studien für Rudolf Bultmann*, ed. Walther Elthester (Berlin: Alfred Töpelmann, 1954), pp. 24–32.

62. Bennett, "Social Interpretation of Christianity," p. 113.

63. On the need for retrieval of the sociohistorical method of the early Chicago school of theology, including the thought of Mathews, see Jerome A. Stone, *The Minimalist Vision of Transcendence* (Albany: State University of New York Press, 1992), p. 143.

64. H. Richard Niebuhr, *Kingdom of God in America*, p. 183.

On the social gospel as a "decentralized, polycephalous movement of clergy and laity," see Smith, "To Reconstruct the World," p. 59.

65. II. Richard Niebuhr, "The Social Gospel and the Mind of Jesus," ed. Diane Yeager, *Journal of Religious Ethics* 16 (1988): 115. For a similar caution regarding attempts to fit Rauschenbusch's theology into the neat schema represented by the category "liberal," see Donovan Ebersole Smucker, "The Origins of Walter Rauschenbusch's Social Ethics," unpubl. Ph.D. diss. (University of Chicago Divinity School, 1975), pp. 11–19, 188–89.

66. Diane Yeager, "Editor's Introduction to the 'Social Gospel and the Mind of Jesus'," *Journal of Religious Ethics* 16 (1988): 109.

67. Robert T. Handy, "George D. Herron and the Kingdom Movement," *Church History* 19 (1950): 97–115. See also "Social Gospel in Historical Perspective," where Handy argues (p. 171) that the demise of neo-orthodoxy opens new perspectives on the social gospel movement.

68. Robert T. Handy, "George D. Herron and the Social Gospel in American Protestantism, 1890–1901," unpubl. Ph.D. diss. (University of Chicago, 1949), p. ii.

69. For a similar argument about Rauschenbusch, see Duke, "Theology Converses with Biographical Narrative," pp. 143–58.

70. William Hutchison, "The Americanness of the Social Gospel," *Church History* 44 (1975): 370, 380.

71. Ibid., p. 380.

72. Gorrell, *Age of Social Responsibility*, pp. 341–42.

73. Ibid., p. 3.

74. For an interpretation of Rauschenbusch's response to consistent eschatology which rebuts the received opinion that Rauschenbusch's kingdom theology was trapped within a progressivist paradigm, and which retrieves this theology as a reinterpretation of apocalyptic Christianity that strengthens the tie between Christian faith and praxis, see Strain, "Rauschenbusch: A Resource for Public Theology," pp. 25–26.

75. On the need for painstaking investigation of the theologies of social gospellers, as a complement to social and cultural histories of the social gospel, see William McGuire King, "'History as Revelation' in the Theology of the Social Gospel," *Harvard Theological Review* 76 (1983): 109–10.

76. The bibliography has been printed with a prefatory note about Mathews's revelance and career in *American Journal of Theology and Philosophy* 5 (1985): 3–26.

77. Stephen H. Wurster, "The Modernism of Shailer Mathews: A Study in American Religious Progressivism," unpubl. Ph.D. diss. (University of Iowa, 1972).

1. SHAILER MATHEWS

1. On the necessity for a "new moment" in Christian moral reflection about war and peace, see the National Conference of Catholic Bishops, *The Challenge of Peace* (Washington, D.C.: USCC, 1983).

2. To date, there is no book-length study of Mathews's life. In addition to NFO, short biographies of Mathews appear in Mathews's article "Theology as Group Belief," in *Contemporary American Theology*, ed. Vergilius T. Ferm (New York: Round Table, 1933), pp. 161–93; Edwin Aubrey, ed., *Shailer Mathews: Selections from the Memorial Service Held in Joseph Bond Chapel* (Chicago: University of Chicago Press, 1941); Robert Eldon Mathews, "Shailer Mathews: A Biographical Note," in *The Process of Religion: Essays in Honor of Dean Shailer Mathews*, ed. Miles H. Krumbine (New York: Macmillan, 1933), pp. 3–14; Bernard Meland, "Shailer Mathews," in *Dictionary of American Biography*, supp. III: 1941–45, ed. Edward T. James (New York: Scribner's, 1973), pp. 514–16; and "Shailer Mathews," in *The National Cyclopedia of American Biography* 10 (New York: James T. White, 1901), p. 74.

In addition, the following published and unpublished sources contain biographical information: Robert Wesley Clark, "The Contribution of Shailer Mathews to the Social Movement in American Protestantism," unpubl. Ph.D. diss. (Southern Baptist Seminary, New Orleans, La., 1960); Cecil Greek, *The Religious Roots of American Sociology* (New York: Garland, 1992); Greek, "The Social Gospel Movement and Early American Sociology," *Graduate Faculty Journal of Sociology* 3.1 (1978): 30–42; Lars Hoffman, "William Rainey Harper and the Chicago Fellowship," unpubl. Ph.D. diss. (University of Iowa, 1978); Hopkins, *Rise of Social Gospel*; Thomas Augustus Ray, "The Life and Thought of Shailer Mathews," unpubl. Th.D. diss. (New Orleans Baptist Theological Seminary, 1957); Smith, "Mathews: Theologian of Social Process"; Smith and Leonard Sweet, "Mathews: Chapter in Social Gospel Movement"; Mark G. Toulouse, "The Birth of the *Journal of Religion*," *Criterion* 23.1 (1984): 10–14; Arthur L. Tracy, "The Social Gospel, 'New' Immigration, and American Culture: An Analysis of the Attitude of Charles Ellwood, Shailer Mathews, and

Graham Taylor toward the 'New' Immigration," unpubl. Ph.D. diss. (American University, Washington, D.C., 1963); and Wurster, "Modernism of Shailer Mathews."

3. Letter, Shailer Mathews to Mrs. Martha Mathews Griswold, Adrian, Michigan, 6 December 1899, University of Chicago Archives, Divinity School Correspondence, box 6, folder 10.

4. "Theology as Group Belief," p. 163.

5. Robert Eldon Mathews, "Shailer Mathews," p. 3.

6. NFO, p. 11.

7. Ibid., p. 1; and "Theology as Group Belief," p. 163.

8. NFO, p. 12.

9. Ibid., p. 7; and Wurster, "Modernism of Shailer Mathews," p. 17.

10. See esp. Tracy, "The Social Gospel, 'New' Immigration"; and Smith and Sweet's useful intellectual biography, "Mathews: Chapter in Social Gospel," which places Mathews's political and economic ideas in a theological and cultural framework.

On the general tendency of social gospel political-economic thought to reformism, see Hopkins, Rise of Social Gospel, pp. 67–78; Greek, "Social Gospel Movement," p. 38 (on Small's gradualism); Vernon K. Dibble, The Legacy of Albion Small (Chicago: University of Chicago Press, 1975), pp. 138, 147 (on Small's preference for class cooperation, social harmony, and governmental control of capital short of socialism).

On the confluence of reformist concerns in the thought of Small, Ely, and Lester Ward, and on biographical connections between all three social gospel thinkers, see Dibble, Legacy, pp. 29, 31–32, 45; Richard Hofstadter, Social Darwinism in American Thought (Boston: Beacon, 1955), pp. 69–70, 107–10, 156–58; Greek, "Social Gospel Movement," 34; and Greek, "Religious Roots," 163f.

11. NFO, pp. 6–8. See also Robert Eldon Mathews, "Shailer Mathews," p. 4, in which Mathews's son speaks of his grandfather's economic views.

12. NFO, pp. 7–8.

13. On this, see Ernest Becker, "The Tragic Paradox of Albion Small and American Social Science," in The Lost Science of Man (New York: George Braziller, 1971), pp. 3–70; Dibble, Legacy, pp. 128–48; and Arthur J. Vidich and Stanford M. Lyman, American Sociology (New Haven, Conn.: Yale University Press, 1985), pp. 181–82, which notes that Small is virtually the only American sociologist to have carried on a lifelong explicit dialogue with the thought of Marx.

For Small's avowal that Marx was "one of the few really great thinkers in the history of social science" and "nearer to a correct diagnosis of the evils of our present property system than the wisdom of this world has yet been willing to admit," see "Socialism in the Light of Social Science," American Journal of Sociology (hereafter, AJS) 17 (1912): 808, 816.

14. See esp. "The Awakening of American Protestantism," *Constructive Quarterly* (hereafter, *CQ*) 1 (1913): 101–2; *The Making of To-Morrow: Interpretations of the World To-Day* (hereafter, *Making*) (New York: Eaton & Mains, 1913), pp. 15–17, 36–39, 44–47; *The Individual and the Social Gospel* (New York: Missionary Education Movement of U.S. and Canada, 1914), p. 45; "Poison Gas and Prohibition," *Independent* 105 (1921): 137–38; "The Christian Faith and the Life of the Community," in *The Christian Faith and Human Relations* (Philadelphia: Judson, 1922), pp. 66–68; and *The Validity of American Ideals* (New York: Abingdon, 1922), pp. 57, 121. On Mathews's attitudes toward immigrants, see Tracy, "Social Gospel, 'New' Immigration."

15. "Theology as Group Belief," p. 164.

16. *NFO*, p. 16.

17. Thomas W Goodspeed, "Albion Woodbury Small," *University of Chicago Record* n.s. 12 (1926): 244.

18. Ibid., p. 249, citing Mathews's personal reminiscences. See also *NFO*, p. 17.

19. On the German historical school of economic thought, see Theo Suranyi-Unger, "Economic Thought: The Historical School," in David L. Sills, ed., *International Encyclopedia of the Social Sciences* (New York: Macmillan, 1968), 4: 454–57.

20. On Small's influence on Mathews, see Smith, "Mathews: Theologian of Social Process," pp. 12–13.

21. *NFO*, p. 18. See also "Theology as Group Belief," p. 164; and "The Kingship of Christ. II: Christ and Education," *The Baptist* 2 (1921): 945.

22. *NFO*, p. 18.

23. "Theology as Group Belief," p. 165.

24. *NFO*, p. 24; "Theology as Group Belief," p. 165.

25. *NFO*, p. 37.

26. Ibid., p. 26.

27. Ibid., pp. 18–19, 26; "Theology as Group Belief," p. 165.

28. *NFO*, p. 28.

29. Ibid., p. 24.

30. Ibid., pp. 32–33.

31. "Theology as Group Belief," p. 166.

32. *NFO*, p. 38.

33. Ibid., p. 41–42.

34. For a persuasive statement of this case, see esp. Smith and Sweet, "Shailer Mathews: A Chapter in the Social Gospel Movement."

35. *NFO*, p. 42. On the importance of the Rankean approach to history in Mathews's theology, see Smith and Sweet, "Shailer Mathews: A Chapter in the Social Gospel," pp. 227–29.

36. *NFO*, p. 42; "Theology as Group Belief," p. 167. On Mathews as primarily a historical, rather than a systematic, theologian, see Edwin Aubrey, "Dean Mathews's Contribution to Theology," in *Memorial Service*, ed. Aubrey, pp. 17–19; on the importance of Mathews's training as a historian for his entire career, see Charles Harvey Arnold, *Near the Edge of the Battle: A Short History of the Divinity School and the 'Chicago school of Theology' 1866–1966* (Chicago: Divinity School Association of University of Chicago, 1966), pp. 36–39.

37. *NFO*, p. 42; "Group Belief," p. 167. For references (both laudatory and critical) to Harnack in Mathews's work, see the review of Renan's *History of the People of Israel*, BW 8 (1896): 412–13; *STJ*, pp. 49, 51; "Professor McGiffert on the Apostolic Age," *BW* 10 (1897): 35–43; "An Outline of the Life of Jesus with References for Reading," *BW* 11 (1898): 328; review of Wernle, *The Beginnings of Christianity*, BW 24 (1904): 389–92; *MHNT*, pp. 138n.1, 145n.1, 197n.1, 261, 311; "The Social Origin of Theology," *AJS* 18 (1912): 296; review of Dewick, *Primitive Christian Eschatology*, BW 42 (1913): 120; "Contemporary Theological Movements in Europe," *Chautauquan* 70 (1913): 309; *JSI*, 92n.19; and *NFO*, p. 283.

38. I am indebted for this information to Kenneth Smith, who told me in an interview (13 April 1984) that Edwin Aubrey often spoke of Wagner's contributions to Mathews's thought. According to Smith, Mathews considered Aubrey his most astute student; thus Aubrey was invited to write the lead essay in Mathews's 1933 *Festschrift, Process of Religion*. Smith also noted that Wagner was a founder of the German Evangelical Social Congress and economic *Verein*, and that he was connected to Bismarck through marriage and assisted in such significant German social reform developments of the 1880s and 1890s as the creation of public housing and the legislation of a graduated income tax.

On Ely's grounding in German historical economics, see Ely, "The Past and the Present of Political Economy," *Johns Hopkins University Studies in Historical and Political Science* 2 (1884): 64f.; and Hofstadter, *Social Darwinism*, p. 146. On the persistent influence of the German historical school on Small, see Dibble, *Legacy of Albion Small*, pp. 2–3. On the German school's contribution to early American sociology in general (noting Ely's [p. 111] and Small's [p. 124] indebtedness to it), see Ross, *Origins of American Social Science*, pp. 104–5. On Ely's influence on Mathews, see Smith, "Social Process," pp. 35–39. On Ward's intent to oppose rigid interpretations of economic growth (as bound by ironclad laws and not susceptible to human creative management), see Hofstadter, *Social Darwinism*, pp. 43–44, 69–70, 76; and on the impact of these historicist presuppositions in Ward's *Dynamic Sociology* (1883) on the entire social gospel movement, see Greek, "Social Gospel," 34.

39. "Theology as Group Belief," p. 167.

40. *NFO*, p. 49; and Robert E. Mathews, "Shailer Mathews," p. 8.

41. *NFO*, p. 50.

42. Ibid., p. 51.

43. On Mathews's predominant concern in his early years at Chicago to apply the methods of historical and sociological study to the New Testament, with particular emphasis on what such application yielded for social reformers, see Wurster, "Modernism of Shailer Mathews," p. 88.

44. On the missionary spirit informing the Chicago school from its foundation, see *inter alia* the following: William J. Hynes, *Shirley Jackson Case and the Chicago school: The Socio-Historical Method* (Chico, Calif.: Scholars Press, 1981); the unpubl. papers of the 1969 Consultation on the Chicago school (Vanderbilt, 1969) coordinated by Robert Funk; Wurster, "Modernism of Shailer Mathews," p. 95 (on the missionary intent of W. R. Harper in creating the AISL to popularize the results of historicocritical work on the scriptures); and John Henry Barrows, "The American Institute of Sacred Literature: A Historical Sketch, 1881–1902," *BW* 19 (1902): 214–22. For Mathews's reflections on Harper's missionary concern expressed in the founding of *BW*, see "William Rainey Harper as an Editor," *BW* 27 (1906): 204–8. On Harper's institution of *BW* deliberately to popularize the theological views of the Chicago school, see Toulouse, "Birth of *Journal of Religion*," p. 12.

45. On this context for the theology of the Chicago school, see esp. Hynes, *Case and Chicago School*, pp. 1–5.

46. *NFO*, p. 52.

47. Mathews, "A Historical Statement," in *The Quarter-Centennial Celebration of the University of Chicago* (Chicago: University of Chicago Press, 1918), p. 123. On Harper as a "tireless Baptist" who wanted to present American Christians with the findings of higher criticism in order to "bring Jesus into history," see Marty, *Irony of It All*, pp. 40–41.

48. Hynes, *Case and Chicago School*, pp. 1–3. On the link between the AISL and Chautauqua, see esp. Barrows, "American Institute of Sacred Literature," p. 218. On the importance of the relationship between Chautauqua and the sociology department at the University of Chicago through George Vincent, an early Chicago sociologist and son of John H. Vincent, one of Chautauqua's founders, see Greek, "Social Gospel Movement," pp. 193–94. On Chautauqua's links to the social gospel in general, see Hopkins, *Rise of Social Gospel*, pp. 163–64.

49. Dorothy Ross, *The Origins of American Social Science* (Cambridge: Cambridge University Press, 1991), p. 123.

50. Hynes, *Case and Chicago School*, pp. 5–12.

51. Thomas S. Kuhn, *The Structure of Scientific Revolutions* (Chicago: University of Chicago Press, 1962); Stephen Toulmin, *Human Understanding*, vol. I: *The Collective Use and Evolution of Concepts* (Princeton, N.J.: Princeton University Press, 1972), pp. 98–125, esp. 106, 116; Toulmin, *The*

Philosophy of Science: An Introduction (New York: Harper & Row, 1960), pp. 105–21; and Toulmin, *Cosmopolis: The Hidden Agenda of Modernity* (New York: Free Press, 1990), pp. 84, 127, 132. On parallels between Mathews's sociohistorical method and Kuhn's thesis about scientific revolutions, see William Dean, *History Making History: The New Historicism in American Religious Thought* (Albany: State University of New York Press, 1988), p. 55.

52. On the Chicago school, see W. Creighton Peden and Jerome A. Stone, *The Chicago School of Theology—Pioneers in Religious Inquiry*, vol. 1: *The Early Chicago School, 1906–1956* (Lewiston, N.Y.: Edwin Mellen Press, 1996). Pp. 119–86 of this volume focus on Mathews.

53. *NFO*, p. 83.

54. Announcements for these courses are in *BW* 5 (1895): 151, 222, 223; and 6 (1895): 229. For similar announcements of an extensive lecture schedule in subsequent years, see 7 (1896): 146, 225, 303, 534; 8 (1896): 311, 396, 497.

55. *NFO*, p. 83.

56. Ibid., p. 90.

57. Ibid.

58. Ibid., p. 93.

59. The editorials are reproduced in *Making*. On the intent of the journal under Mathews's editorship to influence the "social mind" of the day, see Gorrell, *Age of Social Responsibility*, p. 47.

60. *NFO*, pp. 175–78.

61. Ibid., p. 134.

62. *Individual and Social Gospel*, pp. 29–30.

63. *NFO*, pp. 96–97. See *Woman's Citizen's Library*, 12 vols. (Chicago: The Civics Society, 1913–14).

64. *NFO*, pp. 101–2.

65. As with Harnack, Mathews seldom refers to Ritschl by name; when he does so, he tends to distance himself from this liberal Protestant theologian: see the editorial "Certain Hopeful Tendencies in Today's Theological Thought," *BW* 17 (1901): 326; *MHNT*, p. 74; *GMM*, 140f.; "The Christological Problem" (review of Sanday, *Christologies Ancient and Modern*), *AJT* 15 (1911): 136; *Growth of Idea of God*, pp. 179–80; and *NFO*, p. 223.

66. The dominance of theological reconstruction in the thought of American theologians in this period is clearly indicated in *BW* editorials of the prewar years, in which the phrase recurs with almost obsessive regularity. For the confluence of concern for theological and social reconstruction among American theologians of the period, see William R. Hutchison, *The Modernist Impulse in American Protestantism* (New York: Oxford University Press, 1976), pp. 164–84.

67. Hutchison, *Modernist Impulse*, pp. 145–47, 164–84; and Gorrell, *Age of Social Responsibility*, pp. 56–63.

68. The editorial is found in *BW* 40 (1912): 363–65. On the crisis rhetoric of the social gospel as a deviation from liberalism, see King, "'Theology as History'," p. 112. As King notes, this deviation did not escape the attention of H. Richard Niebuhr, who remarks in 1931 that "there was a hiatus between liberal theology and the 'social gospel' which was not accidental but went very deep" (citing "The Social Gospel and the Liberal Theology," *Keryx* 22 [1931], pp. 12–13).

69. *NFO*, p. 248.

70. Ibid., pp. 109–11.

71. Ibid., pp. 76, 116–18, 157.

72. Ibid., p. 260.

73. A good reconstructive historical account of the Foster debacle, told with great sympathy for Foster, is Arnold, *Near the Edge*; see also L. I. Sweet, "The University of Chicago Revisited: The Modernization of Theology, 1890–1940," *Foundations* 22 (1979): 324–51; and E. A. Towne, "A Single-minded Theologian: George Burman Foster at Chicago," *Foundations* 20 (1977): 163–80. On Harper as Rockefeller's "surrogate," see Arthur J. Vidich and Stanford M. Lyman, *American Sociology* (New Haven, Conn.: Yale University Press, 1985), p. 179; see also Ross, *Origins of American Social Science,* p. 126, and Dennis Smith, *The Chicago School: A Liberal Critique of Capitalism* (New York: St. Martin's, 1988), p. 1.

74. *Select Medieval Documents Illustrating the History of Church and Empire, 754 A.D.–1254 A.D.* (New York: Silver, 1892; repr. New York: AMS, 1974).

75. *The French Revolution* (New York: Longmans, 1901).

76. *The Social Teaching of Jesus* (New York: Macmillan, 1897).

77. *History of New Testament Times in Palestine, 175 B.C.–70 A.D.* (New York: Macmillan, 1899).

78. *The Messianic Hope in the New Testament* (Chicago: University of Chicago Press, 1905); hereafter cited as *MHNT*.

79. *NFO*, p. 95.

80. Ibid.

81. Ibid.

82. F. C. Grant, "Ethics and Eschatology in the Teachings of Jesus," *Journal of Religion* (hereafter *JR*) 22 (1942): 359–70. For a recent appraisal of the work and its significance, see William McGuire King, "The Biblical Base of the Social Gospel," in *The Bible and Social Reform*, ed. Ernest R. Sandeen (Philadelphia: Fortress, 1982), pp. 58–84. Another nuanced and sympathetic treatment of the exegetical work of the early Chicago school is to be found in Amos Wilder, *Eschatology and Ethics in the Teaching of Jesus*, rev. ed. (New York: Harper, 1950), pp. 24–30.

83. *The Church and the Changing Order* (New York: Macmillan, 1907). On the book's purpose, see *NFO*, p. 96, 120–21.

84. "The Development of Social Christianity in America during the Past Twenty-five Years," *JR* 7 (1927): 381. On the crisis theology of *Christianity and the Social Crisis*, noting the strong appeal to a present understanding of the kingdom of God in the work, see Gorrell, *Age of Social Responsibility*, pp. 56–59. Gorrell notes that *Church and Changing*'s emphasis on crisis was even more acute than Rauschenbusch's: pp. 59–63. See also Smith, "To Reconstruct the World," p. 41.

85. *The Gospel and the Modern Man* (New York: Macmillan, 1910); hereafter cited as *GMM*.

86. *MHNT*, p. 317n.1 declares that *GMM* is to be a volume of theological reconstruction accompanying *MHNT*.

87. *NFO*, p. 282.

88. *Making*, p. 30.

89. On this, see George M. Marsden, *Fundamentalism and American Culture* (New York: Oxford University Press, 1980).

90. *The Social Gospel* (Philadelphia: American Baptist Publications Society, 1909), p. 65.

91. Ibid., p. 67.

92. Unattributed editorial, "Shall We Take Jesus Seriously?" *BW* 44 (1914): 230.

93. *The Spiritual Interpretation of History* (Cambridge, Mass.: Harvard University Press, 1916), p. viii; hereafter cited as *SIH*.

94. "The Spiritual Challenge to Democracy," *Constructive Quarterly* 5 (1917): 514.

95. See e.g. *Patriotism and Religion* (New York: Macmillan, 1918), pp. 38–39; and "The Moral Value of Patriotism," *BW* 52 (1918): 25–26.

96. *Patriotism and Religion*, p. 103.

97. *NFO*, pp. 198–202.

98. "Present Co-operative Action by the Churches," *BW* 49 (1917): 76; see also *Jesus on Social Institutions* (New York: Macmillan, 1928), pp. 60, 69, 71; hereafter cited as *JSI*.

99. *Patriotism and Religion*, p. 32; see also "Religion and War," *BW* 52 (1918): 167, 175. For a critical appraisal of Mathews's understanding of democracy, see Francis Schüssler-Fiorenza, "American Culture and Modernism: Shailer Mathews's Interpretation of American Christianity," in *America in Theological Perspective*, ed. Thomas M. McFadden (New York: Seabury, 1976), pp. 180–86.

100. "The Christian Faith and the Life of the Community," in *The Christian Faith and Human Relations* (Philadelphia: Judson, 1922), p. 56; see also *Creative Christianity* (Nashville, Tenn.: Cokesbury, 1935), p. 39.

On John Dewey's understanding of democracy as more than a political or economic construct, but a utopian symbol, see Steven C. Rockefeller, "John Dewey, Spiritual Democracy, and the Human Future," *Cross Currents* 39 (1989): 300–21.

101. Gorrell is illuminating with regard to how social gospellers after World War I tended to transform kingdom rhetoric into democracy rhetoric: *Age of Social Responsibility*, pp. 293–97.

102. "The Evolution of Religion," *American Journal of Theology* 15 (1911): 57–82; "The Social Origin of Theology," *American Journal of Sociology* 18 (1912): 289–317; "Generic Christianity," *Constructive Quarterly* 2 (1914): 702–23; "Theology and the Social Mind," *BW* 46 (1915): 201–48; "The Historical Study of Religion," in Gerald B. Smith, ed., *A Guide to the Study of the Christian Religion* (Chicago: University of Chicago Press, 1916), pp. 19–79; "The Functional Value of Doctrines of the Atonement," *JR* 1 (1921): 146–59; and "Theology from the Point of View of Social Psychology," *JR* 3 (1923): 337–51.

On the Chicago school of theology, see Arnold, *Near the Edge*; Larry E. Axel, "Process and Religion: The History of a Tradition at Chicago," *Process Studies* 8 (1978): 231–39; Winthrop S. Hudson, *Religion in America* (New York: Scribner's, 1969), pp. 263–90, esp. 274–77; A. C. McGiffert, "The Chicago School of Theology," in *Encyclopedia of Religion*, ed. Vergilius Ferm (New York: Philosophical Library, 1945); Sidney Mead, "Character and Continuity," *Criterion* 9.4 (Winter 1970): 25–27; Bernard Meland, "A Long Look at the Divinity School and Its Present Crisis," *Criterion* 1.2 (Summer 1962): 21–30; Darnell Rucker, *The Chicago Pragmatists* (Minneapolis: University of Minnesota Press, 1969); Larry I. Sweet, "The University of Chicago Revisited: The Modernization of Theology, 1890–1940," *Foundations* 22 (1979): 324–51; and Daniel Day Williams, "Experience and Tradition in American Theology," in *Religion in Amercan Life*, vol. 1: *The Shaping of American Religion*, ed. James W. Smith and A. L. Jamieson (Princeton, N.J.: Princeton University Press, 1961), pp. 443–95.

103. "Theology and the Social Mind," p. 204.

104. In his memorial appreciation for Lester Ward in *AJS*, Small states, "I would rather have written *Dynamic Sociology* than any other book that has ever appeared in America" (*AJS* 19 [1913–14]: 77).

105. On this, Arnold, *Near the Edge*, pp. 38–39, is particularly enlightening.

106. On this schema, see particularly "Generic Christianity," pp. 702–23. The successive phases of the doctrine of God are worked out in detail in Mathews's well-known *The Growth of the Idea of God* (New York: Macmillan, 1931).

107. "Generic Christianity," p. 717; and "Theology and the Social Mind," pp. 244–46.

108. *SIH*, p. 153.

109. Ibid., p. 207.

110. "Patriotism and Religion," p. 26.

111. "The Deity of Christ and Social Reconstruction," *Constructive Quarterly* 8 (1920): 45. See also "Religion for Democracy," *Independent* 86 (1916): 53–54; "Spiritual Challenge to Democracy, p. 519; and *Validity of American Ideals*, pp; 93-123. For the late Mathews, science, rather than democracy, furnishes the creative social mind for religious thinking: see *Growth of Idea of God*, p. 175, 183–84; *The Atonement and the Social Process* (New York: Macmillan, 1930), p. 181; *Creative Christianity*, p. 69; and "The Church and the Social Order," in *The Church at Work in the Modern World*, ed. W. C. Bower (Chicago: University of Chicago Press, 1935), p. 194.

112. *Patriotism and Religion*, p. 39.

113. *NFO*, p. 207.

114. A brief sketch of Mathews's life and career up to 1930 is to be found in *The Divinity Student* 7 (1930): 3. Various volumes of *Who's Who* in the 1930s and up to 1942 also contain brief biographies.

115. See Erik Erikson, *Identity and the Life Cycle* (New York: Norton, 1959), p. 103; and *Dimensions of a New Identity* (New York: Norton, 1974), p. 124.

116. "The By-Products of a Creative Age," *BW* 44 (1914): 2; see also "The Social Optimism of Faith in a Divine Jesus," *BW* 43 (1914): 154.

117. "The Awakening of American Protestantism," *Constructive Quarterly* 1 (1913): 103–4.

118. Ibid. On the historical origins of the term "fundamentalism"—and distinctions between fundamentalism and premillennialism—see Marty, *Irony of It All*, p. 237.

119. "Ten Years of American Protestantism," *North American Review* 217 (1923): 592.

120. Shirley Jackson Case, *The Millennial Hope: A Phase of War-Time Thinking* (Chicago: University of Chicago Press, 1918).

121. *Will Christ Come Again?* (Chicago: AISL, 1917).

122. Haldeman's tract was privately published, without date; Mauro's was published by Francis Emory Fitch of New York, without date.

123. Toulouse, "Birth of *JR*," pp. 10–11.

124. *Christianity and Social Process* (New York: Harper, 1934), p. 144.

125. "Church and Social Order," p. 209.

126. Ibid.

127. "Development of Social Christianity," p. 385.

128. *Christianity and Social Process*, pp. 99–100.

129. *Creative Christianity*, p. 7.

130. *The Church and the Christian* (New York: Macmillan, 1938), p. 147.

131. Ibid., p. 148. For a historical overview of the interchange between American and European theology in the post–World War I period, see Sydney E. Ahlstrom, "Continental Influence on American Christian Thought since World War I," *Church History* 27 (1958): 256–72; and Robert T. Handy, "The American Religious Depression, 1925–1935," *Church History* 29 (1960): 3–16.

On the interchange between the Chicago school of theology and the Continent in particular, see James Luther Adams, "The Relationship between the Chicago school and the Continent," unpubl. paper at the Consultation on the Chicago school, Vanderbilt, 1969 (organized by Robert Funk).

132. "Unrepentant Liberalism," *American Scholar* 7 (1938): 296.

133. Ibid., p. 307.

134. Ibid., pp. 296–99.

135. Ibid., p. 298.

136. *The Faith of Modernism* (New York: Macmillan, 1924), pp. 283–84.

137. *NFO*, p. 284.

138. *Faith of Modernism*, p. 13.

139. For an extended discussion of Mathews's modernism, especially as it parallels that of European Roman Catholic modernists, see William D. Lindsey, "Shailer Mathews on Doctrinal Development: Parallels between American Protestant Modernism and European Roman Catholic Modernism," *American Journal of Theology and Philosophy* 11 (1990): 115–32. For a recent defense of critical modernism in Christian theology today, see Edward Farley, "The Modernist Element in Protestantism," *Theology Today* 47 (1990): 131–44.

140. "Certain Hopeful Tendencies in Today's Theological Thought," *BW* 17 (1901): 324–25; see also "The Significance of the Church to the Social Movement," *American Journal of Sociology* 4 (1899): 619.

141. "Two Obligations of the Church to a Christian Society," *BW* 18 (1901): 323.

142. *Church and Changing Order*, p. 178.

143. *GMM*, pp. 4–5. See also Mathews's review of Paul Wernle's *The Beginnings of Christianity*, *BW* 24 (1904): 389–92; "Generic Christianity," pp. 709–10; *MHNT*, p. 250; and "Deity of Christ and Social Reconstruction," pp. 40–41. Roy Harrisville thinks that, in defending Paul against the charge that he perverted the message of Jesus, B. W. Bacon was a "unique and often solitary figure" in American New Testament scholarship in the early twentieth century: "Representative Lives of Jesus," in *The Historical Jesus and the Kerygmatic Christ*, ed. Carl E. Braaten and Roy A. Harrisville (New York: Abingdon, 1964), p. 187. But as early as 1904 Mathews was also combating this charge: see esp. *GMM*, pp. 13–24 on this.

144. *Church and Changing Order*, p. 89.

145. "Protestant Liberalism," pp. 300–1.

146. Ibid., pp. 305–7.

147. *Is God Emeritus?* (New York: Macmillan, 1940).

148. On this, see Lindsey, "Social Gospel and Feminism."

149. *Creative Christianity*, p. 15.

150. Ibid., p. 29.

151. Ibid., p. 30.

2. THE SOCIAL TEACHING OF JESUS

1. "The Ideals of Social Reformers," *AJS* 2 (1896–97): 202. On Rauschenbusch's "discovery" of the kingdom of God concept as a bridge between privatized and socially engaged faith, see his essay "The Kingdom of God," *Cleveland's Young Men* 27 (9 January 1913), repr. in Handy, *Social Gospel*, p. 266. For the significance of this essay in Rauschenbusch's biography, see Gorrell, *Age of Social Responsibility*, pp. 17–18; and William D. Nelson, "The Kingdom of God and Walter Rauschenbusch: A Synthesis of Personal Salvation and Social Transformation" unpubl. D. Min. diss. (Wesley Theological Seminary, 1989), p. 24.

2. "Christian Sociology," *AJS* 1 (1895–96): 69–78, 182–94, 359–80, 457–72, 604–17, 771–84; 2 (1896–97): 108–17, 274–87, 416–32.

3. Grant, "Ethics and Eschatology in Teachings of Jesus," p. 359.

4. "The Development of Sociology and the Social Gospel in America," *Sociological Analysis* 30 (1969): 42 (italics added). See in addition Abell, *Urban Impact on American Protestantism*, pp. 232–45; J. Graham Morgan, "Sociology in America: A Study of its Institutional Development until 1900," unpubl. Ph.D. diss. (Oxford University, 1966); and Ross, *Origins of American Social Science*, pp. 102–6. For a critique of Morgan's methodology, see Jeffrey K. Hadden, Charles F. Longino Jr., and Myer S. Reed Jr., "Further Reflections on the Development of Sociology and the Social Gospel in America," *Sociological Analysis* 35 (1974): 282–86.

5. Morgan, "Development," p. 52; and "Sociology," pp. 252–53. On the predominance of clergy and sons of clergy in the first generation of American sociologists, see Dibble, *Legacy*, pp. 3, 223–24n.15.

6. Arthur J. Vidich and Stanford M. Lyman, *American Sociology* (New Haven, Conn.: Yale University Press, 1985), p. 179.

7. Ibid.

8. "Development," p. 47.

9. "Social Gospel Movement," p. 40. See also *Religious Roots*, pp. 51f., 101.

10. Morgan, "Development," p. 43. See also Ross, *Origins of American Social Science*, p. 178, noting Small and Ward's concern for the pragmatist ap-

plications of sociological theory; Smith, *Chicago School*, pp. 5, 211, noting the Chicago school of sociology's predominant concern with applied sociology; and Vidich and Lyman, *American Sociology*, p. 178, on Small's reformist zeal.

11. On the influence on the social gospel movement of Ward's *Dynamic Sociology* (1883) and his critique of Herbert Spencer's and William Graham Sumner's laissez-faire philosophy of social evolution, see Greek, "Social Gospel," p. 34. On Spencer's influence in America, see Hofstadter, *Social Darwinism*, pp. 43–44.

12. Small, "The Significance of Sociology for Ethics," in *Decennial Publications of the University of Chicago* (Chicago: University of Chicago Press, 1903), series 1, 4, p. 119. In the essay, Small critiques Spencer for relinquishing the applicability of social science to a mere theoretical articulation: p. 5.

13. On Ward's sociology as enfolding "an inner-worldly eschatology," and on his understanding of social process as a "transvaluation of theodicy," see Vidich and Lyman, *American Sociology*, p. 23.

14. Small sketches his theory of "volitional social progress" in an 1889 address to the 60th American Institute of Instruction, entitled *The Dynamics of Social Progress* (Concord, N.H.: Republican Press Association, 1889); see Dibble, *Legacy*, p. 27. On Ward's notion of telesis as the conscious direction of evolution, see Greek, "Social Gospel," p. 34; and Hofstadter, *Social Darwinism*, p. 76.

15. On Herron, see Handy, "Herron and Kingdom Movement," pp. 97–115; and "Herron and Social Gospel." For Herron's turn to socialism, see esp. p. 38. See also Greek, *Religious Roots*, pp. 100, 118.

16. Greek, *Religious Roots*, pp. 118–19, citing Benjamin Rader, *The Academic Mind and Reform: The Influence of Richard T. Ely in American Life* (Lexington: University Press of Kentucky, 1966): 134. On Ely as a social gospeller, see Vidich and Lyman, *American Sociology*, pp. 153–57.

17. Abell, *Urban Impact on American Protestantism*, pp. 110–11.

18. On 10 April 1895, Small wrote Ward stating that Herron had "practically wrecked" Ely's Institute of Christian Sociology: see Stern, ed., "The Letters of Albion W. Small to Lester F. Ward: I," *Social Forces* 12 (1933): 171.

19. On Small's concern with the sociological basis of Christian sociology, see Greek, *Religious Roots*, pp. 111–17; Ross, *Origins of American Social Science*, pp. 122–38; Smith, *Chicago School*, pp. 77–78, 85; and Vidich and Lyman, *American Sociology*, pp. 178–94.

20. "The Limits of Christian Sociology," *AJS* 1 (1895–96): 510–11.

21. *An Introduction to the Study of Society* (Chicago: American Book, 1894), p. 32. On this study as an attempt to establish a scientific basis for sociology, see Herman and Julia R. Schwendinger, *The Sociologists of the Chair* (New York: Basic Books, 1974), pp. 236–40.

22. Dibble, *Legacy*, p. 164; the letter is reproduced in its entirety. See also Ross, *Origins of American Sociology*, p. 127.

23. "The Era of Sociology," *AJS* 1 (1895): 15.

24. Greek, "Social Gospel," pp. 35–36. One of Small's earliest writings, an 1893 outline for his Colby sociology course, shows him already concerned with the question of the scientific basis of the new discipline: see Dibble, *Legacy*, p. 10 and pp. 159–62, reproducing a 29 December 1894, letter to William Rainey Harper on the need for a statistician in the Chicago department.

25. "Christian Sociology," *AJS* 1 (1895): 216. See Dibble, *Legacy*, p. 33.

26. On this, see Greek, *Religious Roots*, p. 115; Ross, *Origins of American Social Science*, p. 125; and Smith, *Chicago School*, pp. 77–78. For evidence that Ward's concern to define the new discipline of sociology also arose in part from his alarm at confusion about Christian sociologists' applications of the discipline, see Ward, "Contemporary Sociology," *AJS* 7 (1902): 475–500, esp. 477–78.

27. "Significance of Sociology for Ethics," p. 146.

28. Small, *General Sociology* (Chicago: University of Chicago, 1905), p. 303, spells out the link between superperspectival sociological theory and political application.

29. *Introduction to the Study of Society*, p. 373.

30. *Origins of Sociology* (New York: Russell and Russell, 1924), p. 62.

31. On the "quietist use" of Small's holism, see Ross, *Origins of American Social Science*, p. 127.

32. See Dibble, *Legacy*, pp. 138, 142–47; Smith, *Chicago school*, p. 76; and Vidich and Lyman, *American Sociology*, p. 179.

33. As cited, Dibble, *Legacy*, pp. 26–27.

34. "The Limits of Christian Sociology," pp. 510–11.

35. Ibid., p. 511.

36. Small to Lester F. Ward, 10 April 1895, in Stern, ed., "Letters: I," p. 171.

37. *Between Eras* (Kansas City, Mo.: Intercollegiate Press, 1913), p. 73. See also Small's scathing review of Arthur J. Penty, *Towards a Christian Sociology*, *AJS* 30 (1924–25): 225–226.

38. On the relationship between Small and Mathews, reflected in Mathews's choice of a career and the development of his thought after he arrived in Chicago, as so close that it is impossible to understand Mathews without recourse to Small, see Smith, "Mathews: Theologian of Social Process," p. 13.

39. Synopsis of Z. S. Holbrook, "Christian Sociology," *BW* 4 (1894): 450.

40. Synopsis of John B. Sewall, "The Social Ethic of Jesus," *BW* 5 (1895): 380 (emphasis in original).

41. Synopsis of Holbrook, "Christian Sociology," p. 450.

42. "Editorial: Sociology and New Testament Study," *BW* 5 (1895): 3.

43. "The Captivity of Judah," in *History, Prophecy, and Gospel: Expository Sermons on the International Sunday-School Lessons for 1891*, ed. E. Benjamin Andrews (Boston: Silver, Burdett, 1891), p. 237.

44. Dennis Smith, *The Chicago School: A Liberal Critique of Capitalism* (New York: St. Martin's, 1988), p. 76.

45. "Editorial: Sociology and New Testament Study," *BW* 5 (1895): 1–6.

46. "Editorial," *BW* 6 (1895): 3. *BW* did not have a consistent policy regarding editorial titles in these years; whereas some editorials are titled, others are not.

47. *NFO*, p. 48.

48. Dibble, *Legacy*, p. 29.

49. Wurster, "Modernism of Shailer Mathews," p. 70. See *NFO*, p. 50.

50. Hopkins, *Rise of Social Gospel*, p. 112.

51. Letter, Mathews to E. D. Burton, 22 October 1893, Burton Papers, Divinity School Archives, box 6, folder 13.

52. Letter, Burton to Mathews, 30 December 1893, Burton Papers, Divinity School Archives, box 6, folder 14.

53. Letter, Mathews to Burton, 4 December 1893, Burton Papers, Divinity School Archives, box 6, folder 14.

54. Letter, Mathews to Burton, 1 December 1893, Burton Papers, Divinity School Archives, box 6, folder 14.

55. Dibble, *Legacy*, pp. 2–3, is a short biographical sketch. See also Goodspeed, "Albion Woodbury Small," pp. 240–48.

56. "Christ Comforting His Apostles," in *History, Prophecy, and Gospel*, pp. 380–88.

57. Reviews of Wilbur F. Crafts, *Practical Christian Sociology*; and Washington Gladden, *Ruling Ideas of the Present Age, AJS* 1 (1895–96): 494–98. On the kingdom of God in Small's sociology as the ideal toward which history progresses, see Ross, *Origins of American Social Science*, p. 125.

58. For a recent interpretation of Mathew's theology that emphasizes the sociological foundation of his theological system, and combats the "scientific" interpretation of his thought that has predominated until now (without discounting that influence in his theology), see Creighton Peden, *The Chicago School: Voices in Liberal Religious Thought* (Bristol, Ind.: Wyndham Hall, 1987), pp. 12–23, esp. pp. 22–23.

59. See Smith, *Chicago School*, p. 3.

60. *STJ*, p. l.

61. Ibid.

62. Ibid., p. 2.

63. Ibid., pp. 2–3.

64. Ibid., p. 3.

65. Ibid.

66. Ibid., p. 4.

67. Ibid.

68. Ibid., pp. 4–5.

69. Ibid., p. 5.

70. Ibid., p. 6.

71. On the social anthropology of the social gospel and its concept of social sin as contributions of this theological movement that continue to have significance for Christian theology, see Haight, "Mission of Church in Theology of Social Gospel," pp. 495–96; and Haight and Langan, "Recent Catholic Social Teaching in Light of Social Gospel," pp. 120–23.

72. Ibid., pp. 6–7.

73. Ibid.

74. Ibid., p. 8.

75. For a brief overview of Mathews's exegetical presuppositions in the period leading up to *STJ*, see Wurster, "Modernism of Shailer Mathews," p. 90f.

76. *NFO*, pp. 50–51.

77. See, e.g., "Helps to the Study of the Life of Jesus Christ," *BW* 6 (1895): 524–29; and "An Outline of the Life of Jesus with References for Reading," *BW* 11 (1898): 328–40.

78. "Editorials," *BW* 4 (1894): 161–66, 241–43; 6 (1895): 81–87; 7 (1896): 81–85; 9 (1897): 81–86; 10 (1897): 161–65, 241–45; 11 (1898): 225–28.

79. "Editorials," *BW* 4 (1894): 166; 6 (1895): 81–87; 9 (1897): 81; and 11 (1898): 226.

80. See Lars Hoffman, "William Rainey Harper and the Chicago Fellowship," unpubl. Ph.D. diss. (University of Iowa, 1978), pp. 68–75.

81. "Editorials," *BW* 7 (1896): 81; and 11 (1898): 226–28. See also the review of F. Bruce's *Apologetic*, *BW* 4 (1894): 313.

82. "Editorial," *BW* 11 (1898): 226. See also "Editorial," *BW* 4 (1894): 164. The claim that criticism is destructive as a preparatory phase is found as early as 1893 in "Rebuilding," p. 15.

83. Mathews employs "essence of Christianity" language in this period, but later drops this as he develops his social process theology in the period 1900–10.

84. "Editorial," *BW* 10 (1897): 243.

85. Ibid., pp. 243–44.

86. *STJ*, p. 10.

87. Ibid., p. 11.

88. Ibid.

89. Ibid., p. 142.

90. Ibid., p. 12.

91. Ibid.

92. Ibid.

93. Ibid., pp. 12–13.

94. Ibid., p. 13.

95. Ibid.

96. Ibid.

97. Ibid., pp. 13–14.

98. Ibid., p. 13.

99. Mathews's editorials and book reviews of the period reflect his determination to find a conservative solution to criticism. In his later work, he would often castigate scripture scholars whose desire to display what he calls "cleverness" in their interpretation of biblical texts exceeds the bounds of what he regards as sane scholarship.

100. Ibid., p. 14.

101. Ibid., p. 15.

102. Ibid.

103. Ibid.

104. Ibid.

105. Ibid.

106. "Social Ethics of Jesus," *BW* 6 (1896): 303.

107. *STJ*, p. 40.

108. Ibid.

109. Ibid., p. 41.

110. Ibid. Mathews was among the earliest American scripture scholars to advert to the modern exegetical significance of the Son of Man title and its apocalyptic background.

111. Ibid., p. 42.

112. Ibid.

113. Ibid., p. 43.

114. Ibid., p. 44.

115. Ibid., p. 44n.2.

116. Ibid., p. 45.

117. Ibid., p. 46.

118. Ibid.

119. Ibid., p. 47, citing Julius Kaftan, *The Truth of the Christian Religion*, 2: 377, 379.

120. *STJ*, pp. 48–49.

121. Ibid., p. 189n.1.

122. Ibid., p. 47n.6, citing J. Weiss, *Predigt Jesu*, p. 64.

123. *STJ*, p. 49.

124. Ibid., citing A. Harnack, *Dogmengeschichte*, 1: 62.

125. *STJ*, p. 50, citing Meyer, *Commentary on Matthew*, 3:2, and J. Weiss, *Predigt Jesu*, p. 76.

126. *STJ*, p. 51.

127. Ibid.

128. Ibid., citing Harnack, *Dogmengeschichte*, 1: 58.

129. Ibid., pp. 51–52.

130. Ibid., p. 53.

131. Ibid., p. 54 (emphases in original).

132. Ibid., p. 55.

133. Ibid., pp. 55–56.

134. Ibid., p. 57.

135. Ibid., p. 58.

136. Ibid., pp. 58–59.

137. Ibid., pp. 59.

138. Ibid., pp. 59–62; see also p. 206.

139. Ibid., pp. 62–63.

140. Ibid., pp. 63, 67–69.

141. The conclusion under consideration is *STJ* 4: 70–77; 5: 77–78 are merely a brief concluding statement.

142. Ibid., p. 70.

143. Ibid.

144. Ibid.

145. Ibid., pp. 71–72.

146. Ibid.

147. Ibid., p. 72.

148. Ibid., pp. 75–76.

149. "Awakening of American Protestantism," pp. 17–8.

150. *STJ*, p. 73.

151. Ibid., p. 74.

152. Ibid., pp. 76–78.

153. See "Watershed of American Biblical Tradition," pp. 17–18.

154. *STJ*, pp. 42n.2, n.3; 44–5n.2; 59n.2; 65n.3; 66n.3; 68n.1; 87n.3; 199n.1n.2; 222n.2.

155. "The Process of Social Regeneration," *AJS* 2 (1896–7): 416. The comment is edited out of the text of *STJ*, p. 199.

156. *STJ*, pp. 85n.3; 98n.1; 141n.1; 163n.3.

157. Ibid., pp. 41n.1; 53–5n.l.

158. Ibid., p. 42n.l.

159. Ibid., p. 55n.l.

160. Ibid.

161. Ibid., pp. 49n.1; 51n.2.

162. George Rupp, *Culture Protestantism: German Liberal Theology at the Turn of the Twentieth Century* (Missoula, Mont.: Scholars Press, 1977), pp. 43–51. On American liberal Protestant theology in the same period, see Lloyd J. Averill, *American Theology in the Liberal Tradition* (Philadelphia: Westminster, 1967); Kenneth Cauthen, *The Impact of American Religious Liberalism* (New York: Harper & Row, 1962); William R. Hutchison, *American Protestant Thought: The Liberal Era* (New York: Harper & Row, 1968); Hutchison, "Cultural Strain and Protestant Liberalism," *American Historical Review* 76 (1971): 386–411; and Hutchison, "Liberal Protestantism and the 'End of Innocence'," *American Quarterly* 15 (1963): 126–39.

163. *STJ*, p. 5.

164. "The Significance of Sociology for Ethics," p. 118.

165. *STJ*, p. 27.

166. Ibid., p. 29.

167. Ibid., p. 33.

168. Ibid., pp. 35–36.

169. Ibid., p. 36. See also p. 38.

170. Ibid., p. 127.

171. Ibid., pp. 167–68.

172. Ibid., p. 104.

173. Ibid., p. 134. See also pp. 107, 115.

174. Ibid., p. 116.

175. Ibid., pp. 142–43.

176. Ibid., p. 77.

177. Ibid., p. 23.

178. Ibid., p. 181. See also p. 175.

179. Ibid., p. 168.

180. Ibid., p. 199.

181. Ibid.

182. Ibid., pp. 199–200.

183. Ibid., p. 202.

184. Ibid., p. 203.

185. Ibid., p. 204.

186. Ibid., pp. 205–6.

187. Ibid., p. 206.

188. Ibid., p. 210.

189. Ibid., p. 2lof.

190. Ibid., p. 225.

191. Ibid., p. 277.

192. Ibid., pp. 229–30.

193. Ibid., p. 140.

194. Ibid.

195. Ibid, p. 202.

196. Ibid., p. 212.

197. Ibid., p. 132.

198. Ibid., p. 167.

199. Ibid., p. 168.

200. Ibid., p. 167.

201. Ibid., p. 196.

202. Smith, "Social Process," states that Mathews taught courses on the French Revolution in 1889–90 when he assumed Small's chair in history and political economy at Colby (p. 20).

203. See "Editorial: Sociology and New Testament Study," BW 6 (1895): 2; "The Significance of the Church to the Social Movement," AJS 4 (1899): 612, 614–16; Church and Changing Order, p. ll6f.; The Social Gospel, pp. 120–21, 167–68; "The Sufficiency of the Gospel for the Salvation of Society," BW 41 (1913): 291, 294; Making of To-morrow, p. 25; The Message of Jesus to Our Modern Life (Hyde Park, Ill.: University of Chicago Press, 1915), pp. 190–91; "Theology and the Social Mind," pp. 206–7; review of Walter Rauschenbusch, Christianizing the Social Order, BW 41 (1916): 139; "Moral Value of Patriotism," pp. 25–27; Patriotism and Religion, pp. 37–42, 121–22; "The Minister and Radicalism," Independent 103 (14 August 1920): 178; "Must Religion Steer Clear of Reform?" Independent 105 (19 March 1921): 189–90; Validity of American Ideals, pp. 75–76; "Ten Years of American Protestantism," pp. 588–89; "Development of Social Christianity in America," p. 382; Christianity and Social Process, pp. 99, 139–40, 150–53, 172.

204. STJ, p. 135.

205. Ibid., pp. 142–43.

206. Ibid., p. 144.

207. Ibid., p. 148.

208. Ibid., p. 149.

209. Ibid., pp. 149–50.

210. Ibid., p. 151.

211. Ibid.

212. Ibid., p. 152.

213. Ibid., p. 154.

214. Ibid., p. 155.

215. Ibid, pp. 156–57.

216. Smith, *Chicago School*, p. 85.

217. On the influence of Small and Ely on Mathews's thought, see Smith, "Shailer Mathews: Theologian of Social Process," pp. 13, 35–39.

3. The Eschatological Turn and the Foundation of Social Gospel Theology

1. *NFO*, p. 120.

2. "The Social Teaching of Paul," *BW* 19 (1902): 34–46, 113–21, 178–89, 279–87, 370–77, 433–524; *BW* 20 (1902): 31–47, 123–33, 178–90.

3. Ibid., p. 281.

4. "The Social Teaching of Paul, I: The Social Content of Early Messianism," *BW* 19 (1902): 34–46; "II: The Social Content of Messianism in New Testament Times," pp. 113–21; and "III: The Apocalyptic Messianism of the Pharisees," pp. 178–89.

5. "The Social Teaching of Paul, IV: The Messianism of Paul," *BW* 19 (1902): 279–87.

6. Ibid., p. 280.

7. Ibid.

8. Ibid., p. 281.

9. Ibid., pp. 281–82.

10. Ibid., p. 281.

11. Ibid., p. 280n.1, citing J. Weiss, *Predigt Jesu*, p. 9. The parallel passage in *MHNT* (p. 77) cites the second edition of *Predigt Jesu*, p. 77.

12. "Messianism of Paul," p. 281.

13. Ibid. The parallel passage in *MHNT* is p. 69.

14. "Social Teaching of Paul, VI: The Social Content of Apostolic Christianity," *BW* 19 (1902): 433.

15. "Messianism of Paul," p. 282.

16. Ibid.

17. "The Gospel and the Modern Man," *Christendom* 1 (1903): 300–2, 352–53, 399–401, 446–49, 489–91, 537–39. Mathews refers to the articles as an attempt at theological reconstruction in *MHNT*, p. 317n.1.

18. Ibid., p. 301. For a description of this method, see *NFO*, p. 82.

19. "Gospel and Modern Man," pp. 302, 352, 400–1.

20. Ibid., pp. 352–53.

21. Ibid., p. 352.

22. Ibid., p. 537.

23. Ibid., pp. 538–39.

24. Ibid.

25. Ibid., pp. 400–1.

26. Review of Orello Cone, *Rich and Poor in the New Testament*, *AJT* 7 (1903): 146.

27. Ibid., p. 145.

28. Ibid, p. 146. See also the 1903 review of Paul Wernle, *Die Reichsgotteshoffnung in dem ältesten Christlichen Dokumenten und bei Jesus*, in which Mathews notes with approbation Wernle's contention that, though Jesus and Paul saw the kingdom as not yet present in fullness, they nevertheless saw it as present in power: *AJT* 8 (1904): 817–19.

29. Review of Paul Wernle, *The Beginnings of Christianity*, *BW* 24 (1904): 392.

30. *MHNT*, p. 82.

31. Ibid., pp. 62–66.

32. On the importance of this background to *MHNT*, see Aubrey, "Theology and Social Process," p. 23.

33. *MHNT*, p. 67.

34. Ibid., p. 68.

35. Ibid, p. 68n.2.

36. Ibid., p. 69.

37. Ibid.

38. *MHNT*, pp. 70–83, revising "Messianism of Paul," pp. 281–82.

39. Ibid., p. 70.

40. Ibid., p. 71.

41. Ibid., p. 71n.5.

42. Ibid., pp. 71–73.

43. Ibid., p. 74.

44. Ibid.

45. Ibid.

46. Ibid., p. 75.

47. Mathews never entirely abandons this thesis. In *MHNT*, p. 126, he argues, in fact, that as Jesus expresses his understanding of eternal life, he uses the kingdom idea as a "point of contact" with his audience. For other appearances of this thesis, see *GMM*, p. 12; and "Eschatology," in *The Dictionary of the Bible*, ed. James Hastings (New York: Scribner's, 1909), p. 236.

48. *MHNT*, pp. 75–76.

49. Ibid., p. 77. A footnote names the exegetes Mathews is considering here: J. Weiss, G. Schmoller, E. Issel, G. Schnedermann, P. Wernle, O. Cone, W. Baldensperger, and W. Bousset: pp. 76–77n.3.

50. Ibid., p. 77.

51. Ibid., p. 78.

52. Ibid., pp. 78–79.

53. Ibid.

54. Ibid.

55. Ibid.

56. Ibid.

57. Ibid.

58. Ibid., p. 80.

59. Ibid.

60. Ibid.

61. Ibid.

62. Ibid.

63. Ibid.

64. Ibid., pp. 80–1.

65. Ibid., p. 81.

66. Ibid., p. 82. The emphasis is mine.

67. Ibid.

68. Ibid., pp. 57–61, 225–36.

69. Ibid., p. 58.

70. Ibid., p. 225.

71. Ibid., p. 57. Mathews also questions whether the Aramaic equivalent of *ekklesia* was ever used by the historical Jesus.

72. Ibid., p. 225.

73. Ibid.

74. Ibid., p. 229.

75. Ibid., pp. 2n.2, 72n.4, 76n.1, 118n.2, 229n.3, 232n.2.

76. *Predigt Jesu:* pp. 71n.5, 72n.4, 76n.3, 77n.5, 127n.1, 226n.1; *Das älteste Evangelium:* pp. 57–58n.2, 229n.3, 232n.4; *Markusevangelium:* pp. 57–58n.2, 229n.3; *Apostelsgeschichte:* p. 141n.1; p. 89n.6 incorrectly attributes *Das Leben Jesu* to J. Weiss.

77. *MHNT,* pp. 89n.6, 147n.1.

78. Ibid., pp. 95n.6, 147n.1.

79. Ibid., pp. 3n.1, 28n.6, 35n.1, 39n.1, 40n.1, 48n.4, 68n.1, 71n.5, 76–77n.3, 103n.1 & 2, 182n.2, and 221n.4.

80. Ibid., pp. 57n.1, 65n.1, 67n.1, 71n.1, 82n.2, 123n.1, 261n.2, and 306n.4.

81. Ibid., pp. 27n.4, 43n.7, 62n.1, and 76–77n.3.

82. *Church and Changing Order,* p. 69.

83. Ibid., p. 49.

84. Ibid., p. 79.

85. "A Positive Method for an Evangelical Theology," *AJT* 13 (1909): 43.

86. "The Struggle between the Natural and Spiritual Order as Described in the Gospel of John," *BW* 42 (1913): 31–32.

87. Ibid., p. 31.

88. Ibid., p. 32.

89. Review of Rauschenbusch, *Christianizing the Social Order, BW* 41 (1916): 138.

90. Ibid.

91. "Emil Hirsch's Religion," *Menorah Journal* 12 (1926): 36.

92. *Church and Changing Order,* p. 54.

93. Ibid.

94. "Eschatology," in *Dictionary,* ed. Hastings, p. 237.

95. Ibid.

96. "Struggle between Natural and Spiritual," p. 32. For *GMM*'s discussion of this issue, see below, notes 208–17.

97. Ibid.

98. *Creative Christianity,* pp. 36–37.

99. "Social Origin of Theology," p. 298.

100. "Theology and the Social Mind," p. 210.

101. "Generic Christianity," p. 709.

102. Ibid., p. 719.

103. Ibid., p. 721.

104. Ibid.

105. "The Relation of Belief in Immortality to Conduct," *Proceedings of the Twenty-Fourth Annual Session of the Baptist Congress for the Discussion of Current Questions* (1906), p. 139.

106. Gerald Birney Smith, "AISL Course, II: What Is Christianity?" p. 346.

107. Ibid., p. 108.

108. Grant, "Ethics and Eschatology in Teaching of Jesus," p. 359.

109. "Shailer Mathews: A Chapter in the Social Gospel Movement," p. 153.

110. C. C. McCown, *The Search for the Real Jesus* (New York: Scribner's, 1940), p. 269.

111. Ibid., p. 270.

112. Ibid., pp. 269–70.

113. "Eschatology," in *Dictionary*, ed. Hastings, p. 236.

114. "Messiah," in *Dictionary*, ed. Hastings, p. 611.

115. Ibid.

116. "Eschatology," in *Dictionary*, ed. Hastings, p. 327; see also "Messiah," ibid., pp. 611–12.

117. *GMM*, p. 11.

118. "The Kingdom of God," *BW* 35 (1910): 426.

119. "Doctrines as Social Patterns," *JR* 10 (1930): 5.

120. "Jesus' Experience of God through Facing Apparent Defeat of His Ideal of Establishing the Kingdom of God," in *Through Jesus to God*, ed. Edwin Aubrey et al. (Hyde Park, Ill.: University of Chicago Press, 1931), pp. 84–85.

121. Review of H. K. Booth, *The Great Galilean Returns*, *Christian Century* 53 (8 June 1936): 311.

122. *Church and Changing*, pp. 92, 115. To see the problem in a nutshell—Mathews's continued references to the present kingdom in works in which he also speaks of the kingdom eschatologically—cf. p. 206: "The kingdom of God to which the church looks forward."

123. *Social Gospel*, pp. 19–22.

124. *Individual and Social Gospel*, pp. 20, 59, 62, 81–82.

125. "The Social Optimism of Faith in a Divine Jesus," *BW* 43 (1914): 154.

126. "Present Co-operative Action by the Churches," *BW* 49 (1917): 267–74.

127. Two articles reprinted in the book, both of which speak of the kingdom as present, are "The Significance of the Church to the Social Movement," *AJS* 4 (1899): 603–20, and "The Christian Church and Social Unity," *AJS* 5 (1900): 456–69; these are reprinted as chapters 6 and 4 of *Church and Changing Order*.

128. *Church and Changing*, pp. 54, 206–7.

129. For an unambiguous example of such social gospel rhetorical use of the present kingdom in another post–1905 work, see *GMM*, p. 3. What makes the reference unambiguous, and demonstrates the validity of my thesis, is that this work has discernible theological "layers" in it. When Mathews wishes to speak *qua* "scientific" theologian, he insists on the futurity of the kingdom; but in this section of the text, in which he is patently calling for social gospel activism, he lapses into present-kingdom rhetoric.

130. *Creative Christianity*, p. 39.

131. "The Christian Faith and the Life of the Community," p. 57.

132. "Kingdom of God," p. 426.

133. Ibid. On the continuation of present-kingdom language in social gospel rhetoric in general in the post-war period, see Gorrell, *Age of Social Responsibility*, p. 337.

134. *MHNT*, p. 320.

135. Ibid.

136. Ibid.

137. Ibid., p. 307.

138. Ibid., p. 74.

139. Ibid., p. 122.

140. Ibid., p. 121.

141. Ibid., p. 122.

142. Ibid., p. 125.

143. Ibid., pp. 89–92.

144. Ibid., pp. 96–100.

145. Ibid., p. 123.

146. Ibid., p. 131.

147. For Mathews's reflections on this topic, see *Church and Changing*, pp. 62–69; "Positive Method for Evanglical Theology," p. 25f.; *GMM*, pp. 91–113; "Is Belief in the Historicity of Jesus Indispensable to Christian Faith?" *AJT* 15 (1911): 614–17; and "Emil Hirsch's Religion," p. 36.

148. *MHNT*, p. 131. Note Mathews's persisting tendency to identify the resurrection as a historical datum, a "fact" of the life of Jesus.

149. *Christianity and Social Process*, p. 2.

150. *Church and Christian*, p. 103.

151. *Is God Emeritus?* pp. 7–8.

152. *MHNT*, p. 174.

153. Ibid., p. 189.

154. Ibid., p. 174.

155. Ibid., p. 167.

156. Ibid., p. 177.

157. Ibid., p. 167.

158. Ibid.

159. Ibid., pp. 200–1.

160. Ibid., p. 201.

161. Ibid., p. 213.

162. Ibid., p. 214.

163. Ibid., p. 190.

164. Ibid., p. 200.

165. Ibid., p. 214.

166. Ibid., p. 255.

167. Ibid., p. 223.

168. Ibid., p. 145.

169. Ibid., p. 255.

170. Ibid., p. 274.

171. Ibid., pp. 264–69.

172. Ibid., p. 268.

173. Ibid., p. 288.

174. Ibid., p. 298.

175. Ibid., p. 314.

176. Ibid., p. 288.

177. Ibid., p. 314.

178. Ibid., p. 315.

179. Ibid.

180. Ibid., p. 180. Mathews's attempt to apotheosize democracy as a "Christian" institution is ironic in view of his previous assertion that *no* polity can claim the name Christian.

181. *STJ*, p. 124.

182. The basic motifs of process as a theological system are to be found as early as 1903 in the "Gospel and Modern Man" articles, and in the 1904 "A Scientific Basis for Religious and Moral Education from the Standpoint of Theology," *Proceedings of the Second Annual Convention of the Religious*

Education Association (1904): 115–19. On this, see Aubrey, "Theology and the Social Process," pp. 22–23.

183. *MHNT*, p. 317.

184. *GMM*, p. 293.

185. On the intersection of the theological and social reconstruction projects of the study, see ibid., pp. 315–16.

186. Ibid., p. 245.

187. Mathews regards religion as both a function of social process, and an independent factor in social process. See ibid., p. 44, and *Validity of American Ideals*, p. 359.

188. *GMM*, p. 286. See also "Theology and the Social Mind," pp. 201–5; "Scientific Method and Religion," p. 387; "The Religious Life," p. 39; and *Growth of Idea of God*, p. 208.

189. *GMM*, p. 286. See also "Spiritual Challenge to Democracy," pp. 523–24; "Religion and War," *BW* 52 (1918): 169–76; *Christianity and Social Process*, p. 90f.; and "What Liberty Does Religion Require?" *Religious Education* 32 (1937): 183–85.

190. *GMM*, p. 41.

191. Ibid.

192. Ibid., p. 83.

193. "Eschatology," in *Dictionary*, ed. Hastings, p. 237.

194. *GMM*, pp. 8, 275.

195. Ibid., p. 83.

196. Ibid.

197. Ibid., p. 32.

198. Ibid. See also p. 244.

199. Ibid., p. 300.

200. Ibid., p. 63.

201. Ibid., pp. 63–64.

202. Ibid., p. 71.

203. Ibid., p. 85.

204. Ibid., p. 23.

205. Ibid., pp. 11, 21–23.

206. Ibid., p. 23.

207. Ibid., pp. 82, 232.

208. Ibid., p. 90. See also "The Permanent Message of Messianism," *BW* 49 (1917): 273.

209. *GMM*, p. 83. See also "Permanent Message of Messianism," p. 274.

210. *GMM*, p. 91.

211. Ibid., pp. 76–77.

212. Ibid., p. 283.

213. Ibid., p. 126. See also pp. 91, 120, 184, 236.

214. Ibid., pp. 234, 236. See also "Struggle between Natural and Spiritual," p. 32.

215. *GMM*, pp. 243, 15.

216. Ibid., p. 78. On the necessity to ground Christian faith in the historical Jesus, see also "Permanent Message of Messianism," p. 274. On the historical Jesus as the "very center" of Mathews's theology, see Smith, "Mathews: Theologian of Social Process," pp. 150–55. On Christocentrism in American liberal theology, see H. Shelton Smith, "The Christocentric Liberal Tradition," in *American Christianity*, ed. Smith, Robert T. Handy, and Lefferts A. Loetscher (New York: Scribner's, 1963), 2, pp. 255–308.

217. Mathews's critical concern with Schweitzer's work during this period is also evident in a 1913 book review entitled "More Discussion of New Testament Eschatology," reviewing E. C. Dewick's *Primitive Christian Eschatology*, in which he chides Dewick for having ignored German theologians other than Schweitzer and Harnack: *BW* 42 (1913): 120–21.

218. *GMM*, p. 263.

219. Ibid., p. 11.

220. Ibid., p. 263.

221. Ibid., p. 265.

222. Ibid., p. 256.

223. Ibid.

224. Ibid., pp. 260, 32.

225. Ibid., p. 321.

226. *Creative Christianity*, p. 7.

227. *SIH*, p. 188.

228. Ibid., pp. 67–68. See also pp. 188–96.

229. Ibid., pp. 26–27.

230. Ibid., pp. 25–26, 44–45.

231. On the geographical view, see ibid., pp. 12–16; on the economic view, see pp. 16–25.

232. Ibid., pp. 36–37, 198–201.

233. Ibid., pp. 35–36.

234. Ibid., pp. 35–36.

235. For citations of Small in *SIH*, see p. 12n.1 and 24n.1. In arguing that history is an open-ended process, Mathews is clearly following a trajectory of thought established by Small's sociology.

236. See ibid., pp. 51–57, 57–61, 148, 203–5. On pp. 58–59, Mathews responds to Weber's thesis regarding the connection between the rise of capitalism and Calvinism.

237. Throughout *SIH* Mathews draws on Seligman's 1902 The *Economic Interpretation of History*, which validates Mathews's reading of Marxist analysis by both accepting the economic interpretation of history and attempting to argue that it is an incomplete interpretation. In this regard it is interesting to note that Small's "Socialism in the Light of Social Science," *AJS* 17 (1911–12): 810, praises Seligman's study as "conspicuous in its loneliness" for having given a fair hearing to Marx.

238. *SIH*, pp. 32–34.

239. Ibid., p. 65.

240. Ibid., pp. 32–33.

241. Ibid., pp. 65–66. See also pp. 190–97, applying the argument to Spencer.

242. Ibid., p. 193.

4. JESUS ON SOCIAL INSTITUTIONS

1. For an indication that the turn to eschatological realism is a chief motivating factor in Mathews's decision to revise *STJ*, see (in addition to the passage already cited from *NFO* on this topic) "Church and Social Order," p. 209, which has a bibliography recommending *JSI*, *inter alia*, with the following note: "[*JSI* is] a study of the social significance of the teaching of Jesus from the point of view of the recent studies of his eschatological teaching."

2. Two sections of this chapter—"The Theological Foundation" and "*JSI* as a Social Gospel Foundational Statement"—are substantially reproductions of portions of the 1923 article "What May the Social Worker Expect of the Church?" *JR* 3 (1923): 632–47.

3. In his introduction to the Fortress Press edition of *JSI*, entitled "The Life and Thought of Shailer Mathews," Kenneth Cauthen states (p. liv) that chapter 4, "Jesus as the Exponent of Social Attitudes," is new to the 1928 study. This is incorrect: The material of this chapter in fact reproduces almost verbatim material from chapters 7 and 8 of the 1897 study.

4. Chapter 4, "Jesus as the Exponent of Social Attitudes"; section I, pp. 66–67 = *STJ*, chapter 7, section I, pp. 159–61; section II, pp. 67–69 = *STJ*, chapter 7, section II, pp. 162–65; section III, pp. 69–73 = *STJ*, chapter 7, section III, pp. 165–69; section IV, pp. 72–73 = *STJ*, chapter 7, section IV, pp. 169–73; section V, pp. 73–75 = *STJ*, chapter 8, section I, pp. 176–79.

Chapter 5, "Jesus on the Family": section I, pp. 78–79 = *STJ*, chapter 4, section I, pp. 79–83; section II, pp. 79–80 = *STJ*, chapter 4, section III, pp. 91–93; section III, pp. 80–84 = *STJ*, chapter 4, section II, pp. 84–90. The introductory section and section VI are new to the 1928 edition.

Chapter 6, "Jesus on Wealth": section I, pp. 90–93 = *STJ*, chapter 6, section II, pp. 136–39; section II, pp. 93–94, line 13 is new; section II, pp. 94, line 14 to 97 = *STJ*, chapter 6, section IV, pp. 144–48; section III = *STJ*, chapter 6, section V, pp. 148–55; section IV, paragraph one, p. 101 = *STJ*, pp. 155 and 157; section IV, p. 103, paragraph two, line 5–104 = *STJ*, p. 156. The rest is new to the 1928 volume.

Chapter 7, "Jesus on the State": section II, pp. 107–10 = *STJ*, chapter 5, section II, pp. 115–23; section II, pp. 110–13 = *STJ*, chapter 5, section III, pp. 123–25 and 28–29. The introductory section and sections I, IV, and V are new to the 1928 volume.

5. *JSI*, p. 38.

6. Ibid., pp. 84–87.

7. Ibid., pp. 116–20.

8. Ibid., pp. 114–15.

9. Cauthen, "Life and Thought of Shailer Mathews," p. lv.

10. With exceptions: e.g., p. 13n.1, Lombroso, *La Crime Politique et la Révolution*; p. 68n.14, Brüll, *Trachten der Juden*; p. 35n.5, J. Weiss, *Predigt Jesu.*

11. *JSI*, pp. 42, 38, 32.

12. Ibid., pp. 36–37, 39.

13. Ibid., p. 13.

14. Ibid., p. 12.

15. Ibid., p. 13.

16. Ibid., pp. 14–24.

17. Ibid., p. 25.

18. Ibid.

19. Ibid.

20. Ibid., p. 28.

21. Ibid.

22. Ibid.

23. Ibid., p. 29.

24. Ibid, pp. 16–17.

25. Ibid., p. 30.

26. Ibid., p. 29.

27. Ibid., pp. 29–30.

28. Ibid.

29. Ibid., p. 96n.2 = *STJ*, p. 147n.1. See also ibid., p. 103.

30. *JSI*, p. 41.

31. Ibid, p. 40.

32. Ibid., p. 49. See also pp. 58, 73.

33. Ibid., p. 31.

34. Ibid., p. 32.

35. "The Deity of Christ and Social Reconstruction," *Constructive Quarterly* 8 (1920): 44.

36. Ibid., p. 49.

37. "The Early Followers of Jesus and His 'Way'," in *Jesus' 'Way' of Living*, ed. Gerald B. Smith et al. (Hyde Park, Ill.: University of Chicago Press, 1926), p. 31.

38. *Atonement and Social Process*, pp. 40–41.

39. Ibid., pp. 199–200.

40. Ibid., p. 201.

41. "Jesus' Experience of God in His Contact with the Political Conditions of His People," in *Through Jesus to God*, ed. Aubrey et al., pp. 51–53.

42. *Is God Emeritus?* p. 77. Cf. *The Church and the Christian*, p. 55, in which Mathews depicts Jesus' death as the crucifixion of a "revolutionist."

43. *Is God Emeritus?* p. 77. This passage is drawn largely from "Deity of Christ and Social Reconstruction," p. 49.

44. *JSI*, p. 35.

45. Ibid., p. 35n.5.

46. Ibid., p. 38.

47. Ibid, p. 61. With but little stretch of the imagination, one can conclude that Mathews is referring to socialism, German militarism, and industrial capitalism.

48. Ibid.

49. Ibid., p. 62.

50. Ibid., p. 61n.31.

51. Ibid.

52. Ibid., p. 32.

53. Ibid., p. 32. See *SIH*, pp. 111–8, 168f.

54. *JSI*, pp. 34–35. As may be apparent, this idea harks back to such Romantic lives of Jesus, with their Carlylean hero-figures, as Renan's *Vie de Jésus*.

55. *JSI*, p. 34.

56. Ibid., pp. 65, 32.

57. Ibid., p. 65. Cf. "Why I Believe in Jesus Christ," *BW* 54 (1920): 351.

58. *JSI*, p. 38.

59. Ibid., p. 50.

60. Ibid.

61. Ibid., p. 51.

62. Ibid., p. 127.

63. Ibid., p. 126.

64. Ibid., p. 148. The emphases are in the original.

65. This point of view is basic to "Is Belief in the Historicity of Jesus Indispensable to Christian Faith?" *AJT* 15 (1911): 57–82; "Deity of Christ and Social Reconstruction," pp. 39–54; and "Why I Believe in Jesus Christ," pp. 351–53. See also *Church and Changing*, pp. 81f.; *GMM*, p. 76; and *Faith of Modernism*, pp. 123–24.

66. "Deity of Christ and Social Reconstruction," p. 40. This process argument has affinities with Richard W. Storrs, *The Divine Origin of Christianity Indicated by Its Historical Effects* (New York, 1884), and Loring Brace, *Gesta Christi* (New York, 1882). On these, see Hopkins, *Rise of Social Gospel*, pp. 64–66.

67. "Editorial: The Reality and Simplicity of Jesus," *BW* 16 (1900): 84.

68. Ibid.

69. "The Imitation of Jesus," *BW* 26 (1905): 457.

70. *NFO*, p. 282.

71. *JSI*, p. 149.

72. Ibid., pp. 36–37, 53.

73. Ibid., p. 62.

74. Ibid., p. 37.

75. Ibid.

76. Ibid., p. 38.

77. Ibid., p. 39.

78. Ibid., p. 53.

79. Ibid., p. 102.

80. Ibid., p. 62.

81. Ibid.

82. Ibid.

83. "Spiritual Challenge to Democracy," p. 524. See also "Religion and War," *BW* 52 (1918): 176; and *Validity of American Ideals*, pp. 13–14.

84. *Validity of American Ideals*, p. 35.

85. "Spiritual Challenge to Democracy," p. 514. See also "Christian Faith and Life of Community," p. 68.

86. *JSI*, p. 45.

87. Ibid., p. 77.

88. Ibid., p. 124.

89. Ibid.

90. Ibid., p. 125.

91. Ibid., p. 102.

92. Ibid., p. 114.

93. Ibid., pp. 105, 125.

94. Ibid., p. 52.

95. Ibid., p. 53. In note 23, Mathews acknowledges that this distinction between ideals and attitudes derives from the thought of John Dewey.

96. Ibid., p. 54.

97. Ibid., p. 62.

98. Ibid.

99. Ibid., pp. 62–63.

100. Ibid., p. 63.

101. See ibid., pp. 38–39, 115, 125.

102. Ibid., p. 42. See also pp. 105, 113.

103. Ibid., p. 44. See also pp. 18, 137.

104. Ibid, p. 55.

105. Ibid.

106. Ibid., p. 56. See also p. 124.

107. Ibid., pp. 55–56.

108. Ibid., p. 94.

109. Ibid., p. 123. Cauthen notes (p. 164) that lines in this passage have been transposed.

110. Ibid., p. 113.

111. Ibid., pp. 113–14.

112. Ibid., p. 114.

113. Ibid.

114. Ibid.

115. Ibid.

116. Ibid., p. 115.

117. Cauthen, "Life and Thought of Shailer Mathews," p. lv.

118. *Christianity and Social Process*, pp. 131–32, 144–49, 181–200.

119. Ibid., pp. 144–47.

120. Niebuhr, *Moral Man and Immoral Society*, pp. 71–82.

121. Though *Christianity and Social Process* never explicitly names Niebuhr as a theological sparring partner in Mathews's argument for the love ethic, the work contains many coded allusions to the "cult of pessimism and futility" coming from Europe to American theology, which flirts with socialism and rejects democracy; these are obviously references to neo-ortho-

dox theology, as Mathews saw it: see pp. 2, 20, 35–36, 57–58, 99–100, 215. Mathews's preoccupation with Niebuhr's challenge to social gospel theology in these years is evident in the 1935 article, "The Church and the Social Order," which recommends Niebuhr's *Moral Man and Immoral Society* in a short bibliography appended to the article (p. 209). In addition, the argument of chapter 2 of *Christianity and Social Process* (see esp. p. 20) versus "mechanistic" philosophies attractive to thinkers in the post–World War I period, which promote group coercion, closely parallels that of Mathews's apologia for liberal theology and attack on crisis theology in the 1938 article "Unrepentant Liberalism."

122. Ibid., p. 70.

123. *Creative Christianity*, pp. 33–34.

124. On this see Niebuhr, *Moral Man and Immoral Society*, pp. xv, xix–xx, 79–80.

125. *NFO*, pp. 281–82.

126. Ibid.

127. Ibid., p. 282.

A F T E R W O R D

1. Haight, "Mission of Church and Social Gospel," p. 494.

2. On the sociohistorical matrix of the shift from progressivist idealism in American thought, see Henry May's classic study, *The End of American Innocence* (New York: Knopf, 1959). On the civil rights struggle and the Vietnam period as watershed moments in American history that further confound American myths of innocence, see David O'Brien, *The Renewal of American Catholicism* (New York: Oxford University Press, 1972), pp. 1–9, 14–15, 205.

3. On the social anthropology of social gospel theology as retrievable, see Haight, "Mission of Church and Social Gospel," p. 495; and Carlyle Mauney, "The Significance of Walter Rauschenbusch for Today," *Foundations* 11 (1959): 14–16, 25.

4. Mathews, "Theology and Social Mind," p. 237.

5. Ibid., p. 240.

6. Ibid.

7. Ibid.

8. Ibid., p. 241.

9. Ibid., p. 243.

10. Ibid.

11. Ibid., p. 244.

12. Ibid.

13. Ibid.

14. Ibid., p. 245.

15. Ibid., p. 246.

16. *Creative Christianity*, p. 53. See also "New Apologetic" (editorial), p. 406; *Church and Changing Order*, chapters 5 and 6; *Gospel and Modern Man*, p. 51; "Sufficiency of Gospel for Salvation of Society," pp. 293–94; "Religion for Democracy," p. 53; "Capitalistic Religion," p. 616; "Church and Social Order," pp. 194–95; and *Is God Emeritus?* p. 91.

17. *Christianity and Social Process*, pp. 166–67. On this, see also *Validity of American Ideals*, pp. 60–70, where Mathews argues that the eradication of slavery bequeathed to the United States a new moral problem: the tendency to view workers as commodities. In Mathews's view, "the great issue in civilization today" is to "assure the participation of the wage-earner in the personal control of his contribution to production" (pp. 69–70).

18. Ibid., p. 169.

19. Jähn, *Rauschenbusch: Formative Years*, pp. 14–17, 46.

20. On this, see Stanley Hauerwas, *Against the Nations* (San Francisco: Harper & Row, 1985), pp. 28–29.

21. For defenses of Rauschenbusch's kingdom theology against this charge, see Bennett, "Social Interpretation of Christianity," pp. 117–18; Smith, "To Reconstruct the World," p. 60; Strain, "Rauschenbusch: Resource for Public Theology," pp. 25–27; and Max Stackhouse, "The Continuing Importance of Walter Rauschenbusch," in Rauschenbusch, *The Righteousness of the Kingdom*, ed. Stackhouse (Nashville: Abingdon, 1968), pp. 13–59. Jähn has shown that as early as 1892, Rauschenbusch abandoned the notion that progress was inevitable: *Rauschenbusch: Formative Years*, p. 46. In light of this evidence, one must question Kroeker's recent conclusion that Rauschenbusch was guilty of liberal historicization of the kingdom symbol and anthropocentric immanence: "Theology, Ethics, and Social Theory," pp. 188–98.

22. On this, see King, "'Theology as History'," esp. pp. 118–22.

23. For evidence that the argument against dialectic theology's use of eschatology as an escape from history was not unique to Mathews in the first half of the twentieth century, see C. C. McCown, "In History or Beyond History," *Harvard Theological Review* 38 (1945): 151–75.

24. For a judicious presentation of principles for a critical retrieval of social gospel theology, see Haight, "Mission of Church and Social Gospel," pp. 495–97.

25. "Ethics and Eschatology," p. 359.

26. Ibid., p. 360. C. C. McCown provides corroboration for this reading in his article, "In History or Beyond History," *Harvard Theological Review* 38 (1945): 151–75.

27. Albert Schweitzer, "The Conception of the Kingdom of God in the Transformation of Eschatology," in *Religion from Tolstoy to Camus*, ed. Walter Kaufmann (New York: Harper, 1961), pp. 420, 424.

28. For an overview of this discussion, see Bernard Lee, "The Two Process Theologies," *Theological Studies* 45 (1984): 307–19. See also John B. Cobb Jr., *Process Theology as Political Theology* (Philadelphia: Westminster, 1982), esp. pp. 150–56. It is interesting to note that, as he places process and political theology in dialogue, Cobb calls for a critical retrieval of the social gospel roots of process theology: "As process theology now encounters the challenge of political theology, its roots in the earlier period of the Chicago school take on a new currency and relevance" (p. 22).

29. See Herman and Julia R. Schwendinger, *Sociologists of the Chair*, pp. 222–53, esp. 233, 250–51.

30. See Thorstein Veblen, *The Higher Learning in America* (New York: Huebsch, 1918); and C. Wright Mills, *Sociology and Pragmatism* (New York: Oxford University Press, 1966). On this, see also ibid., pp. 510–18; and Smith, *Chicago School*, p. 6.

31. For critiques of the underlying scientism in Mathews's social process model, see Dean, *History Making History*, pp. 57–58; and Stone, *Minimalist View of Transcendence*, pp. 52, 143.

32. See Max Horkheimer and Theodor Adorno, *Dialectic of Enlightenment*, trans. John Cumming (New York: Herder and Herder, 1972); Horkheimer, *Critique of Instrumental Reason*, trans. Matthew J. O'Connell et al. (New York: Seabury, 1974); Horkheimer, *Eclipse of Reason* (New York: Oxford University Press, 1947); Michel Foucault, *The Archeology of Knowledge*, trans. A. M. Sheridan Smith (New York: Pantheon, 1972); Foucault, *Power/Knowledge*, trans. Colin Gordon et al., ed. Gordon (New York: Pantheon, 1980), esp. pp. 81–86, 114–32; and Jean-François Lyotard, *The Postmodern Condition*, trans. Geoff Bennington and Brian Massumi (Minneapolis: University of Minnesota Press, 1984).

33. On Chicago school social sciences and the Frankfurt school as complementary traditions that would benefit from engaging in dialogue with each other, see Smith, *Chicago School*, pp. 214–20.

34. For a development of this historical argument, which sees first-stage political theology as a "critique of neo-orthodoxy through the eschatological center of Christian faith," see Rebecca S. Chopp, *The Praxis of Suffering* (Maryknoll, N.Y.: Orbis, 1986), pp. 39–41.

35. But see Dorrien, *Reconstructing Common Good*, p. 10, which maintains that both Moltmann and Gutiérrez see Rauschenbusch's work as "the most instructive precedent for a North American theology of praxis." On Metz and liberation theologians as continuing the social gospel project, see Bennett, "Social Gospel Today," pp. 288–93.

36. *Theology of Hope*, trans. James W. Leitch (New York: Harper & Row, 1967), p. 16.

37. Ibid., p. 37.

38. Ibid., p. 325.

39. *Faith in History and Society,* trans. David Smith (New York: Seabury, 1980), p. 73.

40. Ibid., p. 63.

41. Ibid., p. 91.

42. Ibid., p. 117.

43. *A Theology of Liberation,* trans. Caridad Inda and John Eagleson, rev. ed. (Maryknoll, N.Y.: Orbis, 1988), p. 93.

44. Ibid., p. 122.

45. Ibid., p. 95.

46. *Theology of Hope,* p. 16.

47. Ibid., 230; see also 94.

48. Ibid., pp. 18.

49. Ibid., p. 165.

50. Ibid., pp. 224–25.

51. Ibid., p. 338.

52. Ibid., 304–6, 332–35. See also *The Crucified God,* trans. R. A. Wilson and John Bowden (New York: Harper & Row, 1974), p. 172ff.

53. Moltmann's indebtedness to Bloch is particularly evident in *Theology of Hope*'s discussion of the "tendencies" of history: as Moltmann notes, in Bloch, the term refers to a "leaning" toward the future that is not related to the future as cause is related to effect (p. 243). See also *Crucified God,* pp. 99–100. On Bloch's significance for political theology, see Francis Fiorenza, "Dialectical Theology and Hope," *Heythrop Journal* 9 (1968): 142–63, 384–99; 10 (1968): 26–42.

54. Ernst Bloch, *The Principle of Hope,* trans. by Neville Plaice, Stephen Plaice, and Paul Knight (Cambridge, Mass.: MIT Press, 1986), p. 477.

55. Ibid., p. 183.

56. Ibid., pp. 197, 170; see also 144–45.

57. *A Philosophy of the Future,* trans. John Cumming (New York: Herder and Herder, 1970), p. 112.

58. Ibid.

59. *Faith in History and Society,* p. 91.

60. On Metz's critique of evolutionary consciousness, see Chopp, *Praxis of Suffering,* p. 72.

61. *Theology of Liberation,* pp. 98–105.

62. Ibid., p. 99.

63. Ibid., p. 101.

64. Ibid., p. 102. See also pp. 14–15.

65. Ibid., 104.

66. Philip LeMasters badly distorts Gutiérrez's position on the relationship between the *eschaton* and history when he maintains that "Gutiérrez fails to stress adequately the Kingdom's eschatological nature, at least in part due to his claim that history is one" ("Rauschenbusch and Gutiérrez," p. 106). Though LeMasters maintains (p. 106) that this reading of Gutiérrez is derived from Deane William Ferm, *Third-World Liberation Theologies* (Maryknoll, N.Y.: Orbis, 1986), pp. 28–42, Ferm's survey of liberation theologians never claims, as LeMasters does, that Gutiérrez's interpretation of the kingdom is "overly immanent" (p. 107). For a countervailing (and more tenable) view of Gutiérrez's kingdom theology, see Bennett, "Social Gospel Today," pp. 286–87; and *Radical Imperative*, pp. 140–41.

A COMPREHENSIVE

BIBLIOGRAPHY OF

MATHEWS'S WORK

The following bibliography of Mathews's texts is the first bibliography that, as far as I have discovered, seeks to compile a comprehensive listing of all the works Mathews published. It includes books, essays, and journal articles. I have as well appended a list of major book reviews that is by no means exhaustive.

ABBREVIATIONS EMPLOYED FOR
JOURNALS IN WHICH MATHEWS
COMMONLY PUBLISHED

AJS = *American Journal of Sociology*   *CQ* = *Constructive Quarterly*
AJT = *American Journal of Theology*   *Ind* = *Independent*
BW = *Biblical World*   *JR* = *Journal of Religion*
CC = *Christian Century*   *RE* = *Religious Education*
Cdm = *Christendom*   *WT* = *World Today*
Chq = *Chautauquan*

BOOKS, ESSAYS,
AND JOURNAL ARTICLES

1884

"The College Republic." *Colby Echo* 7 (1884): 126–28.

"Said Tom's Father." *Colby Echo* 7 (1884): 78–79.

1888

"The Rhetorical Value of the Study of Hebrew." *Old Testament Student* 7 (1888): 276–80.

1890

Introductory Lectures in European History. Medieval and Modern Periods. Waterville, Maine: Colby, 1890.

1891

"The Captivity of Judah." In *History, Prophecy, and Gospel. Expository Sermons on the International Sunday-School Lessons for 1891.* Edited by E. Benjamin Andrews. Boston: Silver, Burdett, 1891.

1892

Select Medieval Documents Illustrating the History of Church and Empire, 754A.D.–1254A.D.. New York: Silver, 1892. Repr. New York: AMS, 1974.

1893

"Rebuilding the Temple." In *Gospel from Two Testaments: Sermons on International Sunday-School Lessons for 1893.* Edited by E. Benjamin Andrews. Providence, R.I.: E. A. Johnson, 1892. Pp. 10–18.

1894

"Editorial." *BW* 4 (1894): 161–66, 241–43.

Syllabus of Lectures on Economics. Waterville, Maine: Colby, 1894.

1895

"Christian Sociology." *AJS* 1 (1895–96): 69–78, 182, 94, 359–60, 457–72, 604–17, 771–84.

"Editorial." *BW* 5 (1895): 1–5, 81–87.

"Helps to the Study of the Life of Jesus Christ." *BW* 6 (1895): 524–29.

"Introduction to the Gospel of Luke." *BW* 5 (1895): 336–42, 448–55.

1896

"Christian Sociology." *AJS* 2 (1896–97): 108–17, 274–87, 416–32.

"Editorial." *BW* 7 (1896): 81–85, 321–24.

"The Return to Faith." *University of Chicago Record* 1 (1896): 45.

1897

"Bethlehem, The City of Children." *BW* 10 (1987): 473–79.

"Editorial." *BW* 9 (1897): 81–86; *BW* 10 (1897): 161–65, 241–45, 321–25.

"From Jenin to Nazareth: I: The Plain of Jezreel and Beisan." *BW* 10 (1897): 174–82; "II: Gadara and the Jordan Valley." *BW* 10 (1897): 259–71.

"Professor McGiffert on the Apostolic Age." *BW* 10 (1987): 350–65.

The Social Teaching of Jesus. New York: Macmillan, 1897.

1898

"Editorial." *BW* 11 (1898): 65–68, 225–28; *BW* 12 (1898): 1–4.

"History of New Testament Times in Palestine: An Outline." *BW* 11 (1898): 120–25, 188–98.

"In Elijah's Country." *BW* 12 (1898): 162–68.

"The Interpretation of Parables." *AJT* 2 (1898): 293–311.

"The Jewish Messianic Expectation in the Time of Jesus." *BW* 12 (1898): 437–43.

"The Origin of Acts ch. 9:1–19." *BW* 12 (1898): 266–70.

"An Outline of the Life of Jesus with References for Reading." *BW* 11 (1898): 328–40.

"State-Help vs. Self-Help, or Paternalism in Government." *Proceedings of the Sixteenth Annual Session of the Baptist Congress for the Discussion of Current Questions.* Buffalo, 1898. Pp. 116–23.

1899

"Antiochus Epiphanes and the Jewish State." *BW* 14 (1899): 13–26.

"The Conduct of the Adult Bible Class." *BW* 14 (1899): 363–66.

"Editorial." *BW* 13 (1899): 65–67, 145–49, 225–30.

A History of New Testament Times in Palestine, 175 B.C.–70 A.D. New York: Macmillan, 1899.

"Letter to a Sunday-School Superintendent." *BW* 14 (1899): 192–94.

"The Significance of the Church to the Social Movement." *AJS* 4 (1899): 603–20.

1900

"The Christian Church and Social Unity." *AJS* 5 (1900): 456–69.

"Constructive Studies in the Life of Christ" (with E. D. Burton). *BW* 15 (1900): 36–71, 119–42, 193, 212, 273–94, 360–78, 433–53; *BW* 16 (1900): 26–41, 118–36, 210–21, 283–94, 362–77, 451–62.

"The Necessity of Biblical Training for Lay Workers" (editorial). *BW* 16 (1900): 403–6.

"The Reality and Simplicity of Jesus" (editorial). *BW* 16 (1900): 83–86.

"Sunday School Benevolence" (editorial). *BW* 15 (1900): 6–10.

1901

"Bible Study and Religious Interest" (editorial). *BW* 17 (1901): 403–6.

"Certain Hopeful Tendencies in Today's Theological Thought" (editorial). *BW* 17 (1901): 323–26.

"The Decrease in the Number of Theological Students" (editorial). *BW* 17 (1901): 243–46.

The French Revolution. New York: Longmans, 1901.

"Jesus and John: A Suggestion to Reformers," *BW* 17 (1901): 17–21.

The Life of Christ: An Aid to Historical Study and a Condensed Commentary on the Gospels (with E. D. Burton). In *Constructive Bible Studies*. Edited by William Rainey Harper and E. D. Burton. Chicago: University of Chicago Press, 1901.

"Ministerial Virility—And a Suggestion" (editorial). *BW* 17 (1901): 3–5.

"Scientific Ethics and Christian Ethics" (editorial). *BW* 18 (1901): 83–87.

"Simon Peter: A Type of Theological Transition." *BW* 17 (1901): 83–85.

"The Sociological Point of View in Biblical Study" (editorial). *BW* 17 (1901): 83–85.

"Some Implications of the Historical Method in the Study of the Bible" (editorial). *BW* 17 (1901): 163–66.

"Two Obligations of the Church to a Christian Society" (editorial). *BW* 18 (1901): 323–27.

1902

"The Larger Meanings of Biblical Study" (editorial). *BW* 20 (1902): 163–66.

"The Making of a Minister." *WT* 6 (1902): 789–95.

"The New Apologetic—A Forecast" (editorial). *BW* 19 (1902): 403–9.

"The Parting of the Ways" (editorial). *BW* 20 (1902): 3–8.

"The Religious Efficiency of Sunday-School Reform" (editorial). *BW* 20 (1902): 417–21.

"The Social Teaching of Paul." *BW* 19 (1902): 34–46, 113–21, 178–89, 279–87, 370–77, 433–42; *BW* 20 (1902): 31–47, 123–33, 178–90.

1903

"Blessed Are the Peacemakers" (editorial). *Cdm* 1 (1903): 229–30.

"The Boy by the Sea." *Cdm* 1 (1903): 871–74.

"Can Organized Labor Endure Success?" (editorial). *Cdm* 1 (1903): 275–76.

"The Christian and the Changing Order" (editorial). *Cdm* 1 (l9o3): 1–2.

"The Curriculum of Study in the Sunday School." *BW* 22 (1903): 129–38.

"Democracy and Education" (editorial). *Cdm* 1 (1903): 551–52.

"Education in Regard for Law" (editorial). *Cdm* 1 (1903): 638.

"The Gospel and the Modern Man." *Cdm* 1 (1903): 300–2, 352–53, 399–401, 446–49, 489–91, 537–39.

"Must Democracy Abdicate?" (editorial). *Cdm* 1 (1903): 45–46.

"The Negro Problem in Brief" (editorial). *Cdm* 1 (1903): 765.

"On the Obligation to Interpret the Scriptures" (editorial). *BW* 21 (1903): 163–66.

"The President's Interpretation of Democracy" (editorial). *Cdm* 1 (1903): 415–16.

Principles and Ideals for the Sunday School: An Essay in Religious Pedagogy. Chicago: University of Chicago Press, 1903.

"Religious Education in the Home" (editorial). *BW* 21 (1903): 3–6.

Review of *Rich and Poor in the New Testament*, by Orello Cone. *AJT* 7 (1903): 145–47.

"The Revolt against the Boss" (editorial). *Cdm* 1 (1903): 137–38.

"Way for the Leader!" (editorial). *Cdm* 1 (1903): 461–62.

1904

"The Appeal to Brute Force" (editorial). *WT* 6 (1904): 435–36.

"Can the Presidency Be Bought?" (editorial). *WT* 6 (1904): 719.

"College Athletics and College Facilities." *WT* 7 (1904): 1371–72.

"The College, East and West." *WT* 7 (1904): 1006–12.

"Do We Dare Educate Everybody?" (editorial). *WT* 7 (1904): 1245–46.

"Materials for the Interpretation of the New Testament" (review of *Die Reichsgotteshoffnung in den ältesten christlichen Dokumenten und bei Jesus*, by Paul Wernle; and *Sacred Sites of the Gospels*, by William Sanday). *AJT* 8 (1904): 817–19.

"The New Partisanship" (editorial). *WT* 7 (1904): 843–44.

"The Republic That Is an Empire" (editorial). *WT* 7 (1904): 1103–4.

"A Scientific Basis for Religious and Moral Education from the Standpoint of Theology." *Proceedings of the Second Annual Convention of the Religious Education Association.* Philadelphia, 1904. Pp. 115–19.

"Teacher Training" (editorial). *BW* 24 (1904): 243–47.

1905

"The Better Side of Commercialism" (editorial). *WT* 9 (1905): 913–14.

"The Biblical Scholar as Prophet" (editorial). *BW* 26 (1905): 245–47.

"The Call to Modest Leadership" (editorial). *BW* 26 (1905): 243–45.

"Can a Higher Critic Save Souls?" (editorial). *BW* 25 (1905): 247–48.

"Can We Trust Our Legislatures?" (editorial). *WT* 8 (1905): 3–4.

"The Charlatan in Reform" (editorial). *WT* 7 (1905): 457–58.

"Culture in the American West." *WT* 8 (1905): 191–96.

"Democracy in Education: Principles and Practice of President W. R. Harper."
      WT 8 (1905): 432–36.

"Education in Thrift." *WT* 9 (1905): 1066–70.

"The Eschatology of the New Testament" (review of *The Eschatology of
      Jesus,* by Lewis A. Muirhead; and *St. Paul's Conception of the Last
      Things,* by H. A. A. Kennedy). *AJT* 9 (1905): 343–46.

"The Imitation of Jesus." *BW* 26 (1905): 455–58.

The Messianic Hope in the New Testament. Chicago: University of Chicago
      Press, 1905.

"The New Social Conscience" (editorial). *WT* 9 (1905): 799–800.

"The Preacher and the Novel" (editorial). *BW* 26 (1905): 323–24.

A Reading Journey through Palestine. New York: Chautauqua, 1905.

"Reforming Football in the Central West." *WT* 9 (1905): 1221–26.

"The Revolt of the Plain Citizen" (editorial). *WT* 8 (1905): 345–46.

"Uncommercial Chicago." *WT* 9 (1905): 984–90.

"The Undoing of Autocracy" (editorial). *WT* 9 (1905): 1249–50.

1906

"At the End of the Year" (editorial). *WT* 11 (1906): 665–66.

"Expository Study of Lk. 24:36–53." *BW* 28 (1906): 340–41.

"Expository Study of Mt. 13:24–30, 36–43 (The Parable of the Tares)." *BW* 27
      (1906), 313–15.

"Men or Institutions." *BW* 27 (1906): 32–41.

"New-Fashioned Honesty" (editorial). *WT* 10 (1906): 449–50.

"Our Commercialized Christmas" (editorial). *WT* 11 (1906): 1229–30.

"Playing with Social Discontent" (editorial). *WT* 11 (1906): 1117–18.

"Public Service Congressmen" (editorial). *WT* 11 (1906): 891–92.

"Reading Journey through Palestine." *Chq* 43 (1906): 493–560.

"Rebuilding the Nation on Interstate Commerce" (editorial). *WT* 11 (1906):
      773.

"The Relation of Belief in Immortality to Conduct." *Proceedings of the Twenty-fourth Annual Session of the Baptist Congress for the Discussion of Current Questions.* St. Louis, 1906. Pp. 130–40.

"Salvation by Senatorial Courtesy" (editorial). *WT* 10 (1906): 115–16.

"The University President." *WT* 11 (1906): 710–13.

"The Use of the Bible in Public Schools: A Symposium." *BW* 27 (1906): 59–62.

"What Next in the Historical Study of the Bible?" (editorial). *BW* 28 (1906): 83–86.

"William Rainey Harper as an Editor." *BW* 27 (1906): 204–8.

1907

"The Appointment of James Bryce as British Ambassador." *WT* 12 (1907): 196–97.

The Church and the Changing Order. New York: Macmillan, 1907.

"Harry Pratt Judson." *WT* 12 (1907): 384.

"The Mantle of Roosevelt" (editorial). *WT* 13 (1907): 755–56.

"The New President of the University of Chicago." *Ind* 62 (1907): 722–24.

"Our New Battle of the Wilderness" (editorial). *WT* 12 (1907): 227–28.

"Packingtown Today." *WT* 12 (1907): 488–502.

"The Portent of the Far East" (editorial). *WT* 12 (1907): 115–16.

"A Proposed Constitution for a General Baptist Convention." *Standard* 50 (1907): 1083.

"Prosperity Sobering Off" (editorial). *WT* 13 (1907): 1179–80.

"Shall Reform Become Dogmatism?" (editorial). *WT* 12 (1907): 339–40.

The Social and Ethical Teaching of Jesus. Hyde Park, Ill.: American Institute of Sacred Literature, 1907.

"To Hell with Such a Law" (editorial). *WT* 12 (1907): 3–4.

"Whistling Up the Whirlwind" (editorial). *WT* 13 (1907): 955–56.

1908

"Are We Educating Aristocrats?" (editorial). *WT* 14 (1908): 227–28.

"Rational Jingoism" (editorial). *WT* 15 (1908): 177–78.

"The Religious Education Association." *WT* 14 (1908): 248–50.

"Safeguarding a New Epoch" (editorial). *WT* 14 (1908): 335–36.

"S. S. Curry." *WT* 15 (1908): 154–57.

1909

"The Awakened Church: I: The Church and Scholarship." *WT* 16 (1909): 57–61; "II: The Church and Social Service." *WT* 16 (1909): 151–56; "III: The Church and Education." *WT* 16 (1909): 625–28.

"The Council at Jerusalem." *BW* 33 (1909): 337–42.

The Dictionary of the Bible. Edited by James Hastings, with John A. Selbie, John G. Lambert, and Shailer Mathews. New York: Scribner's, 1909.

"Distorting the Nation's Conscience" (editorial). *WT* 17 (1909): 1227–28.

"'Gipsy' Smith—Evangelist." *WT* 17 (1909): 1316–19.

"Maine as a Summer School for the West." *WT* 17 (1909): 714–17.

"Our Heritage in Lincoln" (editorial). *WT* 16 (1909): 115–16.

"A Positive Method for an Evangelical Theology." *AJT* 13 (1909): 21–46.

"Practicing National Mind Cure" (editorial). *WT* 16 (1909): 3–4.

"The Prophet with the Big Stick" (editorial). *WT* 16 (1909): 229–30.

The Social Gospel. Philadelphia: American Baptist Publishing Society, 1909.

"The State University and the Theological Seminary." *RE* 5 (1909): 179–86.

1910

"Belshazzar's Feast of Party Politics" (editorial). *WT* 18 (1910): 453–54.

"The Curriculum of a Theological Seminary as Determined by the Social Task." *RE* 5 (1910): 83–91.

"A Declaration of Allegiance for Boys and Girls" (editorial). *WT* 19 (1910): 1049–50.

The Gospel and the Modern Man. New York: Macmillan, 1910.

"The Kingdom of God." *BW* 35 (1910): 420–27.

"The Lure of the Direct Primary" (editorial). *WT* 19 (1910): 917–18.

"A Religion for Democracy." *Ind* 86 (1910): 53.

"The Triumph of the Middle West" (editorial). *WT* 19 (1910): 801–2.

"The University Professor in Politics." *WT* 18 (1910): 153–54.

"What Mr. Roosevelt Might Become" (editorial). *WT* 19 (1910): 1177–78.

"The Wisdom of Adventure" (editorial). *WT* 19 (1910): 1306.

1911

"Call to American Parents." *RE* 6 (1911): 49–54.

"The Evolution of Religion." *AJT* 15 (1911): 57–82.

"Is Belief in the Historicity of Jesus Indispensable to Christian Faith?" *AJT* 15 (1911): 614–17.

Scientific Management in the Churches. Chicago: University of Chicago Press, 1911.

"The Sufficiency of the Gospel for the Salvation of Society." *Proceedings of the Baptist World Alliance.* Philadelphia, 1911. Pp. 81–88.

1912

"Professional Reading Course on the Efficient Church: Bibliography." *BW* 39 (1912): 116–24, 200–5, 276–81, 414–19.

"The Social Origin of Theology." *AJS* 18 (1912): 289–317.

"Vocational Efficiency and the Theological Curriculum." *AJT* 16 (1912): 165–80.

"William Newton Clarke and George William Knox: In Memoriam." *AJT* 16 (1912): 444–49.

1913

"The Awakening of American Protestantism." *CQ* 1 (1913): 101–25.

"The Beginnings of a New Catholic Unity." *BW* 41 (1913): 8–10.

"Contemporary Theological Movements in Europe." *Chq* 70 (1913): 306–11.

The Making of To-Morrow: Interpretations of the World To-Day. New York: Eaton & Mains, 1913.

"The Sign of the Cross" (editorial). *BW* 42 (1913): 261–62.

"The Social Influence of the Baptists." In *Elements in Baptist Development.* Edited by Ilsley Boone. Boston: Backus, 1913. Pp. 149–62.

"The Struggle between the Natural and Spiritual Order as Described in the Gospel of John." *BW* 42 (1913): 30–35, 76–79, 146–49, 368–72.

"The Sufficiency of the Gospel for the Salvation of Society." *BW* 41 (1913): 291–98.

The Woman's Citizen's Library: A Systematic Course of Reading in Preparation for the Larger Citizenship. Edited by S. Mathews. 12 vols. Chicago: The Civics Society, 1913–14.

1914

"The By-Products of a Creative Age" (editorial). *BW* 44 (1914): 1–2.

"Generic Christianity." *CQ* 2 (1914): 702–23.

The Individual and the Social Gospel. New York: Missionary Education Movement of U.S. and Canada, 1914.

"Leaking at the Top" (editorial). *BW* 43 (1914): 361–62.

"The Message of Jesus to Our Modern Life." *BW* 44 (1914): 225–28, 297–300, 367–72, 431–40.

"Of All Men the Most Miserable" (editorial). *BW* 43 (1914): 217–18.

"The Social Optimism of Faith in a Divine Jesus" (editorial). *BW* 43 (1914): 153–54.

"The Sword of Christ." *BW* 44 (1914): 391–98.

1915

America and the Asiatic World. New York: Church Peace Union, 1915.

"The Functions of the Federal Church." In *The Church and Country Life.* Edited by Paul L. Vogt. New York: Missionary Education Movement of U.S. and Canada, 1916.

"Maran Atha" (editorial). *BW* 45 (1915): 65–66.

"Manufactured Gods." In *University of Chicago Sermons.* Edited by Theodore G. Soares. Chicago: University of Chicago Press, 1915. Pp. 55–67.

"The Message of Jesus to Our Modern Life." *BW* 45 (1915): 56–64, 120–28, 185–92, 250–56, 382–88.

The Message of Jesus to Our Modern Life. Hyde Park, Ill.: University of Chicago Press, 1915. (AISL Outline Bible Study Course).

"Present Opportunities for Physical Education." *American Physical Education Review* 20 (1915): 497–502.

Report on the Christian Embassy to Japan (with Sidney Gulick). Federal Council of Churches of Christ in America, 1915.

"Theology and the Social Mind." *BW* 46 (1915): 201–48.

"The United States and Japan." *Standard* 62 (1915): 1019, 1023–24.

1916

"The Historical Study of Religion." In *A Guide to the Study of the Christian Religion.* Edited by Gerald B. Smith. Chicago: University of Chicago Press, 1916. Pp. 19–79.

"Religion for Democracy." *Ind* 86 (1916): 53–56.

"Some Larger Aspects of the Trade in War Materials." *Journal of Political Economy* 24 (1916): 14–24.

The Spiritual Interpretation of History. Cambridge, Mass.: Harvard University Press, 1916. (The Noble Lectures, Harvard, 1916).

"Theological Seminaries as Schools of Religious Efficiency." *BW* 47 (1916): 75–85.

1917

"Committee of Eleven Report." *Standard* 64 (1917): 997, 1004.

Democracy and World Politics. New York: National Security League, 1917.

"John L. Dearing: An Appreciation." *Baptist Standard* 1917: 581.

"The Permanent Message of Messianism." *BW* 49 (1917): 267–74.

"Present Co-operative Action by the Churches." *BW* 49 (1917): 67–78.

"Propaganda of Reaction" (editorial). *BW* 49 (1917): 201–2.

"The Spiritual Challenge to Democracy." *CQ* 5 (1917): 513–27.

Why the U.S. Is at War. New York: National Security League, 1917.

Will Christ Come Again? Chicago: American Institute of Sacred Literature, 1917.

1918

"The Bible and Christianity" (editorial). *BW* 51 (1918): 65–66.

"A Historical Statement." In *The Quarter-Centennial Celebration of the University of Chicago.* Chicago: University of Chicago Press, 1918. Pp. 122–25.

"The Moral Value of Patriotism." *BW* 52 (1918): 24–40.

Patriotism and Religion. New York: Macmillan, 1918.

"The Place of Denominationalism." *Baptist Standard* 1918: 1022–23.

"Religion and War." *BW* 52 (1918): 163–76.

"To the Strong in Heart" (editorial). *BW* 51 (1918): 129–30.

1919

"Primary and Secondary Christianity." *BW* 53 (1919): 235–40.

"Some Ethical Gains of the War." *BW* 53 (1919): 14–25.

"Why I Believe in the Deity of Christ." *Standard* 66 (1919): 630–31.

1920

"Can a Nation Be Moral?" *Ind* 104, (1920): 50.

"Carpenter's Son." *Ind* 102 (1920): 167–68.

"Changing One's Religious Mind" (editorial). *BW* 54 (1920): 449–50.

"Church Union or Christian Union?" *Ind* 104 (1920): 13.

"The Church and World Peace." *Ind* 102 (1920): 287.

"The Deity of Christ and Social Reconstruction." *CQ* 8 (1920): 39–54.

"Dr. Mathews on the Interchurch World Movement." *Watchman-Examiner* 8 (1920): 20.

"The Duty of the Church." *Ind* 103 (1920): 268, 291.

"Fair Play for the Interchurch World Movement." *Ind* 102 (1920): 359–60.

"The Minister and Radicalism." *Ind* 103 (1920): 178.

"Our War Reaction to Religion." *Ind* 104 (1920): 362.

"Outlook for Protestant Cooperation." *Ind* 103 (1920): 76–77.

"Protestantism in the New Age." *Ind* 102 (1920): 90.

"Salvation Is More Than Rescue." *Ind* 104 (1920): 429.

"Shall We Make the Chinese Drunkards?" *Ind* 104 (1920): 187.

"Soul Saving by Groups." *Ind* 103 (1920): 211.

"Why I Believe in Jesus Christ." *BW* 54 (1920): 351–53.

"Why Mr Hickson?" *Ind* 102 (1920): 321.

"The Woman's Club and the Church." *Ind* 103 (1920): 12–13.

1921

"Can a Nation Be Moral?" In *Christianity in a New World*. Philadelphia: Judson, 1921. Pp. 177–89.

"Capitalistic Religion." *Ind* 105 (1921): 616–17.

"Challenge to Colleges." *Ind* 105 (1921): 108.

"Church Unity vs. Fraternity." *Ind* 105 (1921): 514.

A Dictionary of Religion and Ethics. Edited by Mathews and Gerald Birney Smith. New York: Macmillan, 1921.

"The Functional Value of Doctrines of the Atonement." *JR* 1 (1921): 146–59.

"Is Christian Theology Christian?" *CC* 38 (1921): 9–11.

"The Kingship of Christ: II: Christ and Education." *The Baptist* 2 (1921): 944–46.

"The Missionary's Place in Politics." *Ind* 105 (1921): 66.

"Must Religion Steer Clear of Reform?" *Ind* 105 (1921): 289–90.

"Poison Gas and Prohibition." *Ind* 105 (1921): 137–38.

"The Pope and the YMCA." *Ind* 105 (1921): 264–65.

"Successful Sunday School." *Ind* 105 (1921): 89.

"What the Foreign Missionaries Teach Us." *Ind* 105 (1921): 43.

1922

"The Christian Faith and the Life of the Community." In *The Christian Faith and Human Relations*. Philadelphia: Judson, 1922. Pp. 49–70.

"How Science Helps Our Faith." *The Baptist* 3 (1922): 1108–9.

The Validity of American Ideals. New York: Abingdon, 1922. (The Bennett Lectures, Wesleyan University, 1920–21).

"The Visible Church and Christian Unity." *CQ* 10 (1922): 72–81.

1923

"Ernest Renan." *Homiletic Review* 85 (1923): 89–93.

"The Growth of the Idea of God in the Bible." In *The Truth about the Bible*. Edited by Alexander R. Gordon et al. Hyde Park, Ill.: University of Chicago Press. Pp. 81–93. (AISL Outline Bible Study Course).

"How to Use the Bible." In *Truth about the Bible*. Pp. 121–30.

Jesus and Good-Will. Hyde Park, Ill.: University of Chicago Press, 1923. (AISL Popular Religion leaflet).

"The Opportunity and Task of the Church in View of the Facts and the Experience Which Social Work Now Presents." *Proceedings of the National Conference of Social Work* (1923): 222–28.

"The Seminary View of Training for Social Work." *Proceedings of the National Conference of Social Work* (1923): 235–36.

"Ten Years of American Protestantism." *North American Review* 217 (1923): 577–93.

"Theology from the Point of View of Social Psychology." *JR* 3 (1923): 337–51.

"What May the Social Worker Expect of the Church?" *JR* 3 (1923): 632–47.

1924

"Agencies for Promoting Religion in the Colleges." *JR* 4 (1924): 293–305.

The Contributions of Science to Religion. Edited by Mathews et al. New York: Appleton, 1924.

"The Evolution of Religion." In *Contributions of Science to Religion.* Pp. 351–77.

The Faith of Modernism. New York: Macmillan, 1924. (Repr. New York: AMS, 1970).

"Fundamentalism and Modernism: An Interpretation." *American Review* 2 (1924): 1–9.

"Introduction." In *Contributions of Science to Religion.* Pp. 1–13.

"The Personal Experiment of Faith." In *Contributions of Science to Religion.* Pp. 420–22.

"Science Gives Content to Religious Thought." In *Contributions of Science to Religion.* Pp. 403–22.

"Science Justifies the Religious Life." In *Contributions of Science to Religion.* Pp. 391–402.

"Scientific Method and Religion." In *Contributions of Science to Religion.* Pp. 378–90.

"The Service of the Church to Social Advance." *Journal of Social Forces* 2 (1924): 546–48.

1925

"The Religion of Jesus." In *The Religion of the Bible.* Edited by Julius A. Bewer. Chicago: University of Chicago Press, 1925. Pp. 64–72.

"The Universal Christian Conference on Life and Work at Stockholm." *JR* 5 (1925): 632–36.

1926

"The Early Followers of Jesus and His 'Way'." In *Jesus' 'Way' of Living.* Edited by Gerald B. Smith et al. Hyde Park, Ill.: University of Chicago Press, 1926. Pp. 28–38.

"Emil Hirsch's Religion." *Menorah Journal* 12 (1926): 32–42.

How Science Helps Our Faith. Chicago: American Institute of Sacred Literature, 1926. (AISL Popular Religion leaflet).

"Introduction." In *The Letter to the Galatians.* Translated by Edgar J. Goodspeed. Chicago: American Institute of Sacred Literature, 1926.

"Introduction: Christianity in a New Age." In *The Rise of the Modern Churches*. Vol. 3 of *An Outline of Christianity*. Edited by Mathews. New York: Bethlehem, 1926. Pp. 1–8.

"Jesus' Conception of His 'Way'." In *Jesus' 'Way' of Living*. Pp. 18–27.

"Shall We Have a General Assembly?" *The Baptist* 7 (1926): 324, 351.

"What Constitutes a Baptist Church?" *The Baptist* 6 (1926): 1506–7.

"Would Change Baptist Order, Warns Mathews," *CC* 43 (1926): 563.

1927

"Business as the Maker of Morals." *System* 51 (1927): 291.

"The Development of Social Christianity in America During the Past Twenty-Five Years." *JR* 7 (1927): 376–86. (Repr. in *Religious Thought in the Last Quarter-Century*. Edited by Gerald Birney Smith. Chicago: University of Chicago Press, 1927. Pp. 228–39).

"Harry Pratt Judson: An Appreciation," *The Baptist* 8 (1927): 386–87.

"Jesus—One with the Father." In *Finding God in Human Life*. Edited by William C. Graham et al. Hyde Park, Ill.: University of Chicago Press, 1927. Pp. 103–19. (AISL Outline Bible Study Course).

"Let Religious Education Beware!" *CC* 44 (1927): 362–64.

"Modernism: Why and What It Is." *The Baptist* 8 (1927): 1508–9.

"Paul, the Expositor of the Christian Experience of God." In *Finding God in Human Life*. Pp. 121–33.

"The Scopes Decision" (editorial). *RE* 22 (1927): 101–2.

The Student's Gospels. Arranged by Mathews. In *Constructive Studies*. Edited by Mathews, W. C. Bower, and Edwin E. Aubrey. Chicago: University of Chicago Press, 1927.

1928

Experiments in Personal Religion. Edited E. S. Ames, Mathews et al. Chicago: American Institute of Sacred Literature, 1928.

"The Inception of the Religious Education Association." *RE* 23 (1928): 619–21.

Jesus on Social Institutions. New York: Macmillan, 1928. (Repr. in Fortress Press Lives of Jesus series, 1970).

Modernism, What and Why It Is. Chicago: American Institute of Sacred Literature, 1928. (A Popular Religion leaflet).

"Religious Experience through the Church." In *Experiments in Personal Religion*. Pp. 141–56.

"Religious Experience through the Outer World of Nature." In *Experiments in Personal Religion*. Pp. 1–15.

"What Is the Task of Leadership in Religious Education?" *RE* 23 (1928): 520–21

1929

"G. B. Smith: A Memorial Appreciation." *Divinity Student* 6 (1929): 34–41.

"The Modern Unbeliever's Quest for Religion." *Current History* 31 (1929): 83.

"Music and Morals." *Proceedings of the Music Supervisors' National Conference* 22 (1929): 624–27.

"Protestantism, Democracy, and Church Unity.' *JR* 9 (1929): 169–84.

"The Religious Life." In *Man and His World*, vol. 11. Edited by Baker Brownell. New York: Van Nostrand, 1929. Pp. 37–62.

"Theology and Social Patterns." *Crozer Theology Bulletin* 21 (1929): 142–47.

Why Denominations? Chicago: American Institute of Sacred Literature, 1929. (A Popular Religion leaflet).

1930

The Atonement and the Social Process. New York: Macmillan, 1930.

Building a Moral Reserve, or the Civic Responsibilities of the Christian Citizen. Hyde Park, Ill.: University of Chicago Press, 1930. (AISL Outline Study Course).

"Can We Have Religion without God?" In *Humanism: Another Battle Line.* Edited by William P. King. Nashville, Tenn.: Cokesbury, 1930. Pp. 135–49.

"Doctrines as Social Patterns." *JR* 10 (1930): 1–15.

"Moral Values in Higher Education." *Proceedings of the Ohio State Educational Conference* (1930): 259–64.

"The Philosophy of Religion." In *Proceedings of the Ohio State Educational Conference* (1930): 55–62.

"The Protestant Churches and Charity." In *Intelligent Philanthropy.* Edited by Ellsworth Farris et al.Chicago: University of Chicago Press, 1930. Pp. 112–32.

"The Religious Basis of Ethics." *JR* 10 (1930): 222–31.

1931

"Dean Mathews on the Federal Council." *The Baptist* 12 (1931): 1056–57.

The Growth of the Idea of God. New York: Macmillan, 1931.

"Jesus' Experience of God in His Contact with the Political Conditions of His People." In *Through Jesus to God.* Edited by Edwin E. Aubrey et al. Hyde Park, Ill.: University of Chicago Press, 1931. Pp. 42–54. (AISL Outline Study Course).

"Jesus' Experience of God through Facing Apparent Defeat of His Ideal of Establishing the Kingdom of God." In *Through Jesus to God.* Pp. 82–93.

"Religion and the Growth of Personality." *Institute* 16 (1931): 2–21.

"Religion in the New Age." *Forum and Century* 85 (1931): 98–103.

"Social Patterns and the Idea of God." *JR* 11 (1931): 159–78.

1932

"Religion as the Source of Poise and Power." *Institute* 16 (1932): 152–63.

1933

"The Function of the Divinity School." *JR* 13 (1933): 253–68.

"The Gospel of John." *Institute* 17 (1933): 106–20.

Immortality and the Cosmic Process. Cambridge, Mass.: Harvard University Press, 1933. (The Ingersoll Lectures, Harvard, 1933).

"Nationalism Seen as Help to Peace." *Trans-Pacific* 21 (1933): 13.

"Six Criticisms of 'The Arbitrary as the Basis for Rational Morality'." *International Journal of Ethics* 43 (1933): 144–45.

"Theology as Group Belief." In *Contemporary American Theology.* Edited by Vergilius Ferm. New York: Round Table, 1933. Pp. 161–93.

1934

Christianity and Social Process. New York: Harper, 1934. (The Barrows Lectures, India, 1933–34).

"Jesus Has Religious Significance for the World Today." *Institute* 19 (1934): 35–48.

1935

"The Church and the Social Order." In *The Church at Work in the Modern World.* Edited by W. C. Bower. Chicago: University of Chicago Press, 1935. Pp. 185–209.

"The Co-operation of the Churches." In *Church at Work in the Modern World.* Pp. 53–79.

Creative Christianity. Nashville, Tenn.: Cokesbury, 1935. (The Cole Lectures, Vanderbilt, 1934).

"Faith in God Is Reasonable and a Source of Help." *Institute* 19 (1935): 99–111.

"Is God Emeritus?" *American Scholar* 4 (1935): 389–96.

"Love Is a Practicable Basis for Society." *Institute* 19 (1935): 51–63.

1936

"Jesus and the Social Order" (review of *The Great Galilean Returns* by H. K. Booth). *Christian Century* 53 (1936): 810–11.

New Faith for Old. New York: Macmillan, 1936.

1937

"As Grows the Game: A Case Study in Morality." *American Scholar* 6 (1937): 17–26.

"What Liberty Does Religion Require? The Problem Stated." *RE* 32 (1937): 183–85.

1938

The Church and the Christian. New York: Macmillan, 1938.

"Unrepentant Liberalism." *American Scholar* 7 (1938): 296–308.

1940

"The Church and Social Optimism." In *Theology and Modern Life: Essays in Honor of Harris Franklin Rall.* Edited by Paul Arthur Schilpp. Chicago: Willett, 1940. Pp. 237–45.

"Ira M. Price." *American Journal of Semitic Languages and Literature* 57 (1940): 296–308.

Is God Emeritus? New York: Macmillan, 1940.

"Shall We Have a General Assembly?" *Watchman-Examiner,* 16 May 1940, p. 543.

SELECTED BOOK REVIEWS

1894

Review of Alexander Bruce, *Apologetics, or Christianity Defensively Stated.* *BW* 4 (1894): 309–13.

Review of James Iverach, *Christianity and Evolution,* and William E. McLane, *Evolution in Religion. BW* 4 (1894): 315.

1895

Review of George C. Lorimer, *The Argument for Christianity. BW* 5 (1895): 475–76.

Review of Brooke F. Westcott, *The Incarnation and the Common Life. BW* 5 (1895): 72–73.

Review of William Dewitt Hyde, *Social Theology. BW* 6 (1895): 155–57.

Review of Alexander Mair, *Studies in the Christian Evidence. BW* 5 (1895): 228.

Review of Marvin R. Vincent, *That Monster the Higher Critic. BW* 5 (1895): 393.

1896

Review of A. W. Anthony, *An Introduction to the Life of Jesus. BW* 8 (1896): 517.

Review of George H. Gilbert, *The Student's Life of Jesus,* Lyman Abbott, *The Life of Christ,* and Louise Houghton, *The Life of the Lord Jesus. BW* 8 (1806): 411–12.

1897

Review of R. W. Farrar, *The Bible: Its Meaning and Supremacy. BW* 10 (1897): 229–30.

Review of Phelps-Ward, *The Life of Christ. Dial* 24 (1897): 17.

Review of Bernard Grenfell and Arthur S. Hunt, trans. and ed., *Logia Jesou: Sayings of Our Lord. BW* 10 (1897): 151–55.

Review of Lewis A. Muirhead, *The Times of Jesus. BW* 10 (1897): 394–95.

1898

Review of Washington Gladden, *The Christian Pastor and the Working Church. BW* 12 (1898): 141–43.

Review of D. W. Forrest, *The Christ of History and of Experience. BW* 12 (1898): 219–21.

Review of Edmund Stapfer, *The Death and Resurrection of Jesus Christ. BW* 12 (1898): 461–62.

Review of J. Brough, *The Early Life of Our Lord. BW* 11 (1898): 366.

Review of Elizabeth S. Phelps, *The Story of Jesus Christ. BW* 11 (1898): 58–61.

Review of Walter Locke and Walter Sanday, *Two Lectures on the Sayings of Jesus. BW* 11 (1898): 948.

1899

Review of G. D. Boardman, *The Kingdom. BW* 13 (1899): 220–21.

Review of E. M. Hurll, *The Life of Our Lord in Art. BW* 14 (1899): 460.

Review of T. J. Conaty, *New Testament Studies. BW* 13 (1899): 136.

Review of G. B. Stevens, *The Theology of the New Testament. BW* 14 (1899): 452–54.

Review of W. M. Ramsay, *Was Christ Born at Bethlehem? BW* 13 (1899): 282–83.

1900

Review of James Stalker, *The Christology of Jesus. BW* 15 (1900): 389–91.

Review of Frédéric Krop, *La pensée de Jésus sur le Royaume de Dieu. AJT* 4 (1900): 250.

Review of Rush Rhees, *The Life of Jesus of Nazareth. BW* 16 (1900): 468–70.

Review of George B. Stevens, *The Message of the Apostles. AJT* 4 (1900): 820–23.

Review of D. S. Muzzey, *The Rise of the New Testament. BW* 16 (1900): 472.

Review of George B. Stevens, *The Theology of the New Testament. AJT* 4 (1900): 178–81.

Review of A. T. Innes, *The Trial of Jesus Christ. BW* 16 (1900): 468–70.

1901

Review of Levi Leonard Paine, *A Critical History of the Evolution of Trinitarianism and Its Outcome in the New Christology*. BW 17 (1901): 313–15.

Review of P. C. Simpson, *The Fact of Christ*. BW 18 (1901): 233.

Review of *The First Interpreters of Jesus*. BW 18 (1901): 147–48.

Review of W. L. Crane, *Hard Sayings of Jesus Christ*. BW 17 (1901): 316–17.

Review of F. G. Peabody, *Jesus Christ and the Social Question*. BW 17 (1901): 469–70.

Review of T. C. Hall, ed., *The Messages of Jesus According to the Synoptics*. BW 17 (1901): 390–91.

Review of J. de Visme, *Quelques traits de Jésus de l'histoire*. AJT 5 (1901): 425.

Review of *The Relation of the Apostolic Preaching to the Teaching of Christ*. BW 18 (1901): 314–16.

Review of George Matheson, *Studies of the Portrait of Christ*. BW 18 (1901): 491–92.

1902

Review of Richard Drescher, *Das Leben Jesus bei Paulus*. AJT 6 (1902): 190–91.

1903

"Brief Studies in the New Testament History and Biography," *AJT* 7 (1903): 577–80.

Review of James Denney, *The Death of Christ*. BW 22 (1903): 149–50.

Review of Orello Cone, *Rich and Poor in the New Testament*. AJT 7 (1903): 145–47.

1904

Review of Paul Wernle, *The Beginnings of Christianity*. BW 24 (1904): 389–92.

"Materials for the Interpretation of the New Testament" (review of Paul Wernle, *Die Reichsgotteshoffnung in den ältesten christlichen Dokumenten und bie Jesus*, and William Sanday, *Sacred Sites of the Gospels*), AJT 8 (1904): 817–19.

Review of C. A. Briggs, *New Light on the Life of Jesus*, and G. C. Morgan, *Crises of the Christ*. BW 24 (1904): 237–38.

1905

"The Eschatology of the New Testament" (review of Lewis A. Muirhead, *The Eschatology of Jesus*, and H. A. A. Kennedy, *Saint Paul's Conception of the Last Things*). AJT 9 (1905): 343–46.

Review of Bernhard Weiss, *The Religion of the New Testament*. BW 26 (1905): 392–93.

1906

"The Historical Study of the New Testament." *AJT* 10 (1906): 712–16.

1909

Review of George C. Foley, *Anselm's Theory of the Atonement*. *AJT* 13 (1909): 624–25.

1911

"The Christological Problem" (review of William Sanday, *Christologies Ancient and Modern*). *AJT* 15 (1911): 137–40.

1913

"Forcing the Issue between God and Mammon" (review of Walter Rauschenbusch, *The Sufficiency of the Gospel for the Salvation of Society*). *BW* 41 (1913): 137–40.

"More Discussion of New Testament Eschatology" (review of E. C. Dewick, *Primitive Christian Eschatology*). *BW* 42 (1913): 120–21.

1916

Review of Walter Rauschenbusch, *Christianizing the Social Order*. *BW* 41 (1916): 139.

1925

"Troeltsch's Last Work" (review of Ernst Troeltsch, *Christian Thought: Its History and Application*). *JR* 5 (1925): 325–27.

1932

Review of A. C. McGiffert, *A History of Christian Thought*, I: *Early and Eastern*. *JR* 12 (1932): 581–82.

1933

Review of A. C. McGiffert, *A History of Christian Thought*, II: *Tertullian to Erasmus*. *JR* 13 (1933): 335–36.

1936

Review of H. K. Booth, *The Great Galilean Returns*. *Christian Century* 53 (June 8, 1936): 310–11.

1941

Review of C. Ryder Smith, *The Bible Doctrine of Salvation*. *JR* 21 (1941): 482–83.

INDEX

301

Subject Index